THE MONETARY POLICY OF THE FEDERAL RESERVE

The Monetary Policy of the Federal Reserve details the evolution of the monetary standard from the start of the Federal Reserve through the end of the Greenspan era. The book places that evolution in the context of the intellectual and political environment of the time. By understanding the fitful process of replacing a gold standard with a paper money standard, the conduct of monetary policy becomes a series of experiments useful for understanding the fundamental issues concerning money and prices. How did the recurrent monetary instability of the twentieth century relate to the economic instability and to the associated political and social turbulence? After the detour in policy represented by FOMC chairmen Arthur Burns and G. William Miller, Paul Volcker and Alan Greenspan established the monetary standard originally foreshadowed by William McChesney Martin, who became chairman in 1951. *The Monetary Policy of the Federal Reserve* explains in a straightforward way the emergence and nature of the modern, inflation-targeting central bank.

Robert L. Hetzel is Senior Economist and Policy Adviser in the Research Department of the Federal Reserve Bank of Richmond, where he has served for more than 30 years. Dr. Hetzel's research has appeared in publications such as the *Journal of Money, Credit, and Banking*; the *Journal of Monetary Economics*; the *Monetary and Economics Studies* series of the Bank of Japan; and the *Carnegie-Rochester Conference Series*. His writings provided one of the catalysts for the congressional hearings and treasury studies leading to the issuance of Treasury Inflation Protected Securities, or TIPS. Dr. Hetzel has given seminars or served as a visiting scholar at the Austrian National Bank, the Bank of England, the Bank of Japan, the Bundesbank, the European Central Bank, the National Bank of Hungary, and the Center for Research into European Integration in Bonn, Germany. He received his Ph.D. in 1975 from the University of Chicago, where Nobel Laureate Milton Friedman chaired his dissertation committee.

To my great teacher, Milton Friedman,
and to my steadfast companion in life,
my wife

The Monetary Policy of the Federal Reserve

A History

ROBERT L. HETZEL

Federal Reserve Bank of Richmond

CAMBRIDGE
UNIVERSITY PRESS

CAMBRIDGE UNIVERSITY PRESS
Cambridge, New York, Melbourne, Madrid, Cape Town,
Singapore, São Paulo, Delhi, Mexico City

Cambridge University Press
32 Avenue of the Americas, New York, NY 10013-2473, USA

www.cambridge.org
Information on this title: www.cambridge.org/9780521881326

First published 2008
Reprinted 2010, 2012 (twice)

A catalog record for this publication is available from the British Library.

Library of Congress Cataloging in Publication Data

Hetzel, Robert L.
The Monetary policy of the Federal Reserve : a history / Robert L. Hetzel.
    p. cm. – (Studies in macroeconomic history)
Includes bibliographical references and index.
ISBN 978-0-521-88132-6 (hardback)
1. United States. Federal Reserve Board. 2. Monetary policy – United States. 3. Banks and banking,
Central – United States. I. Title. II. Series.
HG2565.H48   2008
339.5′30973–dc22   2007023447

ISBN 978-0-521-88132-6 Hardback

Contents

Figures

Preface

What is the monetary standard? How does the Fed control inflation? Not only is there little consensus over answers to these questions, but there is also little consensus over how to organize the monetary experience of the twentieth century in a way that can discriminate between competing answers.

As a member of the Money and Banking Workshop at the University of Chicago, I had the privilege of listening to Robert Barro, Stanley Fischer, Robert Gordon, Robert Lucas, Bennett McCallum, Donald Patinkin, and, of course, Milton Friedman. I left Chicago for the Federal Reserve Bank of Richmond in 1975 with several assumptions about monetary economics: (1) the price level is a monetary phenomenon; (2) the price system works; and (3) the public learns to form its expectations in a way that conforms to the Fed's monetary policy (rational expectations).

Paul Volcker demonstrated that not only could the Fed control inflation, but that it could also do so without permanently high unemployment or periodic recourse to high unemployment. Conversely, low stable unemployment did not require monetary management through high, variable inflation. As a result, there is now considerable agreement over assumptions 1 and 2. The central bank, which possesses a monopoly over monetary base creation, controls trend inflation. As described by real business cycle models, the price system works well to offset shocks. However, economists still divide over the nature of inflationary expectations.

Is there inertia in inflationary expectations and in inflation independent of the systematic component of monetary policy? If so, does the central bank exploit that inertia to control inflation through the systematic manipulation of real variables, especially, by moving unemployment relative to a full employment value? In the jargon of economics, is the Phillips curve exploitable? If so, the menu of choice between variability in real output and in inflation defines the monetary standard. In contrast, if no such inertia exists, the central bank must provide a nominal anchor whose nature defines the monetary standard. This book brings empirical evidence to bear on these issues.

As a Fed economist, I learned that Federal Open Market Committee (FOMC) discussions offered no insight into monetary policy understood as systematic behavior, that is, a strategy designed to achieve explicit objectives. Richmond's director of research, James Parthemos, described the 1970s' FOMC as administering funds rate changes in homeopathic doses. That is, Chairman Burns limited FOMC discussion to whether to move the funds rate by $\frac{1}{4}$ or $\frac{1}{8}$ percentage point. The objectives and strategy of policy were the prerogative of the chairman. The language of discretion effectively placed off limits discussion of policy.

As a monetary economist, I found the early years of the Volcker FOMC the most exciting of my life. In 1979, inflationary expectations became unmoored, and long-term bond markets began to shut down. I remember the head of Merrill Lynch in Richmond saying that Merrill was sending analysts to Brazil to learn how to conduct business in a world of endemic inflation. On October 6, 1979, the Fed announced new procedures that would force it to take seriously achievement of its heretofore largely irrelevant money targets. As a quantity theorist, I assumed that money targets would provide the nominal anchor.

By 1983, the Fed had reduced inflation to 4%. However, as the decade progressed, it became clear that the nominal variable that disciplined FOMC actions was the bond rate not money. My colleague, Marvin Goodfriend, invented the phrase "inflation scare" to describe how the FOMC treated discrete increases in bond rates as a challenge to its credibility.

In February 1990, Richmond Fed President Robert Black testified before Congress on Representative Stephen Neal's Joint Resolution 409 mandating that the Fed achieve price stability within five years. Bob Black was a monetarist, and he recommended multiyear M2 targets. As an alternative, I suggested treasury issuance of matched-maturity securities, half of which would be nominal and half indexed to the price level. The yield difference, which would measure expected inflation, would be a nominal anchor provided that the Fed committed to stabilizing it.

The idea came from observing how exchange-rate depreciation in small, open economies constrained central banks because of the way it passed through immediately to domestic inflation. With a market measure of expected inflation, monetary policy seen by markets as inflationary would immediately trigger an alarm even if inflation were slow to respond. I mentioned my proposal to Milton Friedman, who encouraged me to write a *Wall Street Journal* op-ed piece, which became Hetzel (1991). (See also Hetzel 1990b and 1992.) Friedman (Friedman and Friedman 1998, 395) advocated the idea and wrote in a letter to Michael Bruno, governor of the Bank of Israel (Hoover Archives, March 22, 1991):

Hetzel has suggested a nominal anchor different from those you or I may have considered in the past.... His proposal is ... that the Federal Reserve be instructed by the Congress to keep that [nominal-indexed yield] difference below some number.... [I]t is the first nominal anchor that has been suggested that seems to me to have real advantages over the nominal money supply. Clearly it is far better than a price level anchor which ... is always backward looking.

Donald Tucker, chief economist for Doug Barnard, Jr. (D. GA), of the Commerce, Consumer, and Monetary Affairs Subcommittee of the House Committee on Government Operations, arranged congressional hearings on the proposal (U.S. Cong. June 16 and 25, 1992; October 29, 1992). (Tucker had been a professor of mine at Chicago.) Friedman wrote Alan Greenspan encouraging him to consider the indexed-bond idea (Hoover Archives, January 24, 1990). Greenspan (1981) had already advanced a similar idea in the form of treasury securities indexed to the price of gold.

Greenspan and Michael Boskin, Council of Economic Advisers chairman, testified favorably. The treasury agreed to do a study, which meant asking the opinion of an advisory committee of bond traders. Traders never liked the idea of indexed bonds. Because individuals and institutions such as insurance companies and pension funds buy them as long-term investments, they do not generate regular trading revenue. However, by the time the study appeared, Larry Summers was assistant treasury secretary. Summers liked the idea and guided it to fruition as Treasury Inflation Protected Securities (TIPS).

The Fed does not operate with money targets. As a result, for quantity theorists who deny the existence of intrinsic inflation inertia, the nominal anchor that gives money value must be a policy rule that stabilizes inflationary expectations. From nominal treasuries and TIPS of 10-year and 5-year maturity, one can derive expected trend inflation as expected inflation for the 5-year interval 5 years in the future. The consistent part of FOMC behavior that has produced stability in this number since 2003 (Figure 20.1) is the nominal anchor. A rule that makes this measure of expected inflation constant would be analogous to Friedman's (1960) constant money growth rule.

Again, what is the monetary standard and how does the Fed control inflation? Does the FOMC raise the unemployment rate to offset inflation created by inflation shocks and propagated by backward-looking (adaptive) expectations? On a micro level, does the FOMC exercise predictable control over the hiring and firing decisions of employers? Alternatively, has the FOMC created near–price stability through consistent behavior that has created the expectation of price stability? On a micro level, has it created an environment of nominal expectational stability so that the manager of a firm changes the dollar price of his product only when he wants to *change* its relative price? With expected price stability, he does not assume a need to periodically change dollar prices simply to *preserve* his product's relative price. To control inflation, does the FOMC manipulate unemployment discretionarily or manage expectations through rule-like consistency in its behavior?

The change in the willingness of the Fed to accept responsibility for the price level allows economists to think about monetary policies in the twentieth century as a series of experiments. One policy was real bills designed to limit credit creation to productive rather than speculative uses. Another was that of Martin–Volcker–Greenspan lean-against-the-wind. With it, the FOMC moved the funds rate in a persistent way in response to sustained changes in rates of resource utilization subject to the constraint that markets believed that the funds rate changes would cumulate to a degree that would leave inflation unchanged. Another policy was stop–go, which was lean-against-the-wind, but low stable unemployment was the priority rather than low stable inflation. The challenge is to characterize these policies in a way that allows the economist to draw implications that distinguish between competing views of the monetary standard.

The views in this book are those of the author, not the Federal Reserve Bank of Richmond.

ONE

The Pragmatic Evolution of the Monetary Standard

The twentieth century was marked by vast, horrific disasters as well as by widespread, beneficent progress. In the first half of the century, two world wars almost ended Western civilization. In the second half, democracy spread and living standards rose. Throughout, monetary instability interacted with social upheaval and political disorder. Inflation and deflation created feelings of powerlessness in the face of impersonal forces that promoted a search for scapegoats. Hyperinflation and depression contributed to the rise of Nazism in Germany. The stability of the deutsche mark then accompanied the German postwar growth miracle (Hetzel 2002a; 2002b).

In the United States, deflation and depression in the 1930s produced a decade of untold human misery. The Great Inflation of the 1970s spawned wage and price controls, which trampled on due process. The feeling of government's loss of control, symbolized by gas lines, helped propel Ronald Reagan into power. After Paul Volcker led the Fed to accept responsibility for inflation in 1979, an increase in monetary stability accompanied an increase in economic stability.

The success of the twenty-first century will depend upon how well societies learn the lessons of the twentieth century. The grand monetary experiment of the last century was the replacement of a gold standard with a fiat money standard. The failure of central banks to understand their new responsibility to provide a nominal anchor for prices lay at the heart of the spectacular monetary failures of that century. What nominal anchor and what monetary standard are in place at the start of the current century?

I. The Volcker–Greenspan Monetary Standard

The U.S. monetary standard has evolved pragmatically rather than by conscious design. The current standard arose out of the consistent effort by the Volcker–Greenspan (V–G) FOMC to reanchor inflationary expectations unmoored by the experience with stop-go policy. Consistency under duress achieved credibility.

Credibility laid the foundation for the current nominal anchor: an expectation of low, stable trend inflation unaffected by macroeconomic shocks.[1]

Something must "anchor" the public's expectation of the future value of money. For the gold standard, it was the commitment to maintain the par value of gold. Under the gold standard as it existed in the late nineteenth century, money received its value from the Bank of England's commitment to maintain in the future a fixed pound price of an ounce of gold. For the contemporaneous money price of gold to be viable, the public had to believe that the Bank would maintain that value in the future.

To achieve the stability in the expected future price level requisite for contemporaneous stability of the price level, today the public must believe that the central bank will behave consistently. Over the quarter century of the V–G era, the Fed did not follow a rule in the sense that it never departed from consistent procedures for setting the funds rate.[2] Nevertheless, the achievement of near price stability derived from an overall consistency of behavior that emerged out of an effort to restore the expectational stability of the earlier commodity standard.[3]

II. Stop–Go Monetary Policy and Loss of a Nominal Anchor

Experience with a commodity standard created an expectation of price stability that persisted into the second half of the twentieth century. The primacy attached to price stability by the early William McChesney Martin FOMC sustained that expectation into the 1960s. Subsequently, stop–go policy opportunistically exploited it and, in time, destroyed the nominal anchor provided by the expectation of price stability.

Keynesians emphasized discretionary manipulation of aggregate demand. Because they assumed the existence of an inertia in inflation independent of monetary policy, they believed that, subject to the inflation–unemployment trade-offs of the Phillips curve, the central bank could manipulate aggregate nominal demand to smooth fluctuations in real output. The exercise of discretion, however, destroyed the prior nominal expectational stability.

Sherman Maisel (1973, 14, 285), a member of the Board of Governors from 1965 until 1972, expressed the Keynesian view:

There is a trade-off between idle men and a more stable value for the dollar. A conscious decision must be made as to how much unemployment and loss of output is acceptable in order to get smaller price rises. Some price increases originate on the cost side or in particular industries. These cannot be halted by monetary policy, which acts principally on the overall aggregate demand for goods and services.... [E]xperience ... shows that without some type of government intervention in the price–wage bargains struck by labor and industry, the trade-off between inflation and unemployment is unsatisfactory.

Robert Weintraub (U.S. Cong. July 16, 1974, 44) documented the prevalence of these views among FOMC members in the 1970s.[4]

Starting with the Kennedy and Johnson appointments to the Board of Governors, Keynesian views became increasingly prevalent within the FOMC. According to these views, monetary policy should aim for full employment, almost universally assumed to occur at a 4% unemployment rate or less. This figure benchmarked potential output. By 1970, elimination of the resulting presumed negative output gap (actual minus potential output) became a national and an FOMC objective. Furthermore, a nonmonetary view of inflation led the FOMC to believe that monetary policy could be stimulative without increasing inflation as long as the output gap was negative. The inflation that did occur with unemployment in excess of 4% had to arise from cost-push inflation. Failure to accommodate such inflation would require high unemployment.

The loss of expectational stability began in 1966 when the FOMC, unlike 1957, did not move in a sustained way to eliminate nascent inflation. Bond yields began a long, irregular climb to the low double-digit figures reached in the early 1980s. They fell briefly during the 1970 recession but resumed rising in spring 1971. The Nixon administration wanted rapid M1 growth to stimulate output sufficiently to reduce the unemployment rate to 4.5% by summer 1972. Arthur Burns, FOMC chairman, campaigned for wage and price controls as the price of stimulative monetary policy. In their absence, inflationary expectations, Burns contended, would counter the stimulative effects of expansionary policy. On August 15, 1971, Nixon delivered the controls Burns wanted and Burns obliged with expansionary monetary policy (Chapter 8).

Charls Walker (U.S. Cong. November 1, 1971, 36), treasury undersecretary, later summarized the forces leading the Nixon administration to adopt wage and price controls:

[I]nflationary expectations . . . began to come back on us last winter after we had them under some control. Interest rates were going down, and then [they] shot back up again. . . . [L]abor tended to leapfrog into the future and get 3-year contracts to guard against additional inflation. Inflationary expectations are what really got us.

Keynesian aggregate demand management relied on inertia in actual and expected inflation as the lever with which increases in aggregate nominal demand lowered unemployment. By the end of the 1970s, that apparent inertia disappeared. The public's response to price controls offered an early example. Initially, their imposition did assuage inflationary fears and permit stimulative monetary policy. However, as George Shultz (Shultz and Dam 1978, 71), Treasury secretary in the Nixon administration, wrote:

Once the suspicion of permanence sets in, gamesmanship develops between the private and public sectors. It becomes apparent that the controls process is not a one-way street in which the government does something to the private sector; rather, it is a two-way street, with the government taking an action, the private sector reacting to it, the government reacting in turn, and so forth. It is a continual process of interplay and interrelations through which those "controlled" develop ways of doing whatever they really want to do.

Apart from wartime, before 1965, the United States had never experienced sustained high inflation. Experience with a commodity standard had conditioned the public to expect stationarity in prices. However, the sustained rise in inflation produced by stop–go monetary policy changed expectations. As the public learned that policy did not provide for stationarity in either the price level or the inflation rate, an increase in expected inflation increasingly offset the stimulative effect of the expansionary policy followed in the go phases of stop–go policy. By 1979, the Fed found itself operating in the world described by Barro and Gordon (1983) and Kydland and Prescott (1977) where the public believes that the central bank possesses an incentive to raise inflation to lower unemployment below its sustainable value.[5] Forward-looking expectations on the part of the public offset the stimulative effect of monetary policy on the unemployment rate.

Herbert Stein (U.S. Cong. July 30, 1974, 71), Council of Economic Advisers (CEA) chairman in the Nixon administration, foresaw the environment that Volcker inherited upon becoming FOMC chairman in 1979:

If policy or external events slow down the growth of demand, price and wage increases abate little if at all, as everyone is looking across the valley to the next surge of inflation. Because price and wage increases persist at a high rate employment suffers, and governments are driven or tempted to prop up demand, validating the expectation of continued or ever accelerating inflation.

Volcker (December 3, 1980, 4) observed:

[T]he idea of a sustainable "trade off" between inflation and prosperity . . . broke down as businessmen and individuals learned to anticipate inflation, and to act in this anticipation. . . . The result is that orthodox monetary or fiscal measures designed to stimulate could potentially be thwarted by the self-protective instincts of financial and other markets. Quite specifically, when financial markets jump to anticipate inflationary consequences, and workers and businesses act on the same assumption, there is room for grave doubt that the traditional measures of purely demand stimulus can succeed in their avowed purpose of enhancing real growth.

Greenspan (U.S. Cong. February 19, 1993, 55–6) made the same point:

The effects of policy on the economy depend critically on how market participants react to actions taken by the Federal Reserve, as well as on expectations of our future actions. . . . [T]he huge losses suffered by bondholders during the 1970s and early 1980s sensitized them to the slightest sign . . . of rising inflation. . . . An overly expansionary monetary policy, or even its anticipation, is embedded fairly soon in higher inflationary expectations and nominal bond yields. Producers incorporate expected cost increases quickly into their own prices, and eventually any increase in output disappears as inflation rises.

III. A New Nominal Anchor

By summer 1979, the United States had lost the nominal anchor provided by a residual expectation of inflation stationarity. The bond rate fluctuated widely at a level that exceeded 10% until December 1985. The persistent effort to change the inflationary expectations of the public, unmoored in the prior period of stop–go monetary policy, formed the crucible in which Volcker and Greenspan forged a new monetary standard. At the time, the change to a preemptive policy of raising the funds rate in the absence of rising inflation engendered fierce criticism. The abandonment of aggregate-demand management in favor of stabilizing inflationary expectations was a departure for unknown shores.

Volcker and Greenspan had to reduce the expectation of high inflation manifested in the high level of bond rates. Furthermore, financial markets had come to associate inflation shocks (relative price shocks that pass through to the price level) and positive growth gaps (above-trend real output growth) with increases in trend inflation. After the initial disinflation that brought inflation down to 4% in 1983, the FOMC still had to convince markets that a go phase would not follow a stop phase. It had to forego expansionary policy early during economic recovery when inflation had fallen but unemployment had not yet returned to full employment. The V–G expected-inflation/growth gap policy emerged in 1983 when the FOMC raised the funds rate in response to rising bond rates despite the existence of high unemployment and falling inflation. Greenspan reconfirmed the policy during the "jobless recovery" from the 1990 recession when the FOMC lowered the funds rate only gradually to work down the inflationary expectations embodied in long-term bond rates.

As a consequence of responding to the increases in bond rates produced by positive growth gaps, the FOMC replaced an output-gap target with a growth-gap indicator. It raised the funds rate in response to sustained above-trend growth rather than waiting until a perceived negative output gap approached zero and inflation rose. The more expeditious movement in the funds rate eventually convinced markets that FOMC procedures would keep real growth in line with potential growth promptly enough to prevent increases in inflation. As a result, in response to shocks, market participants began to move forward real interest rates embodied in the yield curve continuously in a way effectively estimated to return real output to potential (Hetzel 2006). The alternation of intervals of stimulative and restrictive monetary policy disappeared. Ironically, allowing the price system to work rather than attempting to improve upon it produced more rather than less economic stability.

TWO

Learning and Policy Ambiguity

The Fed does not possess a systematic procedure for acquiring knowledge about the working of monetary policy and for communicating such knowledge to the public. In this chapter, I argue that to learn and communicate in a systematic manner the Fed must use the language of economics to engage in a dialogue with the academic community over the interpretation of monetary history.

I. Disagreement over the Nature of Monetary Policy

Disagreement arises over whether the Fed must choose between stabilizing unemployment and stabilizing prices. In the 1960s, the question was whether achievement of low unemployment required acceptance of inflation (Samuelson and Solow 1960). In the 1980s, when the Fed's primary objective changed from low, stable unemployment to low, stable inflation, the question became whether stability in prices required variability in unemployment (Modigliani and Papademos 1975). For those who answered affirmatively, the empirical correlations of the Phillips curve promised a quantitative answer.

The fundamental disagreement comes from differing views over the nature of price-level determination. Is there a hard-wired (intrinsic) persistence to actual and expected inflation that exists independently of monetary policy? Alternatively, does the behavior of actual and expected inflation derive from the systematic part of monetary policy – the rational expectations assumption? The attempt here is to provide relevant evidence by using different monetary policies over the twentieth century as experiments yielding outcomes useful for testing hypotheses. Especially, does the public learn to form its expectations of inflation in a way that is conformable to the systematic part of monetary policy?

The twentieth century offers two grand monetary experiments. The first came from the Fed's intermittent acceptance of responsibility for the price level. For most of the 1920s, led by Governor Benjamin Strong at the New York Fed, the Fed accepted that responsibility by sterilizing gold inflows. After the 1951 Treasury–Fed Accord, led by Martin, the Fed also accepted it, and it did so again in the V–G era.

6

In contrast, just after World War I, during the Great Depression, and during the stop–go period from 1965 through 1979, the Fed assumed that the behavior of prices derived from market (nonmonetary) forces.

The second grand monetary experiment came from the back-to-back combination of stop–go policy and the V–G policy. With the prior policy, the primary objective was low, stable unemployment sought for in the management of aggregate demand. With the latter, it became low, stable inflation sought for in the establishment of expectational nominal stability (low, stable expected inflation). The underlying premise for stop–go policy was the existence of intrinsic inflation persistence, that is, the hard-wired propagation of today's inflation into tomorrow's inflation absent an increase in unemployment above full employment.

Intrinsic inflation persistence is a two-edged sword. Through its control over aggregate nominal demand, the central bank can exercise systematic control over real aggregate demand and unemployment. However, to control the inflation that arises from inflation shocks, periodically it has to raise unemployment. In the politically and socially charged environment of the 1960s and 1970s, low, stable unemployment became the policy priority. Given this priority, to lessen the presumed cost in terms of unemployment of controlling inflation, policymakers turned to a range of incomes policies from presidential interference in the price setting of corporations to full-fledged wage and price controls. The direct attempt to stabilize real variables destabilized them. In contrast, in the V–G era, stabilization of inflation stabilized output.

The association of monetary and price-level instability in the periods when the Fed rejected responsibility for the price level conforms to the quantity theory hypothesis that the price level varies to endow nominal money with the purchasing power desired by the public. The failure of the inverse relationship between inflation and unemployment to survive stop–go policy and the failure of the inverse relationship between inflation variability and unemployment variability to survive the V–G policy contradict the idea of an exploitable Phillips curve with intrinsic inflation persistence. These outcomes support the Friedman–Lucas natural-rate/rational-expectations hypothesis. First, real variables possess well-defined values ("natural" values that would obtain with perfect price flexibility). Second, rational, forward-looking individuals form expectations conformably with the systematic behavior of the central bank and set prices conformably with those expectations. It follows that the central bank cannot predictably manipulate real variables – real money or unemployment. It can control trend inflation, but it must do so through consistent (rule-like) behavior that creates the expectation of unchanging trend inflation.

II. A Normative Roadmap

Learning requires knowledge of the strategies followed by the central bank. What were the objectives of monetary policy and what consistent behavior underlay the actions that policymakers took to achieve those objectives? Historically, the

Fed has obfuscated the answers. At best, it has revealed only its policy actions, while appealing to "discretion" to avoid clear statement of objectives and strategy. Policy ambiguity in the form of unwillingness to announce explicit objectives and a strategy for achieving them impedes learning. Rather than blaming past mistakes on a failure to learn resulting from this ambiguity, the temptation has been to imbue mistakes with inevitability.

The judgment of inevitability applied to the Great Depression of the 1930s and Great Inflation of the 1970s rests uneasily with the fact that a period of relative stability preceded each. In the 1920s, Governor Strong sterilized gold inflows to preserve price stability. He also moved the Fed in the direction of a lean-against-the-wind interest rate policy directed toward macroeconomic stability. At the same time, however, Strong wrapped himself in the cloak of policy ambiguity.

Irving Fisher (1934, 151) reported a conversation in which he urged Governor Strong to support a bill of Representative Strong's mandating the Fed to stabilize the price level (Hetzel 1985, 8):

In talking with him [Governor Strong], he said, "Don't compel me to do what I am doing. Let me alone and I will try to do it. If I am required by law to do it, I don't know whether I can, and I will resign. I will not take the responsibility." I said to him, "I would trust you to do it without a legislative mandate, but you will not live forever, and when you die I fear this will die with you." He said, "No, it will not."

Fisher then recounted how Governor Strong and Representative Strong, shortly before the former's death, drafted a mandate instructing the Fed to maintain "stable purchasing power of the dollar." However, Governor. Strong felt compelled to seek approval of the Board, which it failed to provide, and Representative Strong's bill came to naught.

Prior to the Great Inflation, Martin presided over a period of low inflation. He reinvented the Fed in a way that looked forward to the V–G era. Instead of a monetary policy focused on financial intermediation and the control of speculation, Martin emphasized economic stabilization. Lean-against-the-wind replaced real bills (Hetzel and Leach 2001a; 2001b). Martin believed that the Fed had responsibility for the purchasing power of the dollar, by which he meant price stability, not low inflation. Although internal division and political attack pushed him off course in the last part of the 1960s, he returned to monetary restriction in 1969. Martin's term, however, ended in January 1970.

Earlier, in fall 1928, before the onset of the Depression, Strong died. Governor George Harrison, who followed Strong, was a weak leader (Hetzel 2002a, Appendix). Arthur Burns, who followed Martin, was a strong but poor leader. Under Burns, the political system wanted the Fed to maintain low unemployment as a way of assuaging the political divisions produced by a variety of distributional shocks. In the 1960s, those shocks included the Vietnam War, the need for higher taxes due to expansion of the welfare state, and disorder in the inner cities. In the 1970s, they included imports that created protectionist pressures and low productivity growth that reduced the revenue growth needed for the expansion of government programs demanded by an activist Congress. Burns believed that monetary policy could give the political system what it wanted, provided the political system gave him the additional instrument of price controls.

Neither Strong nor Martin left a Fed that could cope with the poor leadership of their successors. Policy ambiguity obscured the primacy that Strong and Martin assigned to price stability. The political advantages of policy ambiguity gave way to the longer run disadvantage of confusion about the appropriate role for monetary policy. No internal debate occurred capable of establishing consensus over the role of policy. Faced with external shocks and poor internal leadership, the Fed has foundered. The United States can institutionalize monetary stability. However, to do so, the Fed must be open and promote the necessary debate. Policy ambiguity prevents debate and invites instability.

III. Measurement without Theory

Koopmans (1947) and Lucas (1976) criticized policymaking within an atheoretical framework. In his review ("Measurement without Theory") of Burns and Mitchell's book, *Measuring Business Cycles*, Koopmans (1947, 167) wrote:

> There is no ... awareness of the problems of determining the identifiability of, and measuring, structural equations as a prerequisite to the practically important types of prediction.... Without resort to theory ... conclusions relevant to the guidance of economic policies cannot be drawn.... [T]he mere observation of regularities in the interrelations of variables then does not permit us to recognize or to identify behavior equations among such regularities.

With only the descriptive language of business economics, policymakers cannot make predictions based on cause and effect. With that language, the Fed cannot talk about what macroeconomic variables it controls and how it controls them. Without a framework that yields falsifiable predictions from alternative policies, learning is haphazard.

Like Burns, Greenspan understood monetary policy through the business forecasting perspective, which encourages characterization of optimal policy as the optimal period-by-period choice of policy actions. It focuses on the difficulty of near-term forecasting, which requires the relentless synthesis of a vast amount of disparate information. The constant arrival of unanticipated news makes forecasting inherently difficult. From this perspective, the world is fraught with complexity and uncertainty. The simplifying abstractions of economic models appear irrelevant or naïve.

Nevertheless, those abstractions explain how central banks have succeeded in combining price and economic stability. The price level is a monetary phenomenon: The procedures central banks use to control monetary base creation determine the behavior of inflation. Expectations are rational: The public learns to form its expectations of inflation conformably with the consistent behavior of monetary policy. The price system works to equilibrate macroeconomic activity: Fluctuations in the real interest rate within moderate limits maintain real output in line with potential output over time. These characteristics allowed the V–G FOMC to follow rule-like behavior that both stabilized expected trend inflation and allowed the price system to work (Hetzel 2006).

IV. Concluding Comment

The central bank is responsible for the value of money. Because money's value today derives from the value that individuals expect it to have tomorrow, Lucas's (1980, 255) argument for rules applies naturally to monetary policy:

[O]ur ability as economists to predict the responses of agents rests, in situations where expectations about the future matter, on our understanding of the stochastic environment agents believe themselves to be operating in. In practice, this limits the class of policies the consequences of which we can hope to assess in advance to policies generated by fixed, well understood, relatively permanent rules (or functions relating policy actions taken to the state of the economy). . . . [A]nalysis of policy which utilizes economics in a scientific way necessarily involves choice among alternative stable, predictable policy rules, infrequently changed and then only after extensive professional and general discussion, minimizing (though, of course, never entirely eliminating) the role of discretionary economic management.

Lucas (1980, 255) also noted:

I have been impressed with how noncontroversial it [the above argument for rules] seems to be at a general level and with how widely ignored it continues to be at what some view as a "practical" level.

Concern for nominal expectational stability imparted a rule-like consistency to policy in the V–G era. However, apart from the nonborrowed reserves strategy adopted October 1979, policy evolved pragmatically rather than as a conscious choice of strategy by the FOMC. In no case has it ever involved "extensive professional and general discussion," much less discussion with the academic community utilizing the language of economics. The resulting lack of public understanding of the monetary standard imparts fragility to that standard.

THREE

From Gold to Fiat Money

The centralization of authority in national governments marked the twentieth century. In the realm of money, a fiat monetary standard run by national central banks replaced a commodity standard run largely impersonally. Only after repeated episodes of inflation and deflation did central banks realize their responsibility for the behavior of prices. The greatest episode of monetary instability was the Great Depression. As predicted by Adam Smith in the *Wealth of Nations* in the eighteenth century, the specialization of production allowed the creation of wealth in the nineteenth century. Economic specialization rests on two pillars: free trade and stable money. Stability of the purchasing power of money makes possible roundabout exchange instead of barter. In the Depression, governments and central banks brought down both these pillars.

I. The Gold Standard

In the heyday of the gold standard, the world had a dominant money market – London – and a preeminent central bank – the Bank of England.[1] Britain viewed the gold standard as an extension of its imperial grandeur. A sine qua non for the international gold standard was the freedom to ship gold made possible by the absence of capital controls. That freedom of movement of capital made London the center of the world financial market, just as London was the center of the empire. No one could doubt the commitment of the Bank of England to maintaining the gold price of the pound.

In the latter part of the nineteenth century, all the industrialized countries of the world went onto the gold standard. They associated it with the economic progress that came from the free movement of capital and the integration of world markets through free trade (Yeager 1998). Moderate worldwide inflation after the middle of the 1890s added to the robustness of the pre–World War I gold standard (Figures 4.1 and 4.2). That inflation derived from additions to the gold stock from gold discoveries in South Africa and the cyanide process for extracting gold (Friedman 1992, Chapter 5).

Under the gold standard, periodic fears for convertibility of fiduciary money into gold caused financial panics and suspension of convertibility. The 1907 panic led to a demand for the creation of a central bank. The New York financial community wanted a central bank to aid its challenge to the dominant position of London as the world's financial center (Roberts 1998; 2000). The increasing centralization of power in government during the Progressive era rendered attractive the idea of a central bank.

Politically, the defeat in 1896 by William McKinley of William Jennings Bryan and the populist, free silver coalition that backed him appeared to commit irrevocably the United States to the gold standard. As demonstrated by this election, the country wanted the marketplace through the gold standard rather than the government through paper money to determine prices. That assumption remained unchanged with the creation of the Fed in 1913.

When the Fed began operation, policymakers possessed the businessperson's attachment to the gold standard. They assumed that convertibility of the paper dollar into gold gave paper dollars their value. For them, the gold standard meant the legal commitment to backing currency with gold. They did not understand the self-equilibrating character of the international gold standard. Specifically, they did not understand how gold flows and the associated changes in national money stocks caused price levels among countries to vary to equilibrate the balance of payments.

That ignorance was understandable. The United States had not had a central bank since Andrew Jackson vetoed the charter of the Second Bank of the United States in 1832. Without a central bank, the gold standard functioned automatically.[2] Gold discoveries and international gold flows determined the money stock and the price level. The automatic functioning of the system made unnecessary an understanding of the determination of prices. If the Fed was not going to follow the rules of the international gold standard, however, it needed to devise other rules making it responsible for the price level. Apart from a few economists, no one understood this point.

To achieve the goal of ending financial panics, the Fed's founders adapted the "real bills" rules developed for individual banks. Real bills had arisen to prevent speculative behavior that could lead to insolvency and runs. When expanded to become a theory of financial panics, it held that asset price inflation derived from speculative credit extension for nonproductive uses. Inflated asset prices would inevitably fall.

That fall would initiate forced asset sales and inventory liquidation. Deflation, financial collapse and recession would follow (Hetzel 1985; Humphrey 2001). Experience under commodity monetary standards where price falls had followed price rises reinforced this view. As envisaged by its founders, the Fed would extend credit through the discount window only for real bills – the short-term commercial paper that provided temporary financing of goods in transit from producers to consumers.

In this way, the banking system would proportion credit extended to credit demanded for productive uses. An "elastic" currency would mitigate financial panics, while real bills rules would limit the extension of credit to the legitimate needs of trade. Without a spillover of credit into speculation, financial panics would end. From the real bills perspective, inflation began with a rise in asset prices. Policymakers saw their role as intervening early in boom–bust cycles to limit speculative euphoria and asset price rises. In this way, they would limit the magnitude of the ultimate deflation and economic collapse. In fact, increases in the discount rate to limit perceived speculation required abandoning the rules of the gold standard and left the country without a nominal anchor.

II. Reconstructing the Gold Standard

In the 1920s, Europe tried to reconstruct the gold standard abandoned in World War I. However, creation of the Fed added discretion to the world monetary system. As a public institution that did not need to earn a profit, it could accumulate indefinitely noninterest-bearing gold stocks (Friedman 1961). The Fed's ability to impound gold inflows from the rest of the world meant that international gold flows did not produce a symmetric sharing of the burden of adjustment to balance of payments disequilibria. Gold inflows into the United States did not make U.S. goods more expensive by raising its price level. All the adjustment had to take place through falls in prices of the countries suffering the outflows.

In World War I, governments universally financed war expenditures through the issuance of short-term debt. They abandoned the gold standard in favor of interest rate pegging by the central bank to lower the cost of government debt finance. Cheap money policies and inflation continued after the war. Governments were unwilling to allow their central banks to raise interest rates prior to the refunding of short-term government debt into long-term bonds (Eichengreen 1995, 81, 114; Hetzel 2002a).

In 1919, the U.S. federal budget deficit amounted to 72% of expenditures.[3] The New York Fed kept its discount rate at 4% until the end of 1919, a year after the Armistice of November 1918. Federal Reserve credit (mainly bills discounted with the Fed) continued the rapid growth begun in 1917 (Friedman and Schwartz 1963a, 214–15).[4] From 1915 to 1920, the U.S. price level doubled.[5]

After the war, restoration of the gold standard required a decision about whether to return to the prewar gold parities. In the United States, that parity was $20.67 per fine ounce. To restore the real purchasing power of monetary gold given wartime inflation, the United States could have raised the dollar price of gold. If other countries also raised their gold parities in line with increases in their domestic price levels, the gold standard could have begun operation again with the higher postwar prices.

However, in the real bills environment of the time, restoration of the prewar real purchasing power of gold through such an accounting change was unthinkable.

The Treasury and the Fed viewed the rise in prices associated with World War I as evidence of speculation made possible by credit creation for unproductive purposes. Both agreed to deflation to undo wartime speculative excesses (Roberts 2000, fn. 37; Seay 1922). There was agreement that the banking system should liquidate the credit created to finance the war (Goldenweiser 1951, 132).

From the end of 1919 to June 1920, the New York Fed raised its discount rate from 4 to 7%. The Treasury issued an explanation on November 2, 1919: "The reason for the advance in rates announced today by the Federal Reserve Bank of New York is the evidence that . . . credit . . . is being diverted to speculative employment." The Fed also pressured banks to repay their borrowings (Goldenweiser 1951, 135). Money (M1) fell by 13% over the two-year period from early 1920 to early 1922.[6] Between 1920 and 1922, the level of the CPI fell by 16%, and the wholesale price index fell by 37%.[7] As illustrated by the dramatic move from inflation to deflation by mid 1920 (Figure 3.1), establishment of the Fed inaugurated a long period of nominal instability.

Foreign countries faced a choice of how to deal with U.S. deflation. They could preserve their exchange rate with the United States by deflating along with it. Alternatively, they could avoid deflation by allowing their exchange rate to depreciate relative to the dollar. Countries like France, Belgium, and Italy chose the first course. Others like Britain, Switzerland, and Canada chose the second. Eichengreen (1995, 183) showed that economic recovery proceeded significantly more rapidly in the latter countries. Overall, currency depreciation served to mitigate the shock from the United States to the rest of the world. In contrast, at the end of the decade, a reconstructed gold standard would transmit fully deflationary U.S. monetary policy.

As reconstructed in the 1920s, the international gold standard would have little tolerance for such a shock. Central banks held only small amounts of free gold.[8] One reason was that the United States had absorbed so much of the world's monetary gold stocks. In 1913, the United States held about 22% of world gold reserves. At the time of the armistice in 1918, it held almost 38%.[9] When the United States lifted its gold embargo in 1919, gold flowed out. Overall, it had a balanced trade account, but capital outflows to finance European reconstruction engendered gold outflows.[10] Despite the accumulation of gold during the war, those outflows threatened the adequacy of the gold cover that the Reserve Banks held against their liabilities. The reason was that the wartime rise in the price level had entailed a commensurate increase in the money stock and in the required gold cover.

Even with the 1920–1 deflation, the U.S. price level remained 70% above its prewar level. As a result, the United States retained the gold that it accumulated in World War I. A decline in gold production further exacerbated the problem of a diminished gold supply for the rest of the world. Given the unchanged parity the United States maintained for gold, the rise in the U.S. price level reduced the real price of gold, and gold production fell with the diminished rewards for mining.[11] The 1920–1 deflation caused gold to flow back into the United States. The U.S.

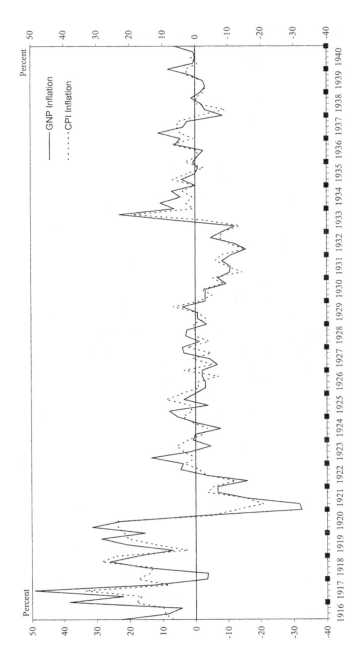

Figure 3.1. Inflation. *Notes:* Quarterly observations of annualized percentage changes in GNP deflator from Balke and Gordon (1986, Appendix B). Consumer Price Index (CPI) inflation data are quarterly observations of annualized percentage changes in monthly average data. Monthly data are from the Bureau of Labor Statistics. Heavy tick marks indicate fourth quarter.

15

monetary gold stock rose from somewhat more than $3.5 billion in early 1922 to $4.5 billion in 1924.[12] These factors reduced the availability of gold outside the United States and rendered more difficult Britain's return to the gold standard at the prewar parity.

III. The Great Depression

In the mid 1920s, the Fed followed a policy that presaged the lean-against-the-wind policy of William McChesney Martin. Governor Harrison (U.S. Cong. April 14, 1932, 499), head of the New York Fed beginning in 1928, testified, "We operated the Federal reserve system with a view, so far as we had power, to stimulating business and prices when they get a little low and to restraining them when they began to consume too much credit." The stock market boom in the last half of the 1920s prompted the next instance of purposeful deflation after 1919–20. In the 1920s, gold inflows rather than advances from the discount window became the primary source of Federal Reserve credit. Policymakers saw the rise in stock prices after 1925 as evidence that gold inflows circumvented the real bills policy.[13] From this perspective, the resulting credit creation, unrelated to the supply of short-term, self-liquidating commercial paper, allowed banks to finance speculation.

Real bills proponents placed the Fed on the defensive by accusing it of having created the stock market boom through an easy money policy (Roberts 2000, Part II). In summer 1924, the New York Fed had made open market purchases and lowered its discount rate to 3% to aid Britain's return to the gold standard. In August 1927, representatives of the Bank of England, the Banque de France, and the Reichsbank persuaded the Fed to undertake open market purchases and to lower discount rates at all the regional banks. In each case, the Fed took those actions following gold inflows. Its actions accorded with the rules of the international gold standard. However, the New York Fed came under attack for creating cheap credit leading to a speculative rise in the stock market.

In early 1928, the Fed initiated a restrictive policy to stop stock market speculation. The Desk undertook open market sales to force member banks into the discount window. With banks in debt to the Fed, the Fed would have leverage to force them to cease making loans for the purchase of stocks on margin. By early 1929, open market sales had pressured banks to the point where all money market rates exceeded the discount rate. (In general, the New York Fed kept the discount rate in the middle of the various money market rates.) The regional Fed Banks interpreted the uniform excess of money market rates over the discount rate not as evidence of contractionary monetary policy but as evidence of an incentive for banks to borrow and speculate (Chandler 1958, 455–9).

Benjamin Strong had been Governor of the New York Fed since its inception. He backed a contractionary monetary policy to bring down the value of the stock market. Strong (Chandler 1958, 329) wrote: "[T]he speculative temper of the American people is not going to be satisfied by a fling in the stock market.... It seems a shame that the best sort of plans can be handicapped by a speculative orgy, and yet the temperament of the people of this country is such that these situations cannot be avoided."

Internal Fed debate centered on whether tying reserve creation to the discounting of real bills allowed the Fed to exercise adequate control over the purposes for which banks extended credit.[14] The New York Fed argued that the fungibility of credit vitiated the effectiveness of tying discount window loans to the discounting of real bills. When speculative fever gripped markets, it believed, the Fed would have to restrain credit extension by high interest rates. An unfortunate but unavoidable side effect would be to force deflation upon the entire economy.

A. Monetary Policy in the Depression

Between May 1928 and August 1929, the New York Fed raised its discount rate from 3.5 to 6%. The stock market crashed October 1929. The contraction that followed worsened with three waves of bank runs (Friedman and Schwartz 1963a). The first began October 1930; the second, March 1931; and the third, January 1933. From 1929 through the cyclical trough in March 1933, nominal income fell by 53%; real income, by 36%; and the money stock, by a third.

Friedman and Schwartz (1963a, Chapter 7) attribute the fall in money to the Fed's unwillingness to engage in open market operations sufficient to offset a bank-ran-induced decline in the money multiplier produced by declines in the deposit-reserves and deposit-currency ratio. It is true that the Fed could have maintained the money stock through an aggressive expansion of the monetary base. However, as summarized in the Appendix ("Borrowed-Reserves Operating Procedures"), policymakers were controlling the level of money market rates by setting the level of the discount rate and member bank borrowing at the discount window. The basic reason for the fall in the money stock was that the Fed maintained a level of interest rates that required monetary contraction.[15]

In congressional testimony in April 1932, Governor Harrison explained why the Fed was unwilling to pursue an expansionary monetary policy. The House Committee on Banking and Currency held these hearings to promote a bill to require the Fed to restore the price level to its predeflation value. Repeatedly, Harrison challenged that goal on the grounds that it would require the Fed to increase bank reserves while the price level was falling even if it believed that banks would use the additional funds for speculative purposes.[16] Harrison (U.S. Cong. April 14, 1932, 485) said:

[S]uppose ... the price level is going down, and the Federal reserve system begins to buy government securities, hoping to check the decline, and that inspires a measure of confidence, and a speculation is revived in securities, which may in turn consume so much credit as to require our sales of Governments. There was that difficulty in 1928 and 1929.

Table 3.1. *Nominal and Real Rate*

Year	Commercial paper rate	Expected inflation	Real rate of interest	Real GNP growth	M1 growth	M2 growth
1929	5.8	−0.9	6.7	6.6	0.9	0.2
1930	3.6	−2.1	5.7	−9.6	−3.5	−2.0
1931	2.6	−7.1	9.7	−7.7	−6.6	−7.1
1932	2.7	−4.1	6.8	−13.8	−12.4	−15.4
1933T1	2.1	−6.1	8.2	−21.3	−17.8	−31.6
1933T2&T3	1.6	5.1	−3.5	14.2	6.0	4.9

Notes: Commercial paper rate is from the Board of Governors (1943, Table No. 120). Expected inflation is from Hamilton (1992, Table 7). Hamilton's figures are for trimesters. The figures are the average of expected inflation for the three trimesters of the individual years. The real rate of interest is the commercial paper rate minus expected inflation. Real GNP growth is annual growth rates from Balke and Gordon (1986, Appendix B). M1 and M2 growth are annual growth rates from Friedman and Schwartz (1970). 1933T1 is the first trimester (four months) of 1933 and 1933T2&T3 is the last two trimesters (eight months) of 1933. For 1933T1, real GNP growth is for 1933Q1. For 1933T1&T2, it is the average of annualized quarterly growth rates for 1933Q2, 1933Q3, and 1933Q4. For 1933T1, M1 and M2 growth are annualized growth rates from December 1932 through April 1933. For 1933T2&T3, they are the annualized growth rates from April 1933 through December 1933.

Also, in fall 1931 the Fed pushed money market rates back up in an attempt to maintain confidence in the gold standard.

Once investors came to expect deflation, the excess of the real over the market interest rate exacerbated monetary stringency (Schwartz 1981). For this period, Hamilton (1992) derived estimates of expected deflation from the behavior of futures prices of commodity markets and the relation of those prices to the aggregate price level. He estimated that the public anticipated about half of the actual price deflation in the years 1929 through 1932. Table 3.1 shows how expected deflation turned moderate market interest rates into high real rates. The most dramatic example occurred in 1931. An expected deflation rate of 7.1% turned a market interest rate of 2.6% into a real rate of 9.7%.

For comparison, over the period 1924 through 1927, the commercial paper rate averaged 4.1% (Figure 3.2). This value is likely also the real interest rate as the CPI remained unchanged over this period. Over the period 1924 through 1927, real GNP grew at an average annualized rate of 2.9% (Balke and Gordon 1989, Table 10). Table 3.1 shows that for the years 1929 through 1932 real GNP growth was below this average value, often dramatically. The negative growth rates in the Depression required low, not the high real rates shown in column 3 of Table 3.1. Monetary contraction, shown in the final columns of Table 3.1, created the high real rates. As a result of using an interest rate instrument, monetary policy fell into a vicious cycle. Monetary contraction produced deflation; deflation produced expected deflation; expected deflation produced high real interest rates; and high real interest rates produced monetary contraction.[17]

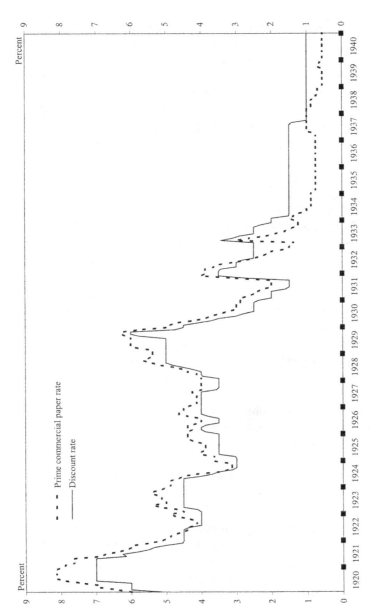

Figure 3.2. Money Market and Discount Rates of Interest. *Notes:* Monthly observations of the prime commercial paper rate and the discount rate are from Board of Governors (1943, Tables No. 115 and 120). Heavy tick marks indicate fourth quarter.

Did the bank failures themselves contribute independently to economic recession beyond the monetary contraction? Bernanke (1983) and Mishkin (1978) argue affirmatively. Friedman and Schwartz (1963a, 352) argue that the bank runs were only the mechanism by which the monetary contraction occurred. Other mechanisms would have produced the same deleterious results for the economy. Friedman and Schwartz cite the case of Canada, which experienced a monetary contraction without bank failures and a recession similar in severity to that in the United States.

B. What If Governor Strong Had Lived?

Friedman and Schwartz (1963a) conjectured that if Governor Strong had not died in 1928 and had instead continued as head of the New York Fed, he would not have allowed the large-scale bank failures and the collapse of the money stock. Representative Strong had convinced Governor Strong in 1928 to back a bill mandating that the Fed stabilize the price level. Economists Irving Fisher and John Commons had drafted the legislation. In Atlantic City in 1928, the two Strongs edited the final version. Representative Strong (U.S. Cong. 1932, 51) later recounted that he had convinced Governor Strong of the desirability of such a mandate by referring to the 1920 deflation. Governor Strong recounted that he had opposed the decision to deflate. Representative Strong got Governor Strong to admit that a mandate to stabilize the price level might have allowed him (Governor Strong) to prevail in 1920 (Hetzel 1985).

Governor Strong died October 7, 1928, on the eve of the stock market crash. Friedman and Schwartz (1963a, 692) argue that had he lived, he would have undertaken vigorous open market purchases to offset the drains on bank reserves. If he had done so, the money stock would not have collapsed, and recession would not have become depression. What intellectual leap would the Fed have had to make to shift the focus away from market interest rates and toward the destruction of the money stock?

The New York Fed did make open market purchases after the market crash. Perhaps Strong, had he lived, would have made even more.[18] In that event, borrowed reserves would have been smaller. However, given the Fed's borrowed reserves procedures, the discount rate placed a floor under market rates (Appendix, "Borrowed-Reserves Operating Procedures"). The Fed was reluctant to lower the discount rate for fear of reviving speculation. Because Strong had supported a deflationary monetary policy to bring the market down, he might have been sensitive to this concern.

More fundamentally, if Strong had lived and had conducted monetary policy as Friedman and Schwartz suggested, he would have had to change radically both the prevailing conception of monetary policy and its operating procedures. To have undertaken open market purchases with the conscious intent of maintaining bank credit and the money stock in order to stabilize the price level, the Fed would have had to have made a reasoned decision to implement a fiat money standard. At the time, only a few academic economists like Irving Fisher and John Maynard Keynes possessed the modern conception of the central bank as a creator of money.[19] The policymaking establishment considered such economists irresponsible (Roberts 2000, 91). Keynes abandoned monetary policy in favor of fiscal policy, perhaps, because of a belief that central banks lacked the conceptual framework and the will to pursue a policy of purposeful money creation (Leijonhufvud 1968, 19).

It is hard to imagine the U.S. political system at the onset of the Depression abandoning the gold standard for a fiat money standard. A currency backed by gold was economic and political orthodoxy. The victory of William McKinley over William Jennings Bryan in the 1896 presidential election appeared to have forever tarred opponents of the gold standard as populist proponents of cheap money who would undermine the established social order. The Glass–Steagall Act of 1932 did give the Fed authority to back its note issues with government securities. However, the United States retained the gold cover requirements for currency issue.

Political attacks on the Fed as an institution also limited its ability to act radically. Senator Carter Glass, who had helped found the Fed, disliked the emergence of the New York Fed as the U.S. central bank. Real bills proponents like Glass blamed the stock market crash and subsequent economic malaise on the discount rate reductions that the Fed had made in 1924 and 1927 (Glass 1932). That criticism undoubtedly made the Fed conservative by requiring it to act with consensus, which limited the ability of the New York Fed to undertake unilaterally open market purchases.

In the real bills environment of the time, policymakers did not think of the Fed as a central bank capable of creating bank reserves. Instead, as E. A. Goldenweiser (1951, 161) explained, the Fed saw itself as a storehouse of the reserves of commercial banks.[20] In the financial panics of the early thirties, its reaction was the defensive one of protecting those reserves:

[T]hat it [a monetary easing] could not have been put into effect is beyond dispute. . . . That Federal Reserve banks could not fail the way commercial banks could as the result of deposit withdrawals, because the Reserve Banks could always issue notes to meet their deposit liabilities [member bank deposits], was not part of the System's thinking of the time. . . . Commercial bank concepts were simply being applied to a central bank to which they are not relevant. . . . A policy of large-scale open-market operations for the purpose of creating money directly and thus maintaining its volume . . . was not one that the System felt itself able to pursue.

Governor Harrison (U.S. Cong. 1932, 517) testified about Fed actions in fall 1931: "It would have been a very unwise and dangerous thing for the Federal reserve system to continue to dissipate its credit in the purchase of Government securities in such a time and yet in that situation last fall we would have had to do it had this bill been law for the price index was going down."

The gold standard also prevented the Fed from understanding its responsibility to manage its asset portfolio to maintain bank credit and the money stock. According to monetary orthodoxy, central banks should respond to gold outflows by raising interest rates. That meant reducing Federal Reserve credit by selling securities. Central banks competed for a given amount of world gold. They did not create their own reserves. In the early thirties, the Fed was trapped intellectually by monetary orthodoxy and real bills. As a practical central banker, it is unlikely that Governor Strong could have acted as Moses to lead the Fed into the land of modern central banking.

C. Transmitting U.S. Deflation through the Gold Standard

The United States had returned to the gold standard March 1919 upon ending its wartime gold embargo. Germany returned at the end of 1923; Britain, in early 1925; and France, in 1926 (Yeager 1976). Allied war debts and the reparations payments required of Germany by the Versailles Treaty added to the fragility of the newly reconstructed gold standard. To make the resource transfers ultimately required by the distribution of international debt, Germany would have had to run a balance of trade surplus with France and Britain. In turn, France and Britain would have had to run a trade surplus with the United States. In the protectionist world of the twenties, that was politically unacceptable. The system stayed together only through capital outflows from the United States to Germany (Eichengreen 1995; Hetzel 2002a; Yeager 1976, 333).

By the end of 1927, it appeared that Europe had successfully reconstituted the gold standard. However, in 1928, the Fed initiated a restrictive monetary policy. Governor Strong understood the problems that such a policy would pose for the Dawes Plan, which attempted to generate the capital flows necessary to make German reparations feasible. In July 1928, in a letter to the official overseeing reparations, Strong (cited in Chandler 1958, 459) wrote: "[T]he continued maintenance of very high rates in New York may ultimately present a real hazard to Europe and especially to the smooth operation of the Dawes plan. It may indeed provoke the very crisis which you seek to avoid."

By early 1929, higher interest rates in the United States forced foreign central banks to raise their discount rates. High U.S. rates disrupted capital outflows from the United States (Eichengreen 1995, 12). By the last half of 1929, foreign debt issued in New York was less than a third of its 1927 level (Chandler 1958, 456). Net capital outflows fell from $700 million in 1928 to $300 million in 1929 and 1930.[21] Gold flows into the United States destabilized the newly reconstructed gold standards of Germany and Austria, which held minimal free gold reserves.

Prior to monetary restriction, the Fed's monetary gold stock had been falling. It went from $4.6 billion in 1927 to $4.1 billion in 1928 (for gold valued at $20.67 per fine ounce). Early in 1929, it began to rise and reached $5 billion in September 1931.[22] France added to the strains placed on the international gold standard by returning to gold at a price that undervalued the franc and sterilizing the resulting gold inflows. Gold stocks of the Banque de France went from $1.1 billion in June 1928, the date of a franc revaluation in terms of gold, to $2.3 billion in September 1931.[23] Inevitably, as the United States and France absorbed gold, banks would fail. In May 1931, the Kreditanstalt of Vienna failed.

In summer 1931, financial panic spread to Germany. The Reichsbank raised its discount rate from 5% in June to 15% on July 31.[24] Believing that German banks were failing because of speculative credit extension, the New York Fed refused to lend to the Reichsbank to allow it to prevent the collapse of its banking system. At New York's urging, the Reichsbank closed its discount window to commercial banks, which had lent to German municipalities in violation of real bills principles (Hetzel 2002a; James 1986). The gold reserves of the Reichsbank, which were $0.65 billion in January 1929, fell to $0.23 billion in December 1931.[25]

Financial panic then spread to Britain, whose banks had considerable exposure to German banks. In September 1931, Britain ceased redeeming sterling in gold. The shock to confidence that followed the end of the gold standard in Britain produced gold outflows from the United States, which lost more than $600 million in gold between August and November 1931. The New York Fed did not offset the gold outflows by purchasing securities. Instead, it raised its discount rate from 1.5 to 3.5% and reduced holdings of bankers acceptances. Market interest rates rose sharply.

D. The Roosevelt Monetary Standard

The United States did not extricate itself from deflation and depression through action by the Fed, which never purchased government securities purposefully to create money. Fed open market purchases (Federal Reserve credit) only accommodated the public's increased demand for currency manifested in bank runs (Figure 3.3). Just as the two recessions that made up the Great Depression involved an active attempt by the Fed to implement its real bill views, the two recoveries required sidelining the Fed as a central bank.

Starting in April 1933, the new Roosevelt administration began to raise the dollar price of gold in order to depreciate the dollar's foreign exchange value. At a press conference, President Roosevelt made clear that the United States intended to depreciate the dollar to raise domestic prices. In May, the Thomas Amendment to the Agricultural Adjustment Act allowed the president to lower the gold content of the dollar by as much as 50%. In September, the treasury began to buy gold to raise its dollar price (Friedman and Schwartz 1963a, 462).

Dollar depreciation, which raised the dollar prices of commodities traded internationally, exercised an immediate impact on prices.[26] From their peak in 1928Q4 through 1933Q1, wholesale prices fell 38.3%, and in 1933Q1, they fell at an annualized rate of 19%. Over the last three quarters of 1933, they rose at an average

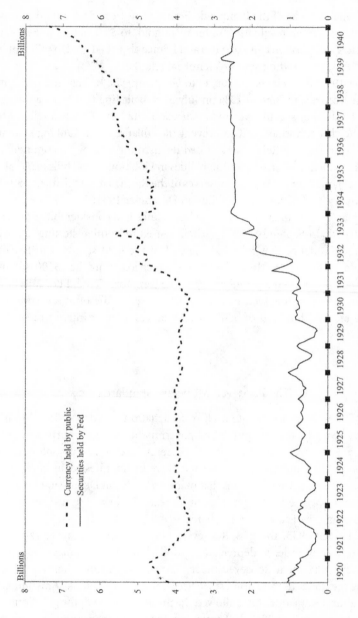

Figure 3.3. Federal Reserve Credit and Currency Held by Public. *Notes*: Observations are monthly. Securities held by Fed is Reserve Bank credit outstanding minus discount window borrowing from Board of Governors (1943, Table No. 102). Currency held by the public is from Friedman and Schwartz (1970). Heavy tick marks indicate December.

24

annualized rate of 25.8%.[27] Over 1928Q4 to 1933Q1, the CPI fell 26%, but rose at an average annualized rate of 5.4% over the last three quarters of 1933.

According to Hamilton's (1992) estimates of expected inflation, this reversal in inflation produced a rise in expected inflation (Table 3.1), which lowered the real commercial paper rate from 8.2% in the first trimester of 1933 to −3.5% in the remainder of the year. The fall in the real rate removed monetary policy as a source of deflation. Money growth went from strongly negative in the first part of 1933 to positive in the remainder of the year.

The complement to using dollar depreciation to raise the domestic price level was gold inflows. For gold inflows to raise the monetary base and stimulate money creation, the Fed could not sterilize them. For that to happen, the Fed had to abandon the borrowed-reserves operating procedures with which it set market interest rates. Events forced that abandonment by removing the Fed as an influence on money market conditions. While banks with eligible collateral could borrow at the discount window to obtain reserves lost through runs, such borrowing stigmatized them as weak. Over time, banks liquidated their commercial loans in an attempt to accumulate excess reserves as a source of emergency funds alternative to the discount window.

When banks ceased obtaining the marginal reserves they needed through the discount window, Fed influence over market rates ceased. Fed irrelevance appears in the excess of the discount rate over the commercial paper rate (Figure 3.2). During 1933, banks practically eliminated their discount window borrowing. While borrowed reserves fell from an average $435 million over the first four months of 1933 to $156 million in the last eight months, excess reserves rose from an average of $360 million to $627 million.[28] May 1933 serves as an approximate date for the end of borrowed-reserves procedures and the beginning of money stock determination within a reserves-money multiplier framework.[29]

The end of interest rate targeting with the breakdown of the Fed's borrowed-reserves procedures made possible the Roosevelt administration's bastard gold standard. After the cessation of the panics in early 1933 and before the rate pegging of World War II, the unwillingness of the Fed to conduct open market purchases resulted in a freezing of the size of its security portfolio (Figure 3.3). With member-bank borrowing minimal, increases in the monetary base derived from gold inflows. Suspension of interest rate targeting meant that the Fed could not sterilize the gold inflows produced by the Roosevelt administration's manipulation of the international monetary standard of fixed exchange rates.

After 1928, the international gold standard transmitted deflationary monetary policy in the United States to other industrialized countries. After March 1933, the United States continued to create deflation for the countries remaining on the gold standard, but it did so in pursuit of domestic inflation. While the United States monetized gold inflows, it eliminated the possibility of a reversal of that monetization. In March 1933, the Roosevelt administration instituted foreign exchange controls and prohibited domestic gold payments.

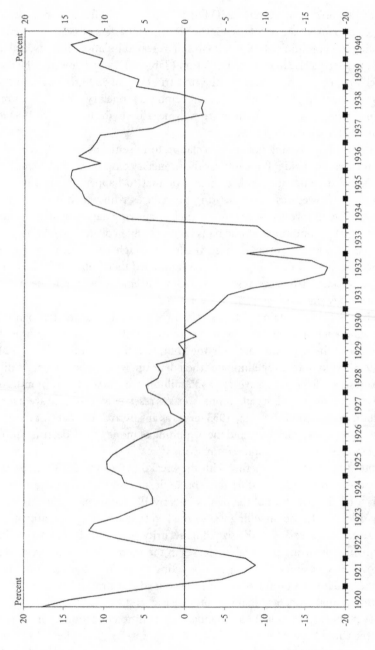

Figure 3.4. M2 Growth. *Notes*: Quarterly observations of four-quarter percentage changes in M2 from Friedman and Schwartz (1970). Heavy tick marks indicate fourth quarter.

26

In January 1934, the United States fixed its purchase price for gold at $35 an ounce – a 59% devaluation. The treasury bought the gold that flowed into the United States. It then delivered a gold certificate to the Fed, which increased the treasury's deposits. The monetary base increased when the treasury drew down its deposits to make purchases (Friedman and Schwartz 1963a, Chapter 8). From 1933Q1 through 1937Q1, M1 and M2 (Figure 3.4) increased at annualized rates, respectively, of 11.5 and 8.1%. Over this same period, real GNP increased at an annualized rate of 10.8%.

Would this growth have happened if the Fed had abjured interest rate targeting and had massively bought assets other than gold like government securities? Until the 1970s, the professional consensus was negative. Most economists believed that an expansion of the money stock would have led to an offsetting reduction in the velocity of money – the Keynesian liquidity trap. However, there is no evidence of a liquidity trap (Bordo, Choudhri, and Schwartz 1995; McCallum 1990). M1 and M2 velocity (Figure 3.5 and 3.6) declined in the 1930s relative to the 1920s, but the decline was in line with a decline in the interest rate opportunity cost of holding money.[30]

The argument that the Fed was powerless to end deflation came from the high level of bank excess reserves after 1933. Policymakers concluded that there was no demand for additional bank credit and, as a result, additional credit creation would go to speculative uses. However, because of runs and the stigma attached to discount window borrowing, banks desired a prudential reserve in the form of excess reserves (Friedman and Schwartz 1963a; Morrison 1966). It follows that increases in reserves from open market purchases beyond the amount desired by banks would have stimulated bank asset purchases and money creation.

E. The Fed Attempt to Reassert Control

After the Fed froze its asset portfolio, the treasury controlled monetary policy. Through its control of gold purchases and sterilization, the treasury determined the growth of the monetary base. With the centralization of control in the new Federal Open Market Committee created by the Banking Act of 1935 and with a new, strong-willed board chairman, Marriner Eccles, the Fed attempted to reassert its prerogatives as a central bank. It did so through an attempt to reinstitute its borrowed-reserves operating procedures. As explained in the Appendix ("Borrowed-Reserve Operating Procedures"), they required the banking system to obtain the marginal reserves it needed through the discount window. As E. A. Goldenweiser (1951, 176) phrased it, to "bring the System in closer touch with the market . . . member banks should not be in a position to expand their operations substantially without being obliged to resort to the Federal Reserve Banks for accommodation."

To again force banks to the discount window, the Fed had to increase required reserves to eliminate the large amounts of excess reserves they had accumulated.[31]

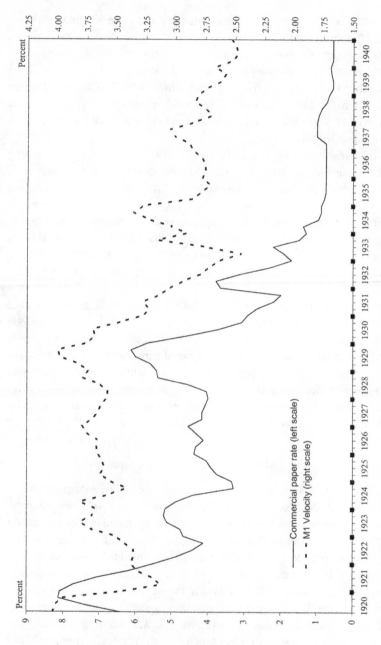

Figure 3.5. M1 Velocity. *Notes*: Quarterly observations of M1 velocity: GNP divided by M1. M1 is from Friedman and Schwartz (1970). GNP is from Balke and Gordon (1986, Appendix B). Commercial paper rate is from Board of Governors (1943). Heavy tick marks indicate fourth quarter.

28

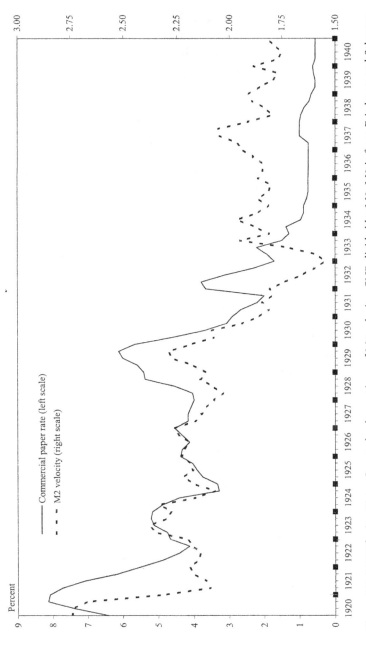

Figure 3.6. M2 Velocity. *Notes*: Quarterly observations of M2 velocity: GNP divided by M2. M2 is from Friedman and Schwartz (1970). GNP is from Balke and Gordon (1986, Appendix B). Commercial paper rate is from Board of Governors (1943). Heavy tick marks indicate fourth quarter.

Those excess reserves exceeded the Fed's holdings of government securities, which it needed to provide income. To avoid open market sales, the Fed turned to massive increases in reserve requirements.[32] Under the influence of real bills, policymakers believed that the banking system's excess reserves could create inflation by allowing banks to extend credit for speculation. Banks would do so to offset the negative effect on their earnings of the low level of interest rates. In his book *Beckoning Frontiers*, Eccles (1951, 288–9) wrote that high levels of excess reserves would allow banks to extend lending "beyond existing or prospective needs of business" and the result would be an inevitable "liquidation of holdings in a painful deflation."

On August 15, 1936, the Board of Governors raised reserve requirements by 50% to eliminate "what was superfluous to the needs of commerce, industry, and agriculture" (Eccles 1951, 290). Also, the treasury began sterilizing gold inflows. The board later increased required reserve ratios to their statutory maximums by imposing an additional 33⅓% increase to take effect in two steps on March 1 and May 1, 1937. From 1937Q1 through 1938Q2, M2 fell at an annualized rate of −1.9%. The economy reached a business cycle peak in May 1937. The trough occurred in June 1938 when money began a vigorous rebound.

After the last increase in reserve requirements, banks again began to accumulate excess reserves. On December 31, 1940, the Fed petitioned Congress to raise the statutory maximums on allowable required reserve ratios. The report stated that "[t]he Federal Reserve System finds itself in the position of being unable effectively to discharge all of its responsibilities." The report also expressed the concern that because of high levels of excess reserves some "interest rates have fallen . . . well below the reasonable requirements of an easy money policy."[33]

IV. The Zero Lower-Bound Problem

When short-term nominal interest rates are zero, the central bank cannot lower the real interest rate by lowering the funds rate. Through use of the moniker "zero lower-bound problem," some economists have suggested that this situation could limit the ability of the central bank to stimulate expenditure.[34] However, the central bank can always stimulate expenditure through the money creation that comes from purchasing illiquid assets. The exogenous money creation that followed the deflationary actions of the Board of Governors in 1936 and 1937 illustrates this possibility.

In the years 1938, 1939, and 1940, the three-month treasury bill rate was essentially zero. It is plausible that the aborting of the recovery along with the return of actual deflation toward the end of 1937 (Figure 3.1) revived the expectation of a return of the deflation of the first years of the decade. Evidence for that assumption comes from the near-zero level of short-term rates. After the cycle trough in June 1938, vigorous growth in real output (Figure 3.7) must have raised the real interest rate and made it positive. Short-term nominal rates, which were not targeted by the Fed (Section III, D), could only have remained at zero through an expectation of deflation in excess of this positive real rate.

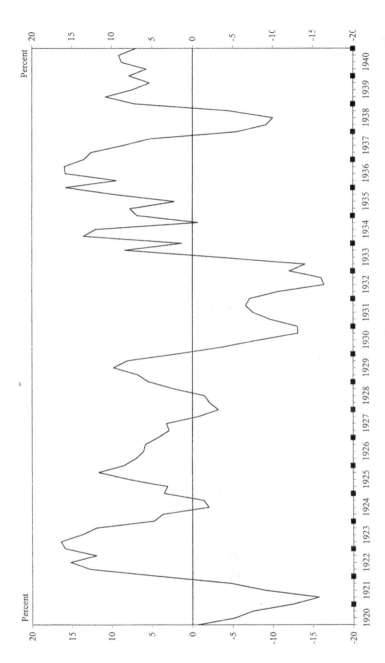

Figure 3.7. Real GNP Growth. *Notes*: Quarterly observations of four-quarter real GNP growth from Balke and Gordon (1986, Appendix B). Heavy tick marks indicate fourth quarter.

At the same time, money growth ($\dot{M}$) was exogenously determined by gold inflows. Growth in monetary velocity ($\dot{V}$) was either moderately negative (Figure 3.5; M1 velocity) or near zero (Figure 3.6; M2 velocity). In terms of the left side of the equation of exchange ($\dot{M} + \dot{V}$), growth in aggregate nominal demand was given. Expected deflation yielded actual deflation ($\dot{P} < 0$) until mid 1939. In terms of the right side of the equation of exchange ($\dot{P} + \dot{Y}$), with deflation, the positive growth in aggregate nominal demand had to appear in positive growth in real output ($\dot{Y} > 0$).

The deflationary spiral that can develop with zero short-term interest rates derives from expected deflation. However, that expectation augments the stimulative force of exogenous money creation. Over the years 1937–9, long-term government security yields averaged 2.5%.[35] Presumably, experience with the gold standard had created the long-term expectation of price stability (Figures 4.1 and 4.2). It follows that if the central bank follows a rule that creates a long-term expectation of price stability, long-term government bonds will yield a positive return. If the short-term interest rate does fall to zero, there will then be government bonds that the central bank can monetize that are illiquid relative to money. Their purchase will force portfolio rebalancing that will stimulate aggregate demand (Hetzel 2004a).

V. Concluding Comment

Congress created the Fed to end the financial crises that had punctuated U.S. history. Ironically, its creation inaugurated a long period of monetary and economic instability. Monetary contraction followed the Fed's attempt in 1920 to lower commodity prices, its attempt in 1929 to lower equity prices, and its attempt in 1936 to immobilize bank excess reserves. Declines in nominal and real output accompanied monetary contraction. Deflation accompanied monetary contraction, and inflation followed monetary expansion (Figure 3.1). With the end of monetary contractions, the economy grew strongly (Figure 3.7).

These facts support a view of the price level as a monetary phenomenon and of the economy as self-equilibrating. Although the economy adjusts with difficulty to a forced, sharp deflation, in the absence of monetary shocks, it grows steadily (Friedman 1997).

APPENDIX: BORROWED-RESERVES OPERATING PROCEDURES

The founders of the Fed, people like Carter Glass and his aide H. Parker Willis, did not believe that they were creating a central bank with the power to create bank reserves undisciplined by market forces. In fact, the New York Fed became the central bank. The New York Fed adopted a variation of the Bank of England's operating procedures. Instead of using the discount rate to control directly money market interest rates, it developed procedures that allowed for indirect control. It adopted these procedures as a way of raising market rates without having to lead with a discount rate hike. In that way, it avoided serving as a lightning rod for domestic political criticism. Governor Strong (U.S. Cong. 1927, 333; quoted in Goodfriend 1991, 21) explained:

> It seems to me that the foundation for rate changes can be more safely and better laid by preliminary operations in the open market than would be possible otherwise, and the effect is less dramatic and less alarming to the country if it is done in that way than if we just make advances and reductions in our discount rate.

The Fed developed these operating procedures starting in 1923 when it noticed that open market operations resulted in offsetting changes in the reserves banks borrowed from it.[36] In particular, open market sales produced increases in borrowed reserves. A rise in money market interest rates accompanied those increases, and conversely. Policymakers assumed that the higher interest rates resulted because higher levels of borrowed reserves placed banks under increased pressure to repay those borrowings.

With these procedures, the Fed constrained the banking system to obtain through the discount window the marginal reserves needed to meet reserve requirements. It also "administered" the discount window by limiting the duration of borrowing. Consequently, short-term market interest rates gravitated around a benchmark equal to the discount rate plus a premium that varied with the level of member bank borrowing.[37] (See also Chapter 13, Appendix: October 6, 1979 Operating Procedures.) Figure 3.2 shows the relationship between the discount rate and the prime commercial paper rate. Board economist Winfield Riefler (1930, chart VII) showed the associated relationship between borrowed reserves and the difference between the paper rate and the discount rate.

Policymakers interpreted these procedures from the perspective of bankers. They believed that the Fed influenced financial intermediation by altering the availability of funds to banks (Brunner and Meltzer 1964). Also, unwillingness of banks to lend limited the influence of monetary policy. Governor Harrison (U.S. Cong. 1932, 504), head of the New York Fed, testified:

> [B]uying securities . . . alone accomplishes nothing because it gives excess reserves to the member banks. . . . It is impossible to be used for expanding credit where it is used for paying off debts of a bank. That does not change the volume of Federal reserve credit at all, but does relieve the Bank under pressure, which tends to make it more liberal. . . . [Y]ou can not expect the bankers . . . to use that excess reserve unless they have reasonable confidence. . . . They are not going into the bond market at all if you have legislation pending in Congress that makes for the unbalancing of the Budget.

FOUR

From World War II to the Accord

The juxtaposition of the Great Depression and World War II raised expectations dramatically of what government stabilization policies could achieve. In 1932, the unemployment rate rose to 23.6%. In 1939, it was still 17.2%. In 1945, the last year of the war, the unemployment rate was 1.9%.[1] The juxtaposition of massive unemployment in the Depression and full employment during World War II provided apparently incontrovertible evidence that government spending could provide a countercyclical stimulus to the economy. The Employment Act of 1946 gave the government responsibility for full employment. However, there appeared to be no place for monetary policy in the arsenal of government policies.

I. A Changed Intellectual Environment

According to real bills, government could do nothing to arrest the painful economic adjustments that inevitably followed the collapse of a speculative mania. Depression had to run its course to eliminate excessive debt and to correct a maladjusted structure of wages and prices. The memoirs of Herbert Hoover (1952, 30) have forever associated this view with his Treasury Secretary Andrew Mellon, whom Hoover labeled a "leave it alone liquidationist":

Mr. Mellon had only one formula: "Liquidate labor, liquidate stocks, liquidate the farmers, liquidate real estate." He insisted that, when the people get an inflation brainstorm, the only way to get it out of their blood is to let it collapse. He held that even a panic was not altogether a bad thing. He said: "It will purge the rottenness out of the system. High costs of living and high living will come down. People will work harder, live a more moral life."

Spurred by the Great Depression, the economics profession began work on macroeconomic theories capable of refuting the pessimistic view that government was impotent to deal with recession once it had begun. The perceived cause of the Great Depression shaped the Keynesian response. Keynes's *General Theory* captured the prevailing sentiment that the Depression arose from a failure of the price

34

system. The economy adjusted to shocks not through price changes but through quantity changes, that is, through changes in output and employment (Friedman 1974, Section 5). Furthermore, the concentration of economic power among large corporations and labor unions made changes in the price level an institutional datum rather than an equilibrating variable.

The view that pessimism about the future could overwhelm the incentives of the price system received the name "elasticity pessimism." Because of the view that monetary policy operated through interest rates, this pessimism contributed to the belief in the impotence of central banks. Economists and policymakers viewed the low interest rates that prevailed during the Depression as confirmation that monetary policy was powerless to offset real disturbances.

In fact, as Table 3.1 shows, when *real* interest rates fell, the economy recovered. Table 4.1 shows the dramatic postwar reduction in both military expenditures and the government deficit. Despite the fall in fiscal stimulus, neither depression nor deflation reoccurred. Even with a massive military demobilization, the unemployment rate remained below 4% in the immediate postwar period. In time, the relative stability of the post–World War II economy made economists receptive to an explanation of the Depression other than the Keynesian one.

Friedman and Schwartz (1963a) offered the alternative. Like the Keynesian response, it also refuted the real bills counsel of despair. Their characterization of monetary policy by the behavior of the money stock rather than interest rates changed the perception of monetary policy in the Depression from easy to highly contractionary. However, the monetarist–Keynesian debate lay ahead (Hetzel 2007a). After World War II, monetary policy was an orphan.

II. Postwar Inflation

Goodwin and Herren (1975, 9) summarize the environment that shaped stabilization policy in the post–World War II period: "America emerged from World War II with deep foreboding about post-war recession. An Elmo Roper poll for *Fortune* magazine in 1945 showed that only 41.0 percent of respondents believed that the United States would 'be able to avoid . . . a widespread depression.'" In fact, inflation not recession turned out to be the primary postwar problem. Inflation soared with the end of wartime price controls. For the 12-month intervals ending June 1946 and June 1947, CPI inflation was 17.6 and 9.5%, respectively. Monetary policy, however, remained on hold.

After the entry of the United States into World War II, in April 1942, the treasury and the Fed agreed to freeze the prevailing term structure of interest rates. Rates went from 0.375% on 90-day treasury bills to 2.5% on long-term bonds. Given the problem with inflation after the war, why did the United States not free the Fed from its obligation to peg rates? The answer lies in the prevailing understanding of inflation, which reflected views formed during the experience with a commodity monetary standard.

Table 4.1. *Postwar Macroeconomic Data*

Fiscal year ending	Military personnel	Ratio of military expenditure to GNP	Ratio of federal deficit to GNP	Real GNP growth	Unemployment rate	Inflation	M1 growth
1945	12,123,455	38.3	-20.4	4.7	1.9	2.8	16.9
1946	3,030,088	22.7	-9.2	-19.9	3.9	3.3	8.8
1947	1,582,999	6.2	2.9	-0.4	3.9	17.6	4.6
1948	1,445,910	4.2	3.5	4.0	3.8	8.0	0.4
1949	1,615,360	5.0	0.4	0.4	4.5	-1.2	-0.7
1950	1,460,261	4.7	-0.8	7.2	6.4	0.8	2.1
1951	3,249,455	6.8	2.3	9.5	3.9	8.4	4.0
1952	3,635,912	12.9	0.0	3.1	3.1	2.3	5.4
1953	3,555,067	13.6	-1.4	5.8	2.8	1.1	3.1
1954	3,302,104	12.9	-0.3	-3.2	4.4	0.4	0.8
1955	2,935,107	10.3	1.0	7.4	5.1	-0.7	3.8

Notes: Data are for fiscal years ending June 30. Military expenditure is from various issues of the Census Bureau's annual *Statistical Abstract of the United States*. Federal deficit and military personnel are from the Census Bureau's *Historical Statistics of the United States*. GNP is from Balke and Gordon (1986). Inflation is 12-month percentage growth in the CPI (June to June). M1 is from Friedman and Schwartz (1970). Growth rates for real GNP and M1 are 4-quarter and 12-month percentage changes, respectively.

That is, the behavior of prices arises from private behavior rather than central bank policy and "what goes up must come down." Figures 4.1 and 4.2 show indices of prices for the United States and England. For the United States, the price level rose and then fell with the War of 1812, the Civil War, and World War I. For England, this pattern appeared during the Napoleonic wars and World War I. Secularly, prices exhibited no trend until World War II.

This stationary behavior of the price level accorded with the real bills view that inflation arose from speculative activity by investors. In hearings on the 1945 Full Employment Act, Senator Robert A. Taft (R. OH) said, "My definition of inflation has always been an activity which is artificially built up to an extent that we cannot permanently maintain" (Goodwin and Herren 1975, 17). Inevitably, deflation followed inflation as asset bubbles burst. In apparent confirmation of this view, people pointed to the recession that followed the post–World War I inflation and the stock market crash and deflation that followed the 1920s boom.

Goodwin and Herren (1975, 44) cite a 1947 report written by prominent economists including John Kenneth Galbraith and Seymour E. Harris "...for a very dramatic expression that unrestrained inflation would lead to a very serious depression." In 1947, in an open letter recommending the veto of a bill reducing taxes, the Board of Governors (Board *Minutes* June 5, 1947, 849) wrote: "The longer inflationary pressures are sustained and readjustment deferred, the more serious the inevitable reaction will be ... the magnitude of which will depend largely upon how long inflationary forces are sustained."

Despite the belief that inflation led to recession, the belief that the central bank neither caused nor could control inflation prevented discussion of Fed independence. Before the war, the Fed had denied responsibility for the behavior of prices. In 1939, an article in the *Federal Reserve Bulletin* (Board of Governors 1939, 258) criticized bills before Congress requiring the Fed to stabilize the price level: "[E]xperience has shown that prices do not depend primarily on the volume or the cost of money; that the Board's control over the volume of money is not and cannot be made complete."

Policymakers believed that powerful, nonmonetary forces determined the price level. In a letter to the Board of the Philadelphia Fed scolding its members for a plea to restrain inflation through central bank action, the Board of Governors (Board *Minutes* May 28, 1947, 811) concluded:

It would be most unfortunate if responsible people in the Federal Reserve System were to create the impression publicly that the System itself could at this late hour materially diminish inflationary forces. The problem is not so simple that it could be dealt with effectively by monetary policy. Outside of the monetary cranks, no one at all informed on the subject would suggest that in the great complex of economic forces there is some simple monetary device that could preserve or restore economic equilibrium.

In steps taken from August 1947 through October 1948, the Fed and the treasury agreed to raise the interest rate peg on short-term government debt. The impetus

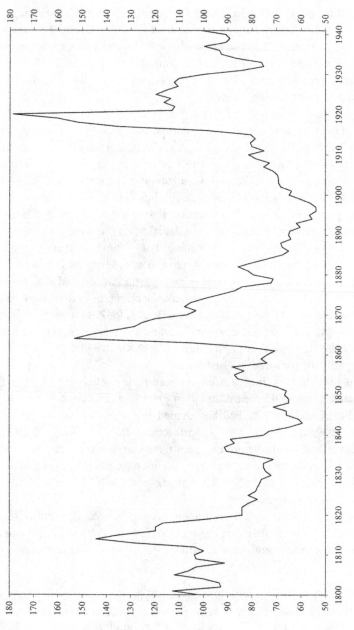

Figure 4.1. Index of Wholesale Commodity Prices, United States: 1800–1941. *Notes:* Jastram (1977, Table 7).

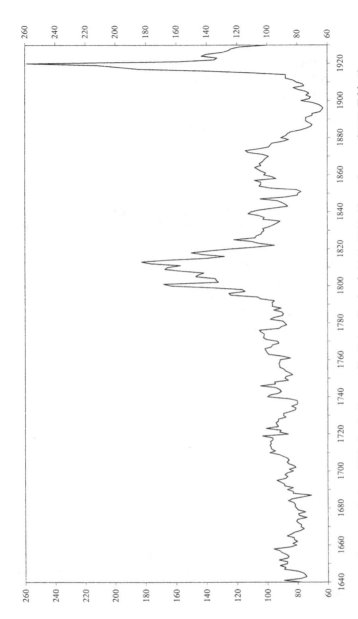

Figure 4.2. Index of Wholesale Commodity Prices, England: 1640–1930. *Notes*: Jastram (1977, Table 2).

was the incompatibility of the 0.375% peg on three-month treasury bills with the 0.875% peg on one-year certificates. Because banks sold short-term debt to the Fed and bought the longer term debt, which was just as liquid given the rate peg, the Fed ended up holding almost all outstanding short-term government securities. Although the short-term peg thus became irrelevant, no one questioned the 2.5% ceiling on bonds.

The Fed chafed at its inability to move short-term interest rates.[2] However, the political environment precluded an open challenge to treasury dominance. Governor Eccles held the common belief that the postwar inflation arose from the government deficits incurred in World War II. To control inflation, he urged Congress to run large surpluses to extinguish government debt (U.S. Cong. November 25, 1947). He also wanted the power to prevent banks from making loans that would add to the stock of debt. He concentrated on a futile effort to persuade Congress to impose a supplementary reserve requirement on banks.

In an essay written before the Korean War, New York Fed President Sproul (1951, 315) expressed the common view that monetary policy could not affect inflation significantly without an unacceptable "contraction of employment and income." Sproul (1951, 298) wrote that the renewal of recession following the Fed's increase in reserve requirements in 1936 and 1937 made it "doubtful that credit policy would thereafter be used vigorously and drastically to restrain inflationary pressures." Sproul also expressed the accepted view that, because of the large amount of government debt outstanding, the Fed had to support the sale of government securities to avoid a "bottomless market" (U.S. Treasury, *1951 Annual Report*, 261).

The Fed could not have won a political contest with the treasury. By the end of the war, the military effort was consuming almost 40% of national output. The fear that reconversion to a peacetime economy would bring a return to depression shaped political views. The Board of Governors expressed its unwillingness to challenge the status quo in its letter to the directors of the Philadelphia Fed, who had urged actions to control the "spiral of expanding credit." Such a course, the Board of Governors (Board *Minutes*, May 28, 1947, 811) argued,

would increase enormously the charge on the budget for servicing the debt. If the Secretary of the Treasury were confronted with any such consequences... he would no doubt take the issue directly to the President who, in turn, would take it to the Congress. . . . There can hardly be any doubt as to what the result would be. The "System's freedom of action" would in all probability be promptly terminated.

III. Explaining Recession with Gold Standard Expectations

The primary postwar monetary puzzle is the decline in money growth and inflation given the Fed's interest rate peg (Friedman and Schwartz 1963a, 577). From 1942Q1 to 1945Q1, average annualized quarterly M1 growth was 23.7%; from 1945Q2 to 1945Q4, 10.3%; from 1946Q1 to 1947Q4, 4.7%; and from 1948Q1 to 1949Q4,

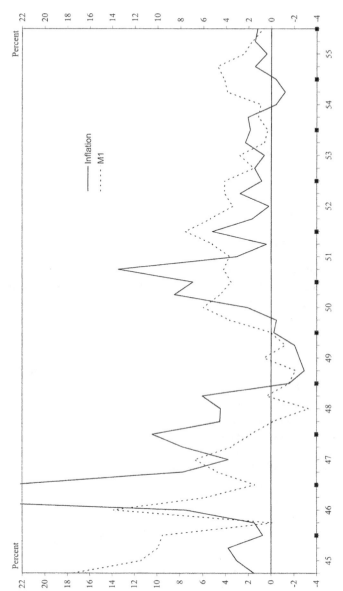

Figure 4.3. Inflation and M1 Growth. *Notes:* Quarterly observations of annualized percentage changes in M1 and prices. From 1945 to 1946, the price level is the CPI. Thereafter, it is the personal consumption expenditures deflator. The observations for inflation for 1946Q3 and 1946Q4, respectively, are 39.3 and 22.9%. M1 data are from Friedman and Schwartz (1970). Heavy tick marks indicate fourth quarter.

41

−.9%. Inflation surged with the end of postwar price controls, and became negative in 1949 (Figure 4.3). For certain, the Keynesian assumption of a hard-wired propagation of realized inflation today into expected and thus actual inflation tomorrow cannot hold. If it did, given the rate peg, inflation would have exploded not fallen. Instead, the expectation of deflation following inflation must have raised the real interest rate. That assumption also explains the recessions that began in November 1948 and July 1953.

In the post–World War II period, inflation created the expectation of deflation. Friedman and Schwartz (1963, 560 and 584) wrote:

[T]he most widely-held expectation at the time was that prices would go down after the war – if this expectation seems unreasonable to us, it is only by hindsight.... The public acted from 1946 to 1948 as if it expected deflation.... The major source of concern about inflation at that time was...that what goes up must come down and that the higher the price rise now the larger the subsequent price fall.

President Truman said in a speech on April 21, 1947 (cited in Goodwin and Herren 1975, 41): "There is one sure formula for bringing on a recession or a depression: that is to maintain excessively high prices. Buying stops, production drops, unemployment sets in, prices collapse, profits vanish, businessmen fail." Starting in February 1946, Truman began to dismantle wartime price controls. In October 1946, he lifted them completely. The single most important reason for their demise, as it would be again for the Nixon controls, was the angry reaction of housewives to the disappearance of hamburger from store shelves (Goodwin and Herren 1975, 34). With the end of controls, inflation surged (Figure 4.3). In 1946Q3 and 1946Q4, respectively, CPI inflation at annualized rates was 39 and 23%. According to the Board of Governor's Survey of Consumer Finances (SCF), in early 1946 before the relaxation of price controls, only 8% of households expected that prices would fall, while 53% expected them to rise.[3] In early 1947 after the inflation accompanying the end of controls, 46% expected prices to fall, while only 13% expected them to rise (Board of Governors 1948, 1357). Ironically, inflation produced a "deflation scare."

Figure 4.4 shows for the Livingston survey the biannual observations for expected one-year-ahead CPI inflation along with subsequently realized inflation. In the five years following the end of World War II, the economists surveyed expected deflation, not despite of but because of the postwar inflation. Figure 4.5 plots a market interest rate and the corresponding real interest rate calculated using the Livingston data on expected inflation. The real interest rates for yearend 1946 and midyear 1947 are, respectively, 6.5 and 8.0%. These high real rates accompanied monetary deceleration and a decline in real output.[4]

The reemergence of expected deflation in 1948 (Figure 4.4) and the corresponding rise in the real interest rate (Figure 4.5) preceded the recession that began after the cyclical peak in November 1948. Measured using Livingston survey data, the real interest rate rose from 1.6% at yearend 1947, to 2.6% at midyear 1948, and to 3.9% at yearend 1948. Monetary deceleration accompanied the rise in the real rate

Figure 4.4. Livingston Survey: Predicted and Subsequently Realized One-Year Inflation. *Notes:* Predicted inflation is the mean of one-year-ahead CPI inflation predictions from the Livingston Survey. The Philadelphia Fed maintains the survey currently. The survey comes out in June and December. The questionnaire is mailed early in May and November. Therefore, the one-year inflation forecast is for the 13-month period from May to June of the following year for the June release and for the 13-month period from November to December of the following year for the December release. The June release inflation forecast is matched with an average of the realized annualized monthly CPI inflation rates starting in June of the same year and ending in June of the subsequent year. The December release inflation forecast is matched with an average of realized annualized monthly CPI inflation rates starting in December of the same year and ending in December of the subsequent year. (See Appendix, "Series on the Real Interest Rates.") The light tick mark is the June release forecast, and the heavy tick mark is the December release forecast.

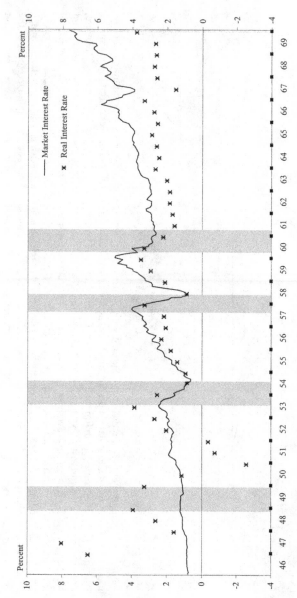

Figure 4.5. The One-Year Market Interest Rate on Government Securities and the Corresponding Real Rate of Interest. *Notes:* The market rate of interest is monthly observations of the yield on U.S. government securities from "Short-Term Open Market Rates in New York City" in Board of Governors (1976), *Banking and Monetary Statistics, 1941–1970.* Through July 1959 the series uses "9– to 12-month issues." Thereafter, it uses "one-year Treasury bills." The series for the real rate of interest is the market rate minus predicted CPI inflation from the Livingston Survey. See notes to Figure 4.4. Shaded areas demarcate recessions. Heavy tick marks indicate the November observation.

44

(Figure 4.3).[5] Even though it is arguable whether monetary deceleration produced the recession that began after the November 1948 cyclical peak, the generally high real interest rates in the postwar period can explain the disinflation that occurred starting in 1948Q3 despite the Fed's low, nominal interest rate peg.

The beginning of the 1950s marked the end of monetary deceleration. Over the year and a half from August 1948 through January 1950, the level of the CPI declined 4.1%. The moderate amount of this decline apparently diminished expectations of deflation and as a result reduced the real interest rate. By May 1950, the real rate had fallen to 1.2% (Figure 4.5).

With the intensification of the Korean War in fall 1950, inflation surged. The possibility of a Third World War generated a worldwide rise in commodity prices. The likely return of price controls and the disappearance of consumer durables caused a surge in consumption. Inflation peaked at 14% in 1951Q1. Although the Fed gained the ability to raise interest rates with the March 1951 Treasury–Fed Accord, the Korean War period possessed a characteristic of the preceding period.[6] Fluctuations in the real interest rate far exceeded fluctuations in the market interest rate (Figure 4.5). Variation in expected inflation rather than purposeful monetary policy actions dominated policy.

Over 1951, inflation fell and ceased by year-end. The fall appeared to confirm the view that price declines follow rises. Accordingly, the expectation of deflation returned (Figure 4.4). The SCF reported that at the beginning of 1953 only 17% of consumers expected price increases, while 31% expected decreases (Board of Governors 1954, 249). Expected deflation raised the real interest rate (Figures. 4.4 and 4.5). Higher real rates produced monetary deceleration (Figure 4.3). Average annualized quarterly M1 growth rates went from 4.25% in 1952 to 2.2% in the first two quarters of 1953 and 0.5% in the last two quarters. A business cycle peak occurred in July 1953.

The Fed's attempt to pursue countercyclical monetary policy began with the 1953 recession. At the time of the accord in March 1951, the market yield on three-month treasury bills was 1.5%. A year later, the Fed began to raise rates, and the bill rate peaked at 2.3% in early June 1953. With the onset of recession, it lowered rates to 0.6% by the June 1954 cyclical trough. Purposeful monetary policy actions rather than variations in expected inflation then came to dominate real interest rates and monetary policy. The era of lean-against-the-wind, that is, of monetary policy dedicated to the stabilization of economic activity, had begun.

APPENDIX: SERIES ON THE REAL INTEREST RATE

Real Rate of Interest (Livingston Forecasts)

Refer to Figures 4.4 and 4.5. The Livingston Survey commenced in 1946 and is currently conducted by the Federal Reserve Bank of Philadelphia. Twice annually in June and December, the survey publishes forecasts from about 50 business economists regarding the level of the CPI at 6- and 12-month horizons. The forecasts of inflation in the paper follow Carlson (1977). Carlson noted that the December survey is mailed early in November when respondents have available the October CPI. The respondents forecast the level of the CPI for the following June. The forecast of inflation, therefore, is assumed to be the annualized rate of growth of the CPI over the 8-month period from October to June. Similarly, the inflation forecast based on the forecasted December level of the CPI for the following year is assumed to be the annualized rate of growth of the CPI over the 14-month period ending in December of the following year.

Real Rate of Interest (Hoey Forecasts)

Refer to Figure 14.2. Richard B. Hoey (1991) in "Decision Makers Poll" conducted irregularly timed surveys of inflation expectations when he worked, respectively, for Bache, Halsey, Stuart & Shields; Warburg, Paribus, & Becker; Drexel, Burnham, Lambert; and Barclays de Zoete Wedd Research. The first 10-year inflation forecast is from September 1978. The survey begins collecting shorter-term (approximately one year) forecasts beginning in October 1980. The number of respondents varied between 175 and 500 and included chief investment officers, corporate financial officers, bond and stock portfolio managers, industry analysts, and economists. The survey dates are dates when the polls were mailed to Hoey. The survey was discontinued in March 1991; it was begun again in March 1993 and ended again definitively after five months.

Real Rate of Interest (Philadelphia Fed Forecasts)

Refer to Figure 14.2. The Survey of Professional Forecasters is currently conducted quarterly by the Federal Reserve Bank of Philadelphia. It was conducted formerly by the American Statistical Association and the National Bureau of Economic Research and began in 1968Q4. In 1981Q3, the survey began collecting forecasts of four-quarter rates of CPI inflation. In 1991Q4, it began to collect forecasts of CPI inflation over the next 10 years.

Real Rate of Interest (Greenbook Forecasts)

Refer to Figure 8.3. The real interest rate is the difference between the commercial paper rate and Greenbook inflation forecasts. The Greenbook contains forecasts of the National Income and Product Accounts (NIPA) prepared by the staff of the Board of Governors before FOMC meetings. The maturity of the real rate varies from somewhat more than one quarter to somewhat less than two quarters. The commercial paper rate is for prime nonfinancial paper placed through dealers (A1/P1). The dates for the interest rates match the publication dates of the Greenbooks. From 1965 through 1969, interest rate data are from the New York

Fed release "Commercial Paper." Subsequently, they are from the Board's FAME database or from Bloomberg. From 1965 through April 1971, the paper rate is for 4- to 6-month paper. Thereafter, if there are fewer than 135 days from the Green-book date to the end of the subsequent quarter, the three-month paper rate is used; otherwise, the 6-month paper rate is used.

Predicted inflation is for changes in the implicit GNP (GDP from 1992 on) deflator until August 1992. Thereafter, the fixed-weight deflator is used until March 1996. Thereafter, the GDP chain-weighted price index is used. A weighted-average inflation rate for the period from the Greenbook date to the end of the succeeding quarter is calculated from the Greenbook's inflation forecasts for the current and succeeding quarter. The weight given to the current quarter's inflation rate is the ratio of the number of days left in the current quarter to the number of days from the Greenbook date until the end of the succeeding quarter. The weight given to the succeeding quarter's inflation rate is the ratio of the number of days in that quarter to the number of days from the Greenbook date until the end of the succeeding quarter. This weighted-average expected inflation rate is subtracted from the market rate of interest.

In the 1960s, the FOMC usually met more than 12 times per year. For example, it met 15 times in 1965. In order to make the real rate series monthly through 1978, if there was more than one meeting per month, an observation was recorded only for the first meeting of the month. The FOMC met only 9 times in 1979. (Because the October 6, 1979, meeting was unscheduled, there was no Greenbook and no real rate is calculated for this date.) It met 11 times in 1980. Starting in 1981, it has met 8 times a year. For this reason, starting in 1979, the observations of the Greenbook real rate series are less frequent than monthly.

The real rate series begins in November 1965 because the Greenbook first began to report predictions of inflation for the November 1965 meeting. Until November 1968, for FOMC meetings in the first two months of a quarter, the Green-book often reported a forecast of inflation only for the contemporaneous quarter. For this reason, for the following FOMC meeting dates, the real rate calculated is only for the period to the end of the contemporaneous quarter, not to the end of the succeeding quarter: November 23, 1965; January 11, 1966; February 8, 1966; April 12, 1966; May 10, 1966; June 7, 1966; July 26, 1966; November 1, 1966; December 13, 1966; January 10, 1967; July 18, 1967; October 24, 1967; November 14, 1967; January 9, 1968; February 9, 1968; April 30, 1968; May 28, 1968; July 16, 1968; October 8, 1968; October 17, 1972; and November 20–21, 1972. For these dates the maturity of the interest rate used to calculate the real rate varies between one and three months. For other dates, the maturity varies between three and six months. For this reason, some of the variation in real rates reflects term-structure considerations. This variation is a consequence of the fact that the FOMC meets at different times within a quarter and the Green-book inflation forecasts are for quarters. See Darin and Hetzel (1995) for data series.

Real Rate of Interest (Global Insight Forecasts)

Refer to Figure 14.2. Observations are monthly. The one-year real rate is the one-year constant maturity treasury bond yield minus the four-quarter predicted inflation. The former is from the Board of Governor's H.15 statistical release "Selected Interest Rates." Inflation forecasts are from Global Insight *U.S. Economic Outlook,* "Summary for the U.S. Economy." The forecasts for a given monthly control date are made at the end of the prior month (say, the end of December for the January control date). Therefore, the interest rate is paired with the inflation forecast by using the interest rate for the last business day of the month preceding the control month. For the first two months of a quarter, the four-quarter inflation forecast begins with that month's quarter. For the last month of a quarter, the four-quarter inflation forecast begins with the subsequent quarter. (In 1996, the NIPA benchmark revisions were occasionally moved from the end of the month to the first few days of the succeeding month. The forecasts were correspondingly postponed. In these cases, the date of the interest rate observations match the date of the NIPA revisions.) Initially, inflation forecasts are for the implicit GNP deflator. Starting August 1992, they are for the fixed-weight GDP deflator, and starting February 1996 they are for the chain-weighted GDP deflator. See Darin and Hetzel (1995) for data series.

FIVE

Martin and Lean-against-the-Wind

After the 1951 accord and through the mid 1960s, approximate price stability prevailed. What produced this stability?

I. From Real Bills to Lean-against-the-Wind

After World War II, policymakers stopped viewing recessions as the inevitable reaction to prior speculative excess. Also, they began to see inflation as a consequence of excess aggregate demand rather than speculative excess. The rise in the price level with the end of wartime price controls and its subsequent failure to fall forced that change. Such inflation could not arise from asset speculation. As FOMC Chairman Eccles (Board of Governors Board *Minutes* November 18, 1947, 1575) reasoned, "Even loans for productive purposes are inflationary if they increase the demand for labor and material that are already in short supply."

The intensification of the Korean War in fall 1950 produced a surge in expenditure and inflation (Figure 5.1). If maintained, the Fed's interest rate peg would have sustained inflation through the monetization of government debt. That experience made clear to the Fed the importance of allowing the central bank, rather than private markets, to control reserves creation. Like World War II, that experience also moved the Fed toward thinking about inflation as resulting from excess aggregate demand rather than speculation.

The accord was a watershed for the Fed. The ideal of a central bank that allows an "elastic currency" passively to "accommodate commerce" disappeared. The Fed moved toward the idea of manipulating short-term interest rates to control aggregate demand and inflation. Governor Eccles (U.S. Cong. January 25, 1951, 158) testified:

As long as the Federal Reserve is required to buy government securities at the will of the market for the purpose of defending a fixed pattern of interest rates established by the Treasury, it must stand ready to create new bank reserves in unlimited amount. This policy makes the entire banking system, through the action of the Federal Reserve System, an engine of inflation.

49

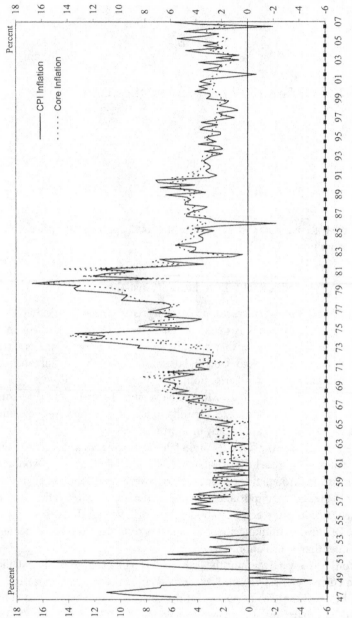

Figure 5.1. CPI Inflation. *Note:* Observations are quarterly annualized percentage changes in the CPI. Core inflation excludes food and energy and is available starting in 1957. Heavy tick marks indicate the fourth quarter of the year.

Eccles (Board of Governors FOMC *Minutes* February 6, 1951, 50–1) told the FOMC:

[We are making] it possible for the public to convert Government securities into money to expand the money supply. . . . We are almost solely responsible for this inflation. It is not deficit financing that is responsible because there has been surplus in the Treasury right along; the whole question of having rationing and price controls is due to the fact that we have this monetary inflation, and this committee is the only agency in existence that can curb and stop the growth of money.

After World War II, a consensus emerged that government had the responsibility to manage aggregate demand. However, because the Keynesian consensus assigned that responsibility to fiscal policy, economists were not interested in monetary policy. After the accord, monetary policymakers had wholly to invent monetary policy. Not since early 1933 had the Fed regularly conducted monetary policy. Martin's views gelled after the 1953 recession and the revival of inflation in 1956. In response to the recession, the FOMC developed lean-against-the-wind procedures whereby it moved short-term interest rates with a view to maintaining aggregate demand rather than disciplining speculative movements in asset prices. In response to the inflation, it moved to preemptive rate increases early during economic recovery.

With respect to lean-against-the-wind, Martin borrowed from the postwar intellectual environment. With respect to preemptive policy, he seemed to borrow from the prior gold standard experience. Namely, the price level possesses a "normal" level. An unsustainable, speculative boom could push it away from its normal level, but an inevitable reaction would follow. For monetary policy to restrain inflation, it had to prevent such booms from developing. At the November 1954 meeting of the FOMC's Executive Committee, only a few months after the May 1954 business cycle trough, Martin (Board of Governors FOMC *Minutes* November 9, 1954, 332) stated that "he had begun to feel that the easy money policy of the Committee was furthering a speculative psychology. . . . There were indications of an exuberance of spirit among intelligent businessmen with respect to 1955 business prospects that seemed to him to be dangerous." Although Martin understood preemptive policy within an anachronistic framework, the substantive change from trying to stabilize the price level rather than asset prices would define modern central banking.

From December 1951 through March 1956, the CPI remained unchanged but then rose 3.5% from mid 1956 through mid 1957. The FOMC then raised rates to restore price stability. In August 1957, the board raised the discount rate despite the earlier plea of New York President Alfred Hayes (Board of Governors FOMC *Minutes* July 30, 1957, 456–7):

[T]he money supply will not show any appreciable net growth for the year as a whole. . . . [W]e must give serious thought to the consequences to the System if we are later blamed for recession and substantial unemployment. . . . It seems to me clear that the prudent course is to continue . . . preventing any national expansion in bank credit and the money supply and allowing reduced liquidity to take effect on the economy.

The timing of the discount rate hike proved unfortunate as the business cycle peaked in August 1957.

The Fed and the Eisenhower administration agreed on the primacy of price stability. Martin (U.S. Cong. February 6, 1959, 467) testified about "the battle against the debasement of the currency with all of its perils to free institutions." Eisenhower wrote in the *1959 Economic Report of the President* (p. 5): "[A]n indispensable condition for achieving vigorous and continuing economic growth is firm confidence that the value of the dollar will be reasonably stable in the years ahead."

The Eisenhower administration's more hawkish stance toward inflation than the Fed's in 1955 following the May 1954 cyclical trough demonstrated the consensus that existed among policymakers over the primacy of price stability (Hargrove and Morley 1984, Burns interview, 104). Bach (1971, 94) wrote about Burns, head of the Council of Economic Advisers (CEA): "Burns, [Treasury Secretary] Humphrey and Eisenhower were agreed in early 1955 that inflation was reemerging as the major problem and that the economy's growth rate could not be sustained. But not until 1956 did the FOMC fully agree with this analysis."

Arthur Burns (Burns and Samuelson 1967, 80) summarized the consensus that developed after inflation rose in 1956 that policy should move aggressively to preempt inflation:

Financial developments during 1958 and the fears which they engendered thus strengthened the determination of governmental authorities to try to prevent, now that the economy was again advancing, the sort of excesses that had led to the inflationary boom during 1956–57.... Having moved too slowly to restrain the preceding expansion, they were ready to move with all necessary speed this time.

Burns (Burns and Samuelson 1967, 7) described the predominant concern with inflation:

[E]mergence of a huge deficit [fiscal year ending June 1959] at a time of rather rapid economic advance was merely the most dramatic of a series of developments that cast doubt on the financial policy of the government.... In the recession of 1957–58 wholesale prices... actually rose, and thus gave fresh support to the widely held theory that we are living in an age of inflation. This somber view about the future was reinforced by the deterioration in the balance of payments. During 1958... our stocks of gold were cut by two billion dollars. More ominous still, foreign financiers, who hitherto appeared to have unbounded faith in American finances, began to whisper serious doubts whether the integrity of the dollar could be counted on in the future.

After the accord, the Fed had encouraged a free market in government bonds capable of conveying information on market sentiment. The Fed experienced an "inflation scare" in 1958 (Figure 5.2). The business cycle peaked in August 1957, and the FOMC pushed short-term rates down sharply (Figures 5.2 and 5.3). The three-month treasury bill rate peaked at 3.7% in October 1957 and reached a low of 0.6% in late May 1958. In April and May 1958, the long-term government bond rate fell to 3.1%. By October, however, it had risen to 3.8% – an unprecedented

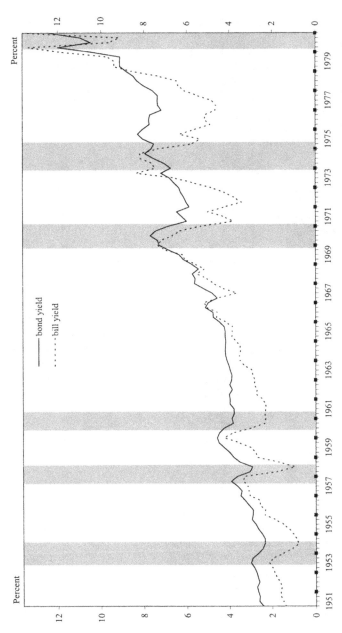

Figure 5.2. Government Bond and Three-Month Treasury Bill Yields. *Notes:* Quarterly observations of U.S. (long-term) government bonds from 1951 to 1953 from Board of Governors (1976) "Banking and Monetary Statistics, 1941–1970." Data from 1953Q1 on are U.S. Treasury 10-year constant maturity bond yields from Board of Governors G13 statistical release "Selected Interest Rates." Shaded areas indicate recessions. Heavy tick marks indicate the fourth quarter.

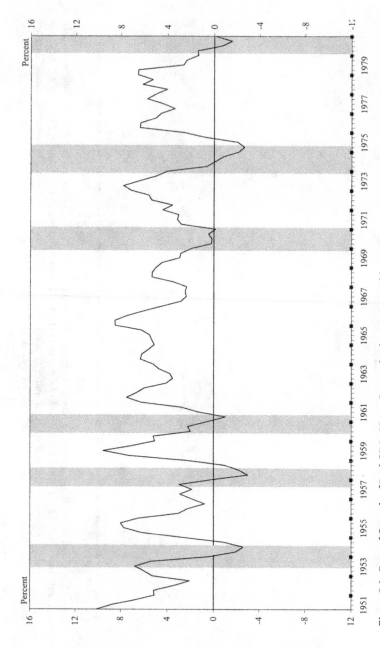

Figure 5.3. Rate of Growth of Real GDP. *Notes:* Quarterly observations of four-quarter percentage changes in real GDP (chained 1996 dollars). Shaded areas indicate recessions. Heavy tick marks indicate the fourth quarter.

increase. At the time, the United States was experiencing gold outflows. Both the Fed and the administration believed that financial markets lacked confidence in the willingness of the government to maintain price stability.[1]

Shortly after the rise in bond rates began, in early August, the FOMC started raising short-term rates. Martin (U.S. Cong. February 6, 1959, 462 and 467) testified:[2]

About this time [summer 1958] inflationary expectations began to spread. The abrupt upward shift of interest levels in central money markets ... reflected investor demand for an interest premium to cover the risk of a depreciating purchasing power of invested funds. ... The experience in the government bond market ... is a vivid example of the influence of inflationary expectations in financial markets. To the extent that such attitudes come to be reflected in decisions on wages, prices, consumption, and investment, they help to bring about their own realization.

There was little lag between the cyclical trough in economic activity in April 1958 and the increase in short-term rates.

The level of the money stock (M1) declined 2% over the 1.5 years from July 1959 through January 1961 (Figure 5.4). The economy went into recession in April 1960. Two back-to-back recessions "routed an inflationary psychology" (Burns in Burns and Samuelson 1967, 9). Bond yields stayed at 4% from 1960 through 1964. The expansionary monetary policy of the 1960s then unfolded in an environment of expected price stability.

II. Martin and the Creation of Modern Central Banking

To economists, Martin appeared old-fashioned. He expressed ideas using metaphors rather than models. Nevertheless, he laid the foundation of modern central banking. He challenged the Keynesian orthodoxy about the impotence of monetary policy and the nonmonetary character of inflation. Although Martin lost the intellectual debate while he was FOMC chairman, the Fed revived his ideas in the Volcker era. The hallmarks of Martin's beliefs, namely, the primacy of price stability for economic stability and the necessity of preemptive policy to maintain price stability, returned after the detour of stop–go monetary policy.

Martin defended his beliefs in part on indefensible real bills views. He defended the rate increases in 1958 by arguing that deflation followed inevitably from prior inflationary excesses.[3] Martin (U.S. Cong. February 6, 1958, 384) argued that if allowed to persist, inflation would create "maladjustments of such severity to lead to a protracted period of liquidation and structural realignment in the economy." Martin (U.S. Cong. February 6, 1959, 469) believed that given the extent of the inflation in 1957 "a recession was ... inevitable." Nevertheless, in the implementation of his views, Martin departed from real bills views in a fundamental way. Instead of trying to prevent "unsustainable" increases in asset prices as a precondition for preventing recession and deflation, he focused on maintaining stability in the price level.

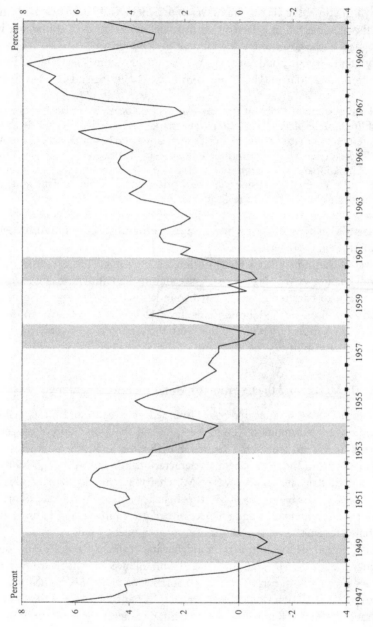

Figure 5.4. Money Growth. *Notes*: Quarterly observations of four-quarter percentage changes in M1. Shaded areas indicate recessions. Heavy tick marks indicate the fourth quarter.

Keynesians interpreted World War II as vindication that government spending could create full employment. Martin instead saw forced monetization of government debt due to a rate peg, suppressed inflation, and price controls that undermined the working of the price system.[4] Martin attributed the failure of depression to follow World War II to the limitless opportunities offered by a free market system for investment. He referred to the time he spent in the Soviet Union in 1942 setting up the lend-lease program. There he unsuccessfully tried to persuade his Soviet friends that the endless stream of Jeeps that America delivered resulted from reliance on a free market.

Keynesians rejected monetary policy as a useful tool based on the assumption that low interest rates had failed to stimulate aggregate demand in the Depression. In general, they concluded that the price system worked only poorly to allocate resources. In contrast, Martin drew on his postwar experiences at the treasury, where he advised Treasury Secretary Snyder that Britain should devalue to deal with its foreign exchange crisis (Bremner 2004, Chapter 5). Martin challenged the view of the British exchequer that it did not have to treat the exchange rate as a price.

In defending the potency of monetary policy, Martin argued that, like the exchange rate, the interest rate is also a price. Just as markets were sensitive to the exchange rate, they were sensitive to interest rates. As a result, the central bank could control inflation through its control over the influence of credit creation on interest rates. Contrary to the Keynesian consensus, the central bank could control inflation without imposing a level of interest rates that would produce recession. The reason for the responsiveness of expenditure to interest rates was the importance of the interest rate as a price affecting the value of future returns on investment.

A flow of credit basically in line with growth of the economy would cause interest rates to move in a way that would provide for macroeconomic stabilization and price stability. Martin attributed the 1953 recession to a failure by the Fed to provide sufficient credit. He attributed the 1956 inflation to a failure by the Fed to restrain sufficiently credit creation. Martin focused on the importance of expectations as a determinant of price setting and believed that the central bank could control expectations. He used the word "confidence" just as central bankers used the word "credibility" in the 1980s. Martin adamantly rejected the idea that inflation would lower unemployment.

III. Eisenhower Conservatism

After the accord, institutional autonomy gave the Fed the ability to control inflation. However, it had to decide whether to exercise its power or to rely on government for that control. In the speeches summarized earlier, Martin expressed his belief in free markets, especially that the interest rate works effectively to ration supply and demand. The Fed can then control inflation through its control over money and credit creation without imposing real costs on society. The belief that government should restrict itself to controlling inflation indirectly through monetary policy defined the Martin era through the early 1960s and also the Volcker–Greenspan era. In contrast, in the stop–go era, the belief prevailed that fiscal policy and direct intervention by government in price setting in markets should substitute for monetary policy.

After the removal of wartime price controls in 1946, government policy toward the control of inflation became a major political issue. President Truman made the reestablishment of price controls an issue in the 1948 presidential election. Although he won the election, a hostile Republican Senate prevented their reestablishment. The issue became moot with the 1949 recession and deflation. Although Congress passed legislation authorizing price controls in early 1951 during the Korean War, it repealed the legislation during the Eisenhower administration.

Eisenhower was willing to exhort corporations to set prices responsibly, but he was unwilling to specify a numerical guideline for changes in wages and prices. He was not willing to intervene in actual price-setting decisions. It followed that the control of inflation had to come from monetary policy. Eisenhower supported the independence of the Fed and acquiesced in the interest rate increases in 1957 and 1959.

A precursor to the 1970 debate that led to price controls occurred in the Eisenhower administration. The coexistence of inflation in 1957 with an unemployment rate at 4% and continued inflation after the onset of recession in August 1957 created political pressure for government intervention in price setting. Many economists concluded that inflation arose due to a rise in the monopoly power of corporations.[5] The best known expression of this belief appeared in the Kefauver Committee hearings on administered prices, which began in July 1957 and ran for three years (Stigler 1962). In 1971, a politically more opportunistic Nixon would make a different decision on controls than the president for whom he had served as vice president. Like his successor Arthur Burns, Martin emphasized the importance to inflation of expectations, but, unlike Burns, Martin believed in the importance of Fed credibility to control those expectations. Martin (May 1958, 541) stated:

[T]he inflationary pressures that had developed in the boom had . . . given rise to the disturbing notion that creeping inflation had become an inevitable condition of modern life. . . . In that atmosphere, Federal Reserve discount rates were raised one-half percentage point in August [1957]. . . . That action . . . served as an indication to the business and investment community that the Federal Reserve rejected the idea that creeping inflation was inevitable.

IV. Concluding Comment

Martin and his adviser Winfield Riefler had views on monetary policy that foreshadowed those of Volcker and Greenspan. They emphasized raising short-term rates in a way that preempts inflation.[6] Greenspan's (U.S. Cong. July 28, 1999, 10) statements sound like Martin: "For monetary policy to foster maximum sustainable growth, it is useful to preempt forces of imbalance before they threaten economic stability." Martin believed that "easy money" allowed an inflationary psychology to develop in financial markets that drove inflation and that such psychology developed early during periods of economic expansion.[7] Consequently, prior to the Johnson administration, the Martin FOMC attempted to stabilize the inflation premium in bond rates (taken as evidence of inflationary psychology) and raised short-term rates early in economic recoveries. The monetary policy of Volcker and Greenspan represented a development of the views of William McChesney Martin, while the views of Arthur Burns were a detour.

SIX

Inflation Is a Nonmonetary Phenomenon

From the mid 1960s through the end of the 1970s, low, stable unemployment became an objective of monetary policy. The resulting experiment in aggregate demand management produced what became known as stop–go monetary policy. The assumption that monetary policy could control the unemployment rate rested on a nonmonetary view of inflation.[1] If real factors controlled inflation, the Fed could manipulate aggregate nominal demand to control unemployment.

I. Inflation at Full Employment

In the Kennedy administration, the conservatism of Treasury Secretary Douglas Dillon, Treasury Undersecretary Robert Roosa, and William McChesney Martin shaped policy. However, the activist Council of Economic Advisers chaired by Walter Heller shaped the intellectual climate. It wanted to make the 1946 Employment Act the organizing force behind economic policy. Although the act mandated "maximum employment" as a national goal, its general language robbed it of substance. As written, it was nothing more than a statement of good intentions.

The CEA made the Employment Act into a driving force for expansionary policy by assigning a number to full employment. "[A]n unemployment rate of about 4% is a reasonable and prudent full employment target for stabilization policy" (*1962 Economic Report*, 46).[2] Henceforth, unemployment rates in excess of 4% generated public pressure for activist policies. Four percent unemployment became the banner for economic activism.[3] Walter Heller (Hargrove and Morley 1984, 176) said later: "Putting ... goals in quantitative terms was ... terribly important.... [Q]uantitative goals ... [got] the president committed to an expansionary economic policy. All during the Eisenhower administration, they talked about full employment but never defined it. We got Kennedy to accept 4 percent as our full employment goal."

A 4% target for unemployment left unanswered the question of what would happen to inflation. To answer it, Samuelson and Solow (1960) adapted for the United States a statistical relationship discovered for Britain by A. W. Phillips (1958).[4]

It showed the change of money wages moving inversely with the unemployment rate. This Phillips curve, with price inflation replacing wage inflation, appeared to offer an explanation of inflation. It did so not with theory, but with an empirical relationship.[5]

Samuelson and Solow (1960) plotted paired observations of nominal wage growth and the unemployment rate and circled postwar observations. The curve drawn through the latter implied that nominal wage growth consistent with price stability required almost 6% unemployment. Inflation had risen in 1956 when unemployment fell to the presumed 4% full employment level (Figure 6.1). Samuelson and Solow divided inflation into the categories of demand-pull and cost-push.[6] For them, the issue of whether 4% unemployment was consistent with price stability turned on which kind of inflation had characterized 1956.

The Samuelson–Solow analysis appeared to give empirical content to the cost-push/demand-pull distinction. If 4% was full employment, the inflation that occurred with an unemployment rate equal to or in excess of 4% was cost-push. The impetus to cost-push inflation could come from private monopoly power or from increases in relative prices arising from factors affecting individual markets. In this case, monetary policy is an inefficient way of controlling inflation because it works through creating unemployment. Government should make use of "incomes policies." That is, it should intervene directly in the markets that caused the inflation by exerting pressure in wage negotiations and pricing decisions.

Demand-pull inflation could arise from any stimulus to aggregate demand. Although restrictive monetary policy could counter excessive demand, so could fiscal policy, and the latter would allow a lower level of interest rates. For Keynesians, inflation was made in Washington only some of the time and the Fed was rarely the right agency for dealing with it. Samuelson and Solow began their article by comparing generals who fight the wrong war with policymakers who fight the wrong inflation. Aggregate demand management could take an unemployment rate of 4% as the objective, but it needed the additional weapon of incomes policies to guard against the emergence of cost-push inflation.

II. The Heller Agenda: Wage and Price Guideposts

The CEA strategy for achieving full employment began with quantification of the output gap – actual minus potential output. The CEA measured potential output by fitting a trend line to real gross national product (GNP). As the base, it selected mid 1955 when the unemployment rate was about 4%. For trend real growth, it used the 3.5% average GNP growth rate from the end of the Korean War until mid 1955. The estimated gap in 1961 was about $40 billion, almost 8% of GNP (*1962 Economic Report*, 47–51). The unemployment rate was then 6%. The *1962 Economic Report* (p. 70) stated "In the last decade, the Nation has lost an estimated $175 billion of GNP (1961 prices) by operating the economy below potential." Arthur Okun developed a relationship between the output gap and the unemployment rate later

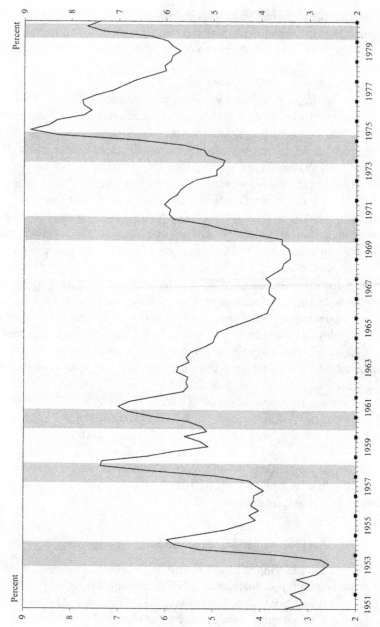

Figure 6.1. Unemployment Rate. *Notes*: Civilian unemployment rate. Shaded areas indicate recessions denoted by the National Bureau of Economic Research. Heavy tick marks indicate the fourth quarter.

known as Okun's Law: A rise in the output gap of 3 percentage points increases the unemployment rate by 1 percentage point (Okun 1969, Interview I, 15).

To eliminate the output gap, the CEA recommended fiscal deficits. The *1962 Economic Report* (p. 81) blamed the premature end of recovery after the 1957–8 recession on a rise in the full employment surplus in 1959. Using a value for the Keynesian multiplier of about 3, the CEA began to make regular estimates of the magnitude of the increase in the government deficit necessary to eliminate the output gap and lower the unemployment rate to 4% (Hargrove and Morley 1984, 205). Figure 6.2 reproduces Chart 2 from the *1962 Economic Report of the President* (p. 52). The chart in the top panel plots real GNP and the CEA's measure of potential GDP. The bottom panel shows the output gap and deviations of the unemployment rate from 4%.

The CEA's strategy for controlling inflation rested on the distinction between demand-pull and cost-push. The *1962 Economic Report* (pp. 44–5) characterized the former as resulting from "excessive aggregate demand," while the latter "may originate in those sectors of the economy where competitive forces are weak and large corporations and unions have a considerable degree of discretion in setting prices and wages." In the section entitled "Guideposts for Noninflationary Wage and Price Behavior," the *1962 Economic Report* (p. 185) called for an "assumption of private responsibility" in price setting in industries where "there is considerable room for the exercise of private power." The *1962 Economic Report* (p. 185) advocated guideposts for setting wages and prices so that an "informed public" could "create an atmosphere in which the parties to such decisions would exercise their powers responsibly."

The CEA blamed the steel and automotive industries for the inflation beginning in 1956. Although the unemployment rate averaged 4.3% over the period 1955–7, CPI inflation rose over these three years from –0.3 to 3.4% (*1962 Economic Report*, 47). Furthermore, over the years 1959–61, CPI inflation was fairly steady at just over 1%, while unemployment averaged almost 6%.

The CEA's "guidepost" policy went back to the Truman years. Emile Despres et al. (1950) had recommended government guidelines to constrain wages to rise at a rate equal to economy-wide productivity growth.[7] Overall price stability would then emerge through stability of unit labor costs. However, firms in an industry would either raise or lower their prices by an amount equal to the shortfall or excess of their specific productivity growth relative to the economy-wide average. In industries with above-average productivity growth, firms would reduce their product prices, and conversely.

To give this policy substance, government had to specify figures for productivity growth both economy-wide and industry-wide. Also, it had to intervene in private wage negotiations and price setting to enforce compliance. Short of actual controls, the government had to marshal public opinion against offenders. The Kennedy administration, basically conservative economically and concerned about support

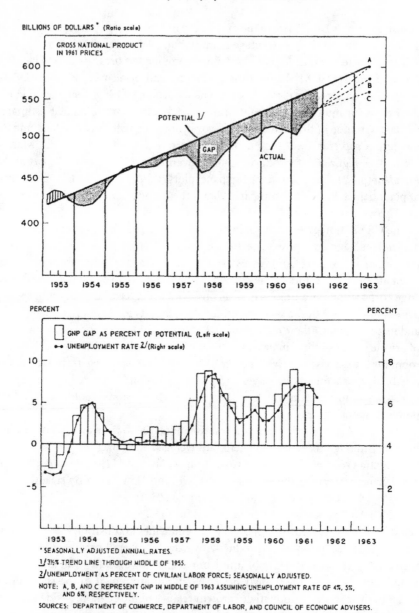

Figure 6.2. Gross National Product, Actual and Potential, and Unemployment Rate. *Notes:*
A, B, and *C* represent GNP in middle of 1963 assuming unemployment rates of 4, 5, and
6%, respectively.
Sources: Department of Commerce, Department of Labor, and Council of Economic
Advisers.

from the business community, implemented the CEA guideposts in a halting way. Kennedy first used them in April 1962 when he forced the steel industry to back down from a price hike. He also used them to intervene in wage and price setting of the automotive industry (Barber 1975).

Strictly enforced, the guideposts would have frozen the ability of the price system to allocate resources. Therefore, the CEA elaborated exceptions to the productivity norm, for example, by allowing for variation where wage rates were "exceptionally" low or high (*1962 Economic Report*, 189). The *Morgan Guaranty Survey* (1964, 10) argued that there was no way to translate these exceptions into practical guidelines. It noted that "it is the Gresham's Law of political communication that simple propositions always drive out complex ones." The practical application of the guidelines would equate "largeness with 'excessive' market power."

The *1964 Economic Report* (p. 118) characterized the guideposts as "general advice as to the pattern of private price–wage decision making that would take account of the public's interest in avoiding market-power inflation." The original guideposts offered no specific number for productivity and wage growth. "General advice" changed to informal coercion after 1965 when the administration became concerned that a full-employment economy could set off an "inflationary spiral," for which "the most likely outcome will be restrictive fiscal and monetary policies" (*1966 Economic Report*, 93). The guideposts then went from cover for behind-the-scenes pressure on the steel and automotive industry to an instrument for general government intervention into wage and price setting. For that purpose, the administration needed to have a single-size-fits-all numerical guideline. In the *1966 Report*, the CEA stated a numerical guide for wage growth of 3.2% (the "weak beer" standard).

Samuelson (Burns and Samuelson 1967, 58) described how George Perry fit a Phillips curve using data through 1963 and then simulated wage and price inflation in the years 1964, 1965, and 1966. Perry found that inflation fell short of what would be predicted in these last years on the basis of the unemployment rate. Samuelson considered three explanations. First, he discussed the possibility that the better Phillips curve trade-off was due to "an investment in sadism" by William McChesney Martin – the restrictive monetary policy pursued in the last term of the Eisenhower administration. Second, he discussed the impact of increased competition from foreign imports into the United States. Third, he discussed the influence of the Kennedy wage and price guideposts. Samuelson concluded that the downward shift in the Phillips curve was due to the latter two factors and predicted that it would not disappear in the future.

III. Exploiting the Phillips Curve

The rise in social tensions unleashed by the civil rights movement and the Vietnam War created a political consensus for low unemployment as a social salve. The inverse relationship between inflation and unemployment shown by the Phillips curve appeared to require unacceptably high unemployment to provide price stability. The issue raised by Samuelson and Solow of whether price stability was consistent with full employment then changed to how much inflation to allow in pursuit of full employment and to what extent government should intervene in private price setting to lower the inflation associated with full employment.

SEVEN

The Start of the Great Inflation

Stop–go monetary policy began in Martin's final years as FOMC chairman. Why did he allow monetary policy to become inflationary?

I. The Spirit of Stop–Go Monetary Policy

In the 1960s, a demand for activist macroeconomic policy arose from a convergence of political imperative and intellectual consensus. An imperative for growth emerged out of the fiscal pressures created by the Vietnam War and the social divisions created by the war and the civil rights movement. President Johnson refused to choose between war expenditures and his Great Society programs. The economy had to grow flat-out to generate the revenues necessary to pay for guns and butter.

Riots in inner cities and the rhetoric of black militants polarized American society. The middle class watched in dismay as the pampered baby boom generation of students burned the American flag in street demonstrations. A political consensus arose on the need to maintain a rapidly growing economy and a low unemployment rate as a social balm for a deeply divided society. At the same time, a consensus existed within the economics profession that government should pursue an activist policy of aggregate demand management to assure steady growth and low unemployment. Keynesian economics promised to deliver the political imperatives of high growth and low unemployment.

With stop–go, policymakers pursued expansionary monetary policy when the unemployment rate was "high" under the assumption that aggregate-demand inflation could not arise with excess capacity in the economy. In general, they assigned the control of inflation to incomes policies of varying degrees of severity. At such times, the flavor of monetary policy was that economic stimulus was the responsibility of the Fed, while inflation control was the responsibility of other government agencies.

The stimulus of the go phases produced inflation. In the stop phases, the FOMC concentrated on reducing inflation. However, given the consensus that inflation reflected cost-push pressures, over time the FOMC ratcheted upward the level of inflation acceptable to it. Prior experience with commodity money had created the expectation that inflation was stationary. Initially, stimulative monetary policy could exploit that expectation. However, by 1979, inflationary expectations became unhinged.

II. Martin versus Heller

Martin believed that the speculative psychology of markets provided an early warning signal of inflation. To preempt inflationary psychology, the FOMC should raise interest rates in the beginning of the recovery phase of the business cycle. If it did not, inflation would follow.[1] The flash point in the conflict between Martin's view and the Keynesian demand-management view was over when the central bank should begin to raise interest rates in economic recovery. While Martin believed that the Fed should raise short-term interest rates at the beginning of recovery, the CEA believed that the central bank should wait until excess capacity disappeared (the output gap went from negative to nearly zero). For example, Arthur Burns (Burns and Samuelson 1967, 36) wrote, "[E]conomic policy during 1965 was still governed by the theory that stimulation of activity was reasonably safe as long as a gap existed between actual and potential output."

Each side interpreted the back-to-back recessions of 1957 and 1960 from its own perspective. As explained by Burns (Burns and Samuelson 1967, 9), Martin and Eisenhower's advisers emphasized the need to banish inflationary expectations:

Financial developments during 1958 and the fears which they engendered thus strengthened the determination of governmental authorities to try to prevent, now that the economy was again advancing, the sort of excesses that had led to the inflationary boom during 1956–57. . . . Having moved too slowly to restrain the preceding expansion, they were ready to move with all necessary speed this time.

Pressure on [bank] reserves was sharply intensified during 1959. . . . [T]he budget moved from an enormous deficit in early 1959 to a sizable surplus 12 months later. Taken together, these fiscal and monetary measures accomplished one of the most violent shifts on record from a policy of stimulation to a policy of restraint. . . . Largely as a result of their actions, the economic expansion that started in April, 1958, came to a premature end. . . . The very abruptness and magnitude of the policy shift routed an inflationary psychology, demonstrated that ours need not be an age of inflation . . . and thus reestablished stability in costs and prices.

The Heller CEA attributed the premature end of the recovery from the 1957–8 recession to the fiscal restraint initiated in 1959 (Stein 1990, 367–8, 400). Concerned about a repetition of the 1960 recession, it espoused tax cuts to eliminate "fiscal drag," the tendency for rising incomes to create fiscal surpluses. For the CEA, the priority was to banish the business cycle, not inflation. However, Martin had allies in the treasury.[2] Treasury Secretary Dillon was a conservative Republican financier and Assistant Treasury Secretary Robert Roosa was a protégé of former

New York Fed President Allan Sproul. The treasury focused on the U.S. balance of payments deficits and gold outflows. Kennedy did not want a gold crisis on top of the international crises he faced with the Soviets in Cuba and Berlin (Pechman 1964). Because of balance of payments problems, the Fed and the administration could come to an agreement over the need to raise short-term interest rates such as in summer 1963.

Furthermore, the CEA concentrated on fiscal policy as the tool for macroeconomic stabilization. From the Fed, the Heller CEA primarily wanted stability in long-term government bond rates to encourage investment. The Fed accommodated with Operation Twist, which entailed lengthening the maturity of its portfolio by buying long-term securities and selling short-term securities. In fact, the public's expectation of price stability delivered the desired stability of bond rates. From the beginning of 1959 until fall 1965, long-term government bond yields remained close to 4%.

III. Martin and Johnson

An explanation for the Great Inflation must deal with Martin's responsibility. Although Martin did not succumb to Keynesian ideas, he had to deal with the Johnson administration. Johnson was a populist who reflexively opposed any increase in interest rates. Also, monetary policy became enmeshed with the politics of financing the Vietnam War and Johnson's Great Society. Both the CEA and the Keynesians on the Board of Governors wanted to coordinate monetary and fiscal policy. In return for a tax increase, the FOMC should refrain from raising interest rates. To raise rates, Martin would have had to face a political system hostile to any increase in rates with his own house divided.

A. A Hostile Political System and a Divided Board

In the Johnson administration, the possibility of bringing the administration on board for interest rate increases by making common cause with the treasury over balance-of-payments deficits disappeared. The Johnson administration resorted to capital controls to deal with the balance-of-payments problem. Early in 1965, the Fed and the treasury joined forces in a "voluntary" credit restraint program that limited the ability of banks to make foreign loans and the ability of corporations to lend abroad.

Johnson, after assuming office in November 1963 with Kennedy's assassination, made passage of the tax cut Kennedy had proposed in spring 1963 his top priority. Its passage in February 1964 initiated Martin's difficulties. When Kennedy submitted the tax cut legislation, Martin had opposed a policy of maintaining interest rates unchanged to accommodate the resulting debt issuance (Martin 1963, 126). However, with passage of the tax cut, Congress and the administration had effectively agreed that reduction in the unemployment rate was a national priority. An increase in interest rates would have appeared to thwart the will of the political system by offsetting the expansionary impact of the tax cut.

Martin confronted a president and Congress united in their hostility to interest rate increases. The situation was untenable for the Fed because it raised the possibility of a political consensus to alter the Federal Reserve Act to limit Fed independence. Internal division on his Board of Governors increased Martin's difficulties. At the October 1965 FOMC meeting, Martin deferred a rate rise. Martin (Board of Governers FOMC *Minutes* October 1965, 1112–13) told the FOMC:

[T]he Administration was strongly opposed to a change in policy. From the discussion today it was evident that the Committee itself was divided in its views. With a divided Committee and in face of strong Administration opposition he did not believe it would be appropriate for him to lend his support to those who favored a change in policy.

Some board members were unsympathetic to Martin's views on the need for preemptive increases in interest rates to prevent economic recovery from turning into an inflationary boom. J. L. Robertson from Broken Bow, Nebraska, had been appointed originally by President Truman in 1952. He had populist sympathies and disliked "high" interest rates. In 1961, Kennedy had appointed George Mitchell, who had liberal Democratic sympathies. Johnson appointed the Keynesian economists Sherman Maisel in April 1965 and Andrew Brimmer in March 1966.

None of these governors were tolerant of inflation, but none were willing to raise interest rates with excess capacity signaled by a "high" unemployment rate. Kennedy made J. Dewey Daane a governor in 1963. He became a stalwart of Martin; however, his loyalties were unclear until the discount rate increase of December 1965. Furthermore, the staff at the board became increasingly Keynesian in the 1960s. Governor Maisel initiated a staff effort to build a Keynesian large-scale, econometric forecasting model – the MPS (MIT–Penn–Federal Reserve System) model.

Martin's problems appeared in the House hearings in January 1964, one month before passage of the tax cut. Congressmen attacked Martin for not excluding an increase in interest rates following passage of the tax act. Representative Reuss (D. WI; U.S. Cong. February 28, 1964, 85) accused Martin of wanting to "vitiate" the effects of the tax reduction on unemployment. In the *1964 Economic Report* (p. II), the president had sent an unprecedented warning to the Fed: "It would be self-defeating to cancel the stimulus of tax reduction by tightening money." Representative Reuss (U.S. Cong. February 28, 1964, 89, 93) presented the Keynesian view that as long as excess capacity existed there was no need for interest rate increases to prevent inflation.[3] Martin (U.S. Cong. February 28, 1964, 87) repeated his view that the Fed should not finance the deficit and should raise interest rates early on during economic recovery to stop "an inflationary psychology" in its "incipient stages."

B. The 1965 Discount Rate Clash

In 1965, Martin became increasingly concerned about the effects of the Vietnam War buildup on future government deficits. In June 1965 in a speech, he indicated his desire to raise interest rates by comparing the current period to the boom period that preceded the 1929 stock market collapse. The issue became enmeshed in the Johnson administration's wage and price guideposts. The administration considered the prime rate paid by banks to be subject to its guideposts, and Johnson had prevented New York City banks from raising the prime rate. The difficulty for the money center banks was that rates on instruments like negotiable CDs had risen to the level of the prime rate. Banks' financial position would weaken without a rise in the prime rate. Also, financing that would have gone through the money market now went through banks. Martin (1965) believed that the resulting expansion of bank credit added to inflationary pressures.

Martin wanted to raise the discount rate to give banks cover for raising the prime rate (Maisel 1973, 74–6). However, during most of 1965, he lacked the board majority to raise the discount rate. In November, he gained a 4-to-3 majority through the support of Dewey Daane, and on December 3, the board raised the discount rate.[4] Johnson reacted angrily. Martin traveled to Johnson's ranch the next day. Gardner Ackley, CEA chairman, was also angry. The CEA had wanted to use the threat of an interest rate increase as an argument to persuade Johnson of the need for a tax increase (Ackley and Okun interviews, Hargrove and Morley 1984, 232, 295).

Heller, the prior CEA chairman, had made the case for a tax cut to stimulate the economy, and the 1964 tax cut appeared to have worked. In December 1965, the unemployment rate had fallen to 4%. However, to be a successful instrument for macroeconomic stabilization, fiscal policy had to be symmetric. Government would have to raise as well as lower taxes. As the CEA's legacy, passage of a tax increase would ensure the use of fiscal policy as the instrument of macroeconomic stabilization.

In summer 1966, with no presidential call for a tax increase forthcoming and with the unemployment rate less than 4%, the FOMC raised interest rates. Furthermore, it accompanied that increase with a letter to banks admonishing them to ration credit quantitatively rather than through raising interest rates. The result was the first credit crunch and disruption in markets such as municipal securities. The economy weakened quickly. The ensuing growth recession gave policymakers at the Fed and in the administration an incentive to compromise.

C. Waiting for a Tax Increase

Martin did not want to finance the Vietnam War's deficits. However, he confronted a political system hostile to interest rate increases. An alternative to a rate increase would be a tax increase that would eliminate the deficit. The Keynesian governors, influenced by the optimal-mix arguments of the Keynesian IS-LM model, would accept an easy monetary policy in return for a tight fiscal policy. Governor Maisel (U.S. Cong. December 13, 1965) made the case for coordination between monetary and fiscal policy.

The August 1966 increase in rates produced an outcry from the housing industry. It also encouraged the belief that the burden of restrictive monetary policy fell on interest-sensitive sectors. The rate increase prompted disintermediation from savings and loans (S&Ls) when savers withdrew funds from passbook savings accounts and redeposited them in higher earning bank CDs. Because S&Ls borrowed short with savings accounts and lent long with home mortgages, raising passbook rates reduced their net worth.[5]

Martin wanted a tax increase (Board of Governors FOMC *Minutes* December 13, 1966, 1420). However, for that he needed the cooperation of the treasury and the CEA to persuade Johnson. That cooperation would not occur if the FOMC raised interest rates. There was a clear political imperative for sustained growth of output at 4%. If fiscal policy was to turn restrictive, monetary policy had to be expansionary. The importance attached to fiscal policy reinforced the administration consensus that a tax hike required a stimulative monetary policy (Fowler 1967a, 209; 1967b, 218).

Ackley expressed this view to Johnson:[6]

There are serious disadvantages in a policy mix where tight money is restricting the economy while fiscal policy is stimulating it. Tight money and high interest rates have a very uneven and inequitable impact, as this year's collapse in homebuilding demonstrated.... [T]he point of bringing higher taxes into the ball game is to bench tight money.... An understanding on this shift in the policy mix should be nailed down before any tax decision is finalized.

In a letter to Johnson, Martin signed on:[7] "[A]n across-the-board increase in taxes should be enacted, promptly.... Somewhat easier money would seem to me desirable if fiscal action is taken to enable it." Thus began a game between Martin, Johnson, and Wilbur Mills, chairman of the House Appropriations Committee. As Okun (Hargrove and Morley 1984, 293) phrased it later:

Martin did a lot of bargaining in the Quadriad [meetings of the heads of the treasury, Budget Bureau, and CEA with the FOMC chairman]. The president attended when the administration wanted to exercise influence over monetary policy. If Johnson made a concession to Martin on fiscal policy ... it damned well better mean that Martin wouldn't tell him that interest rates had to rise during the period.

The FOMC backed off its August 1966 interest rate increase in September after Ackley persuaded Johnson to ask for suspension of the investment tax credit and, Ackley hoped, for a general tax increase in his January State of the Union speech (Hargrove and Morley 1984, 301). However, Martin and administration officials overestimated the difficulty of persuading Johnson to ask for a tax increase (Ackley, Heller, and Okun interviews, Hargrove and Morley 1984, 264, 183, 301). The main problem was that Johnson was not willing to accede to Representative Mills's demand for reductions in expenditures on Great Society programs as a condition for letting a tax bill out of the Appropriations Committee.

The possibility that Johnson would propose a tax increase went on hold when economic activity moderated toward the end of 1966.[8] Martin continued to lower interest rates in the expectation that when the economy recovered, a tax proposal would emerge from the White House. Okun (1970, 85–6) expressed the consensus:

[T]he Federal Reserve and the administration reached a conscious and coordinated decision that the monetary brakes should be released and not reapplied.... Since the tax proposal was specifically designed as an alternative to tight money, a restrictive monetary policy would have undermined the economic and political case for the tax increase.

Johnson did propose a tax surcharge in his State of the Union Message in January 1967, while accompanying the proposal with the condition stated in the *1967 Economic Report* (p. 9) that monetary policy support economic expansion. However, he did not send a tax proposal to Congress.

The economy strengthened after May 1967 while a rise in treasury bond yields produced an "inflation scare." The central banks that maintained the London gold pool began having difficulty preventing a rise in the price of gold. When Johnson hesitated in sending tax legislation to Congress, the FOMC began to raise rates from a low of 3.4% on T-bills in the week of June 10. Inflation returned to 3% in the summer. On August 3, Johnson requested congressional enactment of a 10% surcharge, and the FOMC ceased raising rates. Martin (Board of Governors FOMC *Minutes* September 12, 1967, 1011) argued: "[T]he overriding need at this point was to get some restraint from fiscal policy through a tax increase, and in his judgment that would be less likely if Congress came to believe that adequate restraint was being exercised by monetary policy."

Although Congress spurned Johnson's tax message, a run on the British pound made the FOMC unwilling to raise interest rates. In fall 1967, the Fed worked with the treasury and the International Monetary Fund (IMF) to put together a package of loans to Britain. The Fed could not then raise domestic interest rates and precipitate the very crisis it was attempting to avoid. Furthermore, policymakers feared that if speculators attacked the pound successfully they would turn to other currencies. A competitive devaluation could leave the dollar overvalued (Coombs, Board of Governors FOMC *Minutes* November 14, 1967, 1240, 1253). On November 20, 1967, Britain devalued the pound.

In December 1967, without progress on a tax bill, Martin raised the three-month bill rate to 5%. Political wrangling over the tax hike continued into 1968. Liberal Democrats opposed it as a way of protesting the Vietnam War. Especially after the riots following the death of Martin Luther King, they opposed any economic restraint that would raise unemployment among African Americans. Johnson therefore had to rely upon Republican votes, and Republicans insisted that Johnson cut back on his Great Society programs. Finally, in June 1968 Congress passed the tax surcharge. Senators and representatives used as cover the warnings from Treasury Secretary Fowler and Martin about the precarious international position of the dollar (Okun interview in Hargrove and Morley 1984, 306).

Martin's plea to save the dollar reflected the Cold War view that the central role of the dollar in the system of fixed exchange rates was fundamental to the position of the United States as the leader of the world's free countries. Martin argued that, without a tax increase to restore budget balance, foreign governments would lose confidence in the ability of the United States to control its balance of payments. They would then force dollar devaluation by demanding gold for the dollar deposits of their central banks. Martin (April 19, 1968; *New York Times* April 20, 1968) said:

[W]e are in the midst... of the worst financial crisis that we have had since 1931. [If the United States devalues the dollar] it is going to be a long time before we will be in the position that we now are where the dollar is the counterpart of a great power – diplomatic, military [and] economic. If I thought we would have to devalue, I'd quit.

D. The Tax Surcharge and Fear of Overkill

The Revenue and Expenditure Control Act of 1968, which became law on June 28, 1968, imposed a 10% surcharge on income taxes and a ceiling on federal expenditures. As a result, the budget went from a deficit of 2.9% of GNP in fiscal year 1968 (July 1 to June 30, 1968) to a modest surplus in fiscal year 1969. The prior deficit was the largest in the post–World War II period, approximated only by the 1959 deficit of 2.7% of GNP. Because the CEA believed that the swing from deficit in 1959 to a surplus in 1960 had initiated the 1960 recession, it feared a recession in 1968.[9]

Before 1966, the CEA had not considered monetary policy a tool useful for managing aggregate demand, but viewed it as useful primarily for stimulating investment by maintaining low long-term bond rates. However, after the 1966 credit crunch, the CEA came to see monetary policy as a potent instrument for controlling activity in the housing industry and, therefore, for controlling aggregate demand. Both the Board staff and the CEA believed that without an easing in monetary policy the move to fiscal restraint would produce a recession. The May 22, 1968, Greenbook predicted 7.4% real growth for 1968Q2, the contemporaneous quarter. In contrast, because of the passage of the tax surcharge, the July 10, 1968, Greenbook, predicted only 0.3% real growth for 1968Q3. Dan Brill (Board of Governors FOMC *Minutes* May 28, 1968, 646), director of research at the Board of Governors, told the FOMC:

Given the severity of this fiscal restraint... we have assumed a prompt but moderate shift in monetary policy, one that would permit Treasury bill rates to drop rapidly to about the 5 percent level.... [N]ext year would witness a net swing in this budget of $14 billion to a surplus. By comparison, the movement in the 1958–60 period, often assigned a major role in the recession of 1960, looks relatively mild. And although our economy is larger now than in 1960, it could scarcely take this degree of fiscal restraint – together with the present degree of monetary restraint – without heading into recession.

Martin's lobbying had created the expectation of a reduction in rates with a tax increase. In congressional testimony, Senator Proxmire asked Martin whether a tax increase would allow an "easier policy." Martin (U.S. Cong. February 14, 1968, 203) replied, "[T]here would be a tendency . . . toward lower interest rates." At the August 1968 meeting, Martin (Board of Governors FOMC *Minutes* August 13, 1968, 998) explained: "[He] thought a movement toward a lower level of interest rates was desirable. . . . System officials, including himself, might have contributed to the expectations [of greater monetary ease] that had developed. In the process of working for fiscal restraint, both System and Administration officials might at times have overstated the implications of fiscal restraint for interest rates." Okun (Hargrove and Morley 1984, 304) said later, [Johnson] "sure hated high interest rates and he wanted to get them down, and Martin kept telling him, 'If you can get the tax bill, I can back off on interest rates. I can't do it until you do.'"

Martin wanted to reduce the discount rate to signal the Fed's desire for lower interest rates. Martin (Board of Governors FOMC *Minutes* August 13, 1948, 901) commented, "[A]s other members of the Committee had noted, there had been and continued to be political considerations bearing on monetary policy." On August 16, 1968, the board lowered the discount rate. Monetary policy had become stimulative in 1964, and it remained so until 1969.[10] By yearend 1968, the unemployment rate had fallen to 3.4%. In the last half of 1968, inflation exceeded 5% (Figure 5.1). The next year, in reviewing "the mistakes of these recent years," Martin (May 22, 1969, 7) talked of "the error of an overhasty . . . relaxation of monetary restraint."

IV. Concluding Comment

Martin (U.S. Cong. February 26, 1969, 671, 668, 648) later talked about "the heritage of error" and regretted the gambit of allowing monetary ease in 1967 to encourage a tax increase and the easing in summer 1968 following passage of the increase. In 1969, the FOMC was determined to stick with restraint until inflation and inflationary expectations subsided. Martin (U.S. Cong. February 26, 1969, 651, 668, 669, 685) testified:

Expectations of inflation are deeply embedded. . . . A slowing in expansion that is widely expected to be temporary is not likely to be enough to eradicate such expectations. The experience of early 1967 is a lesson in point. Moderation in economic activity . . . did indeed produce a significant slowing in the rate at which prices advanced. But the moderation was short-lived. As economic activity accelerated after midyear, so did prices. . . . The critical test for stabilization policies in 1969 will be their ability to keep such a rebound in activity and prices from developing. If we were to dissipate again the benefits derived from a reduction in excessive demands, the credibility . . . of Government economic policies would be severely strained. . . . [A] credibility gap has developed over our capacity and willingness to maintain restraint. . . . [W]e have been unwilling to take any real risks. . . . We have raised . . . the ghost of overkill. . . . [W]e have got to take some risk.

Martin's emphasis on the expectational character of inflation and the need for credibility presaged the V–G era.[11] In 1980, the Volcker FOMC would renew Martin's resolve. Martin's successor, Arthur Burns, asked for and received an additional instrument – price controls – for dealing with inflation and inflationary expectations. Controls would substitute for credibility and the 1970s would be a lost decade for the Fed.

EIGHT

Arthur Burns and Richard Nixon

In 1969, newly elected President Nixon promised to lower inflation with only a small rise in unemployment. His CEA head, Paul McCracken, promised a return to price stability by maintaining unemployment modestly above 4%. After all, unemployment rates in excess of 4.5% had always been associated with inflation of less than 2%. Surely the economy could move down the Phillips curve just as it had moved up in the 1960s (Stein 1994, 150).[1] The Phillips curve shown in the *1969 Economic Report* displayed a clear inverse relationship between inflation and unemployment (Figure 8.1). Had not Samuelson and Solow (1960, 1344) said that the Phillips curve was a "reversible behavior equation"? Nevertheless, even though in 1970 the unemployment rate rose to 5% on its way to 6%, the inflation rate remained near 6%. Samuelson and Solow (1960, 1350) had written: "[I]f mild demand repression checked cost and price increases not at all or only mildly, so that considerable unemployment would have to be engineered before the price level updrift could be prevented, then the cost-push hypothesis would have received its most important confirmation."

The experiment in "mild repression" begun in 1969 appeared to demonstrate the existence of cost-push inflation. The comments of Samuelson and Solow (1960, 1352) had appeared prescient where they had talked about the high social costs ("class warfare and social conflict") of controlling cost-push inflation through the creation of unemployment. They referred to "direct price and wage controls" as a way "to lessen the degree of disharmony between full employment and price stability." Samuelson and Solow (1960, 1350) had argued that only a "vast experiment" could tell whether inflation at unemployment rates above 4% was cost-push or demand-pull. With the Nixon wage and price controls, the country did just that.

The rise in the unemployment rate from 3.4% in early 1969 to 6% in 1971 with no abatement in inflation created intellectual consternation among mainstream economists. Later, economists would look for an explanation in inflationary expectations due to the absence of a credible monetary policy. At the time, they turned to explanations of market power by corporations and labor unions. The resulting

77

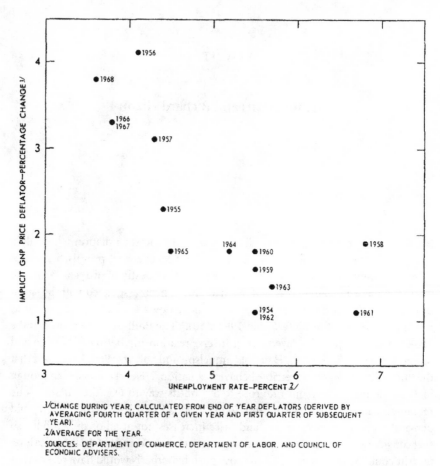

Figure 8.1. Price Performance and Unemployment. *Sources*: Department of Commerce, Department of Labor, and Council of Economic Advisers.

schemes for government intervention in private price setting complemented the "do something" psychology of politics.

I. From Stop to Go

Moderate growth of money was part of Nixon's policy of gradualism. However, an independent Fed controlled monetary policy. Martin's conception of restrictive monetary policy entailed maintaining a high interest rate until the disappearance of inflationary psychology in financial markets, and Martin's term as governor did not expire until January 31, 1970.

After congressional agreement over the tax surcharge in late May 1968, the FOMC had, in early August lowered the three-month bill rate from 5.8 to 5%. Faced with the obvious failure of restrictive fiscal policy to restrain strong real growth, the

FOMC then pushed the bill rate up to 6% by year-end. The FOMC began pushing it up again in early June 1969, and it reached 8% at the beginning of 1970 when Martin retired. M1 growth fell from an average of 6.5% (March 1967 to March 1969) to 2% (April 1969 to April 1970).

In 1969, the FOMC split. Hawks were unwilling to see rates decline until inflation declined. Led by Martin and President Al Hayes (New York), they believed that any reduction in market rates before inflation declined would exacerbate inflationary expectations. Led by Governors Andrew Brimmer, Sherman Maisel, and George Mitchell, the doves wanted rates to fall. Nixon appointed Arthur Burns to succeed Martin, and when he became chairman in February 1970, the doves became a majority. Burns had helped craft the policy of gradualism, and he guided the FOMC into a steady reduction in interest rates. By the end of 1970, the three-month bill rate was less than 5%. However, monetary restriction had already produced a recession with a cycle peak occurring in December 1969.

With the fall 1970 elections in mind, early in 1970, the CEA pushed a macroeconomic strategy to revive real growth. Monetary and fiscal policy would stimulate aggregate demand, but at a moderate rate that would still allow for the reduction of inflation by maintaining an unemployment rate above 4%. Because of the lags in the impact of policy actions on the economy, a strong recovery would begin only in the fall. The CEA stated its policy in the *1970 Economic Report of the President* (pp. 57–8):

The policy problem for 1970 is to take actions in the first half of the year which will place the economy on the sustainable path of moderately rising output and significantly declining inflation in the second half. . . . [B]y mid-1970 the economy, after three quarters of very little increase of real output, would be producing significantly below its potential. Such a GNP gap places a downward pressure on the rate of inflation.

Burns was not a Keynesian, but his views led him to a monetary policy consistent with the Keynesian consensus. Both Keynesians and Burns believed that government could manage aggregate real demand. Keynesians emphasized fiscal policy and, increasingly in the 1970s, monetary policy. Burns wanted to manage the psychology of businesspeople (Hetzel 1998). He believed that by mitigating their concerns about inflationary wage increases, policymakers could simultaneously stimulate real output and reduce inflation. Burns therefore rejected the Phillips curve trade-off. However, like Keynesians, he believed that real phenomena drove inflation. Both believed that the inflation that arose with an unemployment rate in excess of 4% was cost-push.

Burns (U.S. Cong. February 7, 1973, 485 and 504) testified:

Burns: [T]here is a need for legislation permitting some direct controls over wages and prices. . . . The structure of our economy – in particular, the power of many corporations and trade unions to exact rewards that exceed what could be achieved under conditions of active competition – does expose us to upward pressure on costs and prices that may be cumulative and self-reinforcing.

Sen. Proxmire: Would you comment on the monetary policy [in 1972] which seems to have resulted in an extraordinary expansion [in money]?

Burns: [D]uring 1972 unemployment averaged 5.5%. We had considerable slack in the economy in 1972, and I think the Federal Reserve Board served the country well by generating forces of expansion.

Nixon's disappointment with the outcome of the fall 1970 congressional elections made more acute the administration's desire to bring Burns on board with an expansionary monetary policy. Nixon had won the election in 1968 with a campaign that played on middle-class fear of society's "elites," war protestors, and militant civil rights activists. By the time of the 1970 congressional elections, however, erosion of support for the Vietnam War had undermined his coalition of the "silent majority" (Safire 1975, 309). To put together a coalition capable of winning the 1972 elections, Democrats and Republicans both attempted to appeal to the growth of economic insecurity among working Americans. That insecurity arose from the recession and from increased foreign competition due to the decline in the last half of the 1960s of American manufacturing supremacy.[2] For both political parties, 4% or lower unemployment became a rallying cry.

Nixon had never accepted the possibility of recession to lower inflation. With the appearance of recession in 1970, his administration changed its priorities to reducing unemployment rather than inflation, and it looked to the Fed for help. At about the same time, the profession changed its views of monetary policy. From the poor stepchild of aggregate demand management, it replaced fiscal policy as the favored policy tool. A series of monetary experiments demonstrated the potency of monetary policy.

In June 1968, Congress had passed the Revenue and Expenditure Control Act of 1968, which reduced government expenditures and imposed a 10% surcharge on income. The deficit went from 2.9% of GNP in fiscal year 1968 (July 1, 1967, to June 30, 1968) to a small surplus in fiscal year 1969. With the move to fiscal restriction, Keynesians predicted an economic slowdown. However, M1 growth continued unabated. Expansionary monetary policy trumped restrictive fiscal policy, and the economy grew strongly with rising inflation. At yearend 1968, the FOMC began to raise interest rates. Money growth fell in 1969Q2, with annualized M1 growth falling to 2.8% over 1969Q2 to 1969Q4. The Tax Reform Act of 1969 lowered taxes by increasing the standard deduction and the personal exemption and by lowering the maximum marginal rate on earned income. Restrictive monetary policy trumped expansionary fiscal policy, and a recession began December 1969.

Moreover, the politicized struggles in Congress over changes in taxes made clear that fiscal policy as an instrument of economic stabilization was impractical. The 1968 tax surcharge became embroiled in the politics of the Vietnam War. The 1969 act began as an attempt to extend the surcharge but ended as a tax-cutting holiday. By default, monetary policy became the favored instrument for managing aggregate demand. In line with the expectations of most economists and the political system, in the 1970s, the FOMC understood its role as central to an activist macroeconomic policy of sustaining high real growth and low unemployment.

After the fall 1970 congressional elections, the primary objective of the administration became achievement of 4% unemployment. McCracken wrote Nixon in November 1970:[3]

Standing outside government, one would expect a GNP of 1.050 million + next year. This, at best, would mean no decline in unemployment. Re GNP, with a $4\frac{1}{2}$% increase in productivity and a $1\frac{1}{2}$% increase in labor force, a 6% increase doesn't cut unemployment. Add 2% inflation, a 9% GNP increase would only slightly decrease unemployment. We must pick a path and set policies to reach it. It is quite unprobable that a 5% increase in money supply will do this.

In December 1970, administration economists estimated that GNP in 1971 would have to increase to $1,065 to deliver 4% unemployment in 1972. George Shultz at the Office of Management and Budget (OMB) pushed for 6% M1 growth.[4]

Burns was willing to pursue an expansionary monetary policy, but only if he had an incomes policy to control inflation. Burns (Board of Governors Board *Minutes* November 6, 1970, 3116–17) told Board members:

[P]rospects were dim for any easing of the cost-push inflation generated by union demands. However, the Federal Reserve could not do anything about those influences except to impose monetary restraint, and he did not believe the country was willing to accept for any long period an unemployment rate in the area of 6 percent. . . . [I]t was not possible to ignore the unemployment levels that were being reached. . . . [H]e did not believe that the Federal Reserve should be expected to cope with inflation single-handedly. The only effective answer, in his opinion, lay in some form of incomes policy.

In a speech at Pepperdine College on December 7, 1970, Burns argued "that it would be desirable to supplement our monetary and fiscal policies with an incomes policy." Through early summer 1971, heeding the advice of Shultz, Nixon rejected any form of price controls. However, Treasury Secretary John Connally favored them, and he became Nixon's primary economic adviser that summer.

In 1970, the FOMC moved the funds rate down steadily (Figure 8.2). After the October 1970 meeting, the funds rate averaged about 6% and the real rate slightly less than 3% (Figure 8.3). That still left real rates high enough so that M1 growth moderated in the fall. From the November 1970 meeting through the March 1971 meeting, the FOMC consistently saw three-month M1 growth rates at 3.5%, which fell short of its target. By its March 1971 meeting, the FOMC had pushed the funds rate down to 3.5%, which corresponded to a real interest rate close to zero. At the January 1971 FOMC meeting, Burns revealed a pattern of asymmetric concern for M1 growth that would persist for the next two years. He pushed the FOMC hard

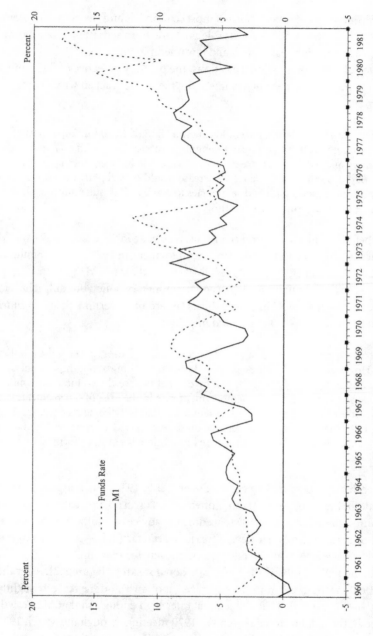

Figure 8.2. M1 Growth and the Funds Rate. *Notes*: Quarterly observations of four-quarter percentage changes in M1. M1 is shift-adjusted M1 in 1981 (Bennett 1982). Heavy tick marks indicate the fourth quarter of the year.

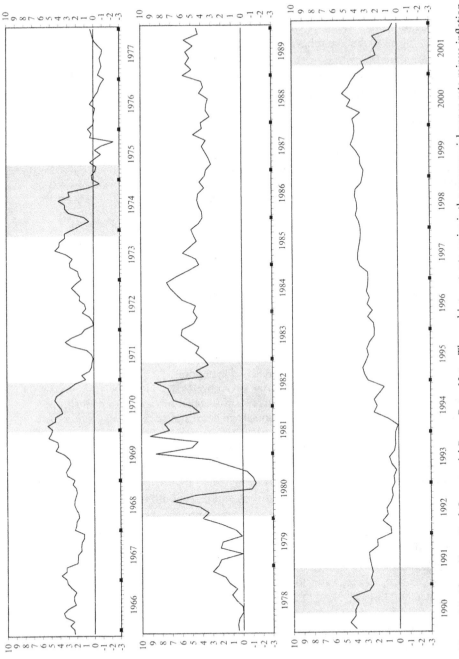

Figure 8.3. Short-Term Real Commercial Paper Rate. *Notes*: The real interest rate series is the commercial paper rate minus inflation forecasts made by the staff of the Board of Governors. Shaded areas indicate recessions. Heavy tick marks indicate December FOMC meeting. The Chapter 4 Appendix, "Series on the Real Interest Rate," describes construction of the series.

to lower the funds rate when M1 growth diminished but expressed reluctance to raise the funds rate when M1 growth surged.

Burns believed that the behavior of money was insignificant for monetary policy. However, the administration cared about M1, and Burns wanted to maintain good relations with the administration so that he could influence incomes policies. Burns (Board of Governors FOMC *Minutes* January 12, 1971, 41, 69) told the FOMC:

[T]he Administration's confidence in the System was weakening as a result of the shortfalls that had occurred in the rates of monetary growth. He was not concerned so much about the loss of System prestige and credibility as he was about the possible impact on other Governmental policies. . . . It was important that System officials never lose sight of the fact that the Federal Reserve was a part of the Government, and whatever the Federal Reserve did or failed to do would have an influence on the actions of the Administration and the Congress.

At its April 6, 1971, meeting, the three-month M1 growth rate jumped to 7%. Although the FOMC set a benchmark for the two-quarter M1 growth rate, its members viewed monetary policy through the lens of interest rates. Daryl Francis, the St. Louis Fed president, was the only exception. Given the FOMC's reluctance to raise interest rates other than gradually, Burns had no difficulty in persuading the FOMC to moderate increases in the funds rate. The *1972 Economic Report of the President* (p. 57) later stated:

[In 1971Q2 M1 grew] faster than desired. . . . [T]emporary "minor firming of money market conditions" was sought. . . . From December 1970 to June 1971, the money stock rose at a seasonally adjusted annual rate of 10.2 percent, and the broadly defined money stock . . . (M2) climbed at a seasonally adjusted annual rate of 16.1 percent.

In spring 1971, foreign central banks had to defend their currencies from appreciating against the dollar. In May 1971, Germany let the mark float, but other countries continued to buy dollars. President Hayes appealed to the FOMC to raise rates to defend the dollar. Ironically, Burns and Hayes both believed that floating exchange rates would recreate the chaotic environment of competitive devaluations that had supposedly exacerbated the Depression. However, raising interest rates to defend the dollar was anathema to U.S. politicians. Burns needed political support to get the incomes policy he wanted and was never willing to jeopardize that support by raising rates to defend the foreign exchange value of the dollar (Gyohten and Volcker 1992, 114).

On August 13, 1971, Britain asked for "cover" for the dollars it was buying to protect against a loss from dollar devaluation. Connally believed the British wanted gold.[5] Since March 1968, the United States had not sold gold except to small countries. However, in his August 15, 1971, Camp David announcement closing the gold window and imposing price and wage controls, Nixon used dollar weakness to make it appear as though he was responding forcefully to a foreign exchange crisis precipitated by foreigners.

II. Controls

Democrats attacked the Nixon administration over failure to lower unemployment and inflation. To embarrass the administration by making it appear indecisive, the Democratic Congress gave Nixon powers it did not believe he would use. In 1970, with the Defense Production Act, Congress gave Nixon power to allocate credit. Credit allocation appeared to allow a restriction in credit extension to lower inflation without the need for an increase in interest rates. In August 1970, Congress gave the administration power to impose wage and price controls.

For $2\frac{1}{2}$ years, until August 1971, the Nixon administration had rejected the intervention in private-sector price setting practiced by the Johnson administration. Why did it finally reverse course and impose controls? By the May 1971 FOMC meeting, an increase in bond rates signaled a rise in inflationary expectations. An expansionary monetary policy would not stimulate growth if undercut by higher inflation engendered by the expectation of inflation.[6]

Burns advised Nixon to exercise presidential leadership to check the union power that had kept inflation high despite high unemployment.[7] Recovery would proceed when businesspeople ceased to fear wage inflation. The rise in bond rates produced by the rise in inflationary expectations would frustrate expansionary monetary policy. Burns suggested a wage–price freeze. Also, in early July, the biannual CEA economic review concluded that economic growth would not achieve the $1,065 goal for GNP in 1971. Consequently, the unemployment rate would not reach the administration's goal of 4.5% unemployment by summer 1972 (*1972 Economic Report*, 21). Although the administration had finally gotten the rapid money growth it desired, it appeared that a rise in bond rates due to inflationary fears would dissipate its stimulative impact.

In Joint Economic Committee (JEC) hearings on July 23, 1971, Burns challenged the administration's desire for a stimulative monetary policy without controls. According to Burns (U.S. Cong. July 23, 1971, 252–4, 259), only by addressing the power of labor to raise wages could the country simultaneously restrain inflation and stimulate recovery:

A year or two ago it was generally expected that extensive slack of resource use . . . would lead to significant moderation in the inflationary spiral. This has not happened. . . . The rules of economics are not working in quite the way they used to. . . . The increased militancy of workers . . . has probably led to wider and faster diffusion of excessive wage rate increases.

Nixon then co-opted Burns. If controls were a condition for expansionary monetary policy, Nixon would deliver them. On August 15, 1971, Nixon announced the measures agreed upon at Camp David. They included closing the gold window, an import surcharge, and wage and price controls.[8] Burns received the incomes policy for which he had so long lobbied. And, by having Burns participate at Camp David as a full partner, Nixon assured his support for the administration's policy of economic expansion. The *1972 Economic Report* (p. 56) stated, "After August 15 the

success of the New Economic Policy became one more goal of monetary policy."
The Camp David program caught Democrats by surprise. Walter Heller expressed
public sentiment when he praised the policy as a change "from a do-nothing to a
do-something policy."[9]

Phase I was a 90-day freeze. Phase II provided for a Cost of Living Council
(COLC), a Price Commission, and a Pay Board with five representatives each from
labor, business, and the public. The Pay Board set a ceiling of 5.5% on annual wage
growth, and the Price Commission set a 2.5% figure for price rises. The difference
of 3 percentage points represented estimated trend growth of labor productivity.
Regulators required approval in advance for wage and price increases from large
corporations. Permission to raise prices depended upon a profit-margin test. Mid-
sized businesses had to report price increases. The remainder were subject to spot
checks but not reporting requirements.[10] Because enforcement relied more on
voluntary cooperation than on a large bureaucracy, the perception of "fairness"
was paramount.

To the public, controls on wages but not interest rates appeared unfair. Congress
at times threatened to pass legislation amending the Economic Stabilization Act,
which reauthorized the controls in fall 1971, to include the control of interest rates.
However, the flow of money from New York to London in 1969 when market interest
rates had exceeded Reg Q ceilings demonstrated the impossibility of regulating
the money market. The administration created the Committee on Interest and
Dividends (CID) to make wage controls politically palatable in the absence of
interest rate controls. Burns became chairman to avoid subjecting monetary policy
to the Cost of Living Council, which was chaired by Connally (Board of Governors
FOMC *Minutes* October 19, 1971, 1011). The CID used "moral suasion" to limit the
dividends corporations paid and to limit increases in "administered" interest rates,
that is, rates on mortgages, consumer credit, and bank loans to small business.

The reason for the price controls was to permit expansionary monetary policy
without raising inflation. At the time of their imposition, inflation was close to 4%,
not far from the 2.5% objective established by the Price Commission. The difference
could not explain a program of invasive, discretionary control that ignored due
process and encouraged the arbitrary exercise of governmental power. However,
"high" unemployment was a potent political issue. In its March 23, 1972, report
on the *Economic Report*, the JEC characterized the February 1972 unemployment
rate of 5.7% as the "nation's most pressing economic problem" (Congressional
Quarterly March 25, 1972, 690).

Congress, the administration, and most economists wanted expansionary monetary policy. Franco Modigliani (U.S. Cong. July 20, 1971, 113–14), future Nobel
Laureate, testified:

[Y]ou have to recognize that prices are presently rising, and no measure we can take
short of creating massive unemployment is going to make the rate of change of prices
substantially below 4 percent. Hence, money income needs to rise by . . . something like
11 percent. . . . So how much must the money supply rise? . . . 10 percent is nothing to
be worried about.

The *1973 Economic Report* (p. 53) stated, "[T]he purposes of the controls were . . . to reduce the fear that the rate of inflation would rise . . . and thus to . . . free the Government to follow a more expansive policy." Burns (U.S. Cong. February 20, 1973, 398) testified: "With an effective wage and price policy in place, the central task of monetary policy was to promote expansion in economic activity on a sufficient scale to reduce the gap between actual rates of production and our full employment potential."

There was no recognition that an objective of 4% for unemployment was unrealistic. In fact, the politically unacceptable 6% unemployment rate of 1971 was not far from full employment.[11] Subsequently, the lowest point reached for the unemployment rate was 4.6% in October 1973, which was achieved through the combination of controls and inflationary monetary policy. There was no public understanding of a positive equilibrium unemployment rate produced by frictional unemployment. For the public, the unemployed stood idly on street corners.

III. Apparent Success

Tension developed between Burns and the White House in fall 1971 when money growth appeared to stall. After the announcement of controls in August 1971, the FOMC left the funds rate unchanged. The announcement lowered expected inflation and raised the real interest rate (Figure 8.3). As the fall went on, the White House became increasingly concerned about the monetary deceleration.[12]

By early 1972, Burns also had problems with the FOMC, especially the New York Fed, which had again become concerned about the viability of Bretton Woods parities. On December 18, 1971, IMF member countries had accepted an effective devaluation of the dollar by 8.6%. By January 1972, this Smithsonian accord was already falling apart. However, at the January FOMC meeting, Burns would allow discussion only of low M1 growth. Prior to the meeting, he informed FOMC members that the only topic of discussion would be the domestic economy. In an unprecedented move, he also advanced the meeting date by one week.[13]

By the February 1972 meeting, FOMC participants feared a repetition of the spring 1971 experience when a sharp reduction in the funds rate had led to rapid growth in money (Board of Governors FOMC *Minutes* February 14–15, 1972, 213). Over the intermeeting period, the Desk had lowered the funds rate target half a percentage point to 3.25%. The Bluebook predicted a sharp rise in M1 growth.[14] At the March 1972 FOMC meeting, the Board of Governors staff was predicting 9.5% annualized M1 growth for the first quarter. Burns opposed significant increases in the funds rate because he feared that an increase in interest rates would discourage the Pay Board from keeping wage increases within its pay guidelines (Board of Governors FOMC *Minutes* March 21, 1972, 338–40).

By the April 1972 FOMC meeting, the funds rate had risen only to 4.25% and M1 was surging. Burns argued against an increase because he feared a rise in mortgage rates that would make the Pay Board less likely to resist wage demands (Board of Governors FOMC *Minutes* April 18, 1972, 417). Governor Brimmer (Board of Governors FOMC *Minutes* April 18, 1972, 448) supported Burns:

The significant point was that the Administration had decided at that time [August 15, 1971] – with the support of the Congress and the Federal Reserve – that the way to solve the problem of inflation was to apply direct controls rather than to slow the rate of economic growth and increase excess capacity. If more effective means of fighting inflation were needed, they should be sought in tighter controls ... not through monetary policy.

By the time of the July 18, 1972, FOMC meeting, M1 growth threatened to exceed the FOMC's targeted M1 growth rate of 6.5% for the third quarter. To avoid raising the funds rate, the FOMC reset its monthly targets for M1 to allow for high growth followed by slow growth. However, by the time of the August 15, 1972, meeting, it was clear that, with no change in the funds rate, the FOMC would miss its third-quarter target and probably the fourth-quarter target as well.

Within the FOMC, Burns had significant support for his position of limiting increases in the funds rate. Governors Brimmer and Mitchell wanted a lower unemployment rate. A few regional bank presidents and governors, especially the newly appointed governors, always supported the chairman. However, Burns still had to be concerned that dissents would advertise a divided FOMC. At the August meeting, Burns told the FOMC that the Fed was part of the government and therefore had to support its incomes policy. That policy limited the FOMC's ability to raise interest rates (FOMC *Minutes* August 15, 1972, 826–7).

By the September 19 FOMC meeting, M1 growth was clearly exceeding its benchmark path. The desk had allowed the funds rate to rise in late August, but only to 5%. However, in September in a departure from its procedures, the Desk had pushed the funds rate back below 5% to reverse an increase in the three-month bill rate. At the September 19, 1972, FOMC meeting, Burns resisted any increase in the funds rate. He told the FOMC that rising interest rates would make the Pay Board less likely to reduce its wage guideline to 4% in early 1973 (Board of Governors FOMC *Minutes* September 19, 1972, 866–7).

Majority sentiment in the FOMC was against Burns. Burns argued that an increase in interest rates would make Congress less likely to place a ceiling on federal expenditures. He also told the FOMC that if it raised interest rates the CID might set guidelines for interest rates (FOMC *Minutes* September 19, 1972, 915). Burns asked the FOMC for a directive that would prevent an increase in the funds rate regardless of the behavior of money. He also told the FOMC presidents not to allow their boards of directors to recommend an increase in the discount rate (Board of Governors FOMC *Minutes* September 19, 1972, 926). The FOMC followed Burns and did not raise the funds rate from its 5% level until the December 19, 1972, FOMC meeting.[15]

M1 growth in 1972 was 8.4%, and M2 growth was 12.8% (fourth quarter to fourth quarter). The combination of controls and expansionary monetary policy produced high real growth and low inflation. In 1972, real gross domestic product (GDP) increased 5.1%, CPI inflation increased 3.2%, and the unemployment rate declined to 5.2% in December. Was Burns politically partisan?

In 1974, with inflation in double digits, critics accused Burns of using expansionary policy to reelect Nixon. However, in 1972, there was near universal support for expansionary monetary policy. For example, comments of economists surveyed regularly by the Boston Fed (contained in the Redbook, the predecessor of the Beigebook – a document circulated to FOMC members prior to their meetings) supported Fed policy. Otto Eckstein, founder of the forecasting firm DRI, and Paul Samuelson commented in the August 9, 1972, Redbook that "monetary restraint at this time would abort the recovery." Neither was concerned about "demand-pull inflation." "Eckstein argued that it is not the Fed's job to solve a structural inflation."

Both the administration and Congress wanted an expansionary monetary policy. Later, Senator Proxmire became Burns's most articulate critic. However, in 1972 he expressed the prevailing view that monetary policy should be expansionary to reduce unemployment. At JEC hearings, Proxmire (U.S. Cong. February 9, 1972, 126) asked Burns, "Shouldn't we take advantage of our wage and price controls . . . to provide for a greater degree of monetary and fiscal stimulation than we could otherwise?"[16]

Burns had strong beliefs about macroeconomic policy, which required administration and congressional support. He believed that the controls program would make possible the simultaneous reduction in unemployment and inflation. Such a result required that the Pay Board set a low wage guideline. To achieve that goal, the FOMC could raise the funds rate only by a limited amount.

IV. Inflation and the End of Controls

Early in 1973, CPI inflation was only modestly above 3%. The *1973 Economic Report* (p. 63) stated that "American anti-inflation policy had become the marvel of the rest of the world." Moderate wage growth and high productivity growth produced moderate growth in unit labor costs in 1972. Based on that fact, CEA chairman Herbert Stein predicted that inflation would fall to 2.5% or less by yearend 1973 (U.S. Cong. February 6, 1973, 6, 7, 9). Accordingly, the administration initiated Phase III of the controls program in January 1973. Under it, firms in most sectors of the economy no longer had to ask for advance approval of price increases. Provided their costs had increased and they passed a profit-margin test, they could raise prices. The administration intended to focus on large corporations and their wage negotiations.[17]

Despite the administration's optimism, inflation soared in 1973. Figure 8.4, which shows Greenbook inflation forecasts and subsequently realized inflation, suggests the extent to which inflation in 1973 surprised policymakers.[18] Quarterly annualized CPI inflation came in at 6.4, 8.6, 8.2, and 10.5%. The fact that the

Panel A

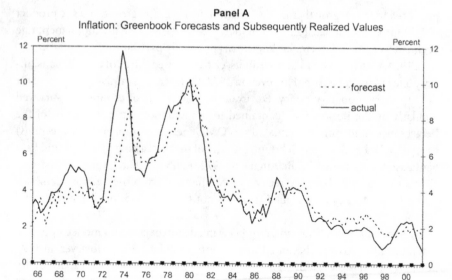

Panel B

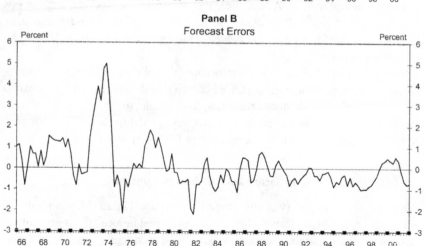

Figure 8.4. Panel A Inflation: Greenbook Forecasts and Subsequently Realized Values; Panel B Forecast Errors. *Notes:* Inflation forecasts are from the Greenbook for the FOMC meeting closest to the middle of a quarter (for Q1 usually end of January, for Q2 May, for Q3 August, and for Q4 November). They are an average of the annualized quarterly predicted inflation rates for the four quarters that begin with the contemporaneous quarter. The realized value is calculated from the "final" figure available in the last month of the quarter that follows the last quarter of the four-quarter forecast. Inflation is for the GNP deflator through 1991Q4, the GDP deflator from 1991Q1 through 1996Q2 and the GDP chain-type price index thereafter. Heavy tick marks indicate the fourth quarter of the year.

increase in inflation derived almost exclusively from the energy and food sectors was irrelevant to the public. Shoppers (at the time synonymous with housewives) were indignant at the rise in food prices in general and meat prices in particular. Although the controls extended to food processing, they did not cover the price of agricultural commodities, which drove the rise in food prices.

The rationale of the controls was that a wage guideline of 5.5% along with normal productivity growth would restrain the cost increases of corporations. A profit-margin test that corporations had to meet before passing through costs would limit the markup of prices over costs. In addition, large corporations had to win approval for price increases. Controls did successfully restrain wage growth. The average rate of growth of unit labor costs from 1971Q4 through 1972Q4 was only 2.4%.[19] Kosters (1975, 37–46) showed that well into 1973, for nonfinancial corporations, price rises followed changes in unit labor costs. Nevertheless, the most extensive controls since World War II failed to control inflation.

Legislation authorizing the controls expired April 30, 1973. Democrats in Congress wanted to make extension into a no-confidence vote on the Nixon administration's implementation of the controls program by forcing a strengthening of the controls. Lobbying by business groups and the administration defeated proposals to roll back price increases, impose rent controls nationally, and freeze interest rates. During the debate, Burns acted to forestall an extension of the controls to interest rates.

By its March 19, 1973, meeting, the FOMC had raised the funds rate to 7% from 5.5% in December 1972. Despite this rise in money market rates, the CID, chaired by Burns, had prevented a rise in the prime rate. When money market rates, which move with the funds rate, moved above the prime rate, corporations abandoned the commercial paper market and turned to banks for funding. Commercial bank credit expanded at an annualized rate of 20% from December 1972 to March 1973.

Burns argued that the FOMC had the freedom to raise money market rates because the CID held down increases in "administered" rates.[20] Administered rates referred to the politically sensitive interest rates on loans to small businesses, consumers, farmers, and home buyers. Limiting the rates that banks charged on such loans created stresses in the financial system. When the FOMC raised the funds rate above the prime rate in early 1973, New York City banks raised the prime rate. Burns forced them to rescind the increase (U.S. Cong. February 20, 1973, 426). On April 16, 1973, the CID established a two-tier prime, which permitted a floating-rate prime tied to money market rates for loans to large corporations. Banks had to continue setting the interest rates on administered loans at below-market rates.

Despite Burns's denials, the Fed did restrain increases in the funds rate as economic activity strengthened in 1972 and early 1973. CEA member Ezra Solomon (U.S. Cong. February 6, 1973, 21) put the behavior of interest rates in 1972 into historical perspective:

The behavior of interest rates in this recovery has been completely different than in any former recovery.... For 3 months' Treasury bills, in the recovery of 1948, they had risen 54 percent. In the recovery of 1954 they rose 199 percent. In the recovery of 1958 they rose 204 percent. In the recovery of 1960 they rose 22 percent. In the current recovery they have declined 9 percent.

The result was M1 growth of 7.1% in 1972, which followed 6.7% growth in 1971. By spring 1973, rapid monetary expansion had created a strong upsurge in inflation.

Starting with its April 17, 1973, meeting, the FOMC began seriously to constrain M1 growth by treating its two-quarter benchmark for M1 growth as an actual target. One reason was the association between rising inflation and high M1 growth. Burns also began to see the responsibility for controlling inflation as resting on the Fed. He was unhappy with what he believed was lax enforcement of the controls under Phase 3. Because in spring 1973 the Watergate scandal had begun to weaken Nixon's moral authority, Nixon could no longer rally the country to controls. Burns (Board of Governors FOMC *Minutes* April 17, 1973, 466; May 15, 1973, 519) told the FOMC, "Trust in government had declined dangerously. Those developments had increased the weight of the System's obligations."

In June 1973, Burns urged Nixon to reassert his leadership by reimposing a price freeze.[21] Politically sensitive food prices continued to rise. The Senate Democratic caucus voted for a 90-day freeze on all prices, profits, and interest rates. Nixon's economic advisers opposed a freeze, but Safire (1975, 507), Nixon's speechwriter, wrote that Nixon wanted to freeze prices because he "needed a dramatic move so as to appear 'Presidential.'" On June 13, 1973, Nixon imposed a 60-day price freeze and controls on agricultural exports. The public saw the move as opportunistic. The conditions that made the first freeze successful no longer existed. Because businesspeople no longer believed that controls were temporary, evasion replaced voluntary compliance.

Because of the strength in economic activity, this time the controls produced shortages. Farmers drowned baby chicks rather than sending them to market at a loss. As the *Congressional Quarterly* (July 21, 1973, 1928) wrote, "You may have chicken prices at 59 cents a pound during the freeze but you may not have any chickens." Meat disappeared from the shelves of supermarkets. Shortages eroded support for controls. The administration began Phase IV on July 18, 1973, with the end of the freeze. With Phase IV, large firms had to provide advance notification of price increases, which the COLC could deny. The practical effect of the program was to prevent a bulge in prices while the administration dismantled the controls program.

At their inception, businesspeople had supported controls enthusiastically. However, by 1973, they had become more concerned about the bureaucratic control that came with them than with labor union militancy. The controls themselves broke down as their enforcement became selective. Finally, they were an obvious failure. In 1973Q4 and 1974Q1, annualized CPI inflation was 10.5 and 12.5%, respectively.

The sharpest price rises were in internationally traded goods like agricultural products, metals, and paper whose prices were not controlled. Controls would only have led to the export of these goods. Restraint on wage growth was the heart of the controls, but the surge in inflation made the wage controls politically untenable. As public support for controls disappeared, Congress began to dismantle them piecemeal through ad hoc legislation. On April 30, 1974, Congress let control authority lapse.

With the outbreak of war in the Middle East in October 1973, the FOMC maintained the funds rate unchanged. Burns wanted the United States to end the embargo through diplomatic pressure, and he did not want to suggest that monetary policy could offset the disruptive effects of the oil shock. He told the FOMC that "any easing of policy at this time could prove mischievous, because it might well be interpreted as suggesting that monetary policy could make a significant contribution toward resolving current economic problems and thus lead to confusion and misdirected effort in the private economy and perhaps in the Government as well" (FOMC *Minutes* November 19–20, 1973, 1232).

The FOMC split on the issue of whether to accommodate inflation caused by the rise in the price of oil. Governor Sheehan (Board of Governors FOMC *Minutes* January 22, 1974, 100) argued for accommodation. "[T]he Committee had no choice but to validate the rise in prices if it wished to avoid compounding the recession." President Clay (Board of Governors FOMC *Minutes* January 22, 1974, 113) from Kansas City disagreed:

[T]his nation had a very long memory for the depression of the 1930's and it lacked any real understanding of the damage that inflation could do to the economy and to the future of people. As a result, actions to halt a developing recession tended to be taken immediately while actions to halt developing inflation were delayed interminably.

Burns (Board of Governors FOMC *Minutes* January 22, 1974, 115) argued that "[T]he economy was suffering from a shortage of oil...rather than a shortage of money." Subsequently, the FOMC concentrated on moving the funds rate to maintain moderate money growth.[22]

Watergate had weakened the president. Without a government that could use its moral authority to intervene in private price setting, the Fed would have to control inflation. Burns (Board of Governors FOMC *Minutes* March 19, 1974, 391) told the FOMC: "[G]overnments were weak in all of the democratic countries.... Because weak governments could not cope with the problem of inflation, the task had become the inevitable responsibility of central banks. Although their ability to deal with inflation was limited, central banks were discharging that responsibility at present."

V. Did OPEC or the Fed Create Inflation?

After 1973, the surge of inflation despite wage controls rendered unsatisfactory wage-push explanations of inflation. Policymakers then turned to special-factors explanations (Hetzel 1998). They believed that these special factors would dissipate in 1974 and that inflation would then decline. However, inflation remained in the low double digits throughout 1974. In the last half of 1974, with inflation unabated, Burns returned to the theme that government deficits caused inflation. The problem with his argument was that deficits had not been especially large. As a percentage of GNP, the government (federal, state, and local) surplus or deficit (−) was 1.1 in 1969, −1.0 in 1970, −1.7 in 1971, −0.3 in 1972, 0.5 in 1973, and 0.2 in 1974. (The 1970 and 1971 deficits reflected recession.)

Many economists have attributed the 1974 inflation to the OPEC price hikes that began in October 1973.[23] However, before the oil-price hikes, expansionary monetary policy had already produced an increase in inflation. The attempt by foreign central banks to prevent their currencies from appreciating by buying dollars propagated expansionary U.S. monetary policy abroad. In G-7 countries broad money growth averaged 16% in 1971 and 17% in 1972 (Hutchison 1991). In fall 1973, Senator Proxmire wrote Burns (1973, 796) asking him to respond to the criticisms of Milton Friedman that the Fed had caused inflation through high money growth. Burns defended Fed policy in 1972 in part by arguing that M1 growth was lower in the United States than in other industrialized countries.[24] However, given that they pegged their currencies to the dollar, U.S inflation determined their money growth.

Money creation generated a worldwide boom that made possible OPEC (Organization of Petroleum Exporting Countries) price hikes (Barsky and Kilian 2001). In G-7 countries, real GNP growth averaged almost 7% in 1972.[25] The boom caused commodity prices to soar. The *Economist* spot index of industrial materials prices doubled between mid-1972 and autumn 1973. The countries of OPEC had limited increases in the dollar price of oil. A measure of the world price of crude oil was at $1.96 in 1971Q2 and $2.32 a barrel in 1973Q3, just before the OPEC price hike. In the first three quarters of 1973, both inflation and the depreciation of the dollar limited the rise in the real price of oil.

With an overheated world economy, OPEC could increase the price of oil dramatically through a reduction in supply. With the outbreak of the Six-Day War between Israel and Arab states on October 6, 1973, OPEC embargoed oil sales to the United States and reduced production by 5%. The OPEC price increases revealed a highly inelastic short-run demand for oil. Jelle Zijlstra, head of the Bank for International Settlements, commented, "If the nations of the world had not embarked on their overstimulative economic policies of 1972–73 . . . the OPEC price increases simply could not have stuck" (cited in Mayer 1980, 215). From September 1973 to March 1974, the price of oil rose from $2.80 to $9.60 a barrel. The United States validated OPEC price hikes through price controls on oil that restricted the expansion of oil production in the United States and encouraged consumption of oil. Price controls kept crude oil prices in the United States at their May 15, 1973, levels. In early 1974, they were about half the level of world prices (Kosters 1975, 81–4).

Already before the October 1973 oil price hike, inflation worldwide was rising (Barsky and Kilian 2001; DeLong 1997). The *1974 Economic Report* (Table 23, 93) listed the following annualized CPI inflation rates by country (December 1972 through September 1973): Japan (18%); Canada, Italy, and the United Kingdom around 10%; France and Germany around 7%; and all other Organization for Economic Co-operation and Development (OECD) countries about 11%. By 1973Q3, average G-7 inflation had risen to 8.8%. In the United States, price controls limited inflation, but even there it averaged 8.4% in 1973Q2 and 1973Q3. The Appendix ("Money Growth and Inflation") shows that the oil price shock adds nothing to an explanation of the longer run behavior of inflation when one accounts for money growth. The other Appendix ("Monetary Policy Procedures under Burns") adds to evidence that the FOMC limited funds rate increases not only to stimulate the real economy but also to influence the controls program, that is, the oil price shock did not cause high money growth.

VI. Concluding Comment

The appendix, "Money Growth and Inflation," shows that money growth predicts inflation. In principle, given a funds rate target, growth in M1 could have just followed an independently determined growth in nominal GDP. The relationship between money growth and nominal GDP and inflation then would demonstrate only stability in money demand not an influence running from money to nominal GDP and inflation. However, the narrative account argues for money as an independent influence. From spring 1973 through fall 1974, the FOMC took seriously its money targets. In the earlier period as well as the later, the FOMC manipulated the funds rate for reasons that had nothing to do with the way that the interest rate works as part of the price system (Chapters 10–11 and 22–25). Money creation then exercised an independent influence on nominal expenditure either as a result of a brief period of purposeful monetary control or as a monetary disturbance. Monetary rather than nonmonetary forces determined trend inflation. "Inflation is always and everywhere a monetary phenomenon" (Friedman 1963, 39).

Why did Burns run an expansionary and ultimately inflationary monetary policy? He did not see himself as politically partisan – both political parties supported expansionary monetary policy to achieve the goal of 4% unemployment. However, Burns politicized monetary policy by using it as a bargaining chip to get the wage guidelines he deemed essential to low inflation. Burns feared that a rise in short-term rates would produce a rise in mortgage rates through a rise in long-term rates (Poole 1979). The Pay Board would then be less able to set a low wage guideline. Burns told the FOMC (Board of Governors FOMC *Minutes* April 18, 1972, 445):[26] "[H]e [Burns] had expressed his concern about the way in which the Government's incomes policy was working, and had suggested that some further tightening of the program might become imperative within the next few months.... [A]ny significant advances in long-term interest rates – particularly mortgage rates – would lead to a difficult problem."

Burns's sensitivity to the effect of a rise in interest rates on the controls program appeared in the Board of Governors' denial of recommended discount rate increases by the reserve banks:[27] "Phase II of the economic stabilization program might tend to be undermined if the Federal Reserve took an action that was followed by an upward movement in a wide range of interest rates.... [I]t was felt that the rates charged by large banks to prime business customers would be especially sensitive to an increase in the discount rate."

Ultimately, however, policy was inflationary not because of the misjudgment of one man but because the Fed delivered the policy that the political system and the economics profession wanted. Society demanded far more from monetary policy than it could deliver.

APPENDIX: MONETARY POLICY PROCEDURES UNDER BURNS

In the last half of the 1960s, the FOMC had sowed high money growth and reaped inflation. In response, it experimented with procedures in the 1970s that made money an explicit factor in the choice of the funds rate. However, the FOMC never gave up setting the funds rate. The spirit of the new procedures was to keep the FOMC aware of the behavior of money. The underlying assumption was that given this awareness the FOMC would set the funds rate at a level appropriate for controlling the real economy while also avoiding the high money growth that led to inflation. The experiment failed. In practice, until October 1979, the FOMC could not consistently tolerate the interest rate increases that appeared necessary to maintain moderate money growth.

In January 1970, at Martin's last FOMC meeting, prodded by the doves wanting a relaxation of monetary stringency, the FOMC began to set targets for M1 growth. Under these procedures, the FOMC set a target range for the funds rate and net borrowed reserves (excess reserves of banks minus their borrowing at the discount window). As described by Governor Maisel (1973, 254), "If the aggregates were not on the targeted path between meetings, the manager would change [money market] conditions slightly." That is, the FOMC continued to target interest rates by specifying money market conditions, but the behavior of money relative to its benchmark would become one factor in setting interest rate targets.

The Bluebook, which the staff of Board of Governors circulated prior to FOMC meetings, offered the FOMC a menu of alternative instructions for the Desk and corresponding general language for the directive. With the February 1970 FOMC meeting, the Bluebook began to present three choices. Each choice offered a specification of money market conditions (funds rate, borrowed reserves, and three-month treasury bill rate) predicted to be consistent with a two-month rate of growth of M1 using the month prior to the FOMC meeting as the base. The staff always included an alternative B with a two-month M1 growth rate equal to the growth rate predicted to occur given the prevailing funds rate. Alternative C would specify a somewhat lower M1 growth rate, and alternative A, a somewhat higher growth rate. If the FOMC wanted to predispose the Desk to raise the funds rate, it would choose Alternative C, and conversely with A. The April 1970 Bluebook was the first to associate each policy alternative with a forecasted monthly path for the quarter ahead for the monetary and credit aggregates as well as a weekly path over the intermeeting period (Hetzel 1981).

Although these procedures made money a factor in setting the funds rate, they did not amount to targeting a monetary aggregate. The six-month benchmark for M1 growth was reset each month using as a base the M1 value for the preceding month. Base drift incorporated into the benchmark for money the contemporaneous miss of money from its benchmark value. Therefore, the FOMC never had an operational target for money. Until later in the 1970s, only the St. Louis Fed supported the idea of substantive money targets.

In late 1970, the Nixon administration became especially concerned about slow M1 growth. Burns blamed low M1 growth rate on foot dragging by the New York Desk in carrying out FOMC directives and threatened to make the System Open Market account manager a board employee. The Desk documented its actions and showed that it had followed the wishes of the FOMC.[28] Burns was scapegoating. The Desk had in fact achieved the funds rate targets desired by the FOMC, but the FOMC had not specified those targets explicitly. To avoid future misunderstanding, in November 1970, the FOMC started to give instructions to the Desk making explicit the desired behavior of the funds rate. Starting with the November 1970 Bluebook, the Board of Governors staff began specifying policy alternatives as paired values of the funds rate alone and associated forecasted money growth.

At its February 14, 1972, meeting, the FOMC had specified new language concerning money growth for instructing the Desk how to implement the directive. The FOMC began to specify numbers for money growth for the current and (starting in May 1972) the succeeding quarter. Based on these numbers, the manager was supposed to respond to "significant deviations from expectations for [the] monetary aggregates." Starting with the October 17, 1972, meeting, the FOMC began to use the word "target" for these quarterly numbers. It instructed the Desk to base its decision on the "combined" quarterly money numbers.

At the February 1972 FOMC meeting, the FOMC adopted procedures for reserves targeting. However, when money growth surged, it abandoned them because Burns wanted to limit the rise in the funds rate. Although the FOMC abandoned these reserves targeting procedures when they called for a higher funds rate, in October 1979, then FOMC Chairman Volcker would adopt the same procedures for reserves control. And he would use them for the reason advanced in early 1972. Bruce MacLaury (vice president Minneapolis) argued:[29]

[T]he case for shifting to a reserve target [assumed]... members were not psychologically prepared to call for changes in interest rates of the size required to achieve the desired growth rates in the monetary aggregates, but that they would permit such changes to occur if they could be described as the by-product of the Committee's pursuit of a reserve target.

President Morris (Boston) added:[30]

[I]n the second half of 1968 . . . in an effort to resist rising interest rates, the System had supplied more reserves than any member would have thought desirable at that time. If the Committee continued to employ a money market strategy it was highly likely to repeat that mistake in 1972, since interest rates probably would come under upward pressure as the economy expanded.

Burns's unwillingness to allow a rise in money market rates before the November 1972 elections appeared in the way that the FOMC backed off of its regular operating procedures. In 1972, the FOMC set M1 targets on a quarterly basis along with consistent monthly paths. At each meeting, as a trigger for changing the funds rate during the intermeeting period, it also gave the Desk a two-month growth rate for M1 ending with the succeeding month. At its July 18, 1972, meeting, the FOMC became aware of a surge in M1 growth in the first two weeks of July. To keep its M1 target of 6.5% for the third quarter and to avoid a rise in the funds rate, the FOMC set a monthly path for M1 of 10.5% in July and 2% in August. Following the July meeting, M1 growth still exceeded its already expansive path. By the time of the August 15 meeting, M1 growth for July had come in at 15.2% and the Board of Governors staff put August growth at 3.5%. Assuming no change in the funds rate, the Bluebook estimated M1 growth at 9 and 8.5%, respectively, in the third and fourth quarters.

At its July 18 meeting, the FOMC had set 5% as the benchmark for annualized M1 growth from June through August. Its procedures were to raise the funds rate if predicted M1 growth exceeded the benchmark. By the August 15 meeting, the New York staff was predicting above-path growth of 6.8% for M1. In response, the Desk raised the funds rate just before the August meeting, but only slightly from 4.625% to 4.75%. At its August 15 meeting, the FOMC raised the July to September M1 path to 7%. Given the high M1 growth in July, rebasing the two-month M1 benchmark growth rate from a June to a July base also raised the effective M1 benchmark.

Immediately after the August FOMC meeting, predicted M1 growth began to come in above the two-month benchmark path. By the time of the September 19 FOMC meeting, the New York Bank was predicting 11.5% M1 growth for the July–September period. Late in August, the Desk allowed the funds rate to rise to 5%. As high rates of growth of money continued, the financial markets anticipated that Desk procedures would produce an additional rise in the funds rate. Correspondingly, the interest rate on treasury bill rates rose.

The Desk, in the statement week ending September 13, pushed the funds rate back below 5% in an attempt to undo the run-up in market rates. At the September FOMC meeting, Allan Holmes, Open Market, Desk Manager, referred to a desire "to avoid a completely unwarranted run-up of interest rates and the risk of disorderly market conditions."[31] President Eastburn criticized Burns for not calling a conference call as stipulated by instructions for instances when "[I]t appears that the Committee's various objectives and constraints are not going to be met satisfactorily."[32]

At the September meeting, Burns asked the FOMC for "the addition of the word 'special' [to the directive] . . . to emphasize that . . . money market conditions were to be given special importance and the Desk was to be given more than the usual degree of flexibility."[33] That is, the Desk would not raise the funds rate. Also, to avoid putting itself in a position where its procedures would call for a funds rate increase, the Desk set the two-month M1 benchmark growth rate for August to October at 11.5%, the same figure the Desk was then predicting for M1 growth.[34] The FOMC kept its funds rate peg at 5% until its December 19, 1972 FOMC meeting.

Finally, Burns told the FOMC presidents that they should not allow their boards of directors to recommend an increase in the discount rate.[35] One of the few ways a Reserve Bank can indicate its disapproval of monetary policy is by recommending a discount rate change. By October 12, 1972, 7 of the 12 regional Banks were in for a discount rate hike. The Board of Governors sent a telegram to the New York Bank stating that it had disapproved its recommendation because it did "not constitute a timely action in furtherance of the economic stabilization effort."[36]

APPENDIX: MONEY GROWTH AND INFLATION

When one accounts for the effect of price controls, money growth predicts inflation. Over the postwar period until financial deregulation in 1981, trend M1 velocity growth averaged 3% per year. Because financial innovation allowed the public to economize on cash balances, the public's nominal expenditure on average grew 3 percentage points faster than M1. Adding 3% to M1 growth then yields a prediction for trend growth of nominal expenditure.

Over the period 1970Q4 through 1973Q1, nominal expenditure grew 10.4%, close to the 10.6% growth predicted by the 7.6% M1 growth. With trend real growth of 3% per year, nominal expenditure growth of 10.4% should have yielded inflation of 7.4%. Over this period, however, inflation grew at only 4% because price controls held down inflation and caused nominal expenditure growth to appear disproportionately as real growth.

However, as the administration began phasing the controls out in summer 1973 and then with their end on April 30, 1974, inflation soared to compensate for its prior suppressed level. To calculate the effect of M1 growth on inflation, one must average over the period of controls and the period following their removal. From 1970Q3 through 1974Q4, M1 grew at an annualized rate of 6.4% (M2 at 9.7%). Nominal GNP grew at 9.7%, which is close to the 9.4% predicted by adding 3% velocity growth to the 6.4% M1 growth. (M2 velocity exhibited no trend growth, and it predicted nominal GNP growth exactly.) With nominal GNP growth at 9.7%, and trend real growth at 3%, inflation should have been at 6.7%. In fact, CPI inflation over this longer period was 6.8%.

NINE

Bretton Woods

In July 1944, the West, under the leadership of the United States and Great Britain, agreed on a postwar international monetary order at Bretton Woods, New Hampshire.[1] The IMF Articles of Agreement required member countries to fix their exchange rates by setting a par value of their currency in terms of the gold content of the dollar. Countries received quotas on which they could draw to offset temporary payments imbalances. The United States committed to pegging the dollar price of gold at $35 an ounce. Success of the new system required U.S. monetary policy to provide the nominal anchor. The United States failed to do so.

For the system to have functioned as a gold standard with gold as the nominal anchor, the United States would have had to allow its price level to vary to give the world's central banks the real amount of gold they desired to hold. Declines in the U.S. price level would have raised the purchasing power of gold and stimulated its production. A simulated gold standard would also have required that the U.S. price level adjust relative to foreign price levels to validate the equilibrium real exchange rate (given that the nominal exchange rate could not change). For the U.S. price level to have behaved in this way, the Fed would have had to allow the monetary base to decline in response to gold outflows. Only briefly in 1959 did it follow this classical gold standard rule.

In the absence of U.S. willingness to allow the price level to fall in response to gold outflows, the system became a dollar standard. For this system to work, the United States had to provide a stable nominal anchor for the dollar other than gold. Although other countries held on to Bretton Woods tenaciously, ultimately inflationary U.S. monetary policy destroyed it. In the late 1920s, the international monetary system had collapsed due to deflationary U.S. monetary policy. In the 1970s, it collapsed due to inflationary U.S. monetary policy.

Because of the belief that the exchange rate devaluations of the 1930s had destabilized the international economic system, the Articles charged the IMF with overseeing a system of fixed exchange rates (Yeager 1976, 375). The designers of this system desired the exchange rate stability of the gold standard. At the same time, the assumption by governments of responsibility for full employment required the

100

independent conduct of national monetary and fiscal policies. This independence required a periodic relaxation of the discipline of fixed exchange rates. Adjustment to balance of payments disequilibria would not automatically entail the inflation or deflation required by the classical gold standard.

The result was a system of pegged rather than fixed exchange rates. The Articles allowed countries to change their exchange rates in response to "fundamental disequilibrium." In practice, the result was a system that produced infrequent, but large devaluations in an environment of crisis.[2] The contradiction of fixed but variable exchange rates allowed imbalances that created one-way bets for speculators to cumulate. One-way bets created destabilizing reserves flows.

Under the pressure of full-employment policies, countries often treated balance of payments disequilibria as real phenomena rather than monetary phenomena requiring corrective monetary policy. The Keynesian intellectual environment impeded an understanding of how, given an exchange rate peg, the price level had to vary to equilibrate the balance of payments. The panoply of ad hoc protectionist measures undertaken to defend overvalued exchange rates in the Bretton Woods period reflected that environment. The extreme example was Britain, which experienced successive crises in 1949, 1951–2, 1955–6, 1966–7, and 1972. Britain devalued the pound in 1949 and 1967 and floated it in 1972. Brittan (1970) described the exchange controls to which Britain resorted during crises.

If the Bretton Woods system encouraged the instability that its founders had hoped to avoid, how did it survive until March 1973? The system of pegged but freely convertible currencies did not begin until December 1958 when the major European countries made their currencies fully convertible for current account transactions. The IMF itself undertook no significant actions until 1956 when it made loans in response to the Suez crisis. Most important, the United States ran the system in a way that did not force deflation on other member countries. After 1949, it maintained an overvalued dollar. The United States could afford to allow persistent gold outflows because it had accumulated most of the free world's monetary gold stocks by the end of World War II.

The United States ended World War II with a huge amount of official reserves, mostly in gold. It then added to them with large balance of payments surpluses through 1949 (Table 9.1). After the war, a consensus existed that a "dollar shortage" would remain an intractable problem. Haberler and Willett (1968, 3) wrote that economists commonly characterized the international payments imbalance as "a perpetual dollar shortage, a deep-seated imbalance incurable by orthodox monetary policies."

In fact, contrary to the Keynesian orthodoxy, balance of payments did respond to changes in real exchange rates. Although not understood at the time, the large devaluation undertaken by U.S. trading partners in 1949 reversed the dollar's undervaluation. In time, the problem became persistent U.S. deficits. In 1950, the United States ran a current account deficit. A string of deficits turned to surpluses with the unusual demand for exports in 1956 and 1957 following the Suez crisis. However,

Table 9.1. *U.S. Trade Balance*

Year	Merchandise net balance	Balance on current account	Balance on current account and long-term capital	Net liquidity balance	U.S. official reserve assets
1946	6,697	4,885			20,706
1947	10,124	8,992			24,021
1948	5,708	1,993			25,758
1949	5,339	580			26,024
1950	1,122	−2,125			24,265
1951	3,067	302			24,299
1952	2,611	−175			24,714
1953	1,437	−1,949			23,458
1954	2,576	−321			22,978
1955	2,897	−345			22,797
1956	4,753	1,722			23,666
1957	6,271	3,556			24,832
1958	3,462	−5			22,540
1959	1,148	−2,138			21,504
1960	4,892	1,774	−1,211	−3,677	19,359
1961	5,571	3,048	−20	−2,252	18,753
1962	4,521	2,446	−1,043	−2,864	17,220
1963	5,224	3,188	−1,339	−2,713	16,843
1964	6,801	5,764	−100	−2,696	16,672
1965	4,951	4,299	−1,817	−2,478	15,450
1966	3,817	1,635	−2,621	−2,151	14,882
1967	3,800	1,273	−3,973	−4,683	14,830
1968	635	−1,313	−2,287	−1,611	15,710
1969	607	−1,956	−3,949	−6,081	16,964
1970	2,603	−281	−3,760	−3,851	14,487
1971	−2,268	−3,879	−10,637	−21,965	12,167
1972	−6,409	−9,710	−11,113	−13,829	13,151
1973	955	335	−977	−7,651	14,378

Notes: Millions of dollars: Data from *1976 Economic Report of the President.* Current-account balance covers trade in commodities and services, including military transactions and earnings on international investments, pensions, nonmilitary foreign aid, and other private and governmental transfers (Yeager 1976, 566). The net liquidity balance is the net change in gold and other official reserves plus the net change in U.S. liquid claims on and liabilities to foreigners. These include bank accounts, short-term securities, and U.S. government securities of all maturities (Yeager 1976, 52)

the deficits returned in 1959. Inflation in the United States in 1956, 1957, and 1958 and a devaluation of the French franc in 1957 and 1958 exacerbated the dollar's problems. Gold losses quickened in 1958 and 1959.[3]

The FOMC raised the bill rate to 4.6% in early 1960. Money (M1) fell slightly over the two-year interval from January 1959 to January 1961. A peak in the business cycle occurred in April 1960, less than three years after the prior peak. In 1960, because of the recession, short-term interest rates in the United States fell compared to those abroad. Furthermore, there was speculation of a revaluation of the deutsche mark. In November 1960, these factors plus nervousness about the position on gold of presidential candidate John F. Kennedy combined to produce a spike in the price of gold on the London gold market. In November 1961, the United States and other European countries joined to sell gold to prevent its price from rising above $35 per ounce. The resulting Gold Pool became a commodity stabilization arrangement to set the dollar price of gold.

Nevertheless, the continuing concern during the Kennedy administration over the balance of payments produced a conservative monetary policy, and the United States experienced near price stability from 1960 through 1964. The current account displayed strong surpluses through 1965. However, long-term capital flowed out of the United States to finance direct investment in Europe. The current account minus capital outflows remained negative from 1960 onward (Table 9.1). The Treasury believed that the deficit was a transitory problem because the long-term investments abroad would generate in time an offsetting return flow of dividends.

In the 1960s, foreign central banks accumulated dollars. Triffin (1960) warned about an insufficient supply of international reserves.[4] He worried that a pyramiding of dollars upon gold would produce a fragile system. At some point, countries concerned about the ability of the United States to redeem dollars in gold would demand gold, and the system would then collapse.[5] The treasury assumed that foreign central banks accumulated dollars because of insufficient growth in international reserves. "Against this background . . . the new Secretary of the Treasury [Henry Fowler] electrified the world in early July [1965] by announcing that the President had authorized him to say that" the United States would negotiate reforms to international monetary arrangements (Solomon 1982, 82). In 1967, the IMF member countries agreed to the creation of special drawing rights (SDRs), which entitled countries to obtain convertible currencies for balance-of-payments needs.

These concerns misrepresented the operation of the dollar standard. The large member countries of Bretton Woods understood that they could not demand gold for their dollars (Yeager 1976, 575). The exception was France, which demanded gold periodically until 1968. The United States continued to lose gold at a moderate rate. However, because other countries pegged their currencies to the dollar, the United States could not devalue. With n countries, only $n - 1$ of them could set an exchange rate. The United States was the nth country. If another country with an overvalued currency ceased supporting its currency, its currency would depreciate in an environment of financial and political crisis. In contrast, if the United States closed the gold window and stopped intervening in foreign exchange markets, nothing would happen.

By the early 1970s, policymakers understood that the United States could neither unilaterally devalue the dollar nor move to floating exchange rates (Shultz and
Dam 1978, 114; Solomon 1982, 170; Volcker and Gyohten 1992, 40). There never
was any willingness to advocate a regime of floating exchange rates. Policymakers continued to adhere to the view that competitive depreciations in the Great
Depression had exacerbated economic instability (Volcker and Gyohten 1992, 7).
Also, businesspeople associated fixed exchange rates and the $35 price of gold with
responsible government policy.

Views within the Fed reflected those of the larger policy community. In response
to a question by Senator Douglas at hearings of the JEC on January 30, 1962, Chairman Martin (April 17, 1962) argued that floating exchange rates were destabilizing:

When the dollar exchange rate began to deviate considerably from its customary level,
the market might well no longer expect a return to that level but rather would count
on progressively wider deviation. Once market behavior became geared to such expectations, it could easily give rise to cumulative movements in financial markets far more
difficult to contain than under a system of fixed exchange rates. . . . These disturbances
would arouse inflationary processes at home. They might set in motion a self-propelling
inflationary spiral, with any increase in inflationary tendencies tending to lead to a further decline in the external value of the dollar.

In the 1960s, there was little understanding of the implications of the dollar
standard. To counter an overall balance of payments deficit, the United States
turned to capital controls. They began with an Interest Equalization Tax, which
imposed a tax on foreign loans and bond issuance in the United States of 1%
to impede capital outflows. In 1965, the Commerce Department implemented a
voluntary, later mandatory, foreign direct investment program to limit foreign
investment.The Fed imposed restrictions on bank lending abroad in the so-called
Voluntary Foreign Credit Restraint Program (Johnson 1966; Meltzer 1966).

Paul Volcker (Volcker and Gyohten 1992, 33–4), Undersecretary for Monetary
Affairs at the Treasury, wrote:

The intellectual concept, beautiful in its simplicity, was smothered in hundreds of paragraphs of regulation. . . . But that turned out to be only the beginning. The supposedly
temporary tax stayed on for more than a decade. . . . The controls greatly encouraged
the development of markets in dollar deposits and securities abroad . . . circumventing
the controls quite legally in what came to be known as the Eurodollar market, which
flourished in London [not New York].

The controls "led inexorably to the displacement of New York as the world's
leading capital market center" (Shultz and Dam 1978, 111). Haberler and Willett
(1968, 22) describe their mind-boggling complexity: "Much time, ingenuity, and
energy are diverted from the productive tasks of improving operations . . . to an
endless struggle with formidable red tape and bureaucracy."

In the Keynesian intellectual environment, policymakers believed that correcting
a balance of payments deficit required reducing aggregate demand. With imports

only about 4% of GNP in the early 1960s, there was no political support for such policies. Mayer (1980, 114) quotes Representative Henry Reuss during testimony before his International Payments Subcommittee in 1962: "To propose paying $30 or $40 billion per year in reduced income to American workers and investors to obtain a $2 billion to $3 billion reduction in the payments deficit is to reduce economic calculus to absurdity."

Because of an unwillingness to tolerate a fall in aggregate demand, the price level could only rise. Increases in prices lowered the real price of gold. Inevitably, the combination of the disincentive to mine gold and increases in the demand for nonmonetary gold threatened the sustainability of the $35 price of gold. Countries, however, held onto a fixed dollar price of gold and fixed exchange rates – symbols of financial conservatism that obscured the reality of monetary and fiscal indiscipline.

Toward the end of 1965, U.S. inflation began to rise. By 1969, CPI inflation was somewhat over 5.5%. After abating in 1971 and 1972, it rose to 8.4% in 1973. Although inflation rose among U.S. trading partners, it lagged behind the United States (Hetzel 1999; 2002a; 2002b). The lag in relative inflation rates made the dollar overvalued and the deterioration in the balance of payments became progressively worse. The net merchandise balance in the five-year periods 1961 through 1965 and 1966 through 1970 went from $5.4 billion to $2.2 billion, while the current account balance fell from $3.7 billion to –$0.6 billion. Including long-term capital, the deficit went from –$0.9 to – $3.3 billion (Table 9.1).

The London gold pool – where national treasuries, chiefly the United States, pegged the dollar price of gold – collapsed in March 1968. Britain had devalued in November 1967. Speculators then bet on a revaluation of other currencies, chiefly the mark, relative to the dollar, and sold dollars for gold. After March 1968, central banks no longer sold gold to the public. Countries went from a de facto to an official dollar standard.

The dollar strengthened temporarily with the student riots and striker unrest in France in May 1968 and a restrictive monetary policy in the United States in 1969. The high interest rates that accompanied restrictive policy attracted short-term capital from abroad. However, with the onset of U.S. recession in 1970, interest rates fell in the United States relative to the rest of the world. Thereafter, in response to short-term capital outflows, foreign central banks had to buy dollars. On average for the years 1965–9, U.S. short-term private capital inflows plus errors and omissions, which hides such flows, amounted to $2.2 billion. In 1970 and 1971, these figures amounted to –$7.7 and –$19.9 billion, respectively (Yeager 1976, Table 27.1).

In 1971, prompted by the difference between U.S. and foreign interest rates and speculative motives, foreign corporations borrowed in dollars, which they used to repay domestic debt. The borrowed dollars ended up at foreign central banks. "The reserves of the Group of Ten [G-10] countries, not counting the United States, but adding Switzerland, rose by almost 31 billion in 1971. . . . In 1971, the total money volume of the ten countries mentioned grew some 18% above its end-period-1970 level" (Yeager 1976, 512). On May 3, 1971, speculative dollar inflows to the Bundesbank forced Germany to float the mark.

For 1971Q2, for the first time in the postwar period, the United States ran a deficit on its merchandise trade balance.[6] By early August, financial markets were acutely nervous about weakness in the dollar. Treasury Undersecretary Volcker informed Treasury Secretary Connally that speculation against the dollar had reached a fever- ish pitch (Volcker and Gyohten 1992, 76). Although dollars flowed into foreign central banks, only small central banks could ask the U.S. Treasury for gold in exchange for dollars.

Forbord (1980, 37) wrote: "There is no evidence that gold conversions of central banks' dollar balances ever threatened the gold/dollar system, not even in August, 1971." Forbord (1980, 162) quoted Bruce MacLaury, treasury deputy undersecre- tary for Monetary Affairs, "The gold window was open in form only, not in fact." He also cites Bergsten (1975, 267): "The U.S. Treasury had convinced European central bankers in 1968 that 'gold would be embargoed in the case of a run on the dollar.'" However, Nixon closed the gold window and imposed a 10% surcharge on imports to give the United States bargaining power in negotiations over new dollar parities.

Because speculators knew that other countries would have to revalue their cur- rencies relative to the dollar, dollars flowed into foreign central banks.[7] Foreign gov- ernments tried to prevent their currencies from appreciating by imposing exchange controls, but they worked poorly.[8] Shultz and Dam (1978, 115) wrote: "In essence, US officials had formed an alliance with the market itself to force a change in the behavior of foreign officials." Leaks from the December 1, 1971, Group of Ten meeting in Rome about Connally's mention of a "hypothetical" 10% dollar devalu- ation reinforced pressures on foreign countries (Solomon 1982, 204). As Secretary John Connally said to Japan, "The dollar may be our currency but it's your problem" (Volcker and Gyohten 1992, 81).

In negotiations with G-10 countries at the Smithsonian in December 1971, the United States agreed to devalue the dollar by 7.89% by raising the official dollar price of gold and to remove the import surcharge. Other countries revalued their currencies by varying amounts. The effective trade-weighted devaluation with the major trade partners of the United States amounted to 10.35% (Yeager 1976, 580). The devaluation was supposed to lead to reflows of dollars into the United States. However, the Fed undermined the devaluation by continuing to lower interest rates. At its December 14 meeting, just days before the Smithsonian meeting, the FOMC lowered its funds rate target to 4.375% from 4.75%. By its February 15, 1972, meeting, the funds rate had fallen to 3.25%, well below European rates. In early 1972, instead of the anticipated return flow of dollars to the United States, foreign central banks again found themselves forced to purchase dollars.

In March 1972, the German Bundesbank reduced its discount rate. For a while, the dollar strengthened, but it again came under attack toward the end of June. Germany debated capital controls, with finance minister Schiller opposed and

Bundesbank President Klasen in favor (Hetzel 2002b). Schiller lost and resigned. On July 18, 1972, the Fed used swap lines to guarantee the value of dollars against depreciation. Even with a renewal of capital controls abroad, "strong speculative pressures against the dollar led to massive flows of funds into various European countries and Japan. Between June 28 and July 14, the inflows came to $6 billion" (Solomon 1982, 223).

The foreign exchange markets were quiet in the last half of 1972, but the crises returned in early 1973. In February 1973, dollar inflows to foreign central banks forced a 10% devaluation of the dollar and a float of the yen. In early March, speculation against the dollar resumed. Faced with monetizing huge amounts of dollars, foreign governments let their currencies float. The Bretton Woods system passed into history.

TEN

Policy in the Ford Administration

On August 9, 1974, with the resignation of Richard Nixon, Gerald Ford became president. In the fall congressional elections, voters angered by Watergate elected an overwhelmingly liberal Democratic Congress. Republicans lost 48 seats in the House and 5 in the Senate. With the fall of Vietnam and, especially, Ford's pardon of Nixon, the Ford presidency became highly partisan.

The Republican administration and the Democratic Congress divided over economic policy. Democrats wanted to use government spending to lower the high unemployment created by recession and were tolerant of the then historically high government deficit. The administration, whose chief economist was Alan Greenspan, wanted to limit government spending to lower long-term structural deficits. It wanted to break a perceived link between government deficits, inflation, and boom–bust business cycles.

I. Administration Economic Policy

At its onset, the Ford administration attempted to reach out to Congress by responding to Senate majority leader Mike Mansfield's (D. MN) resolution requesting a conference on inflation. Addressing Congress just three days after being sworn in, Ford said that "inflation is domestic enemy number 1" (Porter 1980, 10). The administration intended to solicit opinions over how to deal with inflation and how to achieve cooperation between labor and management to defuse a perceived wage–price spiral. Ford presided at the September 27–28 conference, which he termed Whip-Inflation-Now (WIN). At the time, no one predicted the worsening of the recession. Real GDP had fallen in all of the first three quarters of 1974, but only moderately, and bipartisan concern existed over inflation.

Ford's October 8 economic package reflected that concern. It proposed spending measures to aid groups affected by the recession: increased unemployment benefits, an investment tax credit to stimulate investment, and measures for housing. However, it also included a 5% income surcharge on high-income individuals to avoid increasing the deficit. Coming one month before congressional elections on November 5, Congress showed no interest in the surcharge. Also, evidence of further economic deterioration had already begun. The November 13, 1974, Greenbook read: "Declines in economic activity had become deeper and more pervasive in recent weeks, and incoming statistics have begun to display the cumulative downward movement characteristic of a typical business recession."

According to then available figures, real GDP fell at an annual rate of 7.5% in 1974Q4 and 9.2% in 1975Q1. What produced this precipitate decline? After price controls ended April 30, 1974, inflation surged. In 1974Q3, CPI inflation was 14.6%. With nominal output growth restrained by moderate money growth (Chapter 8, Section IV and Appendix, "Money Growth and Inflation"), a rise in inflation forced a fall in real output. The unemployment rate climbed from 5.6% in August 1974 to 9% in May 1975. The February 12, 1975, Greenbook read: "Economic activity has weakened substantially further over recent months . . . It is now clear that we are experiencing the most severe recession since before World War II."

Winter 1974–5 marked the most acute period of stagflation to date. Over the period December 1973 to December 1974, CPI inflation was 12.2%, and the Dow Jones Industrial Average (DJIA) average fell from 828 to 596.5. Greenspan, nominated for CEA head three weeks before Nixon resigned, set administration policy of balancing concern with recession against the longer run need to control inflation. Burns worked closely with the administration (Kettl 1986, 136).[1] He attended meetings of its policy group, the Economic Policy Board (EPB), and there is no evidence of disagreement over policy. Burns (Board of Governors FOMC *Minutes* August 20, 1974, 926) told the FOMC that, in his first meeting with Ford, "the President indicated a firm resolve not to seek direct controls over wages or prices." With the administration opposed to controls, the FOMC necessarily emphasized monetary policy to control inflation.

Greenspan, William Simon (treasury secretary), Roy Ash (OMB), and his successor early in 1975 James Lynn (OMB) remained focused on containing future government deficits by slowing growth in federal spending. Ford, who was an expert on government budgets from his years in Congress, supported his advisers with numerous vetoes of congressional spending bills. Because the administration believed that government deficits drove a cycle of recession and rising inflation, it advocated long-term fiscal discipline. During some of the darkest days, the EPB (December 24, 1974) sent Ford a memo expressing these views.[2] It emphasized "the decline in consumer and business confidence in the economic system." While the EPB recognized the need for "temporary stimulus," future deficits had to be restrained so as not to "trigger renewed inflationary pressures" and "hinder the restoration of consumer confidence." The "adverse impact" of "the overwhelming size of the anticipated deficits . . . on capital markets and on the general level of confidence should not be ignored. . . . The importance of controlling the upward thrust of Federal budget outlays cannot be overemphasized."[3]

According to Greenspan, inflation arose because the Fed monetized deficits to avoid stresses in credit markets.[4] The February *1976 Economic Report* (p. 131) explained:

Rapid and sustained inflation requires a continual inflationary increase of the supply of money. The main reason why expansionary fiscal operations are among the factors generating sustained inflation is that when fiscal deficits are large the monetary authorities, in an attempt to offset the interest rate and credit availability effects of large increases in government debt, tend rapidly to increase their security holdings and hence to inject new money.

With the start of recession, the fiscally conservative Ford administration risked losing the initiative to Congress. Donald Riegle (D. MI) wrote Ford shortly after Detroit announced 60,000 temporary layoffs:[5]

There is no contemporary data to guide us in predicting the kind of public pressure that will arise with [un]employment levels above 7 percent.... As the economic agonies of Michigan spread out to the whole of America ... Congress will be compelled to produce a massive legislative response.... [T]he 75 freshman Democrats are a different breed.... They ... are *determined* to shape the legislative performance.... Their overriding goal is to see the new Congress move quickly and decisively – especially in the area of economic recovery.

To avoid exacerbating the long-run deficit, Ford proposed one-time rebates of 1974 taxes as well as restraints on income transfer programs like Social Security. Congressional Democrats, with their labor base, deepened the tax cuts by combining rebates with withholding reductions and increased outlays for public jobs initiatives. Reluctantly, Ford signed the tax cut in March 1975.

II. Burns and Monetary Policy

Burns shared the same desire as the administration to reestablish the confidence of businesspeople by limiting the size of future government deficits. For him, the major problem was the inflationary psychology of the public. Burns (U.S. Cong. October 10, 1974, 189) testified: "Meaningful progress in combating inflation would lead to a resurgence in consumer buying, a reduction in interest rates, a restoration of financial asset values, and a rebuilding of the optimism and confidence that engender greater willingness to save and invest for the future."

Burns, like Greenspan and Simon, reflecting the views of the business community, believed that lax fiscal policy gave rise to inflationary psychology. That psychology drove inflation, and inflation depressed economic activity through uncertainty. In fall 1974, Burns was unwilling to lower the funds rate for fear that an easier monetary policy would exacerbate inflationary psychology. He was especially loath to lower rates while Congress was talking about increasing spending.

Burns believed additional spending would exacerbate inflationary psychology and worsen both the economic slowdown and inflation.

Burns (U.S. Cong. July 30, 1974, 267) testified: "While our present grave problem of inflation stems from many causes, inadequate fiscal discipline is prominent among them." Burns (U.S. Cong. October 10, 1974, 187–8) testified again:

A still more ominous result of inflation [than high interest rates] is the spread of doubts among businessmen and consumers. They do not know what their future expenses will be in dollar terms. . . . In short, the basic premises for the planning that American business firms and households customarily do have been upset, and the driving force of economic expansion has been blunted. It is not surprising, therefore, that the physical performance of the economy has stagnated. . . . The recent stagnation in real output, and the associated deterioration in employment conditions, are regrettable manifestations of the damage to our economy wrought by inflation.

This logic continued to drive Burns to advocate incomes policies as a way of simultaneously lowering inflation and stimulating output. Burns (U.S. Cong. October 10, 1974, 194) told Congress that "[i]nflation must be brought under control, not only through the exercise of monetary and fiscal discipline, but by a crusade in which all citizens participate." However, because the Ford administration opposed controls, they were unavailable. Burns had another reason for pursuing a restrained monetary policy. In 1974, for the first time, the Fed received public criticism (beyond its handful of monetarist critics) for inflation.

In July 1974, the House Banking Committee asked Fed presidents to testify. Staff member Robert Weintraub had interviewed them and most of the governors. According to Weintraub's (U.S. Cong. July 16, 1974, 5) summary, most admitted that over the period 1965 to 1973 the Fed could have restrained inflation through lower money growth, but they defended high money growth and inflation as necessary to lower unemployment. FOMC members did not view themselves as creating inflation to lower unemployment. Instead, cost-push pressures created inflation, and the unemployment rate high enough to contain them was politically unacceptable.[6] Nevertheless, the association of high money growth and inflation drew attention to monetary policy as the source of inflation.

III. Keeping Calm During Recession

Greenspan and Burns blamed the worsening of the recession that began in fall 1974 on inflation rather than restrictive monetary policy. Burns believed that inflation depressed investment by creating uncertainty over future costs business would face, especially labor costs. Greenspan believed that inflation depressed investment by creating uncertainly through increased dispersion of prices. According to Greenspan, inflation raised the "hurdle rate of return" required of investments. He argued that the economic downturn that began in fall 1974 arose out of a collapse in capital expenditures from the uncertainties produced by high inflation (Hargrove and Morley 1984, 441–3).[7]

Both Greenspan and Burns rejected the inflation–unemployment trade-offs of the Phillips curve. Greenspan said, "Unemployment was never seen as a necessary condition for bringing down the rate of inflation.... [S]ince the unemployment rate and inflation rate both went up together, we always argued that it was possible to bring them both down together" (Hargrove and Morley 1984, 445). Both believed that inflation could fall without a rise in unemployment if a rise in business confidence promoted increased capital expenditures. As a result, Greenspan believed that policy should concentrate on long-run expectational stability rather than aggregate-demand management.

Greenspan (Hargrove and Morley 1984, 417–8, 451) said:

A necessary condition for restoring balanced economic growth . . . was to reduce the instabilities, thereby reducing the risk and hurdle rates, and a necessary condition for that was to bring down the rate of inflation. . . . My underlying policy thrust was to defuse instability in the system gradually and in a sense to be anti-activist because it was precisely the activism . . . which was creating the underlying elements of instability and risk in the system.

Many of my Democratic friends argue that an increase in aggregative demand by increasing the level of economic activity will induce businessmen to invest. I say that the evidence of that is extremely faulty because you're asking them to make a twenty-year investment on the basis of five or three months of expansion in the demand for their product, and you're asking them to generate a facility that will not come on stream for a year to a year and a half.

The administration's emphasis on the long run collided with congressional demands for stimulus to end the recession. Greenspan made the call that the recession, despite its severity, would be short lived. He predicted the start of a sustained revival by mid-summer 1975. Investment continued falling in 1975Q1, but consumption (real durables goods purchases and automobile sales) recovered modestly. With the end of inventory liquidation, Greenspan predicted, real output would again begin to grow.[8] In fact, the reduction in excess business inventories ended in April 1975, and the economy began to recover in 1975Q2 with annualized real GDP growth of 3.3%.

Greenspan (Hargrove and Morley 1984, 448), confident of his forecasting ability, commented:

Pressure was coming from everywhere. It was coming obviously from Congress. I used to put on my bullet-proof vest and armor when I'd go up to the Hill to testify. There was tremendous fear in the Congress. . . . [W]hen I looked at the ten-day auto sales figures and the weekly retail sales, housing permits and starts, some of the new order series, and especially this insured unemployment system, I had enough conviction that we were looking at an absolutely incredible inventory phenomenon, as differentiated from a collapse in final demand. Having that conviction and knowing that there is an absolute limit to the rate of inventory liquidation, I was sufficiently confident that I didn't waffle inside the White House.

IV. Why Was Monetary Policy Disinflationary?

During the Ford administration, monetary policy was disinflationary. Four-quarter M1 growth, which peaked in 1973Q1 at 8.1%, fell to 3.6% by 1975Q1. Although by 1976Q3 M1 growth had recovered to 4.8%, that figure was still relatively low. Thereafter, four-quarter M1 growth rose. By the time Burns left as FOMC chairman in 1978Q1, it was up to 7.5%. Monetary policy at times reflected the fiscal policies that Burns wanted to influence. In 1972, his attempt to influence the pay guidelines of the Pay Board made him reluctant to raise interest rates. In fall 1974, while he attempted to persuade the administration to accompany proposed tax reductions with expenditure decreases, he was reluctant to lower rates.

That reluctance clashed with achievement of the FOMC's money targets. After spring 1973, when Burns could no longer rely on controls to restrain inflation, the FOMC had taken its money targets seriously (Chapter 8). Over the six-quarter interval from 1973Q1 through 1974Q2, annualized quarterly M1 growth rates averaged 5.6%, almost equal to the FOMC's target.[9] In 1974Q1, concern that the oil embargo would set off recession caused the FOMC to allow M1 growth to overshoot its target. However, the weakness in economic activity associated with the oil price rise, which was concentrated in the automotive sector, had dissipated by early summer. During 1974Q2, the FOMC brought down the two-quarter M1 growth rate.

Burns, however, was if anything more interested in fiscal than monetary policy. At the May 21, 1974, FOMC meeting, Burns (FOMC *Minutes* July 21, 1974, 669) said, "While the U.S. inflation was attributable to many causes, a large share of the responsibility could be assigned to the loose fiscal policy of recent years." At the July 1974 FOMC meeting, Burns (Board of Governors FOMC *Minutes* July 16, 1974, 828–9) asked the FOMC to raise the lower bound of the funds rate range.[10]

Chairman Burns said his purpose could be simply stated. If the funds rate . . . were to decline . . . the drop would be likely to be interpreted by the market as an easing of Federal Reserve policy. Such an interpretation would be unfortunate. . . . In private conversations with both Administration officials and Congressmen, he had been urging that some steps be taken in the direction of fiscal restraint. . . . [T]hat possibility would be reduced if at this juncture the System were to take actions that were publicly interpreted as easing.

At the August 20, 1974, FOMC meeting, weak M1 growth in July should have produced a fall in the funds rate. However, Burns (Board of Governors FOMC *Minutes* August 20, 1974, 926) told the FOMC:

[A]t President Ford's invitation, he had attended a . . . meeting of legislative leaders. . . . [T]he President's objective was to work toward an expenditure total of under $300 billion for fiscal 1975. That would be a difficult task. . . . [M]easures being considered in the Congress could easily push the total up.

Governor Mitchell (Board of Governors FOMC *Minutes* August 20, 1974, 928) "observed that in light of the Chairman's remarks the Committee might well temporize with its policy posture." President Hayes (Board of Governors FOMC *Minutes* August 20, 1974, 933) said "that he respected the Chairman's reading of the mood of the country and the Congress. . . . Consequently, he believed that this would be the wrong time to ease."

By the September 10, 1974, FOMC meeting, weakness in M1 growth had prompted the Desk to reduce the funds rate. However, Peter Sternlight (Board of Governors FOMC *Minutes* September 10, 1974, 989), Deputy Manager of the Desk, commented that "[o]vert action to produce a significant further easing would have risked a breakout of over-ebullient expectations." Several members urged the FOMC to move the funds rate sufficiently to achieve its money targets. However, Hayes (FOMC *Minutes* September 10, 1974, 1017) countered that "fiscal restraint was not yet by any means assured, and a relaxation of monetary policy in advance of its realization could be taken as an implied reduction in the need for fiscal restraint."

The FOMC continued a pattern of grudging funds rate reductions through the remainder of the year. Concerned that Congress would pass a tax reduction resulting in an overly expansionary fiscal policy, it accepted weakness in money growth. For example, at the October FOMC meeting, Dallas Fed President Coldwell (Board of Governors FOMC *Minutes* October 14–15, 1974, 1133) commented that "until it was clear that Federal expenditures would be held down, he would hold to a policy of restraint." At the December FOMC meeting, Burns made a plea for restraint in reducing the funds rate to achieve money targets.

The importance Burns attached to the budget cuts in the Ford tax package appeared in a question to the board staff at an FOMC meeting. Burns (Board of Governors FOMC *Minutes* December 16–17, 1974, 1261) asked the staff to predict the effects of "a simultaneous decrease of, say, $20 billion in both Federal expenditures and business taxes." The staff responded with the standard balanced budget multiplier result of Keynesian economics "that such a policy was deflationary, on balance, because it would result in a rise in savings." Burns countered that "the effects would be strongly expansionary rather than deflationary; a $20 billion tax cut would create a wholly new environment for business enterprise, and businessmen would react by putting their brains, their resources, and their credit facilities to work." Also, Burns did not want interest rates to fall and then have to raise them when such a policy produced economic recovery.

Burns (Board of Governors FOMC *Minutes* December 16–17, 1974, 1319) told the FOMC:

[A]ny drastic change in that policy course [to ease money market conditions gradually] would be a great mistake. . . . Monetary policy was only one of the policy instruments available. At present the Administration was engaged in a serious and thorough reappraisal of economic policy, and significant steps would be taken to limit the recession and to initiate forces of recovery.

In 1975Q1, annualized quarterly M1 growth fell to only 2.4%. However, Burns believed that the behavior of the velocity of money rather than money itself was more important for monetary policy. Velocity was a reflection of the fundamental determinant of behavior – the confidence of the businessperson. Burns (Board of Governors FOMC *Minutes* December 16, 1974, 1339) told the FOMC:

Fundamentally, velocity depended on confidence in economic prospects. When confidence was weak, a large addition to the money stock might lie idle, but when confidence strengthened, the existing stock of money could finance an enormous expansion in economic activity.

Greenspan wanted the Fed to maintain moderate, steady growth of money. In the darkest hour of the recession, the EPB (March 24, 1975, Alan Greenspan Files, FL) sent Ford a memo expressing a desire for monetary restraint:

The Chairman [Greenspan] expressed hope and confidence that the Federal Reserve would persist in its policy of steady, reasonable growth in reserves to permit expansion of the monetary aggregates. Such a policy path would provide adequate reserves to support a recovery in economic activity . . . while avoiding serious disruption of financial markets or expectations that could rekindle inflation and choke off the economic recovery.

In May and June 1975, money growth rose when taxpayers deposited the $10 billion in tax rebates provided for in the Tax Reduction Act of 1975. Despite the proximity of the March 1975 business cycle trough, the FOMC raised the funds rate from 5.25% in June to 6.375% by September. Burns was willing to give Greenspan the moderate money growth the latter desired as long as Burns got what he wanted, a deceleration of projected growth in government outlays that would limit the size of future deficits.

V. A Close Election

March 1975 marked the business cycle trough. However, in June 1976, weakness appeared and continued through the 1976 presidential election. The November 10, 1976, Greenbook (p. 1) reported that "[e]conomic growth has slowed further . . . from the reduced pace of the previous half-year. Industrial production apparently declined in October, there was little evidence of strength in the demand for labor, and the unemployment rate remained on the high plateau of the prior three months."

In a close election, many issues are pivotal. Although the most controversial issue remained Ford's pardon of Nixon, economic issues also were critical. Fiscal policy remained controversial. In October 1975, Ford proposed a $28 billion tax cut, which extended the 1975 tax reductions. However, he linked those reductions to future expenditure reductions by Congress. Ford promised to veto any tax cut that did not limit fiscal 1977 spending to $395 billion.

Porter (1980, 206) wrote later:

There were attempts, a few successful, to circumvent the EPB. The President's $28 billion tax reduction proposal in October 1975 was the single most dramatic example of this form of end run. . . . During July, August, and September 1975, White House chief of staff Donald Rumsfeld and his deputy Richard Cheney met frequently with CEA Chairman Alan Greenspan, OMB director Jim Lynn, and his deputy Paul O'Neill to discuss possible tax reduction initiatives and budget strategies. . . . One senior official revealed: "The notorious end run was that dollar for dollar tax cut thing by Greenspan and/or Lynn . . . It cost us the election. . . . In effect the end runners . . . had dictated the course of action which imprisoned us. It was a terrible mistake."

Ford's reversal on a common-site picketing bill hurt him with labor. Ford originally backed a bill to legalize common-site picketing, which would allow a union with a complaint against a single contractor to picket and close an entire work site. In 1951, the Supreme Court had ruled such a practice illegal. However, Ronald Reagan ran against Ford in the primaries and used the common-site controversy to rally conservatives. In response, Ford vetoed the bill Congress passed. Although Ford received the nomination, the Reagan challenge split the Republican Party.

Even though the recovery was back on track by the end of 1976, it was too late to help Ford, who lost a close election to Jimmy Carter. The halting recovery of 1976 failed to lower the unemployment rate, which began the year in January at 7.9% and finished the year at 7.8%. The Congressional Quarterly *Almanac* (1976, 357) wrote: "Carter's speeches on unemployment may have sounded like a broken record to some of the American electorate – but not to organized labor. . . . With voter turnout low in most parts of the country, labor's efforts to bring out the union vote in key industrial states clearly helped save Carter from defeat."

Greenspan had argued that pauses commonly occurred during economic recoveries. "Nevertheless, the administration's earlier optimism that the economy would be much improved by the November elections clearly had gone awry. . . . Carter used the [preelection] data to argue his case that the Republican's handling of the economy was having the effect of worsening unemployment and inflation, and that a change was needed in the White House" (Congressional Quarterly *Almanac* 1976, 39). With Jimmy Carter in the White House, there was no longer a Greenspan to insist on moderate money growth.

ELEVEN

Carter, Burns, and Miller

The assumption that monetary policy had a responsibility to manage aggregate demand to maintain low unemployment reached its high point in the Carter administration. The activist consensus also held that inflation was a nonmonetary phenomenon. Until 1980, the administration, constrained by labor union aversion to wage controls, considered moral suasion its primary tool for inflation control. The last experiment in classifying inflation as demand-pull or cost-push and tailoring policy accordingly occurred in 1979 when the FOMC decided to accommodate the price-level rise produced by the December 1978 oil price shock. That accommodation took the form of leaving the funds rate unchanged as inflation rose. In the event, the public's expectation of inflation rose; the real rate of interest fell; and money growth surged. Financial markets began to talk about Latin American style inflation.

I. Humphrey–Hawkins

The activist spirit peaked in the first half of the Carter administration. The deepest economic downturn since the Depression created a demand for economic stimulus to lower unemployment. Almost all members of the FOMC shared a commitment to "low" unemployment. Although Congress and to a lesser extent the administration pressured the Fed for a stimulative policy, stimulative monetary policy derived from the common intellectual environment of the time rather than from political pressures.

The Humphrey–Hawkins full employment bill exemplified the activist character of the times.[1] Representative Augustus F. Hawkins (D. CA) and Senator Hubert H. Humphrey (D. MN) introduced it in 1974. As reported out from the House Education and Labor Committee in 1976, it provided for joint planning by Congress and the administration to achieve a 3% unemployment rate for persons 20 years and older within 4 years. The bill also provided for federally funded jobs programs making the government the employer of last resort.

The original bill required the president in the *Economic Report of the President* to set numerical goals for employment, production, and prices. The president also had to specify the fiscal and monetary policies necessary to achieve these goals. The bill required the Fed to submit to Congress a statement of its goals for the coming year with a justification for any discrepancy between its goals and the administration's. If the president believed that the Fed's policies were inconsistent with administration goals, he had to submit to Congress a remedy to make monetary policy conform.

FOMC chairmen had always opposed basing monetary policy on explicit objectives. Such objectives, they feared, would be set by the political system, and the Fed would lose its independence. As illustrated by the Humphrey–Hawkins legislation, FOMC chairmen had good reason to fear that the political system would set unrealistic objectives for unemployment.[2]

II. Carter and Economic Stimulus

Carter came into office committed to economic stimulus. His economic advisers were Keynesians. Larry Klein of the University of Pennsylvania, creator of large-scale econometric models, was the godfather (Biven 2002). Reducing unemployment was a consistent theme of Carter's presidential campaign. In an interview in *U.S. News & World Report*, Carter said that he would set a goal of 4 to 4.5% for the unemployment rate.[3] In a position paper, he said: "An expansionary policy can reduce unemployment without reigniting inflation, because our economy is presently performing so far under capacity.... There are far more humane and economically sound solutions to curbing inflation than enforced recession, unemployment, monetary restrictions and high interest rates." Carter told the editors of *Fortune* magazine: "I would proceed aggressively, with the first emphasis on jobs. My economic advisers and I agree that until you get the unemployment rate down below five percent, there's no real danger of escalating inflationary pressures." Carter's CEA assumed that government could engineer the kind of strong growth that occurred in the Kennedy and Johnson administrations. Stein (1994, 216) wrote: "The Carter team . . . had come to repeat the Kennedy achievement of 'getting the economy moving again.' . . . Kennedy could exploit the expectation of price stability, which allowed him to get a great deal of output increase and only a little bit of price increase by rising demand. Carter had no such margin."

Carter's advisers believed that in 1977 like 1961 the economy possessed a significant negative output gap. However, they overestimated the magnitude of the gap for two reasons. First, stimulative monetary policy had artificially increased output and productivity growth. Real output had grown above trend in the 1960s because of the combination of expansionary monetary policy and an environment of expected price stability and, in the early 1970s, because of the combination of expansionary monetary policy and price controls. Also, trend output and productivity growth did fall. From 1961 through 1973, productivity growth (output per hour in the nonfarm business sector) was 3.0%. It then fell to 1.2% from 1973 through 1979.

On January 31, 1977, Carter submitted a stimulus package to Congress. He asked for a rebate of $50 on 1976 taxes for each taxpayer and dependent as well as for Social Security recipients. On March 8, the House approved the package. Republicans voted against it because they preferred permanent reductions in tax rates. Democrats disliked the rebate but felt they had to support the President. Just four days before the Senate was to start deliberation on the rebate bill, Carter withdrew it. Although he said that a revived economic recovery had made the rebate unnecessary, he may well have feared its defeat.

Charles Schultze (Hargrove and Morley 1984, 480–1), Carter's CEA chairman, said later of the rebate: "[A]ll the Congress hated it. For some reason it struck them as immoral. We just hand a $50 check to people.... [T]here were a lot of people who really didn't like it but who had taken a political position on it to please Carter. Then the first thing he did was suddenly to reverse course." Burns was the most prominent critic of the rebate. When asked by the House Banking Committee what he thought of the rebate, Burns (U.S. Cong. February 3, 1977, 92–3) replied: "I was hoping and praying that I would not be asked this question.... I was born some years ago.... I have inherited certain attitudes. I still believe that people should not receive any gifts of money from their government. I still believe the people should earn the money they receive." The committee chairman, Henry Reuss, replied that he had "never seen such a rash of head-nodding and partner-nudging as went on during that statement."

III. Arthur Burns and Monetary Policy

In his own way, Burns shared in the Keynesian consensus that policymakers had to manage aggregate demand to ensure full employment and that fiscal policy was essential. Moreover, he shared the prevailing nonmonetary view that because inflation originated in cost-push pressures reducing it through excess unemployment would be socially costly.[4] Incomes policies were therefore indispensable (Burns 1979). However, with his background in the Wesley Clair Mitchell NBER, Burns viewed the psychology of the businessperson rather than the price system as the coordinating mechanism for economic activity (Hetzel 1998). As Burns (Board of Governers *Transcripts* January 17, 1978, 18) told the FOMC, "What happens in the sphere of profits – and what expectations are with regard to profits – is still the main driving force of the economy." Burns also disliked inflation intensely. Greenspan (Board of Governors *Transcripts* January 31, 1995, 57) recounted that "Arthur Burns, with whom I used to visit quite often and whom I had known since graduate school, would speak against inflation like none of us is used to hearing. If one looks at what the Federal Reserve did in this period, that anti-inflation attitude is scarcely to be seen."

The hypothesis used here to explain this seeming contradiction highlighted by Greenspan is the same as that advanced to explain policy in the Nixon administration. Burns wanted to influence the fiscal and incomes policies of the Carter administration as a way of bolstering the confidence of businesspeople and their willingness to invest. He wanted a balanced budget and an incomes policy that would both stimulate output by giving businesspeople the confidence that their future costs would remain under control and that would restrain (cost-push) inflation at a socially acceptable cost. Later, Burns recounted to Kettl (1986, 167) how his interest in influencing Carter's fiscal policies derived from the belief that the combination of slow economic recovery and high inflation originated in businesspeople's fears of inflation, which were driven by fears of excessive government spending.

With the new administration, Burns' influence with the president again became tenuous. He reverted to his Nixon strategy of public criticism tempered by the desire not to alienate the president to the point where he (Burns) would cease being an adviser. Monetary policy again came to have the aspect of a bargaining chip – available if the administration did not pursue what Burns believed were desirable fiscal and incomes policies. These concerns when combined with the desire by FOMC members to promote economic recovery eliminated the possibility of strong action to control inflation.

At the recession's trough, Burns (FOMC *Minutes* March 18, 1975, 338) had made a prophetic comment. "[T]he recovery might appear to be so delicate, fragile and uncertain that it would be hard to face up to a course that would bring about rising interest rates." That reluctance would appear in overshoots of the newly established targets for money forced on the Fed by Congress in early 1976. Congress's intent had been to pressure the FOMC into a more stimulative monetary policy (Woolley 1984). In the event, the targets exercised no influence.[5]

Already by the time of the December 21, 1976, meeting, the FOMC was aware of rapid money growth.[6] At the January 18, 1977, meeting, in a discussion of whether to lower the Fed's long-term money targets, Burns told the FOMC that "any actions by the Fed to reduce the monetary aggregates now would be considered as frustrating the [administration's] fiscal package."[7] Governor Coldwell echoed Burns's sentiment, "Congress will harass us for any reduction in targets at this time, seeing it as frustrating fiscal policy."[8] The other side of the unwillingness to lower high money growth was a reluctance to raise the funds rate. At its March 15, 1977, meeting, Burns noted that an unchanged funds rate "has been most helpful in his dealings with Congress.... Congress considers that we frustrated its will in 1975 by increasing the Fed funds rate at the time of the rebate."

The April 1977 meeting illustrated FOMC concern for administration policy. Prior to the meeting, Art Broida, FOMC secretary, circulated a memo pointing out that since the institution of the congressionally mandated long-run money targets, money growth had come in at the top of the ranges.[9] At the time of the meeting, the FOMC's current long-run target range for M1 was 4.5 to 6.5%. Over the prior 6- and 12-month periods, M1 had grown at an annualized rate of 6%. If the FOMC wanted to restrain inflation, Broida noted it would need to reduce the growth of the aggregates. Broida would not have distributed the memo without Burns's prior approval. Furthermore, Burns had delivered this message in congressional testimony.

At the meeting, Burns's comments began in the spirit of the Broida memo. He pointed out that in the 2 years that the long-run target for M1 had been in effect the FOMC had reduced the midpoint of the target by only 0.75%. At that rate, it would take 10 years to make the money targets consistent with price stability. Furthermore, despite the decline in the midpoint, there had been no decline in actual M1 growth. Burns said that he had been ready to reduce the M1 target range by 0.5%.

However, Burns then told the FOMC that he was unwilling to lower the M1 range or raise the funds rate. He said that he was concerned about the effect that the proposals in Carter's speech on energy the previous evening would have on increasing the uncertainty of businesspeople. Burns said that he was "deeply concerned about [the program's] complexity; Congress will not easily grapple with it or understand it; the increased uncertainty that it will add to business investment decisions is unfortunate."[10]

The program was Carter's National Energy Plan. The first part was to decontrol the price of "new" oil, that is, oil discovered after 1975. Its price would rise to the world price over a period of three years. "Old" oil would remain subject to price ceilings. Starting in January 1978, a "crude oil equalization tax" would raise the price of controlled oil to the world level. The government would distribute its revenues to the public through tax rebates (Biven 2002, 158–60).

The emphasis on conservation and the demand-side without incentives for production reflected Carter's Democratic constituency for which decontrol was anathema. Carter had then made two difficult decisions: the withdrawal of the tax rebate and oil price decontrol. Burns's public opposition had contributed to the former. It is likely he had supported the latter decision also. At the time, economists were especially concerned about the effect of the controlled price of oil on energy consumption, oil imports, the U.S. trade deficit, and dollar depreciation.[11]

The administration opposed any increase in interest rates.[12] If Burns had raised rates after having prevailed on the rebate and the energy bill, he would have strained his relationship with the administration. Governor Partee supported Burns. "Fiscal policy has been tightened by removal of the rebate [proposal]. We should not simultaneously tighten monetary policy." President Volcker (New York) commented, "Ideally, we should be reducing monetary aggregates this meeting, but with the removal of the rebate it would be unseemly to follow that with a further restriction on monetary policy." Moreover, Burns had made progress toward getting an administration incomes policy. In April 1977, Carter announced a program "to convince labor and business to cooperate voluntarily in moderating price and cost increases" (Biven 2002, 130). *Newsweek* described it as including "a laundry list of contributions the government itself could make to keep prices down" (Nelson 2005, 23).

Despite strength in the real economy, the FOMC raised the funds rate only very cautiously. It pushed the funds rate to 5.375% at the May meeting from 4.75 %. It then waited until its August meeting to raise the target to 6%. FOMC reluctance to raise the funds rate accorded with majority views among macroeconomists. The March 9, 1977, Redbook reported:[13]

[Paul] Samuelson ... is concerned that money growth may be insufficient to maintain the pace of the recovery.... It is best that monetary policy be ready to accommodate exogenous price increases.... This is no time to put the economy through another wringer.... [D]on't meet irrational apprehensions by sacrificing real growth.... [M]oney growth may have to exceed stated targets in 1977; otherwise, the risks of jeopardizing real growth in 1978 are considerable.

[Robert] Solow ... would be "appalled" if rising interest rates jeopardized even this modest growth performance. Only if inflation were increasing rapidly at the end of the year, should tighter monetary policy lead to increasing interest rates. It would take another recession to push inflation below the 5 to 6 percent range, and that is more than a depressed economy should pay.

[Otto] Eckstein believes that ... "Monetary policy should let economy move into a period of stimulus...." Until there is evidence that fiscal policy threatens an unmanageable boom, the Federal Reserve should accommodate growth. This may require that the money aggregates exceed upper bounds.

FOMC attitudes reflected the assumption that the existence of excess capacity implied that inflation arose from cost-push pressures or expectational inertia rather than from excess aggregate demand.[14] Similarly, excess capacity allowed a stimulative monetary policy without exacerbating inflation. In 1977, the FOMC focused on economic stimulus while accommodating whatever inflation emerged. The July 1977 FOMC meeting exemplified the unwillingness of the FOMC to raise interest rates for fear of restraining economic recovery. The Board of Governors staff reported 7% real growth in the second quarter and forecast 6% inflation in 1978. The alternative that Burns offered the FOMC was a move in the funds rate from 5.375 to 5.5%. The FOMC resisted, and only three voting members supported an increase.

At the July 1977 FOMC meeting, in discussing the long-term monetary aggregate ranges, Burns noted that since their introduction in March 1975, actual money growth had risen despite a reduction in the ranges. Some members drew attention to the way that base drift in the money targets allowed higher money growth. That is, by rebasing its money targets each quarter, the target rose in line with misses. Burns agreed: "We permit, through our short-run decisions excessive money growth." However, he opposed a reduction in the upper limit of the ranges for money growth.

Burns noted: "I think it is dangerous to reduce the upper end of the M1 range because of the potential pressure on interest rates. Monetary policy cannot do away with changes in minimum wage laws and oil wellhead taxes." He also added: "I see [money growth at] the upper limit as an insurance policy which will help us through a difficult legislative period." Presumably, Burns was referring to the Humphrey–Hawkins bill as well as to proposed legislation that would submit the Fed to GAO audit. On July 12, the House Government Operations Committee had reported out such a bill. Burns (Congressional Quarterly *Almanac* 1977, 151) opposed it, stating that "[e]xemption from GAO audit is one of the main pillars of Federal Reserve independence."

The August 16, 1977, FOMC meeting highlighted the dilemma of controlling money or interest rates. President Roos (St. Louis) asked the staff, "Can't we control M1 rather than just predict M1?" The staff answered that the FOMC could if it were willing to accept increases in interest rates. Burns said that the FOMC should not apologize for its "concern about interest rates" given "that our knowledge of the monetary aggregates and the relation to income and prices is foggy." At the September 1977 meeting, Burns commented: "We worship at the shrine of economic performance, not the monetary aggregates." Presidents Roos and Balles expressed the view that high money growth would lead to inflation. However, Governor Wallich expressed the majority view that FOMC influence worked through the way it controlled excess capacity: "The major policy dilemma at the moment is that high levels of unemployment are not acting as a depressant on the inflation rate. Therefore, we must try something else to lower the inflation rate, such as some form of incomes policy."

At its October 1977 meeting, Burns noted that government policy and low profits were sapping the confidence of business and that "the economy is more important than the monetary aggregates."[15] Although the FOMC raised the funds rate to 6.5%, the Greenbook was predicting 12% annualized nominal GNP growth for 1977Q4, which broke down into 5.2% real growth and 6.8% inflation, and predictions for 1978 were similar (Figure 8.8). Despite funds rate increases starting in May 1978, the real rate remained consistently below 1% until September 1978 (Figure 8.3).

Although the FOMC never explicitly decided on a strategy, one can think of the FOMC as having an intermediate target for nominal output growth high enough to eliminate a negative output gap. The inflation component equaled existing inflation, assumed given by expectational inertia and cost-push factors. Money growth had to be sufficient to limit a rise in monetary velocity large enough to produce a more than normal cyclical interest-rate increase and stifle recovery. In explaining this viewpoint, Governor Partee (Board of Governors *Transcripts* July 18, 1978, 26) concluded the FOMC would have to accept above-target M1 growth: "[T]he honest, rational, intelligent thing to do is to recognize that M1 growth has exceeded the target over a protracted period and that is because there has been a great deal of inflation in the system, which is induced by wage increases and government actions and things like that."

IV. G. William Miller

With G. William Miller, who became chairman of the Board of Governors starting February 1978, the Fed had both a head and governors sympathetic to the goals of the Carter administration. Board members believed that expansionary monetary policy did not cause inflation as long as the unemployment rate exceeded a number like 5.5%. They also believed that a rise in interest rates indicated a policy tightening. Although M1 growth in 1977, 1978, and 1979 exceeded that in any other three-year interval of the postwar period, there was little concern among governors and most Federal Reserve Bank presidents that monetary policy was inflationary.

For these reasons, the FOMC was slow to raise the funds rate relative to the inflation rate as economic recovery progressed. In 1976, CPI inflation was 5.2% (quarterly average annualized). It rose to 6.6% in 1977. In 1978Q1, it was 7.1% and then averaged 9.6% in the last three quarters of 1978. The FOMC pushed the funds rate down to its cyclical low of 4.625% at the end of 1976. The increase through August 1978 to 7.875% was still significantly less than the increase in inflation.

Miller was reluctant to raise the funds rate out of a fear of hurting the economy. The Board of Governors only reluctantly approved the recommendations of the regional bank boards for discount rate increases. From mid-January to early May 1978, it denied requests based on a "preference for a market-following move rather than an anticipatory increase that might signal a more restrictive monetary policy" (Board of Governors, Record of Policy Actions Board, *Annual Report* 1978, 91). Although from mid May to mid October the board approved increases, it kept the discount rate at an unusually low level below the funds rate. In that way, "a higher discount rate was widely anticipated and increases . . . [would] have little or no impact on other interest rates" (Board of Governors, Record of Policy Actions Board, *Annual Report 1978*, 92).[16]

Given its priority of strong real growth, the FOMC raised the funds rate only cautiously. The May 16, 1978, FOMC meeting offered an example. According to the *Record of the Federal Open Market Committee Policy Actions*, the FOMC realized the economy was growing strongly, inflation was rising, and money growth was vigorous. It nevertheless agreed to only a quarter percentage point increase in the funds rate (Board of Governors, *Record of Policy Actions FOMC, Annual Report* 1978, 176, 177):[17] The FOMC decided on "a very cautious approach to any further firming" to avoid "provoking dislocations in financial markets that would contribute eventually to the onset of a downturn."

Miller, along with most FOMC members, accepted the view that inflation originated in private wage setting rather than in money creation. At the March 1978 meeting, President Willis (Minneapolis) asked, "What are the chances for an effective anti-inflation policy from the administration?" Miller replied that "[i]f the administration doesn't act, inflation will be left to the Federal Reserve and that is bad news." Under Miller, the Federal Open Market Committee continued to assume that monetary policy could be stimulative as long as the unemployment rate exceeded its full-employment level, which in 1978 the Board of Governors staff estimated as 5.5%. Governor Partee called a 5.75% unemployment rate unacceptable politically.[18] The unemployment rate did not fall to 5.5% until 1988.

In 1978, the administration continued to urge the FOMC not to raise rates. It advocated incomes policies to deal with inflation (Biven 2002, 140). In April

1978, Carter announced a deceleration strategy under which businesses would voluntarily restrain wage and price increases to less than their average increases in the past two years. Schultze (Hargrove and Morley 1984, 488, 497) said:

"[D]eceleration"... was Barry Bosworth's very clever way of getting around numerical guidelines.... If everybody decelerated... inflation would generally move down.... I presented the report to the assembled Economic Policy Group... and all of a sudden... all the politicians in the room and everybody else got all excited. "Great idea; we've got something new now.... We have a new Carter initiative."... The proposal ran into ... [a] reception, ranging from hostility to indifference."

Schultze wrote Carter that the proposal should "make [G. William] Miller feel monetary restraint was less necessary."[19] Later, in the summer, to convey his concern that monetary policy might tighten to the point of causing a recession, Schultze arranged a meeting between the members of the CEA and the Board of Governors In a January 16, 1978, memo, Schultze wrote Carter: "We see no sign that inflation is heating up again, or is likely to do so over the next two years." Also, in early 1978, the administration proposed a tax cut. Although Carter disliked the end result of the congressional tax cut, especially, the cut in capital gains taxes, in a September 27, 1978 memo, Schultze urged him to sign the tax cut bill "to maintain the upper thrust of the economy."

The U.S. current account deficit became negative in 1977. The Carter economists attributed it to a more vigorous economic recovery in the United States than in other countries. The administration put pressure on Germany and Japan to implement expansionary policies to stimulate their imports. In the last part of 1977, the dollar depreciated sharply against other currencies.[20] It continued to decline through fall 1978 despite large-scale intervention by the United States and other countries. The Fed sterilized U.S. dollar purchases to prevent monetary tightening, but the Bundesbank lowered short-term interest rates and allowed its money stock to expand. Foreign countries saw the dollar devaluation as giving the United States an unfair competitive advantage. Congressional Quarterly *Almanac* (*Almanac* 1978, 218) wrote: "Pressured by other Western nations, and by domestic political realities as well, Carter strengthened his anti-inflation stance on Oct. 24 [1978] by calling for wage and price guidelines." Carter also proposed rebates for workers in companies agreeing to the wage guideline if inflation exceeded 7%.

Markets reacted negatively to Carter's proposal and the dollar plummeted. Mayer (1980, 293) wrote, "By Friday, October 27, [1978,] there was no international exchange market: everybody was offering dollars, and nobody was bidding." In response, the Treasury and the Fed put together a program to strengthen the dollar. Treasury Undersecretary Anthony Solomon organized a massive foreign exchange intervention to buy dollars. On November 1, 1978, Carter announced the creation of a $30 billion fund of foreign currencies available for the purchase of dollars on the foreign exchanges.

On the same day, the Fed raised the discount rate by 1 percentage point and the dollar strengthened. Between the August 15 and November 21, 1978, meetings, the FOMC raised the funds rate 2 percentage points from 7.875% to 9.875%. M1 growth, which had been at 10.7 and 8% in 1978Q1 and 1978Q2, respectively, moderated to 5.5% from 1978Q3 to 1979Q1. However, CPI inflation, which had finished 1978 at about 9.5%, rose to 10.25% in 1979Q1 and averaged 13.5% over the last three quarters of 1979. On December 16, 1978, OPEC announced a 14.5% increase in the price of oil spread over 1979. In the first half of 1979, the FOMC concerned that the oil price rise would precipitate a recession became unwilling to raise the funds rate. By the time of the August 14 FOMC meeting, the funds rate at 10.25 % was only slightly higher than in December. As inflationary expectations rose in 1979, the real rate fell (Figure 8.3), and rapid M1 growth resumed.[21]

At the April 17, 1979, FOMC meeting, dissent began to develop and Governor Wallich and Presidents Coldwell and Volcker dissented. Volcker (Board of Governors *Transcripts* April 17, 1979, 16) commented: "[T]he expected rate of inflation has increased somewhat in the last six months and the nominal rate of interest has not. Therefore, the real rate of interest has declined." Wallich (Board of Governors *Transcripts* April 17, 1979, 17) said: "[W]e've had several months now of status quo and in that several months we've had at least a 3 percentage point increase in the inflation rate."

The Carter CEA continued to believe that excess capacity would restrain inflation. Later, Schultze (Hargrove and Morley 1984, 482) noted that Greenspan (President Ford's CEA head) in his last *Economic Report of the President* redefined potential output as output consistent with an unemployment rate of 5% instead of 4%. Schultze said: "We reluctantly came around to accept that." However, even 5% turned out to be unrealistically low. Schultze (Hargrove and Morley 1984, 483) later stated that "excessive demand stimulus" only contributed "perhaps one-half percent" in the movement from a "core 6 percent to a core 10 percent [inflation] rate" in the Carter presidency.

Schultze (Hargrove and Morley 1984, 479, 475) blamed inflation on shocks to food and energy prices and argued later that the administration should have adopted a tougher incomes policy: "[I]t would have been worth taking a bigger risk . . . and being willing to be 'presidentially unfair.' I mean by this . . . we never did have a nice dramatic steel confrontation. . . . You, or a given union, are going to be presidentially excoriated. . . . Guidelines are a Democratic president's problem. . . . [H]e's always scared to take on organized labor." However, by early 1979, Schultze believed that the rate of growth of output was reducing excess capacity at an undesirably fast rate. He and Treasury Secretary Blumenthal leaked stories that administration officials desired tightening. As Schultze (Hargrove and Morley 1984, 485) related, Carter ended the leaks: "[W]e got a very nasty note from the President . . . saying, lay off. Democratic presidents, even fiscal conservatives, are also populist on interest rates."

Because of the rise in oil prices in 1979, the FOMC became unwilling to raise the funds rate.[22] Between February and July 1979, M1 grew at an annualized rate of 9.7%, but the FOMC raised the funds rate over this interval by only half a percentage point. As reported in the *Record* (Board of Governors *Record of Policy Actions FOMC Annual Report 1979*, 166), "[I]n view of many indications of weakening in economic activity . . . Chairman Miller recommended that the Manager be instructed to continue to aim for a federal funds rate of about 10 1/4 percent." Leonard Silk of the *New York Times* reported (Biven 2002, 144): "[I]n mid-April 1979, Miller told me an economic slowdown was in progress and he had no intention of tightening monetary policy further. He said he didn't think the inflation, which had gone back up to double-digit rates in the first quarter, reflected excessive demand for goods." However, the relentless rise in inflation throughout 1979 (Figure 5.1) exacerbated inflationary expectations and reduced the real rate, which fell from 3% in January 1979 to close to 1% by June (Figure 8.3). Volcker (December 1979, 958) recounted: "Virtually all economists were either predicting a recession or felt a recession had already started. As the summer ended, however, signs began to emerge of a surprising degree of strength in spending. . . . [I]t seemed to reflect . . . a "buy now" attitude spurred by an intensification of inflationary expectations."

V. Changing Consensus on Inflation

Until Volcker brought inflation down and kept it down at a socially acceptable rate of unemployment, the consensus within the economics profession was that nonmonetary forces drove inflation. James Tobin (September 6, 1974) expressed the prevailing view in a *New York Times* essay entitled "There are Three Types of Inflation: We Have Two." He began with the statement "Three decades of experience tell us that inflation is endemic to modern democratic industrial societies." He went on to "distinguish three types of inflation: (a) "excess demand inflation," (b) "the wage–price–wage spiral," and (c) "shortages and price increases in important commodities." Tobin argued that inflation was a mix of the last two types.

According to the prevalent nonmonetary view of inflation, even if inflation were of the excess-demand type, it was not necessarily due to monetary policy. Any stimulant to spending that caused aggregate demand to strain the capacity of the economy to produce could generate inflation. In his essay, the only inflation Tobin attributed to excess demand occurred "in 1966, when President Johnson and Secretary of Defense Robert McNamara piled war demands onto an economy already operating close to capacity and ignored economists' pleas to raise taxes." Franco Modigliani (1975, 179) wrote:

I hope that no one is rediscovering that inflation is money determined. . . . The first appearance of inflationary developments is typically the result of an excess demand relative to capacity, and this may be due either to overexpansive monetary or fiscal policy. . . . If the excess demand is maintained, then the inflation will continue, possibly at an accelerating rate, but it is correct to say that it is money determined only if it is maintained through an overexpansionary monetary policy.

In a passage reminiscent of Burns (1979), *The Anguish of Central Banking*, Tobin (1974, 232) wrote:

[T]he tormenting difficulty is that the economy shows an inflationary bias even where there is significant involuntary unemployment. The bias is in some sense a structural defect of the economy and society, perhaps a failure to find and to respect orderly political and social mechanisms for reconciling inconsistent claims to real income. Chronic and accelerating inflation is then a symptom of a deeper social disorder, of which involuntary unemployment is an alternative symptom. Political economists may differ about whether it is better to face the social conflicts squarely or to let inflation obscure them and muddle through. I can understand why anyone who prefers the first alternative would be working for structural reform, for a new social contract. I cannot understand why he would believe the job can be done by monetary policy. Within limits, the Federal Reserve can shift from one symptom to the other. But it cannot cure the disease.

Economists at the Universities of Chicago and Minnesota continued with the monetary theory of inflation but supplemented it with the assumption that the public uses information efficiently (rational expectations). Taken together, these ideas imply that monetary policy shapes the public's expectations of inflation. The popular idea of a wage–price spiral then appeared empty without some assumption about monetary policy. Also, the attribution of stagflation to a rise in the monopoly power of unions appeared unsatisfactory. In the absence of an accommodating monetary policy, monopoly power would alter relative prices, not the price level. Stagflation appeared as the consequence of a lack of credibility on the part of the Fed to pursue a sustained noninflationary monetary policy. Stagflation derived not from a change in the rules of economics, as Burns had argued in 1971 (Chapter 8), but from how the experiment with activist aggregate-demand management changed the way that the public formed its expectations of inflation.

The combination of sustained high unemployment in the Depression followed by low unemployment in World War II had created an intellectual environment receptive to Keynesian ideas. After the 1964 Kennedy tax cut, the United States created another back-to-back experiment that tested these ideas. However, the activist experiment envisioned by Samuelson and Solow of aggregate-demand management to control unemployment combined with incomes policies to control inflation ended in failure. Two decades of experiments with incomes policies ranging from moral suasion to outright wage–price controls produced one inescapable conclusion: Only the central bank can control inflation. When central banks turned disinflation into durable low inflation and unemployment remained low and stable, the intellectual and political environment changed again. Governments turned the control of inflation over to their central banks and endowed them with instrument independence: freedom to move interest rates to whatever extent required to maintain trend inflation unchanged at a low level.

APPENDIX: DID THE FOMC TARGET MONEY IN THE 1970s?

The Fed's 1970s operating procedures made money one determinant of the funds rate.[23] Rapid money growth would raise the funds rate, and conversely. However, the FOMC routinely concluded that achievement of moderate money growth would require unacceptably large increases in interest rates. Not until 1979 did the FOMC have substantive money targets. Before then, base drift, where target misses were incorporated into the subsequent base, vitiated money targets. The FOMC lacked any procedure for deriving short-run money targets from substantive long-run targets. Finally, it imposed constraints on the magnitude of changes in the funds rate that prevented achievement of moderate money growth.

In March 1975, Congress passed House Concurrent Resolution 133, which expressed congressional intent that the Fed report its objectives for growth of money over four-quarter periods to the Congress. As a result, the FOMC changed the targeting interval for the monetary aggregates from two to four quarters. To lessen the possible impact of money targets on its ability to manage the funds rate, the FOMC also began to specify money targets as a range rather than as a single value. The FOMC left in place the base drift that arose when it missed its money targets. M1 growth exceeded its target range from 1977Q3 through 1978Q4.

Since October 1972, the FOMC at each meeting had specified tolerance ranges for the two-month growth rate of M1. The Desk moved the funds rate peg in response to deviations of forecasted money growth from the tolerance ranges. A "money-market" directive called for a change in the funds rate between FOMC meetings if predicted two-month M1 growth deviated significantly from the tolerance range. A "monetary-aggregates" directive called for a change in response to a smaller deviation. In practice, these contingent changes in the funds were somewhat more important than the changes made at FOMC meetings. At the June 20, 1978, meeting, the FOMC emphasized that the tolerance ranges set for money were not targets. "It was noted that, perhaps because of the manner in which the directive was worded, the two-month ranges of tolerance for M1 and M2 were subject to misinterpretation as embodying the Committee's short-run targets for these aggregates, intended to be achieved by appropriate changes in the funds rate" (Board of Governors, *Record of Policy Actions FOMC, Annual Report 1978,* 189). How did the FOMC choose the tolerance ranges?

At its meetings, the FOMC possessed a Board staff estimate of the two-month growth rate of money consistent with no change in the funds rate. If the FOMC considered money growth undesirably high, it set a tolerance range with a midpoint usually 1 percentage point below the midpoint of the staff benchmark estimate, and conversely. In that way, there was a better than even chance that predicted money growth in the intermeeting period would produce a change in the funds rate in the direction necessary to offset the undesirably high or low money growth. By making the timing of changes in the funds rate coincide with high or low money growth, these procedures built in a rationale for funds rate changes useful in dealing with populist attacks.

Although these procedures produced changes in the funds rate in the right direction for offsetting undesirably high or low money growth, the magnitude of the changes allowed was inadequate to achieve the money targets. Over the course of the 1970s, the FOMC narrowed significantly the range of allowable fluctuation set each meeting for the funds rate. The FOMC also never set a tolerance range with a negative lower bound as it would have had to do if it had wanted to offset base drift. Furthermore, the FOMC imposed the constraint that funds rate changes be unidirectional over phases of the business cycle. The FOMC did so because it considered the funds rate, not money growth, as revealing the stance of policy. For example, Burns (August 1974, 557) said: "If the Federal Reserve tried to maintain rigid monetary growth rate . . . interest rates could fluctuate widely, and to no good end. The costs of financial intermediation would be increased, and the course of monetary policy might be misinterpreted."

At the February 15, 1977, meeting, in response to a suggestion that the FOMC include its short-run and long-run monetary ranges in the directive, Governor Wallich recommended using the word "targets" before the long-run ranges. He argued that especially in an inflationary environment monetary aggregates were a better guide to policy than interest rates. Partee responded that he disliked the word "targets" "because we are primarily interested in the real economy and not in the monetary aggregates." Although the FOMC agreed to put the monetary target ranges in the directive, only President Balles (San Francisco) agreed with Wallich that the word "target" should describe the long-run ranges.

The Full Employment and Balanced Growth Act of 1978 (the Humphrey–Hawkins Act) required the Fed to report objectives for growth of the monetary aggregates in *The Monetary Policy Report* submitted semiannually to Congress. The *Report* was supposed to relate those objectives to the short-term macroeconomic goals of the administration published in the most recent *Economic Report of the President*. At the initial and midyear FOMC meetings, individual members of the FOMC submitted forecasts of the economic variables that the law required the administration to specify as goals in the *Economic Report*. In the semiannual oversight, the FOMC chairman furnished the range of these predictions for nominal and real output, inflation, and the unemployment rate. By reporting a range, the numbers inevitably encompassed the administration's goals. Also, the use of predictions avoided the implication that the FOMC sets macroeconomic goals. Thus, the Fed avoided the accusation that it set macroeconomic goals incompatible with those of the administration.

These predictions lacked content. They were contingent predictions based on what the individual members assumed about how they and other members of the FOMC would conduct monetary policy in the coming year. However, they did not make explicit any assumptions about this behavior. From the beginning, events rendered Humphrey–Hawkins useless as a way of conveying information to the public about policy. Immediately after its passage, the Carter administration began to place priority on reducing inflation rather than unemployment. In 1980, to avoid providing an explicit goal for unemployment, which would have appeared unacceptably high, it substituted a prediction for the required goal.

TWELVE

The Political Economy of Inflation

Macroeconomic miscalculations by policymakers cannot alone account for the decade and a half of high inflation following 1965. The desire of the political system to use inflation as a tax was a major factor. Friedman (1975, 149) explained: "From time immemorial, the major source of inflation has been the sovereign's attempt to acquire resources. . . . Inflation has been irresistibly attractive to sovereigns because it is a hidden tax that at first appears painless or even pleasant, and above all because it is a tax that can be imposed without specific legislation. It is truly taxation without representation."

The political environment within which the Fed operated changed radically after the November 3, 1964, election. The election provided the mandate and the congressional votes to undertake a broad expansion of income redistribution programs. In the election, Democrats had campaigned for a national medical care program (Medicare) and a strong Social Security program. Republicans had campaigned for Social Security coverage limited to the needy elderly and financed out of general revenues. The elections gave the Democrats a 295–140 majority in the House and a net increase of 42 northern Democrats. The conservative coalition of Republicans and Southern Democrats that had blocked social legislation crumbled. In 1965, the Vietnam War defense buildup began. The political system demanded a rapidly growing economy that would generate continuous increases in revenue. For the Fed, that concern translated into pressure for "low" interest rates.

Although the cost of low interest rates was inflation, in the new political environment, the cost was offset by the benefits of inflation. Inflation generated revenue through its interaction with a non indexed tax code. The difficulty in deciding how to finance the income transfer programs that expanded after the mid 1960s made an inflation tax attractive.

I. Political Pressure for Low Interest Rates

Since 1933, Reg Q had imposed ceilings on the rates banks could offer on time and savings deposits. The ceilings had been irrelevant until 1958 when a rise in interest rates produced the shift in funds from banks to the money market known later as disintermediation. Thereafter, until 1966, the Board of Governors raised Reg Q ceilings regularly in order to keep them above market rates. In the first half of 1966, the combination of restrictive monetary policy actions that raised market rates and strong loan demand by corporations that caused banks to raise CD rates produced a sharp fall in the rate of growth of time and savings deposits at S&Ls. Housing starts fell from 1.47 million in 1965 to 1.17 million in 1966. Congress considered a variety of bills to prevent commercial banks from competing for S&L deposits, for example, bans on bank issuance of negotiable CDs or time deposits less than $15,000 and statutory maximums for rates on bank time and savings deposits (Congressional Quarterly Almanac 1965–8, 259–60).

In September 1966, Congress passed legislation that allowed the Board of Governors to impose lower Reg Q ceilings on small (consumer) bank time deposits than on large (business) time deposits. The legislation also extended Reg Q to S&Ls. The Fed, the FDIC, and the Federal Home Loan Bank Board then imposed Reg Q ceilings on savings and small time deposits that were lower at commercial banks than at S&Ls. This use of Reg Q to allocate credit from commercial banks to S&Ls, in combination with an easy stance of monetary policy in 1967, produced a strong revival of deposit flows to S&Ls.

Allan Sproul (1980, 39), formerly president of the New York Fed, commented:

The administration of general monetary policy has been partially diverted from broad pervasive measures, which interfere as little as possible with the decisions of reasonably competitive markets, toward attempts to channel credit into the housing industry. By using the power to fix ceiling rates on the interest which banks can pay on savings and time deposits . . . the authorities have sought to promote the competitive position of those nonbanking institutions which have been large investors in home mortgages.

At the time, the Fed believed that different Reg Q ceilings, by assuring a flow of credit to S&Ls, would allow it to raise market rates in order to restrain inflation (Robertson 1966). Ironically, once in place, Reg Q itself provided a major source of pressure for inflationary policy. First, Reg Q ceilings, once extended to S&Ls, proved almost impossible to raise because of the adverse impact on S&L earnings. Regulators set the ceiling rate on commercial bank savings deposits at 4% in 1966, 4.2% in 1970, 5% in 1973, and 5.3% in 1979. In contrast to this 1.3 percentage point rise from 1966 to 1979, the three-month treasury bill rate rose almost 5 percentage points, from about 5 to 10%. When market rates rose above Reg Q ceilings, funds flowed out of S&Ls and politicians pressured the Fed not to increase interest rates.

Second, Reg Q made inflation into an instrument for transferring income from savers to homeowners and the construction industry. The rise in trend inflation from 1965 through 1980 turned Reg Q ceiling rates into negative real rates for small savers. They lacked alternatives because investment in money market instruments had to be made in large denominations. For example, commercial paper was only available in multiples of $100,000. Beginning with the rise in market rates in 1969, small savers began to buy treasury bills, as evidenced by a rise in noncompetitive tender offers submitted at weekly auctions.

In order to prevent savers from holding treasury bills instead of S&L deposits, in February 1970, the treasury raised the minimum denomination for issuance of treasury bills from $1,000 to $10,000. It also kept the rate paid on Series E savings bonds below the rate of inflation in the 1970s. The rate on these bonds was raised from 4.25 to 5% in December 1969. After a rise to 6% in December 1973, it remained unchanged through 1979. Only in one year after 1972 (1976) did inflation fall as low as 6%.

The high level of market rates produced disintermediation from S&Ls in 1969 and 1970, 1973 and 1974, and again in 1978. To offset the outflow of funds, the Federal National Mortgage Association (FNMA) and the Federal Home Loan Bank (FHLB) borrowed from the public and relent the funds to S&Ls. Because the government charters the FNMA and the FHLB, financial markets view their debt as implicitly guaranteed by the government; therefore, they can borrow at rates only slightly higher than on treasury issues.

Pressure from the political system for low interest rates increased dramatically after the imposition in 1971 of wage and price controls. The popular perception was that the controls would require sacrifices of the common person. Such sacrifices would have been unacceptable politically if they had been accompanied by interest rate increases. Many considered such increases as evidence that large banks were not sharing the burden of reducing inflation. This perception provided powerful leverage for political constituencies desiring low interest rates. As an alternative to the direct control of interest rates, the Committee on Interest and Dividends, formed in October 1971 with Arthur Burns as its head, exercised informal pressure to restrain increases in dividends and interest rates.

In 1972, the FOMC wanted to prevent a rise in short-term rates that would push long-term rates above the level prevailing at the time of the imposition of controls (Woolley 1984, 173). Burns (FOMC *Minutes* April 18, 1972, 417; August 15, 1972, 826–7) told the FOMC:

The key question was whether increases in short-term rates would spread to the long-term market – particularly to rates on mortgages.... If that tendency continued, the Committee on Interest and Dividends would undoubtedly come under mounting pressure to stabilize such rates at existing levels.

Given the framework of the Government's incomes policy . . . there was widespread opposition to higher interest rates. Thus far the record on interest rates had been extraordinarily good, and while the System could claim only a small part of the credit for that record, it had made its contribution. Nevertheless, voices had been raised to advocate ceilings on interest rates.... In the circumstances, the Federal Reserve should not be eager to raise interest rates.

Market rates rose in early 1973, and banks raised the prime rate in February. Against a background of congressional threats to impose explicit controls on interest rates, Burns criticized the rise in the prime, and banks halved the size of the original rises. The prime rate remained about 1.5 percentage points below the rate banks were paying on large CDs. As a consequence, bank credit expanded strongly. In response, in April 1973, the CID decreed the "dual prime." For corporations, there would be one prime that would increase with market rates. According to the CID press release (April 16, 1973), there would be a lower prime, with increases "decidedly smaller" and "less frequent," at which banks would "meet legitimate credit needs of home buyers, consumers, small businesses, and farmers" (cited in Kane 1974).

The ability to impose low real rates on savers through the combination of interest rate ceilings and inflation eroded after 1978. Money market mutual funds, which allowed individuals to hold money market instruments in small denominations, emerged in 1974, but marked time when rates declined after 1974. They began to grow rapidly in 1978, however, with the rise in market rates. Earlier in the 1970s in New England, state regulators had allowed savings banks to offer NOW accounts. Although NOWs were legally savings accounts from which payments could be made by check, they were in fact demand deposits labeled as savings deposits in order to avoid the prohibition of payment of interest on demand deposits. Commercial banks, which could not offer NOWs, were at a competitive disadvantage in attracting consumer deposits. In 1976, they persuaded Congress to allow all financial institutions in four New England states to offer NOWs. In November 1978, regulators allowed financial institutions in New York to offer NOWs.

In 1976, credit unions had begun to offer withdrawal of funds from share accounts by check (a share draft). With the rise in market rates in 1978, the number of credit unions and their membership grew rapidly. A U.S. district court ruled share drafts illegal, but gave Congress until January 1980 to enact legislation legalizing them. Credit unions in 1979 mounted a significant letter-writing campaign to Congress seeking legalization of share drafts and interest-bearing checkable deposits in general.

Early in 1978, the rise in market rates began to revive disintermediation from thrifts. In June, banks and thrifts were allowed to issue money market certificates (MMCs) of six-month maturity in minimum denominations of $10,000. The certificates could pay a rate of interest equal to the discount rate on six-month treasury bills. The regulatory authorities intended them as a temporary expedient, which would be eliminated when the rise in market rates subsided. The MMCs, however, were surprisingly popular. By June 1979, $158 billion were outstanding.

The spread of MMCs not only caused a political lobby to form to maintain them as a permanent instrument but also caused resentment that they were not available in small denominations. The organization of consumer groups concerned about the interest rates paid to individual savers caused a change in the attitude of politicians (Axilrod 1988, 59). As William Gibson, chief economist for RepublicBank in Dallas, noted, "It used to be that if a politician wanted to go to Washington, he could campaign on lower interest rates. It isn't that simple anymore" (McGinley 1985).

In 1979, the implicit tax imposed by Reg Q on individual savers rose when inflation rose to 9.5%. The ceiling on savings deposits, which was 5% in the first half of 1979, was raised to only 5.3% in July 1979. The imbalance of forces in favor of low interest rates ended in 1979 when lobbies for the elderly weighed in against Reg Q. Senator Proxmire (U.S. Cong. June 27, 1979, 2) noted: "Secretary Blumenthal cited one estimate that between 1968 and 1979 . . . savers over the age of 65 lost $19 billion in interest because of Regulation Q. That is almost a $2 billion per year tax on older citizens. Should the older citizens be taxed to subsidize borrowers, even if they are home buyers?"Groups such as the American Association of Retired Persons and the Gray Panthers organized lobbying campaigns against Reg Q. The latter issued buttons and bumper stickers that read: "Saving may be dangerous to your wealth." In response, Congress passed the Depository Institutions Deregulation Act (DIDA) in March 1980, which provided for the phase-out of Reg Q over a six-year period.

After 1980, subsidies to S&Ls changed form. Deposit insurance lowers the cost of funds to financial institutions by reducing the risk premium required by investors. With DIDA, Congress increased the limit for an insured deposit from $40,000 to $100,000. Because deposits of $100,000 or more escaped Reg Q ceilings, so-called hot money could then flow in huge amounts to individual S&Ls regardless of their solvency. At the same time, the act allowed thrifts new portfolio powers. In 1982 in the Garn-St. Germain Depository Institutions Act, Congress allowed S&Ls to make commercial loans and nonresidential real estate loans. Expanded deposit insurance and portfolio powers increased the value of thrift charters. Although these changes exacerbated the problem of S&L insolvency, they facilitated legislation to end Reg Q.

II. Inflation as a Tax

Inflation allowed Congress to run a shadow fiscal system that circumvented the constitutional requirements for explicit approval of taxes. Inflation interacted with a tax code not indexed for inflation to generate large increases in government revenue. By pushing taxpayers into higher tax brackets, inflation increased the progressivity of the tax system. By the end of the 1970s, the public had come to understand that Washington rather than labor unions and corporations caused inflation. A tax revolt produced a change in the political environment that elected Ronald Reagan, forced indexing of the tax code, and enabled Volcker to disinflate. Burns (U.S. Cong. July 30, 1974, 279) commented on inflation as an engine for increasing tax revenue: "Inflation, in combination with the progressive income tax, causes an upward drift in income tax rates that increases the share of income going to government. It has been estimated that for every one percent increase in taxable individual income, Federal income tax revenues increase by approximately 1.3 percent."

How much did inflation increase government revenue? The Appendix ("Revenue from the Inflation Tax") answers that question for 1974 (Hetzel 1990a). It reviews quantitative estimates of the increase in federal revenue in 1974 due to the inflation that year of 11%. If the tax code had been indexed for inflation, federal revenue would have been less by $33.9 billion. In 1974, federal government revenue, exclusive of Social Security taxes, was $198 billion. In 1974, therefore, 17% of revenue derived from inflation. Congress reduced tax rates on an ad hoc basis to keep the overall tax burden relative to GNP fairly steady. These reductions, however, occurred only sporadically. The ongoing increase in real revenue produced by inflation combined with occasional reductions in tax rates raised the average tax rate.

Federal revenues and expenditures were roughly in balance from 1951 through 1966 at about 18% of GNP (Figures 12.1 and 12.2). Expenditures then began to rise irregularly and reached 23% of GNP in 1987. In contrast, revenues as a percentage of GNP exhibited little trend over the period from 1951 to 1987. Until the Reagan administration, the political system dealt with the fiscal tension caused by the trend increase in expenditures relative to revenue by recourse to inflation to raise revenue.

Figures 12.3, 12.4, and 12.5 show the sources of growth in federal government expenditure. Figures 12.3 and 12.4 divide federal government expenditure into three classes: domestic social programs, defense, and all other. From 1951 through 1987, the source of growth in expenditure was domestic social programs, which rose, relative to GNP, by 8 percentage points. Figure 12.5 shows that growth of federal government transfer payments to individuals drove this growth. These transfer payments, relative to GNP, also rose by 7 percentage points over the period from 1951 through 1987.

The driving force behind the expansion of transfer payments was a desire to redistribute income. For this reason, it was difficult to establish a consensus over the acceptable level of taxation for effecting such transfers. The use of inflation as a source of revenue arose as a temporizing measure taken by the political system while searching for this consensus. This view of the origin of inflation is supported by the behavior of federal government expenditures and revenue (Figure 12.1). Relative to GNP, revenues showed little trend since the early 1950s. In contrast, expenditures began to trend upward in the mid 1960s, at the same time that inflation began to rise. As shown in Figure 12.6, relative to GDP, expenditures out of general revenue on domestic social programs grew rapidly beginning in 1967. Apart from the short-lived 10% surtax on income taxes enacted in 1968 and the windfall profits tax on oil enacted in 1980, however, there was no significant legislation raising tax rates.

The growth of transfer payments increased in 1967 with the implementation of the Great Society programs. An opening of the political system to a greater diversity of the electorate preceded these programs. In 1962, the Supreme Court passed down its one-man one-vote decision requiring that voting districts contain approximately the same number of voters. In 1964, the 24th Amendment abolished the poll tax, and in 1965 Congress passed the Voting Rights Act. Subsequently, states simplified complicated voting registration requirements that had disenfranchised

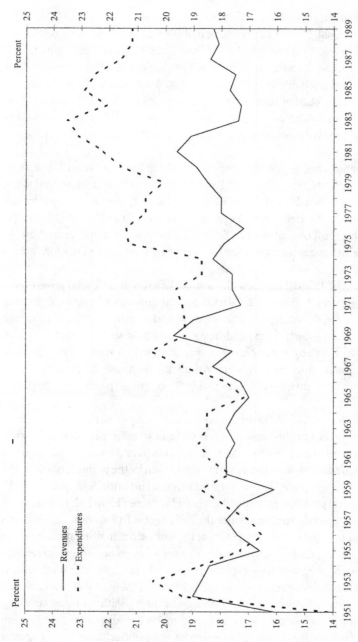

Figure 12.1. Federal Revenues and Expenditures (percentage of GDP). *Notes*: Revenues and expenditures are total of on- and off-budget items. In Figures 12.1 through 12.7, years are fiscal years, which are designated by the year in which they end. Prior to fiscal year 1977, the fiscal year runs from Q3 through Q2. Subsequently, it runs from Q4 through Q3. In Figures 12.1 through 12.7, data are from OMB Historical Tables, Budget of the U.S. Government.

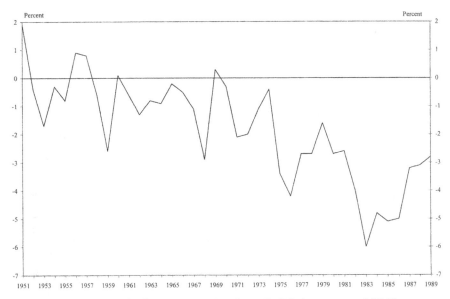

Figure 12.2. Federal Government Surplus or Deficit (percentage of GDP).

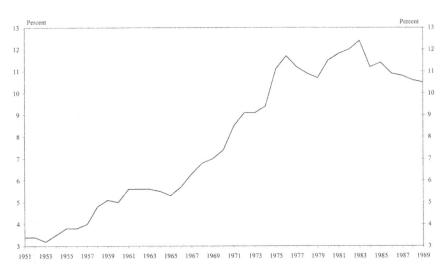

Figure 12.3. Federal Expenditure on Domestic Social Programs (percentage of GDP). *Notes:* The series is the category Human Resources in the Table "Outlays by Superfunction and Function" in OMB Historical Tables. It comprises the subcategories of education, training, employment, and social services; health; Medicare; income security; Social Security; and veterans benefits and services.

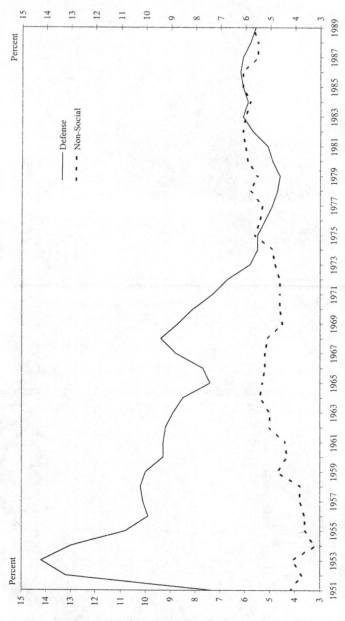

Figure 12.4. Federal Expenditures on Defense and Expenditures Other Than on Domestic Social Programs (percentage of GDP). *Notes:* Expenditures other than on domestic social programs comprise expenditures on physical resources (energy, natural resources, commerce and housing credit, transportation, community and regional development); other functions (international affairs, general science, agriculture, justice, general government); and net interest.

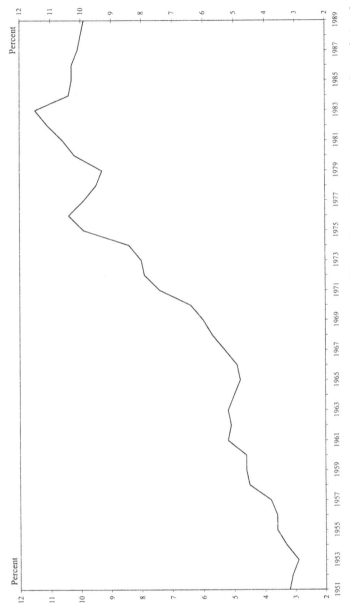

Figure 12.5. Federal Transfer Payments to Individuals (percentage of GDP). *Notes*: Federal government expenditures designed to transfer income and for which no current service is rendered. Data are from the table "Summary Comparison of Outlays for Payments for Individuals" in OMB Historical Tables. The components comprise primarily health, Medicare, income security, Social Security, and veterans benefits.

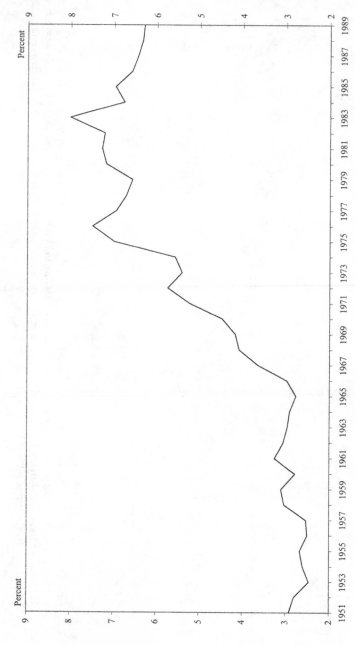

Figure 12.6. Federal Expenditures Out of General Revenue on Domestic Social Programs (% of GDP). *Notes:* The series comprises the following subcategories of Human Resources: education, training, employment, and social services; health; veterans benefits and services; income security (federal employee retirement and disability, unemployment compensation, housing assistance, food/nutrition assistance, and family support payments to states); and transfers from general revenue to social security.

many poor and minority voters. The incentive to use income transfer programs for redistributive purposes was reinforced by a change in the demographic composition of the population that increased the political influence of older voters.

Initially, the political costs of deferring consensus over how to pay for increased government expenditures favored an inflation tax over deficit spending. It is clear to the public that a deficit merely purchases a deferment of taxation. The cumulative experience with inflation in the 1960s and 1970s, however, changed the political calculus of relative costs. Experience with inflation eventually made clear that inflation is made in Washington. By 1980, the political system could no longer blame inflation on private forces like increases in commodity prices or wage-push pressures.

III. The Interplay between Inflation and Fiscal Pressure

The year 1967 marks a break with the monetary policy that followed the Korean War. Inflation in 1966 had attained a level of about 3%, the same as in 1957. In 1966, as in 1957, in response to the behavior of inflation, monetary policy became restrictive, and inflation began to abate in 1967. Based on earlier behavior, monetary policy should have remained restrictive until inflation fell. Instead, monetary policy became expansionary in 1967, and inflation began an irregular upward climb that lasted until 1980. What changed to make inflation acceptable to the political system?

In 1965, both federal government expenditure and revenue were 17.5% of GNP. The combination of increased spending on Social Security and Medicare, defense, and domestic social programs financed out of general revenue caused federal government expenditure as a percentage of GNP to rise to 21% in 1968. Inflation provided the revenue to finance this rise in expenditure. Personal income taxes as a percent of personal income had fluctuated around 10% after the Korean War (Figure 12.7). The Revenue Act of 1964 reduced this figure to 9% in 1964.

Because the progressive tax rates of the personal income tax applied to income in dollar terms, inflation pushed taxpayers into higher tax brackets and increased the proportion of income paid in taxes. By 1969, personal tax receipts as a percentage of personal income had reached 10.75%. (To isolate revenue due to inflation, this figure excludes revenue raised by the 1968 income tax surcharge.) The rise in revenue produced by inflation plus the income tax surcharge brought the federal budget into balance in 1969.

In the early 1970s, fiscal pressures eased. Expenditure on domestic social programs continued to rise, going from 7% of GNP in 1968 to 9% in 1973. Defense expenditures as a percentage of GNP, however, declined from 10 to 6%. Total federal government expenditures as a percentage of GNP fell about 2 percentage points over this period. The Tax Reform Act of 1969 offset the increase in personal income taxes caused by inflation, and personal income taxes as a percentage of personal income fell from their peak in 1969.

The underlying imbalance between steady revenues and growing expenditures reemerged in the last half of the 1970s. From 1965 to 1974, federal government

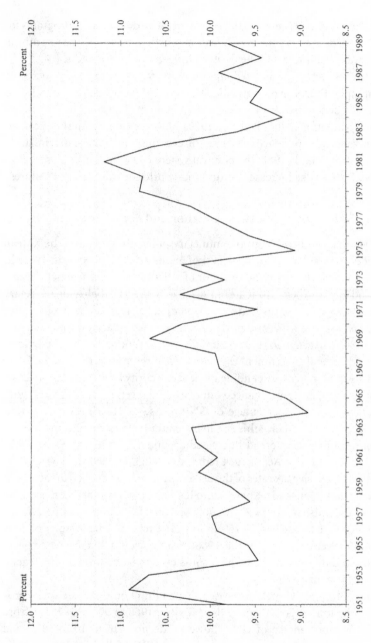

Figure 12.7. Personal Income Taxes as a Percentage of Personal Income. *Notes:* Data are from the national income and product accounts. An adjustment is made to eliminate the effects of the income tax surcharge in 1968, 1969, and 1970. The ratio in these three years is divided, respectively, by 1.075, 1.1, and 1.025.

expenditures as a percentage of GNP rose to 19.4% and, from 1975 to 1979, to 21.3%. In contrast, over this entire period, federal government revenues as a percentage of GNP remained at about 18%. In the Tax Reduction Act of 1975, Congress reduced tax rates sufficiently to undo the revenue-increasing effects of inflation since the late 1960s. Personal income taxes as a percentage of personal income fell almost to their 1964 level. Congress concentrated reductions on middle and lower income groups (Fellner, Clarkson, and Moore 1975). While federal expenditures on domestic social programs as a percentage of GNP continued to increase from the first half of the 1970s to the second half, defense expenditures began to decline more slowly. Fiscal tensions arose in the Carter administration because a fall in defense expenditures no longer allowed rising social welfare expenditures.

CPI inflation, which had fallen to 6% in 1976, began to increase in 1977 and reached a peak of 11% in 1980. Monetary policy became stimulative again in 1977, even though inflation remained historically high. The political system continued to desire a stimulative monetary policy to deal with fiscal pressures. Inflation raised the level of personal income taxes as a percentage of personal income from 9.2% in 1975 to over 11% in 1981, despite the tax reductions in the Revenue Act of 1978. Even with the revenue increases yielded by inflation, increased expenditures caused the deficit to rise to historically high levels.

From 1977 to 1980, the size of the deficit put both the Carter administration and the Democratic majority in Congress on the defensive. Sensitivity to the deficit increased pressure for stimulative monetary policy. A growing economy produces tax revenues that lower the unemployment rate and the deficit. The Congressional Budget Office or CBO (U.S. Cong. CBO, 1980, xvii) estimated that in 1980 a decrease in the unemployment rate of 1 percentage point would decrease the deficit about $27 billion (1% of GNP).

After 1976 especially, the political system needed to maintain the employment base for the payroll tax that financed the Social Security trust funds. Prior to the 1970s, the expansion of Social Security had derived from increases in coverage through provisions for disability, health care, and early retirement. The increase in average real monthly benefits followed the increase in real wages (Figure 12.8). Beginning in 1970, Congress voted large increases in benefits. By 1977, Social Security accounted for 33% of the income of families with a head aged 65 and over, up from 7% in the first half of the 1960s (U.S. Social Security Board, 1977–9).

In 1972, Social Security added indexing provisions to preserve benefit increases from erosion through inflation. The indexing provisions, however, calculated retirement benefits as the product of a percentage, adjusted for inflation, and a wage base calculated as an average of past wages. Because wages move with inflation, both the rate and the base of the benefits formula increased with inflation. The formula therefore overcompensated for inflation and caused benefits to rise over time by more than inflation for new retirees. Beginning in 1975, OASDI began to run a deficit.

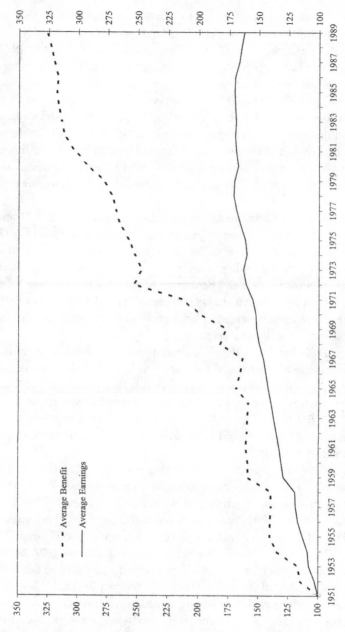

Figure 12.8. Indices of OASI Average Monthly Benefit and Average Hourly Earnings in Manufacturing (1951 = 100). *Notes*: Old Age and Survivors Insurance (OASI) average monthly benefits is from the *Social Security Bulletin*. Average hourly earnings in manufacturing is from the Bureau of Labor Statistics' establishment survey. Both series are deflated by the personal consumption expenditures implicit price deflator (1996 = 100). Index numbers are constructed by dividing the series by the 1951 value.

The relationship between unemployment and Social Security deficits was evident. Reno and Price (1985, 31) comment:

The major preoccupation in social security policy since the mid-1970s has been the financing of the OASDI Trust Funds. The program trust funds are financed almost exclusively from . . . payroll taxes. . . . [U]nemployment was seen as one of the causes of the financing problems for the retirement and disability insurance programs, rather than as a problem to be solved by these programs.

Congress worked on a solution to the financing of Social Security in 1977. A stimulative monetary policy that encouraged employment growth, rather than reduced the inflation rate, bought time for Congress to find consensus.

IV. Tax Revolt

Congress had begun to debate indexation of the tax code in early 1974. At the urging of Milton Friedman, Representative Crane in the House and Senator Buckley in the Senate introduced legislation to index the tax code. Congresspeople disliked indexation because of a desire to take credit for the periodic tax cuts made possible by the increases in revenue due to inflation. Senator Long, chairman of the Senate Finance Committee, in floor debate in 1976 over a proposal by Senator Taft to index the personal income tax argued against indexation because of the need to raise revenue and the unwillingness of Congress to raise revenue through explicit tax increases (U.S. Cong. April 24, 1978, 32, 34):

This amendment would mean that every time we have a 6 percent inflation, we will lose $5 billion in revenue . . . when we already have an absolutely uncontrollable government deficit. It is difficult . . . to get senators to vote for tax increases. . . . Inflation is one thing that does tend, somewhat automatically, to help bring the budget into balance. . . . One of the few things we have going for us to give us the chance to balance the budget is that inflation does tend to bring in more revenues for the government.

In the last half of the 1970s, inflation generated large increases in revenue. (Figure 12.7). Moreover, the changes in the tax code made to offset the effects of inflation benefited mainly lower income families. In 1967, 24.1% of taxpayers faced a marginal tax rate of 21% or higher. By 1979, this figure had risen to 60.2% (Sanders and Greene 1980, 25). As of 1980, the tax code built in large future increases in revenue. In early 1980, the CBO forecast a rise in inflation to 11% in 1980 and then a decline to somewhat under 8% by 1985. With this forecast, federal government revenues as a percentage of GNP were forecast to rise from 20.6% in 1980 to 23.9% in 1985 (U.S. Cong. CBO, February 1980, xv).

With the passage in June 1978 of California's Proposition 13, which reduced property taxes and limited the ability of local governments to raise future taxes, movements began across the country to limit the growth of taxes. The reaction by the middle class to higher taxes influenced the 1980 election in which Ronald Reagan defeated Jimmy Carter. Although Democrats retained control of the House, they lost 33 seats to the Republicans. In the Senate, the reelection rate for incumbents fell to 55.2% from 69.8% in the previous three presidential-year elections. Control of the Senate passed to the Republicans.

After 1980, it became politically unacceptable to use inflation to raise personal income tax rates. The Economic Recovery Tax Act of 1981 reduced personal income tax rates by 25% over 33 months. It also indexed personal income tax brackets for inflation beginning in 1985. Congress set the reduction in the tax rates on personal income at a level that eliminated the rise in revenues that would have occurred with the inflation forecast for the three years before indexing was to take effect in 1985. A final rise in expenditures relative to GNP began in 1980. The tax revolt and the election of Ronald Reagan in 1980, however, rendered recourse to an inflation tax politically unacceptable. The underlying trend imbalance in expenditures and revenues then appeared in a sustained rise in the deficit (Figure 12.2).

APPENDIX: REVENUE FROM THE INFLATION TAX

The figures detailed in this appendix for the separate components of the revenue increases due to inflation in 1974 add to $33.9 billion. First, the outstanding stock of base money (currency in circulation and member bank reserves) in 1974 was $111 billion. With inflation at 11% in 1974, the public had to add an additional 11% to holdings of base money in order to maintain its real value. This addition to base money is equivalent to a tax collected by government in that it allows the government to finance additional expenditures. Seigniorage in 1974 amounted to about $12.2 billion ($111 × 0.11).

Second, in June 1974, treasury debt paid an average of 6.56%. The average maturity of debt was three years. The market rate of interest on a three-year treasury note was 8.33%. The difference in the market rate and the average rate paid (1.77) is an estimate of the extent to which past issues of federal debt failed ex post to have incorporated adequately a premium for future inflation. With $254.5 billion of debt held by private investors, the gain to the government from unanticipated inflation in 1974 was $4.5 billion (0.0177 × $254.5).

Third, inflation increased the real revenue raised by the personal income tax. Inflation eroded the real value of the standard deduction, the personal exemption, and the low-income allowance. Because the rate structure of the personal income tax was progressive before 1985 with respect to nominal income, inflation increased real revenue by increasing individuals' nominal income. Fellner, Clarkson, and Moore (1975) used a stratified sample of tax returns from the IRS to calculate the increase in revenue in 1974 due to inflation. To these returns they applied the actual tax code in 1974 and also a hypothetical inflation-adjusted tax code. They concluded that inflation in 1974 increased revenue from the personal income tax by $6.7 billion.

This figure is close to an estimate from aggregate figures. Between 1973 and 1974, nominal personal income increased 9.7%. Because CPI inflation rose by 11%, real income declined by about 1%. An indexed tax code that caused changes in real revenue to reflect only changes in real personal income would have produced an increase in nominal personal tax receipts of about 8.7% (9.7%−1%). In fact, personal tax receipts rose by 14.3%. These figures suggest an elasticity of real revenue from the personal income tax with respect to inflation of (14.3−8.7)/8.7 or 0.64. In 1973, personal tax receipts were $107.3 billion. The real tax increase due to inflation then was about $6 billion ($107.3 × 0.087 × .64), which is close to the Fellner et al. figure.

Fourth, inflation increases the real revenue raised by the capital gains tax because increases in the dollar value of assets due to inflation are taxed as real, rather than nominal, gains. Feldstein and Slemrod (1978) estimated that inflation caused the tax on capital gains to generate an additional revenue of $.5 billion in 1973. (This figure is a lower estimate of the revenue gain for 1974, when the inflation rate was higher than in 1973.)

Fifth, inflation raises the real revenue from the corporate income tax. Fellner, Clarkson, and Moore (1975) calculated the increase in corporate taxes in 1974 due to inflation. They adjusted corporate depreciation allowances for inflation so that depreciation was at replacement rather than historical cost. They also reduced profits due to the nominal gain in inventories caused by inflation. They estimated that inflation increased corporate taxes in 1974 by $10 billion. This figure may be an underestimate. Feldstein and Summers (1979) estimated that inflation in 1977 of only 6.8% increased the taxes of nonfinancial corporations by $32 billion. That is, in 1977, inflation raised the effective corporate tax rate from 41 to 66%.

The percentage shares of the inflation tax contributed by the separate parts of the tax code in 1974 were seigniorage 36.0; depreciation of existing government debt, 13.3; personal income tax excluding capital gains, 6.7; capital gains, 1.5; and corporate tax, 29.5. These relative shares, however, underestimate the importance of the personal income tax component of the inflation tax. A constant inflation rate would generate the same amount of revenue each year from the other components. In contrast, revenue increases from the personal income tax were cumulative because each year taxpayers were forced into higher tax brackets. The cumulative increase in revenue was only limited because of the limit on the top marginal tax bracket of 70%.

THIRTEEN

The Volcker Disinflation

The appointment of Paul Volcker as chairman of the Board of Governors on August 6, 1979, changed the policymaking environment of the Fed. Burns and Miller had taken the Fed on a detour away from Martin's belief that the Fed was responsible for inflation. Volcker made low inflation the objective of policy. Consistent with his early background in financial markets at the New York Fed and with his oversight of the Bretton Woods system at the treasury, Volcker focused on expectations. Moreover, he acted on the belief that credible monetary policy could shape those expectations.

With that belief, Volcker challenged Keynesian orthodoxy, which held that the "high" unemployment of the 1970s demonstrated that inflation arose from cost-push and supply shocks. Expectations in the form of a wage–price spiral propagated that inflation. Because of the nonmonetary origin and built-in propagation of inflation, an attempt to control it through monetary policy without incomes policies would create unacceptably high levels of unemployment. The rational expectations revolution became so only with the demonstrated success of the Volcker disinflation. *The 1979 Joint Economic Report* (U.S. Cong. March 22, 1979, 45) expressed the prevailing view:

Inflation ... cannot be dealt with ... through demand restriction alone without exacting intolerable costs in terms of lost output and high unemployment. ... Clearly, demand restriction does not address supply-related inflation triggered by rising energy and food costs, increases in government regulation, substandard productivity gains, and a declining international value of the dollar – which is propelled onward by subsequent spirals of wages and prices attempting to keep up with each other.

Today, it is hard to imagine the birth pains required to bring forth a new, credible monetary regime. For Volcker, the imperative was to restore stability to inflationary expectations through credibility.[1] If low inflation required a recession, then credibility meant cessation of the pattern of go phases following stop phases. Policy would have to be preemptive in that rates would have to rise before public concern shifted from unemployment to inflation. Volcker first turned to a visible commitment to low money growth to establish credibility. Volcker (December 3, 1980, 9) said:

[E]xpectations, as they are reflected in wage bargaining, in pricing policies, and in financial decision-making, have in the past few years... fed the inflationary process.... Our own sense of conviction in restraining money – and even more a demonstration of success measured realistically over a reasonable period of time – will be among the crucial ingredients in changing those expectations.

Volcker (January 2, 1980, 3, 10, 11) explained how the FOMC adopted the new operating procedures of October 6, 1979, with the intent of changing expectations through credible commitment:

Our policy... rests on a simple premise – one documented by centuries of experience – that the inflationary process is ultimately related to excessive growth in money and credit.... [T]he question I receive most frequently is... "Will the Fed stick with it?"... My own short and simple answer... is yes. "It" is restraint of the money supply.... [O]ne expectation that has come to be almost universally shared is that prices would move higher – and so long as that expectation is held it tends to become a self-fulfilling prophecy.... To break that cycle, we need to change expectations. One indispensable element in the process is singularly in the domain of the Federal Reserve – we must have a credible and disciplined monetary policy that is characterized by sustained moderation of growth in money.

The visible commitment to achieving the money targets committed the FOMC to raising interest rates by whatever extent necessary to lower inflation (Volcker 1994, 160).

I. The Fed Assumes Responsibility for Inflation

Volcker was a product of the New York Fed. In the 1950s when Robert Roosa was at New York, he had worked at the Open Market Desk. In the 1960s, he had worked as treasury undersecretary for Treasury Secretaries Dillon and Fowler. After leaving in fall 1965 for Chase Manhattan Bank, he returned in the Nixon administration to work for Treasury Secretaries Kennedy, Connolly, and Schultz. Volcker, who was the guardian of the Bretton Woods system, had to watch helplessly as it disintegrated in March 1973. Volcker (Volcker and Gyohten 1992, 113) recounted later a conversation with Arthur Burns in an emergency meeting on March 9, 1973, in Paris: "[Burns] feared floating with a passion. [He] made one last appeal to turn the tide [in favor of saving Bretton Woods]. To me, it simply seemed too late, and with some exasperation I said to him, 'Arthur, if you want a par value system, you better go home right away and tighten money.' With a great sigh, he replied, 'I would even do that.'"

Volcker wrote (Volcker and Gyohten 1992, 103): "As I came to know later... Burns... was extremely sensitive to charges that international considerations were influencing domestic interest rates. Hence, despite his enthusiastic support of fixed exchange rates, he seemed to me to have a kind of blind spot when it came to supporting them with concrete policies." Volcker (2001, 443) said of the breakdown of Bretton Woods, "It's a sad story, engraved on my mind."

Volcker became FOMC chairman in August 1979 when Miller became treasury secretary. The dollar was depreciating rapidly. Later, Volcker (Volcker and Gyohten 1992, 151) wrote: "[T]he insistent question arises whether it would have been more appropriate to have paid attention much earlier to the warning signal sent by a falling exchange rate." In summer 1979, intervention failed to halt the dollar's decline. Mayer (1980, 303, 308) wrote:

In February 1978, the expenditure of $750 million in marks in ten days had been considered extraordinary by all participants; in mid July 1979, American purchases of marks ran as high as $500 million a day. And the markets would not stabilize. . . . On September 19, the dollar in one day lost 2 percent of its exchange value against the Swiss franc and the currencies of the D-mark bloc.

At his first meeting as FOMC chairman, Volcker gave a speech outlining the primacy of restoring credibility at a time when participants believed the economy was entering into recession. Volcker (Board of Governors *Transcripts* August 14, 1979, 21) assumed responsibility for shaping inflationary expectations:

[I]f a tightening action is interpreted as a responsible action . . . long-term rates tend to move favorably. . . . [E]conomic policy in general has a kind of crisis of credibility. . . . Can we restore the feeling that inflation will decline over a period of time? . . . [Recession is] manageable . . . for us if long-term expectations are not upset . . . by any decline in interest rates.

In September 1979, Volcker returned early from IMF meetings in Belgrade. Shortly thereafter, at a secret meeting held on October 6, 1979, the FOMC adopted new operating procedures.[2] According to Volcker (Volcker and Gyohten 1992; 2001), on the way to Belgrade, he drew support from Helmut Schmidt, chancellor of West Germany, and Otmar Emminger, president of the Bundesbank. Volcker briefed G. William Miller and CEA chairman Charles Schultze. Neither liked the idea of the new procedures, but Volcker inferred that President Carter would not challenge their adoption.

Volcker needed to unite a divided FOMC. The September 18, 1979, FOMC meeting highlighted the anguishing choices. On the one hand, the Greenbook (September 12, 1979, 1–3) reported that "Inflation has continued at double-digit rates in recent months, boosted by energy prices." The Bluebook (September 14, 1971, 1) reported that "[o]ver the August–September period growth of M1 is projected to be above the upper end of the Committee's 4 to 8 percent range." On the other hand, recession appeared likely. The Greenbook reported that 1979Q2 real GNP had fallen at an annualized rate of 2.5% and projected little change for the contemporaneous quarter followed by an annualized decline for the next three quarters of 1.25%. For the end of 1980, the Greenbook forecast an unemployment rate of 8%.

The FOMC voted for a "slight increase" in the funds rate (Board of Governors, *Record of Policy Actions FOMC, Annual Report 1979*, 193–4, 196). Four members dissented. Presidents Balles, Black, and Coldwell wanted additional tightening, and Governor Rice objected to any tightening. On the same day, the Board voted 7 to 3 to raise the discount rate with Partee, Teeters, and Rice dissenting. Even though Volcker could count on a majority in both bodies, especially with the appointment of Frederick Schultz as vice chair in July, he was in an untenable position because a divided Fed invites attack. Representative Henry Reuss and Senator Lloyd Bentsen, chairman of the JEC, wrote Volcker opposing any further increase in rates (Mayer 1980, 308).

The internal division appeared visibly in a split over an increase in the discount rate. Volcker (2001, 447) said later:

What really propelled me to make the change [in operating procedures] . . . was when we raised the discount rate. . . . The vote was 4–3. . . . The response was, "[T]hat's the last increase . . . we'll see." So the market reacted badly. . . . Then I realized we had this credibility problem worse than I thought. That got me off and really thinking . . . about the other approach.

Volcker took the funds rate decision away from the FOMC. He told the FOMC (Board of Governors *Transcripts* January 8–9, 1980, 13), "While we still worry about what the federal funds rate is doing, when it doesn't go according to our preconception, we at least avoid making a concrete decision."[3] Volcker (Volcker and Gyohten 1992, 170) acknowledged that without the new procedures he could not have achieved FOMC support for the high interest rates actually realized.

The new procedures dealt with internal divisions and lack of credibility by focusing attention on money targets rather than the funds rate. Volcker wrote (Volcker and Gyohten 1992, 167–8):

Among the most important [benefits] would be to discipline ourselves. Once the Federal Reserve put more emphasis on the money supply, not just by publicly announcing the target but by actually changing its operating techniques to increase the chances of actually hitting it, we would find it difficult to back off even if our decisions led to painfully high interest rates. More focus on the money supply also would be a way of telling the public that we meant business. People don't need an advanced course in economics to understand that inflation has something to do with too much money.

Volcker was a natural leader who responded to a crisis. Volcker (*Financial Times* October 23–24, 2004) said later, "It was a good time to be chairman because there was a sense of national crisis." He was also an intellectual who followed academic debate. By 1979, he accepted the monetarist position that only a central bank can control inflation. Volcker (Volcker and Gyohten 1992, 164) wrote: "[O]ne thing was clear to me at the time. If all the difficulties growing out of inflation were to be dealt with at all, it would have to be through monetary policy." Volcker (Volcker and Gyohten 1992, 166) also understood the difficulties of using an interest rate instrument given volatile inflationary expectations.

As Volcker (U.S. Cong. October 17, 1979, 1) told the JEC, the imperative was to control inflationary psychology, which manifested itself in speculative activity in commodity and foreign exchange markets and threatened to spread to wage setting:

Inflation feeds in part on itself, so part of the job of returning to a more stable and more productive economy must be to break the grip of inflationary expectations. We have recently seen clear evidence of the pervasive influence of inflation and inflationary expectations on the orderly functioning of financial and commodity markets and on the value of the dollar internationally.

To control expectations, the FOMC needed to avoid overshooting the four-quarter target ranges for money. "[I]t was clear by early fall that the growth in money and credit was threatening to exceed our own targets for the year and was nourishing inflationary expectations" (Volcker, December 1979, 959).

Based on interviews with governors and board staff, Woolley (1984, Chapter 5) observed that targeting money offered solutions to the Fed's immediate problems. First, a credible anti-inflationary stance would require a significant rise in interest rates, but there was uncertainty over the magnitude of the rise required. A resolution was to allow the funds rate to rise by whatever amount necessary to prevent an overshoot of the M1 target range. Second, the new procedures allowed use of the language of monetary control in communicating to the public the need to raise rates.

Richard G. Davis (1981, 19–20), special adviser to the president of the New York Fed, commented: "[T]he use of money stock targets . . . provides a means of communicating the objectives of policy. . . . [T]he possibility of defining an anti-inflationary strategy in terms of a long-term path for intermediate money growth rate targets, with its attendant advantages for internal and external communication, apparently has no analog in interest rate targets."

Although the new procedures allowed the FOMC to make large changes in interest rates, they did not gain it credibility. Credibility would be tested periodically for the next one and one-half decades. Volcker (U.S. Cong. February 19, 1980, 9–11) could only commit to an unspecified moderation in money growth: "In the past . . . we have usually been more preoccupied with the possibility of near-term weakness in economic activity . . . than with the implications of our actions for future inflation. . . . The broad objective of policy must be to break that ominous pattern. . . . I see no alternative to a progressive slowing of growth of the monetary aggregates."

At the time, the public could not know whether these statements represented only one more stop phase in a recurrent go–stop cycle. No one knew whether the political system would support disinflation. Only when the Fed did not initiate a subsequent go phase did it begin to gain credibility. In fact, Volcker found support among politicians. Representative James Blanchard (D. MI), commented (U.S. Cong. February 19, 1980, 129): "If Arthur Burns had advocated the policies you discussed, we would have probably had a lynch mob in the hallway." The next president, Ronald Reagan, also supported Fed independence. Volcker (Volcker and Gyohten 1992, 175) wrote: "[U]nlike some of his predecessors, he [Reagan] had a strong visceral aversion to inflation and an instinct that ... it wasn't a good idea to tamper with the independence of the Federal Reserve."

II. Credit Controls and the 1980 Roller Coaster

Despite the new procedures, the FOMC made no progress in reducing inflationary expectations by year end 1979. Prior to its October meeting, the 30-year bond rate was 9.3%. Two months later in December, it had risen to 10%. After the Soviets invaded Afghanistan in December 1979, President Carter proposed more spending for defense. Skeptical over forecasts of eventual budget balance, bond markets handed Volcker his first inflation scare. The bond rate began rising sharply in the last half of January 1980 with the report that the CPI had risen 1.2% in December and 13% for 1979. The bond rate rose above 12.5% in the last half of February.[4]

The FOMC hesitated in responding to the challenge to its credibility. Volcker (Volcker and Gyohten 1992, 171; Volcker 1994, 147) wrote that he had wanted to raise the discount rate but that the Carter administration persuaded him to wait. The funds rate rose sharply only in mid February 1980. From 13.6% after the February FOMC meeting, it rose to 17.8% after the March meeting.

In response to double-digit inflation, Carter promised to resubmit a budget with additional fiscal restraint. At the time, Carter believed that he would be running against Kennedy in the primaries and he wanted something in his anti-inflation plan that would give it a "liberal" rather than a completely "conservative" cast. In response, his advisers came up with credit controls.[5] Schultze (Hargrove and Morley 1984, 494) wrote:

We ... resubmitted the budget in March of 1980, along with an ill-fated request for a tax on gasoline. ... We did some silly things along with it. ... I let some of the political types persuade us that while we were doing so many illiberal things in this package, cutting so much out of spending, putting a tax on energy which would hurt the poor people, all this business – that we should do something liberal. And the something liberal was selected credit controls.

The political appeal of credit controls came from the assumption that quantitative restrictions on credit would limit the rise in interest rates needed to control inflation and mitigate the impact on housing. The populist character of controls appeared in the board press release stating that the purpose of the Special Credit Restraint Program (SCRP) was to prevent "use of available credit resources to support essentially speculative uses of funds." Volcker told bankers on March 25, 1980:[6]

The Fed's credit restraint program is a substitute for higher interest rates, which were having a very disruptive effect on certain sectors of the economy. There appeared to be no shortage of funds to large businesses.... Money market mutual funds... were channeling funds from areas which were short of funds, such as small banks, small businesses in rural areas, into areas that already had sufficient quantity of funds, large banks and large corporations.

The Credit Control Act, passed in 1969, gave the Board of Governors authority to limit "any or all extensions of credit." Knowing that Nixon would not invoke the controls, Congress wanted only to embarrass him. Whether the president could force the Fed to implement controls was unclear. On March 30, 1979, when Miller was still board chairman, Treasury Secretary Michael W. Blumenthal sent President Carter a memo urging him to invoke controls. He did so at a time when the treasury and CEA were urging the Fed to pursue a more restrictive policy (cited in Schreft 1990, 30):

The Federal Reserve has been reluctant to increase restraint on the banking system.... Our concern is that much further delay in exercising restraint will permit and encourage a surge in both business and consumer spending that will add significantly to the already poor prospects for prices.

The Credit Control Act of 1969 *permits* the Federal Reserve Board to impose such controls on your authorization, but you *cannot* order them to do so. The Board will have to be persuaded of the wisdom of this action. [italics in original]

Volcker felt he had to accede to the president's request to implement controls. He was involved in discussions on revising the budget both within the administration and between Congress and the administration (Volcker and Gyohten 1992, 172; Volcker 1994, 147). Carter had followed Volcker's advice to reduce the projected deficit (Volcker and Gyohten 1992, 171). Schultze (Hargrove and Morley 1984, 494) wrote: "We pulled them [the Fed] kicking and screaming into that [credit controls].... But having gotten himself into the process [of revising the budget] one of the prices of the gentleman's agreement is that you play by the outcome. You make your case and if you lose you still play good soldier, which he did."

Also, the Fed itself was trying to control credit extension. Volcker (U.S. Cong. July 14, 1983, 48) said: "Some parts (of the credit controls) were quite acceptable to us in terms of what we call voluntary restraints on banks." The motivation for the new procedures derived in part from monetarist arguments about the need to control money. However, Volcker and most FOMC members were not monetarists. As a result, the measures taken October 6, 1979, included steps to control credit. "And we placed a special marginal reserve requirement of 8% on increases in managed liabilities of larger banks... because that source of funds... has financed much of the recent excessive buildup in bank credit" (Volcker, December 1979, 960). Managed liabilities – which included time deposits of $100,000 and over, Eurodollar borrowings, repurchase agreements and Fed funds borrowing from banks not Fed members – were not part of M1 or M2.

Volcker had brought on board the Keynesian governors (Partee, Teeters, and Rice) with the argument that increased variability of the funds rate under the new operating procedures would discourage speculation.[7] Also, the Board urged banks not to extend credit for speculative purposes. "The Board of Governors has particularly stressed its own concern that, in a time of limited resources, banks should take care to avoid financing essentially speculative activity in commodity, gold and foreign exchange markets" (U.S. Cong. October 17, 1979, 4). Volcker (Volcker and Gyohten 1992, 172) wrote that in early 1980 the Board was considering stronger measures to curb credit. Since "we were by no means ideologically pure," it was harder to say no to the administration's credit controls. The Board announced the SCRP on March 14, 1980.[8]

The credit controls exacerbated sharply the economic downturn (Schreft 1990).[9] Volcker (2001, 448) commented:

[W]e put them [controls] on one day, with a big White House announcement by the President, and the economy collapses the next day.... [T]o the very day, to the very week, there was a sharp reaction. Suddenly the stuff that was covered, like I guess automobile trailers or mobile homes, sales went to zero the next week. People were tearing up their credit cards, and sending them in to the White House. "Mr. President we want to be patriotic." Consumption just collapsed.

Charles Schultze (Hargrove and Morley 1984, 494) said:

We got the steepest decline in one quarter in our history.... [P]eople felt guilty about using credit... and as soon as the President said something about credit, they didn't bother to read the regulations... the public just stopped using credit. We had merchants calling in to complain that all their customers thought that the President declared consumer credit illegal, immoral, unpatriotic. There were huge temporary drops in appliance sales. It had an incredible impact.

As economic activity sank, so did money (Figure 13.1). Because the FOMC continued to implement its monetary control procedures, interest rates fell precipitately.[10] With the economy clearly in recession, the board lifted the controls on July 3, 1980. The next surprise was the way that the economy roared back. Figure 13.2 shows how the board staff underestimated growth in 1980.

When the economy revived with the end of the SCRP program, the funds rate was at too low a level to prevent a monetary acceleration. From May through August, M1B grew at an annualized 16.9%. By midsummer, a consensus still existed that a recession was under way. Because the strength in money did not accord with this perception, the FOMC did not initially implement its procedures in a way that produced a significant rise in the funds rate (Levin and Meek 1981, 35). From the July through the October meeting, the FOMC raised the intra-yearly target for M1 from the bottom to the top of the four-quarter target range. The Board raised the discount rate a percentage point on September 26, but postponed additional increases and significant reductions in the target for nonborrowed reserves until November.[11]

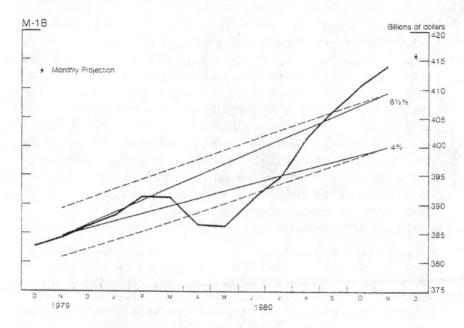

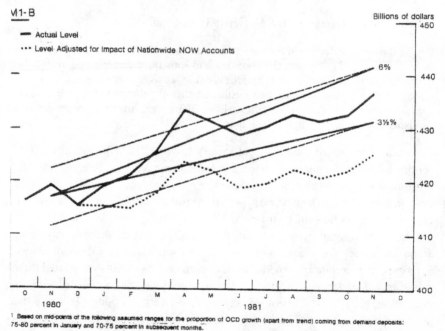

Figure 13.1. Money and Target Ranges. *Notes:* Reproduced from December 1980 and December 1981 Bluebooks. The FOMC set the target ranges as required by the Humphrey–Hawkins legislation. The figures express them as cones and parallel lines. In the bottom figure, the dotted line is shift adjusted M1.

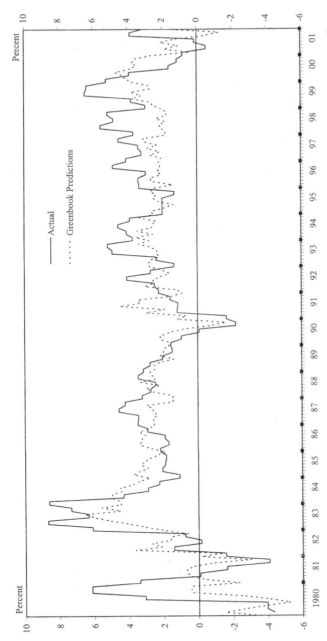

Figure 13.2. Actual and Predicted Real Output Growth. *Notes*: Observations correspond to FOMC meetings. Predictions are from the Greenbook and are for the annualized two-quarter rate of growth of real output (GNP before December 1991 and GDP thereafter). If an FOMC meeting is in the first two months of a quarter, the predicted growth rate is for the contemporaneous and succeeding quarter. If it is in the last month of a quarter, the predicted growth rate is for the succeeding two quarters. Actual growth is the subsequently realized growth rate, measured using the data available at the time of the publication of the "final" GDP estimate for the final quarter of the two-quarter growth rate. The final estimate is released in the last month of the quarter following a particular quarter. Heavy tick marks indicate a December FOMC meeting.

As the fall progressed, it became clear that the recession of late spring and summer had only been a temporary reaction to the credit controls and that the economy was growing strongly. The FOMC then permitted its procedures to increase the funds rate sharply. It rose about 3 percentage points in each of the months November and December, reaching a peak of 20% early in January 1981. The monetary acceleration of the last half of 1980 pushed money above the four-quarter target cone by year-end (Figure 13.1).

As indicated by the behavior of bond yields, the FOMC ended 1980 with no increase in its credibility. Democrats believed that the Fed behaved in a partisan way by raising interest rates and the discount rate before the November election. Republicans believed that it behaved in a partisan way by allowing money to surge before the election (Volcker and Gyohten 1992, 173). For the Fed, 1980 was a lost year. Volcker (2001, 449) said:

The economy just took off as fast as it had gone down. Then we really got behind the eight ball.... It was a sad experience, because we basically lost ... 8 months.

Mehrling: So it took 3 years instead of 2 years before you could really change expectations.

Volcker: Exactly.

Later, Volcker (1994, 148) commented, "It was ... a mostly wasted year [for] restoring credibility in the attack on inflation."

III. Confronting Inflationary Psychology

The recovery that began in 1980Q3 extended into 1981. Real GNP grew by an annualized 8.6% in 1981Q1. The irregular slowing of growth of various price indices provided mixed evidence on whether inflation was slowing.[12] With this uncertainty, the FOMC continued to display a firm anti-inflationary posture. Volcker (August 1981, 617) testified to Congress: "[A] crucially important round of union wage bargaining begins next January, potentially setting a pattern for several years ahead. That is one reason why we need to be clear and convincing in specifying our monetary and fiscal policy intentions and their implications for the economic and inflation environment."

Monetary policy was strongly restrictive in 1981. Shift-adjusted M1 decelerated in 1981 (Figure 13.1).[13] M1 grew (fourth quarter to fourth quarter) at about 8.3% in 1977 and 1978. In 1979 and 1980, it grew at 7.5 and 7.3%, respectively. In 1981, growth of shift-adjusted M1 fell to only 2.3%. The monetary deceleration that began toward the end of 1980 caused shift-adjusted M1 to remain below its four-quarter target cone in 1981Q1.

As a result, the FOMC's operating procedures pushed the funds rate down to 14.7% in March 1981. M1 grew strongly in April, but still remained only at the lower boundary of the four-quarter target cone. Nevertheless, in early May the board raised the discount rate and the surcharge on the basic discount rate, and the Desk reduced substantially the target for nonborrowed reserves. This episode possesses the distinguishing characteristics of the Volcker policy regime – a strong response to inflation scares. From about 12% in March, bond rates shot up to 14% in early May. At its May meeting, the FOMC overrode the automatic part of its procedures and pushed the funds rate up to 20%.

At the May 1981 meeting, the FOMC highlighted its anti-inflationary resolve (Board of Governors *Record of Policy Actions Annual Report* 1981, 111): "The indications of some slowing of the rise in the consumer price index did not appear to reflect as yet any clear relaxation of underlying inflationary pressures, and emphasis was placed on the importance of conveying a clear sense of restraint at a critical time with respect to inflation and inflationary expectations." To prevent weakness in M1 from lowering the funds rate, the FOMC adopted an open-ended directive with respect to the extent that growth in shift-adjusted M1 could decline (Board of Governors *Record of Policy Actions Annual Report* 1981, 112).[14] In June and July the funds rate was at 19%, and in August it was still almost 18%. Shift-adjusted M1 remained well below its four-quarter target cone throughout most of 1981. Throughout 1981, the FOMC's desire to convey its anti-inflationary resolve affected the implementation of policy. The *Record of Policy Actions* for the November 17, 1981 FOMC meeting (Board of Governors *Record of Policy Actions Annual Report* 1981, 138) reported that "a decline in short-term rates could exacerbate inflationary expectations and abort a desirable downtrend in bond yields."

In February 1982, another inflation scare challenged Fed credibility. In the last part of 1981, the Reagan administration projection of a balanced budget unraveled. In this environment, bond rates, which had fallen below 13% at the end of November 1981, rose and peaked in early February 1982 at 14.75%. The FOMC pushed the funds rate up from 12.5% after its December 1981 meeting to 14.5% after its February 1982 meeting.

IV. Abandoning the October 1979 Procedures

Through early 1982, policy focused on assuaging inflationary fears. However, as 1982 progressed, a moderation in inflation became evident. Volcker (March 1982, 167–8) testified: "Now we can see clear signs of progress on the inflation front.... [W]e are also seeing signs of potentially more lasting changes in attitudes of business and labor toward pricing, wage bargaining, and productivity.... I believe the pattern is likely to spread, 'building in' lower rates of increase in nominal wages and prices."

At the same time, evidence became clear that the economy had entered a recession. (The cyclical peak occurred in July 1981.) In this environment, the FOMC could relax its concern for credibility and respond to economic weakness. A key assumption behind the new operating procedures was the establishment of credibility through achieving money targets. In an environment in which concern for inflationary expectations was less pressing and in which the predictability of the relationship between M1 and nominal GNP had diminished, the FOMC questioned the desirability of attaining M1 targets (Volcker July 1982, 406–7).

Concern over the international debt situation became the catalyst to the phasing out of the October 1979 operating procedures. The sharp appreciation of the dollar in 1982 as well as the continued high level of interest rates made numerous emerging-market countries unable to pay their external debt. The FOMC began negotiating with the Bank of Mexico in June to furnish reserves under the existing swap arrangement (Board of Governors *Record of Policy Actions Annual Report* 1982, 120). The fear arose that defaults by large debtor nations would threaten the world financial system (Volcker December 1982, 747; March 1983, 170).

Coping with the international debt situation required a reduction in the level of U.S. interest rates. First, because much of third-world debt was of short maturity, lower rates would reduce the burden of interest payments. Second, because this debt was denominated in dollars, lower U.S. interest rates would facilitate repayment by limiting dollar appreciation. Third, lower rates would spur the U.S. economy and increase the exports of debtor nations. Finally, lower U.S. rates would allow central banks of other industrialized countries to lower rates to stimulate their economies and increase imports. "[A]n environment of sustained recovery and expansion in the industrialized world is critically important" (Volcker February 1983, 82).

In mid July 1982, the FOMC began to lower the funds rate through reductions in the discount rate and increases in the target for nonborrowed reserves. From the end of June to the end of August, the funds rate fell from about 15% to about 9%. At the time, M1 was just within the four-quarter target cone. At its October 5, 1982, meeting, the FOMC formally dropped the M1 target. When the FOMC lowered the funds rate in the last half of 1982, the bond market rallied initially under the assumption that the level of rates necessary to control inflation had fallen. The sustained reduction in inflation in 1982 had increased Fed credibility. The reduction in rates ended in December 1982 when a reduction in the discount rate failed to produce a fall in bond rates.

V. Creating a New Monetary Standard

In 1980, as a result of the interaction between the SCRP and the new operating procedures, the FOMC produced a small version of the stop–go cycle it was determined not to repeat. That experience fortified its resolve not to initiate an expansionary policy in response to recession.[15] The FOMC remained focused on establishment of credibility. Volcker told the FOMC (Board of Governors *Transcripts* February 2–3, 1981, 129): "Everybody likes to get rid of inflation but when one comes up to actions that might actually do something about inflation . . . one says: 'Well, inflation isn't that bad compared to the alternatives.' . . . The history of these things in the past . . . is that when we come to the crunch, we back off."

Early 1982 tested FOMC resolve. Although the economy was contracting, the FOMC raised the funds rate. It focused on achievement of the M1 target as a litmus test of its commitment not to allow "go" periods of policy to follow "stop" periods. Governor Schultz (Board of Governors *Transcripts* February 2, 1982, 94, 108) commented: "To me...credibility...is really critical....We have not yet changed...inflation expectations because everybody thinks that we are going to cave in to the political pressure that is going to be on us."

For Volcker (U.S. Cong. February 25, 1980, 10, 22), money targets were a commitment device to constrain the FOMC to maintain a long-run focus on inflation rather than on economic stabilization: "[T]here is little doubt that inflation cannot persist in the long-run unless it is accompanied by excessive expansion of money and credit." Money was an "automatic pilot" that would raise interest rates in response to inflation. In his statement, Volcker (U.S. Cong. February 25, 1980, 7–17) emphasized how the commitment to monetary control would lower inflation by controlling expected inflation:

[W]e have usually been more preoccupied with the possibility of near-term weakness in economic activity...than with the implications of our actions for future inflation.... The result has been our now chronic inflationary problem, with a growing conviction on the part of many that this process is likely to continue. Anticipations of higher prices themselves help speed the inflationary process.... [I]nflationary anticipations have tended to rise once again.... We cannot simply rail at "speculators" in foreign exchange, or gold or commodity markets if our own policies seem to justify their pessimism about the future course of inflation.... Rising demands for wages and cost-of-living protection, anticipatory price increases, skyrocketing gold and commodity prices, sharply declining values in the bond markets – all of these are symptomatic of the inflationary process and undermine the economic outlook. But none of them are inevitable, provided we turn around the expectations of inflation.

In his first two years as chairman, Volcker experienced repeated instances in which the funds rate fell and then the bond rate rose (Figure 13.3).[16] That sequence made clear that inflationary expectations could thwart the real effects of expansionary monetary policy. With the fall in bond rates in the last half of 1982, which accompanied the fall in the funds rate, the FOMC passed an important test. The next test would come in late spring 1983 when bond rates began to rise with an unchanged funds rate. Despite falling inflation, the FOMC increased the funds rate.

With that increase, Volcker started creation of a new nominal anchor. It was not the money target urged by monetarists, but rather the expectation of low, stable inflation. Later, Volcker (U.S. Cong. July 21, 1987, 97) defined the Fed's objective in expectational terms. "[W]hatever the precise [inflation] statistics are, people should not be planning on inflation." Greenspan gave the same expectational definition (Chapter 15, n. 4). Inherent in these statements is the working assumption that monetary policy can shape the expectational environment in which price setters operate. Although neither Volcker nor Greenspan made the rational-expectations connection that associates the systematic part of monetary policy with the public's formation of inflationary expectations, in practice it guided their conduct of

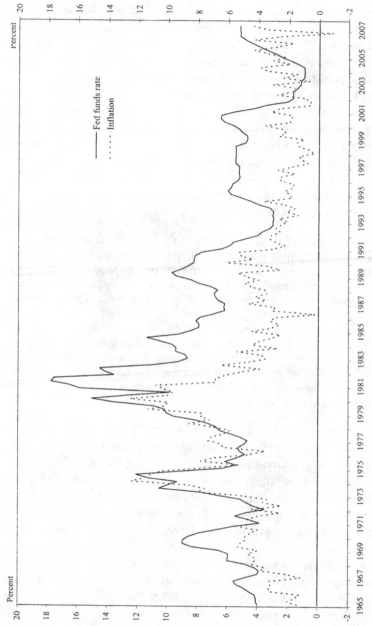

Figure 13.3. Fed Funds Rate and Inflation. *Notes*: Quarterly observations of annualized percentage changes in the personal consumption expenditures deflator.

monetary policy. However, the failure of the FOMC to articulate its inflation objective and to highlight the consistency with which it pursued that objective made learning and the ultimate acquisition of credibility a long process.[17]

Although the rational-expectations implication that the public forms its expectation of inflation conformably with monetary policy is testable in the case of dramatic monetary reforms (Sargent 1982), the Volcker disinflation did not offer such an experiment. In 1980, the first full year of the new operating procedures, the FOMC repeated the stop–go cycle. Governor Gramley (Greider 1987, 219) recalled the skepticism in 1980 that the Fed would disinflate: "I got nowhere. For years, the public had heard these ringing speeches from the Federal Reserve about fighting inflation. The Federal Reserve was always fighting inflation and nothing ever happened. They just didn't believe the words."

In 1979, no one knew whether the political system would support Fed independence if disinflation imposed high costs. Without at least the tacit support of the president, Volcker's policy was just a statement of good intentions. Greider (1987, 185–7) contrasted the Fed's announcement of its anti-inflation program with Carter's announcement of the credit controls:

On March 14, with the dramatic flourish available to the Presidency, Jimmy Carter announced to the nation that urgent measures were being invoked.... Within days, consumer spending slowed drastically.... On October 6, when Volcker launched his major offensive, the announcement had been couched in the obscure language of finance. Not surprisingly, very few citizens who were not financiers understood what he meant. Not grasping the significance, the general public... did not change [its]... behavior.... [W]hen credit controls were announced, the language was blunt and melodramatic.... [T]his time the government spoke clearly and ordinary citizens responded.

VI. Articulating the Monetary Standard

The Fed has yet to articulate the monetary standard created in the V–G era. The Fed's responsibility in a democracy to explain how it has exercised the delegation of authority from Congress to create the monetary standard entails such an effort. What is required? With Volcker, FOMC chairmen began to take responsibility for inflation. However, they never explain in terms of monetary policy the behavior of realized inflation that occurs under their tenure. Explication of the monetary standard will require a willingness on the part of the Fed to use the causal language of economics to explain how monetary policy determines the realized behavior of inflation. Use of the language of economics to explain inflation will require willingness to debate both the theoretical abstractions embodied in models and the consistency the FOMC imposes on its individual funds rate changes.

The resulting combination of theory and policy must explain why after the Volcker disinflation both nominal and real stability increased. This result overturned the Keynesian consensus and moved the economics profession toward acceptance of three abstractions, each seemingly at odds with descriptive reality. First, the price level is a monetary phenomenon in that the central bank, which controls only a nominal variable (the monetary base), determines trend inflation. Second, the price system works in that moderate changes in the real interest rate keep output at potential (in the absence of monetary shocks that force unanticipated changes in the price level). Third, expectations are rational in that the public learns how to make its expectation of inflation conform to the consistent part of monetary policy. Together, these abstractions imply that a credible central bank can deliver price stability through conditioning the expectations of forward-looking price setters rather than through periodic recourse to the creation of excess unemployment.

The rational-expectations abstraction remains especially controversial.[18] The emphasis here is on the evidence that despite the failure of the Fed to articulate the consistent part of its behavior the public has adjusted its inflationary-expectations formation to that behavior. The monetary history of the twentieth century is that of the loss of the nominal anchor provided by a commodity standard and the fitful, often disastrous attempt to replace it with a paper standard. The initial failure of the Fed to accept responsibility for inflation and its continuing failure to explain the realized behavior of inflation in terms of monetary policy have made learning about monetary policy extremely difficult. Nevertheless, the public has adapted its expectations formation to monetary policy.

In 1983, inflationary expectations proxied for by bond rates replaced money as an intermediate target. Volcker never articulated the change in procedures.[19] Greenspan, through his continued focus on shaping the expectational environment, turned Volcker's experiment into a new monetary standard. However, Volcker and Greenspan dealt with a succession of crises, and they interpreted monetary policy accordingly. The task of articulating the monetary standard they created must fall to their successors.

APPENDIX: OCTOBER 6, 1979 OPERATING PROCEDURES

This appendix explains the October 6, 1979 operating procedures (see Hetzel 1982; Lindsey 2003; Lindsey, Orphanides, and Rasche 2005; Chapter 3, Appendix, "Borrowed-Reserves Operating Procedures"). With a nonborrowed-reserves target, the reserves-supply schedule (R_s) possesses a vertical section at the value of the nonborrowed-reserves target (Figure 13.4). Banks obtain reserves beyond the amount of nonborrowed reserves from the discount window. Because the nonpecuniary cost of borrowing varies with the amount of borrowing, the marginal cost of borrowed reserves exceeds the discount rate. Through arbitrage, the funds rate also rises above the discount rate. The positively sloping section of the reserves-supply schedule shows the positive relationship between borrowed reserves and the difference between the funds rate and the discount rate. Figure 13.5 shows the empirical relation between borrowed reserves and the difference between the funds rate and the discount rate.

Funds Rate

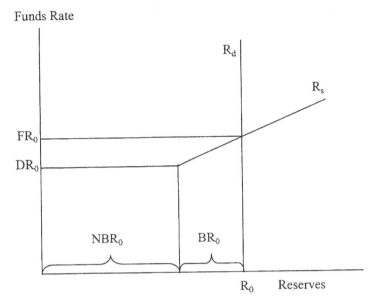

Figure 13.4. The Market for Bank Reserves. *Notes:* The market for bank reserves. R is bank reserves. R_d is the reserves demand schedule of the banking system and R_s the reserves supply schedule. FR is the funds rate. DR is the discount rate. NBR and BR are nonborrowed and borrowed reserves. The 0s denote particular values.

With lagged-reserves accounting, the reserves-demand schedule (R_d) is vertical. Required reserves are predetermined because they depend upon deposits held two weeks in the past rather than upon deposits held in the current statement week. Also, desired excess reserves are interest insensitive. The intersection of the reserves supply and demand schedules determines the funds rate.

Consider the effect of a reduction in nonborrowed reserves. With the quantity of reserves demanded fixed in a given reserves-accounting period, borrowing from the discount window rises by an amount equal in magnitude to the reduction in nonborrowed reserves. As a result, the marginal effective rate of interest on borrowed reserves rises. In Figure 13.6, R_s shifts leftward to R_s' and intersects the unchanged R_d schedule at a higher funds rate. An increase in the discount rate produces the same increase in the height of the reserves supply schedule and, consequently, the same increase in the funds rate. (R_s' shifts upward to R_s''.) Figure 13.7 shows the relationship between the funds rate and the discount rate for the period of nonborrowed reserves targeting.

Lagged reserves accounting renders infeasible a target for total reserves by making the reserves-demand schedule interest inelastic (vertical). With a total-reserves operating target, the reserves-supply schedule is also interest inelastic. An attempt to target total reserves would produce a razor's edge situation. A reserves surplus would force the funds rate to zero and a reserves deficiency would force the funds

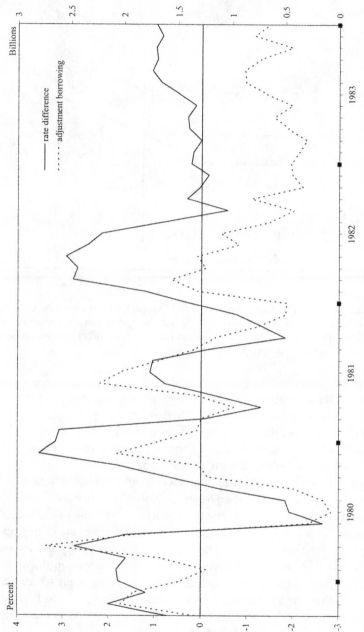

Figure 13.5. Adjustment Borrowing and the Difference between the Funds Rate and the Discount Rate Plus Surcharge. *Note:* Heavy tick marks indicate December.

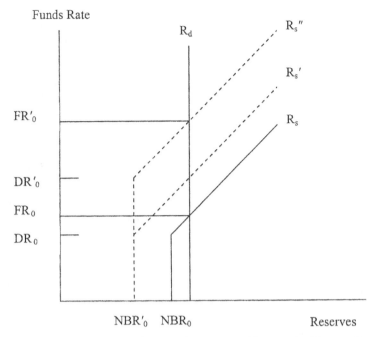

Figure 13.6. Decrease in Nonborrowed Reserves and Increase in Discount Rate.

rate up to a point where banks would be willing to default on their holding of required reserves.

Implementation of the procedures began with specification by the FOMC of an intrayearly target for M1 growth. From this target, the Board of Governors staff derived a target for the average level of total reserves for the intermeeting period. The FOMC also specified an initial target for borrowed reserves, usually the prevailing target for borrowed reserves. The difference between the total-reserves and borrowed-reserves targets determined the target for nonborrowed reserves.

Note the identity

$$NBR - RR = ER - BR$$

where NBR is nonborrowed reserves, RR is required reserves, ER is excess reserves, and BR is borrowed reserves. (Transposing the negative terms gives the identity total reserves equal total reserves.) Because of lagged-reserves accounting, required reserves are given for a particular statement week. Given a projection for excess reserves, the target for nonborrowed reserves then determines a target for borrowed reserves. Consequently, the Desk used nonborrowed reserves and borrowed reserves interchangeably as targets.

In the intermeeting period, the staff made regular M1 forecasts. Based on them, it projected total reserves. The Desk subtracted the target for nonborrowed reserves from the revised estimates of total reserves in order to arrive at a new target for

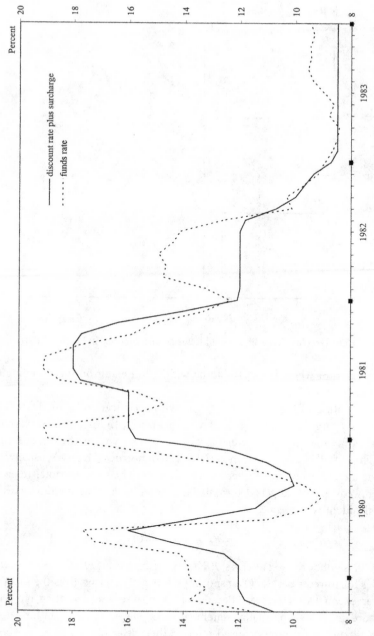

Figure 13.7. Funds Rate and Discount Rate Plus Surcharge. *Notes*: Discount rate for the Federal Reserve Bank of New York. Heavy tick marks indicate December.

borrowed reserves. As a consequence of targeting nonborrowed reserves, deviations of money from its targeted path produced, via associated movements of total reserves, changes in borrowed reserves. Changes in borrowed reserves, in turn, produced changes in the funds rate that mitigated the miss from the money target.

The FOMC made discretionary changes in response to misses of the money target. It could, at FOMC meetings, raise or lower the initial target for borrowed reserves relative to the prevailing level, thereby lowering or raising the initial target for nonborrowed reserves. It could also change the target for nonborrowed reserves between meetings. The Board of Governors could change the discount rate.

Although the FOMC never characterized its policy as monetarist, many outside the Fed interpreted the new procedures as a monetarist experiment. They also argued that monetary control introduced the volatility in this period into interest rates. For example, Nordhaus (1982) wrote:

The first step [of a new economic policy] would be to bring down the curtain on the disastrous monetarist experiment of the last two years. The Federal Reserve should be directed to cease and desist its mechanical monetary targeting and to set monetary policy with an eye to inflation and unemployment.... The technique of emphasizing supply of bank reserves rather than interest rates since October 1979 has produced greater volatility of both interest rates and the money supply.

However, in contrast to "monetarist" monetary control procedures (Burger 1971), the October 1979 procedures worked through indirect control of the funds rate rather than the control of total reserves. The combination of lagged reserves accounting with a nonborrowed reserves target rendered impossible monetary control through a reserves-money multiplier relationship. The FOMC debated a move to contemporaneous reserves accounting, but rejected the idea presumably because of unwillingness to surrender control of the funds rate. Furthermore, the behavior of the funds rate did not derive primarily from the automatic interaction between misses of the money target and a given target for nonborrowed reserves. Instead, as Cook (1989, 15) concluded, "movements in the funds rate from October 1979 to October 1982 were largely determined on a judgmental basis." However, as noted by the board staff, the discretionary movements in the funds rate due to discount rate changes reinforced the funds rate movements produced by the automatic part of the procedure for controlling M1.

FOURTEEN

Monetary Policy after the Disinflation

Volcker was a crisis manager whose immediate goal was to prevent a surge in inflation from permanently raising inflationary expectations. On October 9, 1979, Volcker (cited in Lindsey, Orphanides, and Rasche, 2005, 205) told the American Bankers Association that "the immediate challenge is to avoid imbedding the current rate of inflation in expectations and wage and pricing decisions, before the current bulge in prices subsides." However, the road to restoring credibility for low inflation was long and difficult. The bond markets provided the most sensitive measure of inflationary expectations, and bond rates rose during economic recovery when real growth rose above trend.

At his first FOMC meeting as chairman, Volcker (Board of Governors *Transcripts* August 14, 1979, 21, cited in Goodfriend and King 2005, 27) explained the consequences of the loss of credibility: "I am impressed myself by an intangible: the degree to which inflationary psychology has really changed. . . . That's important to us because it does produce . . . paradoxical reactions to policy. . . . [T]he ordinary response one expects to easing actions . . . won't work if they're interpreted as inflationary; and much of the stimulus will come out in prices rather than activity." Sensitivity to market expectations pushed the FOMC to raise the funds rate when the growth gap became positive not when a negative output gap approached zero. Bond market vigilantes pushed the FOMC to create a new monetary standard based on stable expected inflation as the nominal anchor.

Money targets had advertised the FOMC's commitment to lower inflation. After 1981, however, money proved a flawed indicator for moving the funds rate to control aggregate demand. Volcker then signaled the commitment to control inflation by raising the funds rate in response to increases in expected inflation evidenced by increases in bond rates. That commitment required raising the funds rate in the early stages of recovery. Earlier, as New York Fed president, Volcker (Board of Governors *Transcripts* April 17, 1979, 21, cited in Goodfriend and King 2005, 16) had foreseen how economic recovery would test the FOMC's resolve to remain focused on expectational stability: "[T]he difficulty in getting out of a recession . . . is that it conveys an impression that we are not dealing with inflation."

I. Expected-Inflation/Growth Gap Targeting

The FOMC brought inflation (core PCE – personal consumption expenditures ex food and energy deflator) down steadily after 1981 until it reached 3.75% in 1985 (Figure 14.1). In 1981 and the first half of 1982, both short- and long-term real rates averaged about 7% (Figure 14.2). In the postwar period, only at the onset of the 1970 recession (with real rates of 5%) did real rates approach such heights (Figure 8.3).[1] Despite disinflation and high real rates, the continued high level of nominal bond rates demonstrated the limited level of Fed credibility (Figure 14.3).

The 30-year bond rate began to rise after the November 1982 trough in the business cycle. It climbed from 10.5% on that date to 13.4% in May 1984, just short of the 14.2% peak in January 1982 (Figure 14.3). Volcker (February 1984, 97, 100) highlighted the high level of bond rates relative to inflation as evidence of the lack of credibility:

[I]nflation has tended to worsen during periods of cyclical expansion. But that need not be inevitable.... [W]e can shape disciplined policies.... [W]e ... recognize that the battle against inflation has not yet been won – that skepticism about our ability ... to maintain progress toward stability is still evident. That is one of the reasons why longer-term interest rates have lingered so far above the current inflation levels. After so many false starts in the past, the skepticism is likely to remain until we can demonstrate that ... the Federal Reserve is not prepared to accommodate a new inflationary surge as the economy grows.

The abandonment in fall 1982 of the nonborrowed-reserves procedures led in 1983 to expected-inflation/growth gap procedures. With the latter, the FOMC raised the funds rate in response to increases in inflationary expectations proxied for by increases in bond rates. Sensitivity to the bond market also caused it to reduce the cyclical lag in the funds rate relative to nominal output growth. It began to raise the funds rate when a positive growth gap first appeared. These changes appeared in a dramatic way in 1983 when the FOMC raised the funds rate from 8.5 to 9.5% from the March to the August 1983 meeting (Figure 14.3).[2] This rise, prompted by a rise in the bond rate from 10.5% in mid May to 12% at the end of August, took place during the early stage of economic recovery with an unemployment rate in March 1983 of 10.3%.

With its May 1983 meeting, the FOMC had to make the tormenting choice between the obvious imperatives of aggregate demand management and the unknown benefits of expectational stability.[3] In referring to the international pressures that had led the Fed to lower the funds rate beginning in mid 1982, President Corrigan, Minnesota (Board of Governors *Transcripts* May 24, 1983, 27) stated the issue:

Internationally, the case is overwhelming that we would be better off with lower interest rates and a lower exchange rate.... What will happen to bond rates if we do snug up a little, recognizing that they have already increased 50 basis points in the last two weeks? On the other hand, what would happen to bond rates if we didn't do anything? ... [T]hat is the $64 question.

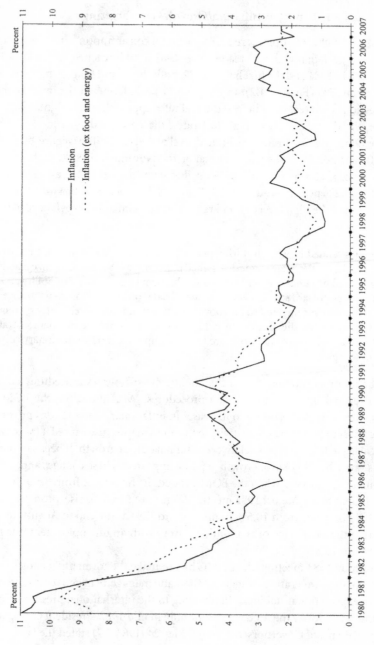

Figure 14.1. PCE Inflation and PCE Inflation ex Food and Energy. *Notes*: Quarterly observations of four-quarter percentage changes in the PCE deflator and PCE deflator ex food and energy. Heavy tick marks indicate the fourth quarter of each year.

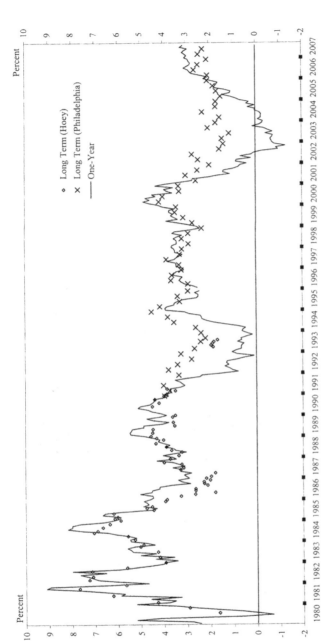

Figure 14.2. Long- and Short-Term Real Treasury Security Rates. *Notes:* The long-term (Hoey) real rate is the 10-year constant-maturity U.S. Treasury bond yield minus the predicted 10-year inflation rate from the "Decision Makers Poll" conducted in the 1980s by Richard B. Hoey. Starting in October 1991, the long-term real rate (Philadelphia) is the 10-year constant-maturity U.S. Treasury bond yield minus the predicted 10-year inflation rate from the Survey of Professional Forecasters. This survey is conducted quarterly by the Federal Reserve Bank of Philadelphia (formerly conducted by the American Statistical Association and the National Bureau of Economic Research) and measures expected CPI inflation for a 10-year horizon. The 1-year real rate is monthly observations of the 1-year constant maturity U.S. Treasury yield minus predicted one-year ahead inflation from Global Insight. See Chapter 4, Appendix, "Series on the Real Interest Rate." Heavy tick marks indicate the last observation of the year.

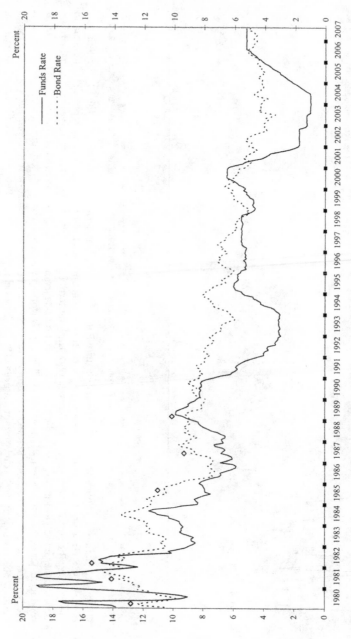

Figure 14.3. The Funds and Bond Rate. *Notes*: Monthly Observations of the funds rate and the bond rate. Prior to 2000, the bond rate is the 30-year treasury constant maturity series; thereafter, it is the 10-year series. Diamonds mark the following dates: March 1980, May 1981, February 1982, May 1987, February 1989. Heavy tick marks indicate December meetings.

The following exchange (Board of Governors *Transcripts* May 24, 1983, 35–8) captured the drama of navigating when deciding whether to try a new compass:

Solomon (N.Y. Pres.): We're going to be perceived as going against the consensus view of all the governments, including our own, to encourage a worldwide recovery, because people judge that the inflationary problem is considerably reduced.

Gov. Wallich: There's a certain inconsistency between saying we want to snug up because the economy is strong and then saying moreover that that's going to hold down the long-term rate.

Balles (San Francisco Pres.): [L]ong-term rates are heavily influenced by expectations of future inflation.

Solomon: It will look as though we're trying to spoil the recovery.... [P]eople are just not going to understand.

Roberts (St. Louis Pres.): [S]nugging would be positively interpreted... we would more likely to get a decline in [long] rates than an increase.

Gov. Teeters: I have never seen the short-term rates go up without the long-term rates going up.... If we want the long rate down... we need to lower the federal funds rate, not increase it.

As long as inflation remained at historically high levels, the FOMC had remained united behind Volcker. However, with inflation falling and an unemployment rate still in excess of 10%, the FOMC split. Although the FOMC tightened, four members dissented.

Although Volcker did not believe that there was a rule that could govern funds rate changes, his speeches uniformly conveyed a sense of the need for public officials to exercise discipline, which would ultimately banish inflationary expectations.[4] The test of that discipline would come during economic recovery. To restore expectational stability, the FOMC had to convince the public that inflation would not follow recovery. Volcker (December 28, 1983, 4, 5, 7, 9, 11, 12) said in a speech:[5]

The years of inflation... have understandably left deep scars.... As the economy grows... there will be stronger temptations to anticipate inflation.... [P]rogress against inflation is... typically reversed in the second year of expansion, with further acceleration expected before the next recession.... [T]he need remains to convey a sense of conviction.... [G]rowth in nominal GNP and money and credit will need to be reduced over time.... [B]oth our policy decisions..., and your expectations, should be strongly conditioned by that broad objective and strategy – I am tempted to say by that "general rule."

A renewed rise in bond rates in spring 1984 again tested FOMC resolve to master inflationary expectations. From 12.5% in mid March, bond rates rose to almost 14% by the end of May. Reacting to the inflation scare, at its March 1984 meeting, the FOMC raised the funds rate from the 9.375% set at the January meeting to 10.25%. By the August meeting, it had raised the funds rate to 11.625%. Strains in financial markets created by high interest rates made evident the severity of the test of FOMC resolve. In May 1984, after a run on its deposits, Continental Illinois turned to the discount window. By August, its borrowings reached $7.5 billion.[6]

Furthermore, readings on the economy called for ease. In 1984Q1, the unemployment rate averaged 8%, while inflation continued to fall. Despite a negative output gap, Greenbook predictions of declining real growth (Figure 13.2), and falling inflation (Figure 14.1), the FOMC waited three months after the peak in bond rates in June 1984 before allowing the funds rate to decline at its October meeting. Board Staff Director Steve Axilrod (Board of Governors *Transcripts* November 7, 1984, 4) noted, "[L]onger-term inflationary expectations have probably improved – according to one poll by 1 to $1\frac{1}{4}$ quarter percentage point since last winter." The rapid decline of the 30-year bond rate to 7.25% in July 1986 signaled a victory of the new monetary standard. The steady fall in the unemployment rate and an economic expansion that lasted the remainder of the decade increased political acceptance of the standard's preemptive character – funds rate increases without a prior increase in inflation.[7]

The year 1985 should have been a time of satisfaction for the FOMC. It had brought down trend inflation to 4% (Figure 14.1). With dramatic increases in the funds rate is 1984, it had confronted and subdued the inflationary expectations created by strong economic recovery. Moreover, it had done so without derailing the recovery. By the end of 1985, the funds rate had fallen 4 percentage points from its August 1984 peak. Still, what must have seemed like the perfect storm began to form.

The "imbalances" that worry central bankers seemed everywhere. In almost every speech, Volcker beseeched the political system to reduce the deficit. A strong dollar and large current account deficit produced a rust-belt recession in the Midwest while Louisiana and Texas suffered from low oil prices. Pressures for protectionism festered. The LDC (less-developed-country) debt crisis continued. Outside the United States, economic recovery limped along. The Board of Governors reduced the discount rate with the intention of pressuring the German and Japanese central banks to lower rates. For example, the announcement accompanying the July 10, 1986, reduction stated: "[A] reduction in the System's rate might encourage easing measures abroad later, if not immediately" (Board of Governors *Record of Policy Actions Board, Annual Report 1986*, 82).

With the continued decline of the funds rate in 1986, the short-term real rate drifted down to 3% in early 1987 (Figure 8.3), while longer term real rates fell more strongly (Figure 14.2). As a result, from 1983 through 1987, aggregate nominal demand growth remained at a level somewhat too high to maintain inflation at less than 4%. Figure 14.4 shows velocity-adjusted M2 growth, which is a proxy for aggregate nominal demand growth (see Appendix: "Velocity-Adjusted M2 Growth"). From 1963 through 1978, aggregate nominal demand growth trended upward. It trended down thereafter, but stabilized above 7% for the years 1983 through 1987.[8] Although consistent with moderate inflation during the strong economic recovery, in 1988 it led to a revival of inflation (Figure 14.1).[9]

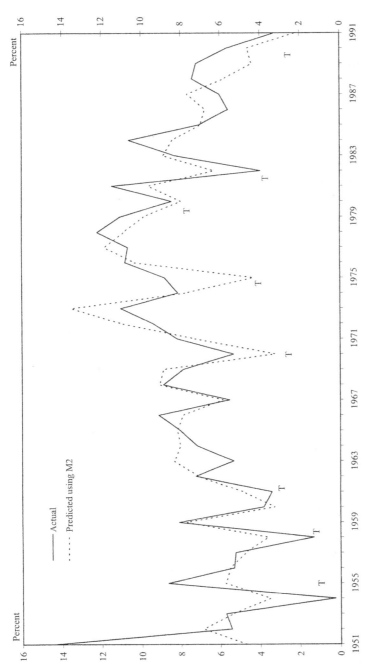

Figure 14.4. Annual Nominal Output Growth: Actual and Predicted Using Velocity-Adjusted M2. *Notes*: Predictions of nominal GDP growth are from the M2 indicator variable $\Delta m + \Delta v^p$, where Δm is the percentage growth in M2 and Δv^p is the predicted percentage growth in M2 velocity due to changes in the opportunity cost of holding M2: $1.6\Delta(R_t - RM2_t)$. R is the six-month commercial paper rate and $RM2$ is the own rate on M2 (a weighted average of the rates paid on the components of M2). The coefficient 1.6 is the semilog elasticity of M2 velocity with respect to the opportunity cost of holding M2. See Appendix: "Velocity-Adjusted M2 Growth." Ts mark business cycle troughs: 1954, 1958, 1961, 1970, 1975, 1980, 1982, and 1991.

II. The Road to the Louvre Accord

To address the politically divisive international and domestic imbalances, Volcker (Volcker and Gyohten 1992, Chapter 8) imagined a grand solution that required international coordination of policies among countries. The story of those imbalances begins with the large current account surpluses for the OPEC countries created by the oil price rise in 1973. They placed their oil revenues in international banks, which recycled the funds to the LDCs that imported oil. Latin America, where nationalist sentiment prevented foreign direct investment, especially accumulated large amounts of dollar-denominated, short-term bank debt. The low real interest rates of the 1970s made the debt burden bearable. However, when real rates rose after 1979, many LDCs could no longer service their debt. Domestic and foreign protectionism, which limited the size of the LDCs export sectors, restricted their ability to generate the foreign exchange necessary to repay debts. In summer 1982, Volcker became concerned that default by large sovereign debtors would disrupt the international banking system (Board of Governors *Transcripts* August 24, 1982, 18).

U.S. recovery from the early 1981–82 recession proceeded faster than in other countries. Most other OECD countries pursued restrictive monetary policies to suppress inflation, while LDCs restrained demand in order to generate balance of payments surpluses. In addition, the Reagan tax cuts, which reduced taxes on capital, made the United States an attractive place to invest. These forces produced a rise in the U.S. current account deficit.[10]

That deficit created protectionist pressures, which threatened the ability of LDCs to export to the United States and, consequently, their ability to repay external debts. A general debt default by these countries would have made a number of large international banks insolvent.[11] In 1985, Volcker expressed a desire for more stimulative policies in other developed countries. Volcker (U.S. Cong. July 17, 1985, 26) said:

[M]uch of the world has been dependent . . . on expanding demand in the United States to support its own growth. Put another way, growth in domestic demand in Japan, Canada, and Europe has been less than the growth in their GNP, the converse of our situation. . . . As a consequence, the demand of others for our products has been relatively weak. . . . In the meantime, the flood of imports, and the perceptions of unfairness which accompany it, foster destructive protectionist forces.

Volcker emphasized the importance of stimulative policy by European countries and Japan (U.S. Cong. July 17, 1985, 27, 55): "The needed adjustments would be eased as well if other industrialized countries became less dependent on stimulus from the United States for growth in their own economies. . . . We have a home-grown expansion. It is flowing abroad. The foreign countries need home-grown expansion."

Volcker's (U.S. Cong. February 26, 1985, 99, 117) favorable comments with regard to intervention in the foreign exchange markets represented recognition that foreign willingness to undertake more stimulative policies required a mitigation of the strength of the dollar on the foreign exchanges:

[T]here are opportunities in . . . countries . . . with the strongest external positions – Japan, Germany . . . to take some stimulating action, perhaps by way of reducing taxes.
  [I]ntervention can be a useful tool. . . . [I]t certainly is a tool . . . that ought to be in our armory. . . . At the same time, I don't think intervention is likely to be the answer to these problems standing alone. It has to complement . . . more basic actions and more basic directions.

With Secretary Donald Regan, the treasury had opposed foreign exchange intervention. However, under Secretary James Baker and Deputy Secretary Richard Darman, a newly activist treasury organized the September 1985 Plaza Accord.[12] The United States, West Germany, Japan, Britain, and France agreed to intervene jointly to lower the value of the dollar, which had already begun to depreciate in February 1985. Against a background of central bank intervention in the foreign exchange markets, the dollar fell against the other G-5 currencies. From February to the end of November 1985, the dollar fell by 20% against the Japanese yen and by about 15% against the deutsche mark and the French franc.[13]

However, when dollar depreciation did not reduce the U.S. current account deficit, international and domestic pressures aligned to produce the Louvre Accord.[14] U.S. trading partners wanted "tight" fiscal policy and "easy" monetary policy in the United States. Policymakers believed in the "twin deficits" problem, that is, the government deficit in the United States created the need for foreign inflows of funds, which created the strength in the dollar.[15] Foreign governments therefore wanted a reduction in the U.S. deficit. They also wanted low U.S. interest rates to limit the strength in the dollar and the corresponding weakness in their currencies. Any increase in the funds rate in the United States would make it more difficult for foreign central banks to lower their discount rates.

The LDC debt crisis remained. In early 1987, Brazil threatened to renege on its debts. IMF lending to the LDCs to buy time while they opened their economies and sold off state-owned enterprises had not worked. Regional U.S. banks wanted to write off their LDC debt. By creating market prices for this debt, this action would have revealed the insolvency of some large money center banks. Industrialized countries were unwilling to open their domestic markets any further to the exports of debtor nations. By default, the only politically feasible policy appeared to be world economic stimulus to increase demand for LDC exports.

Domestic pressure arose from the rise in 1986 of the trade deficit to $166 billion. As a result, the free trade coalition in Congress that in the past had blocked protectionist legislation disintegrated. The *Wall Street Journal* (April 27, 1987) reported:

The movement toward tough trade legislation has become a stampede. . . . The new mood partly reflects the continuing erosion of the coalition of multinational corporations that for decades staunchly opposed any curbs on trade. Some import-battered companies, such as Chrysler Corp., Motorola Inc. and Ford Motor Co. have deserted the free-trade fold and are backing a controversial measure that automatically limits imports from countries having large trade surpluses with the U.S.

[T]he 1986 election put control of both houses of Congress in Democratic hands for the first time in six years, and the Democrats have decided to make trade a key test of their power. . . . Democratic congressional leaders have concluded that the trade issue should get top political priority and could be a key issue in the 1988 presidential election.

Volcker (U.S. Cong. July 29, 1986, 26) testified: "We cannot continue to increase our trade deficit. . . . [P]olitical pressures are not going to permit it in terms of protectionist action." Congresspeople pressured the Fed to lower the funds rate in order to depreciate the dollar. Dollar depreciation became a rallying point because politicians viewed strength in the dollar as destroying jobs by stimulating imports and depressing exports. They felt constituent pressure to aid a long list of depressed sectors such as agriculture, energy, manufacturing, and mining. All the political players lined up in favor of economic stimulus.

There was also pressure from administration figures for a return to fixed exchange rates.[16] Because they viewed the dollar as overvalued, dollar depreciation appeared to be a first step to returning to fixed rates. Representative Leach's (D. IA) comment to Volcker conveyed the political sentiment (U.S. Cong. July 17, 1985, 46): "An eased monetary policy has implications for fairness as well as for the economy at large, and a little bit of inflation and a reduction in the value of the dollar may well be the greatest way to avoid protectionist efforts from a congressional perspective, and this ought to be a serious concern of the Federal Reserve Board."

The decline in the dollar on the foreign exchanges in 1986 and early 1987 provided the catalyst for a revival of what was known as the locomotive strategy in the Carter administration. The result, the Louvre Accord, turned into a major source of global instability. Commentary by Fannie Mae (January 16, 1987) foreshadowed how the willingness of the administration to use the dollar as a weapon to pressure Japan and Germany for stimulative policy would backfire through higher bond rates:

A huge decline in the value of the dollar was the catalyst for a general weakening in bond prices this week. The dollar plunge followed reports that the Administration, concerned about the prospects for protectionist legislation and frustrated by its inability to get our major trading partners to follow more stimulative monetary and fiscal policies, wanted the dollar to move lower.

In February 1987, the United States, Germany, Japan, France, Britain, and Canada signed the Louvre Accord. The countries with large trade surpluses, Germany and Japan, would stimulate their economies to increase imports. Because the disinflation of the first half of the 1980s and the transitory effect of declining oil prices had virtually restored price stability (Figure 14.1), stimulus appeared acceptable. The United States would reduce its fiscal deficit, which other countries believed caused its current account deficit. All agreed to foreign exchange intervention to halt further declines in the dollar. Volcker supported intervention.[17]

Louvre became a loose cannon whose careenings knocked down the stock market on Black Monday October 17, 1987. It rested on two miscalculations. First, Louvre's credibility depended upon the willingness of the United States to reduce its fiscal deficit.[18] The 1986 Gramm–Rudman legislation had made the U.S. pledge to reduce the deficit credible. However, a Supreme Court decision invalidated the provision for automatic spending cuts. By fall 1987, it had become clear that the administration and Congress could not agree on how to fix the law. The Reagan administration feared that congressional Democrats wanted to use the legislation as a lever for forcing a tax increase and reductions in defense spending. By fall 1987, Congress had also demonstrated its ability to circumvent the law through budgetary sleights of hand (*Wall Street Journal* August 10, 1987).

Second, Louvre depended upon an economic environment that did not require a rise in U.S. interest rates. That constraint came from the U.S. desire to persuade the German Bundesbank and the Bank of Japan (BoJ) to lower their discount rates. The Bundesbank feared that higher U.S. interest rates would weaken the mark and increase inflationary pressures in Germany (Hetzel 2002b). Japan, in contrast, wanted a weaker yen to help its exporters. Its desire to prevent further appreciation of the yen disposed it to reduce interest rates (Hetzel 1999). Nevertheless, Washington did not want Japan to believe that it could get a weaker yen through higher interest rates in the United States rather than lower rates in Japan. The *Wall Street Journal* (April 22, 1987) reported:

The Federal Reserve is refraining from nudging U.S. interest rates higher because it doesn't want to take pressure off the Bank of Japan to ease credit, according to a senior U.S. official. The official asserted that U.S. and Japanese monetary authorities are engaged in a struggle "almost like a game of chicken" over how to stabilize the dollar. He contended that there's a high risk of global recession if Japan and the other major industrial nation with a trade surplus – West Germany – fail to stimulate their economies quickly. The Fed could help boost the dollar by jacking up U.S. interest rates. But the senior official noted that such a move would eliminate an important motive for the Japanese to ease credit, since they are particularly anxious to avoid a further drop in the U.S. currency.

III. An Inflation Scare and the Stock Market Crash

In 1987, an inflation scare challenged the FOMC and, unlike 1983–84, it temporized due to Louvre. The scare came from an inflation shock produced by dollar depreciation. Depreciation in 1986 had occurred with falling headline inflation due to declining oil prices. However, in 1987 when that effect wore off and inflation rose, depreciation revived inflationary fears in the bond markets. In the spring, with a weak economy, they recovered. In the fall with a strong economy, the FOMC would not be so lucky.

Almost a decade earlier in 1978, when the economy recovered and the dollar depreciated, inflation had surged. In the earlier period as well as the latter, markets believed that the treasury talked down the dollar to pressure Germany and Japan to accept its locomotive strategy. Solomon (1982, 345) cited Secretary Blumenthal's "infamous statement" of "talking down the dollar." Volcker (Volcker and Gyohten 1992, 260) complained that "the secretary of the Treasury [Baker] . . . seemed to be inviting further dollar depreciation."[19]

With the announcement of the Louvre Accord February 22, 1987, foreign-exchange markets stabilized. However, the dollar resumed its decline after March 27 when the United States threatened Japan with 100% tariffs on its electronic products. The *Wall Street Journal* (March 31, 1987) reported: "The dollar's sharp drop sent shock waves through the credit markets again yesterday as Treasury bond markets took their biggest tumble in about six months. . . . [T]he dollar's plight is having a "chilling impact" on the bond markets. . . . [T]he dollar's steep slide has aroused renewed concern that inflation will increase as imports become more expensive."

Dollar depreciation raised bond rates in two ways: first, by exacerbating inflationary fears and, second, by diminishing the willingness of the Japanese to invest in dollar-denominated assets.[20] Because in 1986 the United States exported about $370 billion and imported more than $520 billion of goods and services, the financial inflows associated with the current account deficit exerted significant influence on U.S. capital markets.

In part, strength in the stock market in the first three quarters of 1987 came from Japanese investment. The Japanese government had relaxed capital controls in order to mitigate strength in the yen. Initially, Japanese investors invested heavily in the United States in order to diversify their portfolios. In the beginning, investment went primarily into fixed-income securities. However, in response to the fall in bond rates in 1986, they began to invest more in real estate and in stocks. Rising Japanese land prices and high P/E ratios on the Tokyo exchanges also made U.S. stocks appear attractive.[21]

In April 1987, a rise in the 30-year bond rate to 8.5% from 7.4% at the start of the year signaled an inflation scare (Figure 14.3). In response, in an intermeeting move, Volcker raised the funds rate (raised borrowed reserves) to 6.5% (Board of Governors *Transcripts* April 29, 1987, 4).[22] The full FOMC then moved the rate to 6.75% at its May 19 meeting.[23] However, the bond rate remained high and averaged 8.6% in July and 9% in August. It peaked at 10.25% in October. In a departure from its procedures for reversing increases in inflationary expectations, the FOMC left the funds rate unchanged at 6.75%.

Volcker (Volcker and Gyohten 1992, 284) later wrote: "To my subsequent regret, I resisted the idea of raising the discount rate. . . . The confidence of financial markets that the Federal Reserve would resist any resurgence of inflationary pressures . . . might have ebbed a bit." Ironically, Volcker (1994, 150) also wanted to end the dollar depreciation.[24] However, Louvre worked against the necessary funds rate increases. The U.S. desired to achieve stimulus in Germany and Japan by pressuring them into resisting dollar depreciation through reductions in their own interest rates rather than through rate increases in the United States.[25] Volcker (Board of Governors *Transcripts* May 19, 1987, 2) talked about "embarrassing" them.

During the inflation scare, President Reagan failed to reappoint Volcker, whose departure came as a surprise to the markets. Although his replacement, Alan Greenspan, had been President Ford's CEA head and had headed a national commission on Social Security reform, he lacked Volcker's stature and credibility. Many in financial markets doubted whether Greenspan would be independent of the administration, and he lacked credentials as a central banker (*Wall Street Journal* June 3, 1987).

In August, the dollar began to depreciate again. Commentary attributed the associated rise in bond yields to fears of inflation and to foreigners' reluctance to hold bonds.[26] In his last testimony, Volcker (U.S. Cong. July 21, 1987, 21, 23) summarized the challenge confronting Greenspan because of the inflation scare: "[W]e've had a burst of prices ... related to the oil and external situation. ... Now do we relapse back to a lower rate of inflation ... or does that get built into ... expectations?" Greenspan (U.S. Cong. March 5, 1985, 163) had already acknowledged the FOMC's focus on inflationary expectations: "The Fed is presumably keeping an eye on long-term interest rates as a gauge of inflation expectations. Should these show signs of beginning to rise steeply, the Fed could be expected to respond expeditiously with policies more heavily focused on fighting inflation."

As FOMC chairman, Greenspan (*Wall Street Journal* October 5, 1987) warned on *This Week with David Brinkley* of "dangerously high interest rates" if financial markets' fears of accelerating inflation "start to mushroom." He continued: "[T]here seems to be ... a fear that ... the next step is to get it [inflation] out of control again. ... [I]t's quite conceivable that if everybody gets it into his head that inflation is inevitable, they will start taking actions which will create" higher inflation.

Because a "sharp rise in long-term interest rates ... had raised questions about the outlook for inflation," on September 4, the Board of Governors raised the discount rate and the FOMC increased the funds rate to 7% after its September 22 meeting (Board of Governors *Record of Policy Actions Board, Annual Report 1987*, 73). The 30-year bond rate, however, continued rising and peaked at 10.25% on October 19. That level of rates left the stock market overvalued, and it crashed that day. Figure 14.5 shows the 10-year bond yield and the ratio of forecasted earnings for the S&P 500 companies to the S&P 500 price index. The rise in bond rates preceded the market crash. Dollar politics determined the timing of the crash. In the week before, the dollar, stocks, and bond prices all fell on news of the August trade deficit. Although never publicly announced, the Louvre Accord had set "rather precise ranges" for the dollar exchange rate (Volcker and Gyohten 1992, 260). On October 15, as noted in an FOMC briefing by Sam Cross (Board of Governors *Transcripts* November 3, 1987, 2), Secretary Baker "signaled displeasure with interest-rate trends in Germany, and there were press reports suggesting that

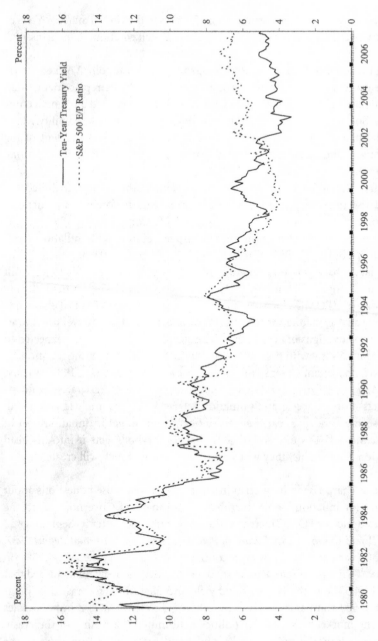

Figure 14.5. S&P 500 Earnings/Price Ratio (Forward) and 10-Year Treasury Bond Yield. *Notes:* The bond yield is the 10-year treasury constant maturity yield. The earnings–price ratio is the I/B/E/S International, Inc., consensus estimate of earnings over the coming 12 months divided by the S&P 500 price index. Observations are monthly and reflect midmonth prices.

the target range for the dollar would be lowered, or even that cooperation among the G-7 countries was breaking down. The dollar moved down abruptly against the mark . . . on the weekend of October 17."[27] The *New York Times* (October 18, 1987) reported:

In an abrupt shift . . . , the United States is allowing the dollar to decline against the West German Mark, a senior Administration official said today. This means that the government is following through on Treasury Secretary James A. Baker 3d's comments Thursday implying that the United States would let the dollar fall in reaction to higher West German interest rates. Mr. Baker said today that West Germany "should not expect us to sit back here and accept" rises in German interest rates. . . . Analysts and another senior Administration official . . . said Mr. Baker's remarks . . . meant that the Administration and the Federal Reserve Board would not interfere if market pressures start pushing the dollar down somewhat against the German mark.

The *New York Times* (October 19, 1987) reported:

As Treasury bond yields rose above 10 percent last week and stock prices plummeted, the financial markets were focused on the dangers from abroad and unimpressed by assurances from senior government officials that interest rates were needlessly high and based on exaggerated fears of inflation. . . . [An] adviser to the Deutsche Bank [said], "[T]he reason for the higher bond yields is the impaired inflow of foreign capital to the United States. . . . " Foreign buying of Treasury bonds has already subsided this year, and there were periods, such as in September, when Japanese institutions were actually net sellers of bonds.

On Monday, October 19, the Dow Jones industrials fell 22.6%.

Lack of credibility for government policies produced destabilizing shifts in investor sentiment in 1987. The promise of deficit reduction foundered with the failure of Gramm–Rudman. The breakdown of the Louvre Accord re-created the discrete changes in exchange rates that had characterized the fixed-rate Bretton Woods system. An inflation shock in the form of dollar depreciation set off an inflation scare.

Treasury Secretary Baker's public disputes with the Bundesbank and the Fed created doubts about the willingness and ability of the United States to maintain the value of the dollar. Baker expressed his unhappiness at the Board's September increase in the discount rate unmatched by reductions in interest rates in Germany and Japan. Governor Angell (*Wall Street Journal* May 2, 1994) later commented: "The precipitating factor in the 1987 stock market crash was the notion that the administration would accept a depreciating currency." Angell (*New York Times* August 24, 1997) also said, "I think there was a question about the Federal Reserve's credibility."

On Monday morning, October 19, when the market opened lower and continued to fall, the Desk engaged in nonstop telephone conversations involving the president of the New York Fed and several governors.[28] In the afternoon, the Desk and the full FOMC held a telephone conference. The Desk concentrated on supplying the additional reserves that banks demanded. Presidents of the Reserve Banks made clear that their discount windows were open. New York Fed president, Gerald Corrigan, made certain that brokers and dealers in the government securities market could continue to get credit to finance their operations regardless of market fears that the fall in stocks might have rendered some of them insolvent. The New York Fed notified government securities dealers that they could borrow government securities from the Desk's portfolio to collateralize repurchase agreements with banks.

Board Vice Chairman Manuel Johnson expressed concern that a rise in the funds rate above its previous level would indicate that the Desk was not fully meeting additional reserve demand. The Desk entered into a round of repurchase agreements Monday morning that supplied reserves in excess of what the prior week's projection indicated would be needed. Those repurchase agreements represented the Desk's only action before the afternoon telephone conference with the full FOMC. The issue never arose of reducing the borrowed reserves target to lower funds rate. The Fed concentrated on meeting unusual demands for liquidity. Only with the reduction in the funds rate on October 29 from 7.375% to 6.875% did the Fed associate its role in a crisis with an easing of policy rather than simply providing ample liquidity at an unchanged funds rate.

Central bank orthodoxy as distilled by Bagehot holds that in a financial crisis the central bank should provide liquidity at a high interest rate. There was no established precedent before Greenspan of lowering the funds rate in response to market volatility. For example, at its May 26, 1970, meeting, the FOMC had to deal with the crisis created by the Cambodian invasion. The DJIA had fallen 12% from beginning of year, its lowest level in six years. At the June 23 meeting, the Penn Central bankruptcy threatened the commercial paper market. Although the FOMC continued with the moderate decline in the funds rate begun in February, it reacted primarily by allowing banks to borrow freely at the discount window and by eliminating Reg Q ceilings on bank deposits of $100,000 or more (Maisel 1973, 38–45). Similarly, from October 26 through December 5, 1973, the DJIA fell 20% while the funds rate remained unchanged at 10%. Finally, during the collapse of Continental Illinois, which began in May 1984, the FOMC raised the funds rate from $10^1/_4$% in April to 11.625% in August.

Over 1988, core PCE inflation rose from 3.75% to 4.75% (Figure 14.1). In retrospect, to avoid exacerbating inflation, the FOMC should have limited its response to the stock market crash to liquidity provision at an unchanged funds rate instead of creating stimulus through a funds rate reduction. The FOMC lowered the funds rate from 7.375% before the October 1987 stock market crash to 6.5% after its February 1988 meeting. Although growth had revived in early 1987, the funds rate did not rise significantly until late spring 1988 (Figure 14.6).[29] Only after May 1988 did the real rate rise significantly (Figure 14.2). Although the Greenbook had predicted weakness, by spring 1988, it was clear that output was growing at an unsustainable rate (Figure 13.2).

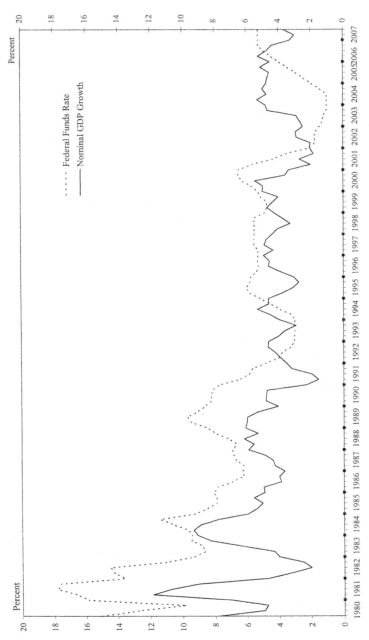

Figure 14.6. Funds Rate and Nominal Output Growth. *Notes*: Quarterly observations of funds rate and four-quarter percentage changes in nominal GDP. Heavy tick marks indicate the fourth quarter of each year.

189

IV. Concluding Comment

Despite the mild go–stop cycle that began with Louvre, the FOMC's overall focus on stabilizing expected inflation created an environment of low inflation and economic stability. Continuation of that policy in the 1990s created the benign combination of low inflation and economic stability.[30] The Keynesian Phillips curve with backward-looking expectations failed to offer policymakers useful predictions on two dimensions. Not only did low inflation not require high unemployment, but reduced variability of real output did not require increased variability of inflation.

APPENDIX: BORROWED-RESERVES OPERATING PROCEDURES AFTER 1982

With the October 1979 procedures, given the discount rate, the FOMC controlled the funds rate by controlling borrowed reserves. With total reserves demand basically predetermined with lagged reserves accounting, the FOMC's target for non-borrowed reserves determined borrowed reserves. Borrowed reserves in turn determined the premium of the funds rate over the discount rate (Appendix, "October 6, 1979, Operating Procedures" in Chapter 13). After 1982, with the abandonment of M1 targets, the FOMC targeted borrowed reserves directly (Lindsey 2003). These procedures possessed many of the characteristics of the earlier procedures.

With borrowed-reserves procedures, the funds rate equals the discount rate plus a positive increment, which increases as borrowed reserves increase. The Desk sets a level of nonborrowed reserves less than the desired (required plus excess) reserves of banks so that banks collectively must borrow from the discount window. The Fed rations over time the amount of reserves a bank can borrow. Given their borrowing history, banks will take that borrowing when they believe that current market rates are high relative to expected future market rates. If banks believe that they are likely to be in the window in the future, they would be reluctant to go in today, and the funds rate would rise (Goodfriend 1983). Consequently, there exists a (noisy) positive relationship between borrowed reserves and the difference between the discount rate and funds rate. An increased target for borrowed reserves increases the difference and increases the funds rate.

For a given borrowed reserves target, a change in the discount rate initially changes the funds rate by the same amount. The Board packaged discount rate changes to convey information about future funds rate changes (Cook and Hahn 1988). For example, a reduction in the discount rate accompanied by language expressing a concern for economic growth implied that additional reductions in the funds rate were likely. Because such reductions will lower the difference between the funds rate and the discount rate at a given level of borrowed reserves, they will produce a decrease in the funds rate that exceeds the decrease in the discount rate.

Borrowed-reserves procedures continued to allow for the indirect funds rate targeting that created some separation between the actions of the FOMC and short-term interest rates. Because the FOMC did not announce its target for borrowed reserves immediately, financial markets had to learn of changes over a period of several weeks. When the FOMC changed the target for borrowed reserves, market rates then moved to their new values only gradually. The gradual change in rates limited their newsworthiness (Dotsey 1987).

With these operating procedures, market interest rates moved ahead of FOMC actions. As noted, with a borrowed-reserves target, the funds rate–discount rate difference depends upon the current level of borrowed reserves and the levels that banks anticipate will prevail in the future. In the event that economic data come in strong, banks anticipate an increased incentive to borrow in the future and higher interest rates. The funds rate would rise with no change in the FOMC's borrowed reserves target (the "degree of reserve pressure" announced to the public with the release of the directive). In this way, the Fed could raise short-term interest rates and attribute the rise to market forces.

However, especially in the case of weakness in economic activity, the Fed might want to draw attention to its role in lowering market interest rates. It could demonstrate visible concern for the economy by a reduction in the discount rate accompanied by a message expressing concern for economic weakness.[31] Such reductions are highly visible. FOMC members sometimes called these changes "the gong effect." In sum, by targeting the funds rate indirectly through a borrowed-reserves target, the Fed gained the flexibility to package funds rate changes as reflecting either market forces or its own actions.

Although FOMC members knew the funds rate was the instrument, Volcker insisted that the FOMC set a target for borrowed reserves without reaching explicit agreement over the intended funds rate. In that way, he had some ability to move the funds rate between FOMC meetings without a telephone conference authorizing his action. The directive talked only of changing the degree of reserve pressure on the banking system rather than of the intended funds rate. The Desk, in consultation with the chairman or his representative Steve Axilrod, made an ongoing choice of whether to look through the proximate borrowed-reserves target to the effective funds rate target. If the Desk did look through the target, it would make an adjustment to that target to achieve the desired funds rate target.[32] In the mid 1980s, the FOMC gradually phased out borrowed-reserves targeting and began to set a target for the funds rate directly. When Greenspan became FOMC chairman, he permitted the FOMC to debate and to set a funds rate target.[33]

APPENDIX: MONETARY POLICY ACTIONS IN 1986

In 1986, the Board of Governors, not the full FOMC, dominated policy. Borrowed-reserves targeting gave the board control of the funds rate through its control over the discount rate. Because the FOMC set only the target for borrowed reserves, the board could then move the funds rate independently of FOMC actions. The new Reagan appointees to the board desired a more stimulative monetary policy than did the regional bank presidents.[34] Although the latter had a cautious attitude toward reducing rates, the Board moved the funds rate down aggressively through reductions in the discount rate.

In 1986, reductions in the funds rate occurred through reductions in the discount rate, despite directive language predisposing the Desk toward no change. At its February 11, 1986, meeting, the FOMC decided against any change in the funds rate and adopted contingent language for the directive designed to render funds rate changes unlikely in the subsequent intermeeting period. The directive instructed the Desk to "maintain the existing degree of pressure on reserve positions." It was also symmetric. That is, its contingent language did not predispose the Desk to change the funds rate in the intermeeting period either up or down (Board of Governors, *Record of Policy Actions FOMC Annual Report 1986*, 102).

Nevertheless, on February 24, 1986, in a split 4-to-3 vote, the board voted a decrease in the discount rate of half a percentage point. The vote was startling in that the chairman was in the minority. Later in the day, the board rescinded the action (Board of Governors, *Record of Policy Actions Board Annual Report, 1986*, 81). On March 6, it voted unanimously to reduce the discount rate. According to the *Record of Policy Actions of the Board of Governors*, the critical factor in making the vote unanimous was the willingness of key foreign central banks to lower their discount rates also. Volcker believed that a coordinated lowering of discount rates would avoid a further, sharp depreciation of the dollar.

As noted earlier, the decisions made at the February FOMC meeting indicated a majority sentiment in favor of no change in the funds rate. Although the contingent language of the Directive is vague, it indicated an emphasis on incoming data from the real sector. Both inside and outside the Fed, the most widely watched statistic on the real sector is the monthly nonfarm civilian payroll employment figure from the Labor Department. This statistic is the first available, comprehensive indicator of the behavior of real output. On February 7, the employment figure registered a gain of 566,000, the largest gain in the entire decade. This statistic is fairly volatile from month to month. Its average gain in the previous three months of 210,000, however, indicated steady growth in the economy (Figure 14.7).

On March 6, the board nevertheless approved a reduction in the discount rate by half a percentage point, which carried through to a reduction in the funds rate. The board desired to move toward a more stimulative monetary policy. Reducing the funds rate via a discount rate decrease allowed it to do so without the dissents that could have arisen in forcing the issue at an FOMC meeting.

This situation recurred at the April 1, 1986, FOMC meeting. The *Record of Policy Actions* indicates that at the meeting FOMC members were divided on whether to emphasize the transitory disruption to energy-producing regions caused by the fall in the price of oil or the longer run positive effects for the overall economy of

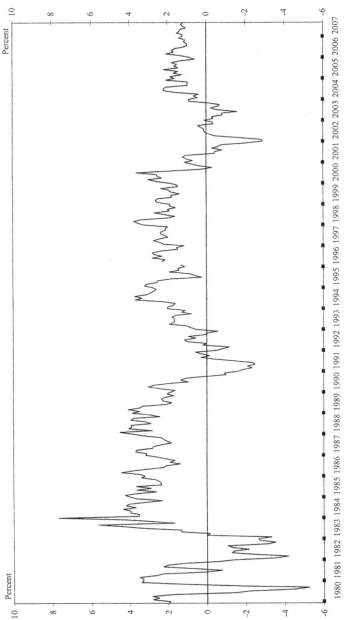

Figure 14.7. Contemporaneously Available Three-Month Growth Rate of Payroll Employment. *Notes:* Observations are annualized three-month growth rates of total employees on nonagricultural payrolls (establishment survey) taken from the original releases from the BLS. There was no contemporaneous release of data for January 1996 because of an ice storm. Heavy tick marks indicate last month of year.

lower energy prices. The *Record* notes that "[t]he staff projection presented at this meeting had suggested that the expansion in real GNP would strengthen by the second half of the year, after the relatively modest growth in the first half" (Board of Governors, *Record of Policy Actions FOMC Annual Report 1986*, 106). The directive asked the Desk to "maintain the existing degree of reserve pressure" and not to lean toward changing the funds rate in the intermeeting period either up or down. ("Somewhat lesser reserve restraint or somewhat greater reserve restraint might be acceptable.") The payroll employment figure available after the FOMC meeting indicated a continuation of moderate growth. The increase announced April 4 was 192,000, which followed a revised increase for the month earlier of 153,000. On April 18, the board nevertheless moved the discount rate down from 7% to 6.5% and reduced the funds rate to 6.875%.

At the May 1986 meeting, the FOMC again voted for an unchanged borrowed reserves target (and by implication an unchanged funds rate) and for a symmetric directive. At its July and August meetings, respectively, the FOMC voted to "decrease somewhat" and to "decrease slightly" the "existing degree of pressure on reserve positions." At both the July and August meetings, it adopted a symmetric directive. The use of the adverbs "somewhat" and "slightly" suggested a reduction in the funds rate of 0.125 to 0.25 of a percentage point. In each case, however, after the FOMC meeting, the Board lowered the discount rate and the funds rate by half a percentage point. It also accompanied the discount rate reductions by language drawing attention to slow economic growth. In that way, it announced publicly an intention to stimulate growth. Between January and late August 1986, the funds rate fell from 8 to $5\frac{7}{8}$%. The board generated that fall entirely by a 2 percentage point reduction in the discount rate. Also, the reductions in the funds rate were large – half a percentage point rather than the usual 0.25 or 0.125 of a percentage point.

APPENDIX: VELOCITY-ADJUSTED M2 GROWTH

In the 1980s, the difficulty of using M1 as an indicator became apparent. In the pre-1981 period, its growth rate had been a good measure of the impact of monetary policy on aggregate nominal demand. With the nationwide introduction of NOW accounts in 1981, M1 demand became interest sensitive. The lack of experience with the newly defined M1 made estimation of that interest sensitivity impossible. The resulting inability to predict changes in M1 velocity made problematic prediction of aggregate nominal demand growth from M1 growth.

The redefinition of M2 to include retail money market mutual funds raised the possibility that its demand function would become unstable. In fact, the demand for M2 remained a stable function of its interest rate opportunity cost. Until the M2 demand function shifted leftward starting in 1990, M2 could serve as an indicator of the stance of policy (Hetzel and Mehra 1989; Mehra 1993). I construct a monetary

Table 14.1. *M2 Velocity Regression*

$$\Delta \ln VM2_t = 0.10 + 2.8 * K + 1.6\Delta(R_t - RM2_t) + e_t$$
$$(0.3) \quad (2.1) \qquad (5.3)$$

$\mathrm{CRSQ} = 0.45, \mathrm{SEE} = 2.2, \mathrm{DW} = 1.9, \mathrm{DoF} = 38, \text{Dates: 1951–1991}$

Notes: Observations are annual averages. *VM2* is the ratio of GDP (gross domestic product) to M2; *R* is the four- to six-month commercial paper rate; *RM2* is a weighted average of the own rates of return paid on components of M2; *K* is a shift dummy with the value 1 in 1951, 1952, and 1953 and zero otherwise. Before 1959, M2 is M4 in Table 1 of Friedman and Schwartz (1970). ln is the natural logarithm; Δ is the first-difference operator. t-statistics are in parentheses. CRSQ is corrected R-squared; SEE, standard error of estimation; DW, Durbin-Watson statistic; DoF, degrees of freedom.

indicator variable for nominal GDP growth based on the behavior of changes in M2 and on predicted changes in M2 velocity. The indicator derives from the quantity equation:

$$\Delta m + \Delta v^p = \Delta y^p \tag{1}$$

Adding quarterly percentage changes in M2, Δm, to quarterly percentage changes in predicted M2 velocity, Δv^p, creates an indicator variable of nominal GDP growth, Δy^p. Table 14.1 shows a regression of percentage changes in M2 velocity on changes in the opportunity cost of holding M2 (the difference between the commercial paper rate and the own rate on M2). The product of the estimated coefficient (the semilog elasticity of M2 demand) and the change in the M2 opportunity cost yields the predicted change in velocity. The dashed line in Figure 14.4 shows the resulting measure of the monetary (M2) determinants of annual percentage changes in nominal output. The solid line shows actual percentage changes in nominal output (GDP) growth.

In 1990, M2 velocity began rising due to the flight of small time deposits to bond and stock money market mutual funds (Darin and Hetzel 1994). M2 velocity, which had been stable at about 1.65, rose through 1994 to about 2.

FIFTEEN

Greenspan's Move to Price Stability

Volcker and Greenspan shared an intense dislike of inflation and a concern for inflationary expectations (Chapters 10 and 13). Their common desire to reestablish the nominal expectational stability lost with stop–go imposed a "rule-like" character to the FOMC's standard lean-against-the-wind procedures. The essence of the V–G standard was a rule that both created a nominal anchor through the expectation of low, stable inflation and moved the funds rate in a way that allowed the price system to work.

Core PCE inflation fell from 4.5% in 1990 to 2% in January 2006 when Greenspan left the Fed. Greenspan never took any credit for the decline in inflation during his tenure as FOMC chairman. Indeed, he never offered any general vision of how central banks control inflation. Greenspan's (May 2004) characterization of the Fed was that of crisis manager. When Greenspan left, the Fed had not yet articulated the nature of the monetary standard created over the last two decades of the twentieth century. The characterization offered here highlights the similarity of the Greenspan and Volcker years that arose from the emphasis placed on expected inflation measured by bond market behavior.

I. The Absence of an Articulated Greenspan Standard

The Greenspan FOMC never discussed strategy. The role of the FOMC was to accept or reject Greenspan's funds rate recommendations.[1] Public characterization of monetary policy was also the chairman's prerogative – a characterization that reflected his nonmonetary view of inflation and inflationary expectations. Specifically, monetary policy is only one contributing factor to trend inflation and inflationary expectations. Greenspan testified (U.S. Cong. February 25, 2004, 28): "[T]he low inflation rate . . . is the consequence of a number of things, largely globalization and the competition that has come from globalization and a whole series of structural changes, including . . . the bipartisan deregulation that has been going on for a quarter of a century."

Greenspan (Board of Governors *Transcripts* January 31, 1995, 58) told the FOMC that it could only pursue the objective of price stability in a way that took advantage of nonmonetary forces that restrained inflation, as opposed to the implicit alternative of raising unemployment: "[T]hat objective [price stability] has not been implemented in a straight line because we have recognized ... that the Congress would not give us a mandate to do that ... I do not think we have the philosophical, cultural, or political support in our society for that. There still is a short-term Phillips curve."

The failure of the FOMC to specify an inflation target and to place individual funds rate decisions in the context of a strategy requires economists to infer the character of monetary policy. The hypothesis here is that Greenspan pursued price stability as a "provisionally" desirable long-run objective until the Asia crisis.[2] The July 1996 FOMC meeting is an exception to the rule that FOMC chairmen do not allow the FOMC to discuss a numerical value for an inflation objective. At this meeting, as a result of a debate between Governor Yellen and President Broaddus (Richmond), the FOMC reached a consensus over an "interim" target for CPI inflation of 2%.[3]

In an exchange with Governor Yellen, Greenspan revealed a desire to achieve price stability. Greenspan (Board of Governors *Transcripts* July 2, 1996, 50) asked the FOMC, "Is long-term price stability an appropriate goal?" Yellen asked Greenspan to "define 'price stability'" and he replied that it "is that state in which expected changes in the general price level do not effectively alter ... decisions."[4] Yellen then asked, "Could you please put a number on that?" Greenspan replied, "I would say the number is zero, if inflation is properly measured." One can infer that his provisional, personal objective for inflation was a value equal to the amount of upward bias in measured indices, about 0.75%.[5]

The hypothesis here is that Greenspan's desire to restore price stability through lowering and stabilizing inflationary expectations gave monetary policy a rule-like character. In contrast, Greenspan himself depicted monetary policy as an ongoing exercise in discretion. His "risk-management" characterization of the FOMC as a crisis manager (Chapter 18) together with his nonmonetary view of inflation was reminiscent of stop–go. Namely, the FOMC controls the economy while powerful nonmonetary forces control inflation (Hetzel 2007b). What is at issue in these contrasting characterizations of monetary policy is the nature of the V–G monetary standard.

II. Disinflation

In early 1989, Greenspan (U.S. Cong. February 22, 1989, 167–8) testified to Congress:

[L]et me stress that the current rate of inflation [4–4.5%], let alone an increase, is not acceptable, and our policies are designed to reduce inflation in coming years. This restraint will involve containing pressures on our productive resources and, thus, some slowing in the underlying rate of growth of real GNP is likely in 1989. The central tendency of GNP forecasts for this year of Board members and Reserve Bank presidents is 2–1/2 to 3 percent; abstracting from the expected rebound from last year's drought losses, real GNP is projected to grow closer to a 2 percent rate.

One can infer that FOMC members hoped to keep real growth enough below trend to raise unemployment but still high enough to prevent recession.[6] However, the FOMC never implemented a strategy to effect such a soft landing. It never specified a NAIRU (nonaccelerating inflation rate of unemployment or full employment) value and a path for unemployment relative to NAIRU that would serve as an intermediate target path the way that money had served in the post-October 1979 period. Basically, the FOMC raised the funds rate steadily to a value that made monetary policy restrictive and then lowered it only cautiously when the economy went into recession. The disinflationary strategy was "opportunistic" in that it avoided any direct association between increases in the funds rate and in the unemployment rate.

Between its March 1988 and May 1989 meeting, the FOMC raised the funds rate from 6 $\frac{1}{2}$% to 9 $\frac{7}{8}$%. The March 28, 1989, FOMC *Record* (Board of Governors, *Record of Policy Actions FOMC, Annual Report 1989*, 87) mentioned "growing market concerns about inflation" and from the end of January to mid March, the 30-year bond rate rose about $\frac{1}{2}$ a percentage point. The short-term real rate moved above 4% in August 1988 and above 5% in early 1989 (Figure 8.3). At the July 1989 meeting, with a fall in the Greenbook prediction of real GNP growth for 1989Q3 to 1.5% and a fall in the 30-year bond rate from a peak of 9.3 to 8.1%, the FOMC lowered the funds rate. However, a general reluctance to lower the funds rate while the bond rate remained high kept the short-term real rate high. It averaged 5% from late 1988 through early 1990.

Initially, real growth declined moderately. From 1986Q3 through 1989Q1, real GNP had grown at an annualized rate of 4.1%. From 1989Q1 through 1989Q4, it grew at an annualized rate of 2.1%. However, the FOMC failed to prevent recession, which began in July 1990 the month before the rise in oil prices set off by the invasion of Kuwait by Iraq.

III. A Soft Landing Becomes a Soft Recovery

The FOMC brought trend inflation down from 5% in 1990 to below 1.5% by the end of 1997 (Figure 14.1). An explanation requires an understanding of the stability of aggregate nominal demand growth from 1990 through 1997, with the exception of the recession year 1991. As a measure of nominal demand (expenditure) growth, Figure 15.1 plots the annual measure of final sales to domestic purchasers. The height of the bar divides into real expenditure growth and inflation. In 1990, this nominal demand growth necessitated a recession given the high inflation rate.

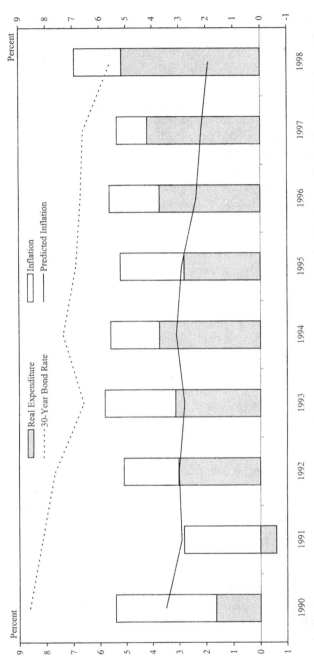

Figure 15.1. The 30-Year Bond Rate, Predicted Inflation, and Growth Rates of Nominal and Real Expenditure. *Notes:* Nominal expenditure is final sales to domestic purchasers (nominal GDP minus the change in business inventories and minus net exports). Real expenditure is real final sales to domestic purchasers. Predicted inflation is an average of four-quarter predicted inflation rates from the 12-monthly forecasts of a year in Global Insight's (formerly Standard & Poor's DRI) *Review of the U.S. Economy,* "Quarterly Summary of the U.S. Economy (Control −)." Until July 1992, the forecast is for the GNP implicit price deflator; from August 1992 to January 1996, it is for the GDP fixed-weight deflator; and from February 1996 on, it is for the chain-weighted GDP price deflator. If the control date is the first or second month of the quarter, the initial forecast quarter is the contemporaneous quarter. If the control date is the third month of the quarter, the initial forecast quarter is the following quarter.

However, it eventually forced a moderation in inflation, which allowed real growth to resume.

With the onset of recession, the FOMC followed a "soft-recovery" strategy in that Greenspan focused on reducing expected inflation. In the absence of credibility, the high real growth normal in recovery would have raised expected inflation. During the recovery from the 1990 recession, preventing a rise in expected inflation (and promoting an eventual decline) required subpar real growth for a recovery.[7] With bond rates above levels consistent with low expected inflation inducing a reluctance to lower the funds rate, not until a year and a half after the July 1990 cycle peak did the FOMC lower the funds rate sufficiently to push down short-term real rates significantly from their prerecession level (Figures 8.3 and 14.2). Stable (rather than rising) expected inflation induced moderate inflation.[8] Moderate (rather than above-trend) real growth combined with moderate inflation to create moderate, stable nominal demand growth. Monetary policy lowered inflation through both an extended negative output gap and a reduction in expected inflation.

Greenspan consistently focused on working down the level of bond rates rather than focusing on them only during inflation scares. In the recovery from the 1990 recession, Greenspan (April 19, 1993) stated as a "goal" the reduction of long-term rates: "The goal of low-to-moderate long-term interest rates is particularly relevant.... We have eased in measured steps ... to reassure investors that inflation is likely to remain subdued, thereby fostering the decline in longer-term interest rates.... [M]onetary policy ... has given considerable weight to encouraging the downtrend of such rates." The FOMC watched the bond market for evidence that its disinflationary policy was credible. A Fed watcher wrote: "The monetary authorities were pleased that long yields declined in anticipation of the Federal Reserve's easing moves. The declines signaled that the long markets believe inflation is waning and that they do not view Federal Reserve easing as a weakening of the central bank's determination to bring inflation under control" (*Washington Bond and Money Market Report* September 13, 1991). The *Wall Street Journal* (July 31, 1992) reported: "[Governor] Angell sees the bond market as a rolling referendum on the Fed's commitment to reducing inflation."

Pressed by President Black (Richmond), Greenspan offered insights into the nature of his disinflation strategy. Black (Board of Governors *Transcripts* November 17, 1992, 45–6) questioned whether the FOMC could use the M2 target range, which the chairman presented in his Hamphrey–Hawkins testimony, to signal a credible commitment to price stability if it moved the range down to accommodate changes in money demand.

Greenspan: [T]here is no debate within this Committee ... that a non-inflationary environment is best.... [W]e have seen that to drive nominal GDP, let's assume at 4-1/2 percent, in our old philosophy we would have said that [requires] 4-1/2 percent growth in M2.... I'm basically arguing that we are really ... using a nominal GDP goal of which the money supply relationships are technical mechanisms to achieve that.

One can infer that Greenspan had an interim 2% inflation target. Between the cyclical peaks 1973Q4 and 1990Q3, productivity averaged about 1.5%.[9] With labor force growth of 1%, a common estimate for trend real GDP growth was 2.5%. Nominal GDP growth of 4.5% would then imply 2% inflation.[10] Black replied:

I agree [establishment of a noninflationary environment] that that's exactly the position of everybody in this room, but I'm not sure that the public is completely convinced.

Greenspan: That may be. They will be convinced only after a period of time; and we will know they are convinced when we see the 30-year Treasury at 5-1/2 percent.

With an estimate of the long-term real interest rate of 3.5%, a 30-year treasury yield of 5.5% would imply expected inflation of 2%. Implicitly, Greenspan suggested that nominal GDP growth or expected inflation (proxied for by the bond rate) had replaced money as an intermediate target. Later, the unpredictability of productivity growth and thus trend real growth left expected inflation as the intermediate target and nominal anchor.[11]

In 1990, the FOMC balanced concern for revived inflationary expectations against weakness in economic activity. In 1988, inflation had begun to rise. CPI inflation was 4.1% in 1988, 4.8% in 1989, and 6.1% in the first half of 1990. In early 1990, monetary restriction began to produce a decline in real activity. The growth rate of payroll employment peaked in March 1990 and then fell steadily through March 1991. The business cycle peaked in July 1990. Concerned about inflation, over the first half of 1990, investors pushed up bond rates (Figure 14.3). In August, Iraq invaded Kuwait. With the rise in oil prices, bond rates jumped.

Although the cycle peak occurred in July 1990, FOMC concern over inflationary expectations delayed significant reductions in the funds rate until late fall. The *Record* (Board of Governors, *Record of Policy Actions FOMC Annual Report 1990*, 142) for the October 2, 1990, FOMC meeting stated: "A number of members expressed strong reservations about any easing.... [T]hey were concerned that any easing in the near term would worsen inflationary expectations.... [S]uch easing might well have the unintended effects of generating upward pressures on long-term interest rates." The first half-point reduction in the funds rate from 8 to 7.5% occurred at the November 13 meeting after the 30-year bond rate declined to 8.6% from its August peak of 9%.

Because the funds rate had peaked at a high level, real rates remained high for a considerable period (Figure 14.2). The FOMC had raised the funds rate to 9.875% after its May 1989 meeting, while core inflation never quite reached 5% (Figure 14.1). The real rate still averaged 4.6% between July 1989 and the cycle peak in July 1990 (Figure 8.3). In the last 5 months of 1990, it averaged 3.5%, only moderately lower than its value at the July peak of 4.3%. After 1990 the real rate declined slowly and did not fall below 2% until December 1991.

The economy experienced a "jobless recovery" from its March 1991 trough. The rise in payroll employment growth from negative values faltered twice – in late

1991 and in fall 1992 (Figure 14.7). Not until April 1992 did employment growth become significantly positive. The unemployment rate peaked in June 1992 at 7.7%. In October 1992, the funds rate reached a low of 3%, where it remained until early 1994. The 1991 economic recovery stands out among postwar recoveries for its weakness (Figure 15.2). In the four prior postwar recoveries (excluding the short-lived recoveries from the 1957 and 1980 recessions), during the three years following the year containing the trough, real GDP grew at about 5% annually. The figure for 1992 through 1994 was only 3.6%.

Despite the weak recovery, the FOMC faced a moderate inflation scare when inflation picked up over the first four months of 1993. Core CPI inflation rose at an annualized rate of 4.5%, up from 2.9% in the last half of 1992. Bond yields, which had fallen to about 6.7% in early March, backed up to 7% in late May. At its May meeting, the FOMC kept the funds rate at 3% but specified an asymmetric directive in favor of tightness. Greenspan (U.S. Cong. July 20, 1993, 47–9) noted:

The process of easing monetary policy ... had to be closely controlled and generally gradual because of the constraint imposed by the marketplace's acute sensitivity to inflation. ... The role of expectations in the inflation process is crucial. Even expectations not validated by economic fundamentals can themselves add appreciably to wage and price pressures for a considerable period, potentially derailing the economy from its growth track. ... The FOMC became concerned that inflation expectations and price pressures, unless contained, could raise long-term interest rates and stall economic expansion.

Subsequently, CPI inflation moderated, bond rates declined after mid June, and the funds rate remained at 3%.

IV. The 1994 Inflation Scare

In 1994, a resurgent economy tested the FOMC's resolve to attain price stability. By September 1993, the economy had begun to grow more strongly and bond rates rose (Figure 14.3). With an unchanged funds rate, the short-term real rate fell. From September 1993 through February 1994, it averaged 0.2% (Figure 8.3). By the February meeting, many FOMC members wanted to raise the funds rate by $\frac{1}{2}$ percentage points. However, Greenspan was willing to move only cautiously.[12] Early in 1994, Greenspan (Board of Governors *Transcripts* February 4, 1994, 55) opposed a significant funds rate increase:

It is *very* unlikely that the recent rate of economic growth will not simmer down largely because some developments involved in this particular period are clearly one-shot factors – namely, the very dramatic increase in residential construction and the big increase in motor vehicle sales. ... I've been in the economic forecasting business since 1948, and I've been on Wall Street since 1948, and I am telling you I have a pain in the pit of my stomach. ... I am telling you – and I've seen these markets – this is not the time to do this [raise the funds rate 50 basis points]. (italics in original)

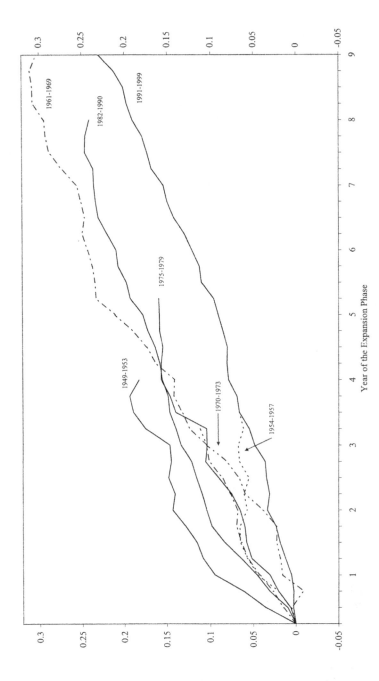

Figure 15.2. Per Capita Output during Economic Recoveries. *Notes*: Observations are the logarithm of quarterly values of real GDP per capita normalized by dividing by the NBER trough value. The graph omits the short-lived recoveries from the 1957 and 1980 recessions.

In the event, the economy did not "simmer down" with a small funds rate increase. The FOMC moved the funds rate up by a quarter percentage point at each of the February and March meetings. Starting in late spring 1994, it began to raise the funds rate decisively. A series of increases left the funds rate at 6% in February 1995 – double its cyclical low of 3%.

In 1994, measures of resource stress flashed red. Capacity utilization rose from just over 80% in mid 1993 to 85% by yearend 1994. Vendor performance (the Institute of Supply Management or ISM measure of delivery times) moved from around 51 in 1993 to 65 by year-end. A consensus existed in the forecasting community that, if the unemployment rate fell to a value somewhat above 6% (the NAIRU), labor costs would begin to rise. The May 1994 Greenbook was unusual in that it gave an explicit number for the NAIRU – 6.5%. The economy passed that threshold when the unemployment rate fell from 6.6% in 1994Q1 to 5.6% in 1994Q3.

Financial markets continued to fear that the FOMC might let inflation revive. Citibank's *Economic Week* (June 13, 1994) stated: "Capacity utilization ... has been edging up toward 85%, the level at which inflation usually starts to heat up.... [T]he remaining slack in the U.S. economy could be used up by year end.... [I]nflation ... will begin to heat up soon."

The 30-year bond rate, which reached a trough on October 15, 1993 of 5.8%, rose to 8.2% on November 4, 1994. The FOMC raised the funds rate at its February and March 1994 meetings in 0.25 percentage point increments from 3 to 3.5%. The dramatic rise in bond rates through most of 1994 conveyed the message from the markets that the FOMC was not moving aggressively enough to counter incipient inflationary pressures. Greenspan abandoned his hallmark quarter-point funds rate changes, and the FOMC raised the funds rate 0.75 percentage points after the May 1994 meeting; 0.5, after the August meeting; 0.75, after the September meeting; and 0.5 again after the February 1995 meeting. In 1994, the FOMC raised the funds rate without first seeing a rise in inflation. Between 1993 and 1994, CPI inflation (year-over-year) fell from 3.0 to 2.6%. That behavior earned the term "preemptive strike."[13] Greenspan (U.S. Cong. February 22, 1994, 12) likened raising the funds rate only after inflation had risen to "looking in a rearview mirror."

For Greenspan (U.S. Cong. June 22, 1994, 23, 11–12), the association between above-trend growth and rising inflationary expectations implied a failure to restore credibility:

[T]he rise in long-term rates has been partially an expectation of ... increased inflation. After World War II ... tightened markets became increasingly associated with rising inflation expectations.... [T]here remains a significant inflation premium embodied in long-term interest rates, reflecting a still skeptical ... view that American fiscal and monetary policies retain some inflation bias.... Having paid so large a price in reversing inflation processes to date, it is crucial that we do not allow them to reemerge.

V. Credibility

The slowness with which the FOMC lowered the funds rate coming out of the 1990 recession kept the lid on nominal expenditure growth in the recovery. In 1994, when the economy began to grow strongly, the FOMC raised the funds rate sharply, restrained nominal expenditure growth, and offset a rise in inflationary expectations. The combination of the 1990 recession, the restraint imposed on expenditure growth in the recovery, and the restrictive actions of 1994 created the conditions for a decline in inflation. From 1995 to 1996, inflation (year-over-year change in chain-weighted GDP deflator) fell from 2.3 to 1.9%. At the same time, real GDP growth rose from 2.3 to 3.4%.

Figure 15.1 exhibits the change from an unfavorable to favorable mix of real growth and inflation that began in 1996.[14] That change occurred with stable nominal expenditure growth around 5.5%. The behavior of inflationary expectations is the key to understanding the change. As shown in Figure 15.1, in the first half of the decade, a modest decline in the bond rate required subpar real growth during economic recovery. In 1994, bond rates rose when real growth rose. In contrast, starting in 1996, the bond rate fell while real growth rose. The 30-year bond rate, which averaged 7.4% in 1994, declined to 5.6% in 1998. The bottom solid line records one-year-ahead inflation forecasts from Global Insight.[15] They fell from an average of 2.9% for the years 1991 through 1995 to 2.4, 2.2, and 1.9%, respectively, in 1996, 1997, and 1998. By the end of the decade, financial markets had stopped associating high real growth with a resurgence of inflation. The Fed had defeated the "bond market vigilantes."

SIXTEEN

International Bailouts and Moral Hazard

In 1995, the treasury led an IMF bailout of foreign investors in Mexico. The bailout set off a chain of destabilizing events. The amount of money potentially made available to prevent default by Mexico on dollar-denominated debt made banks willing to hold large amounts of short-term debt in U.S. allies. That debt made possible the Asia crisis. Banks made what looked like sure one-way bets in lending to Asian banks and then abandoned them en masse when currency devaluations caused insolvencies large enough to threaten the international safety net. The FOMC responded to the Asia crisis with expansionary monetary policy, which exacerbated an unsustainable rise in asset prices. The fall of lofty equity valuations created the 2000 recession.

I. The Mexico Bailout

By late 1994, the Mexican peso had become overvalued due to an unwillingness of the Mexican government to allow the exchange rate to depreciate sufficiently to compensate for domestic inflation. From 1990Q1 through 1994Q3, the Mexican CPI doubled. Over this same period, the U.S. price level rose by 18% and the peso price of the dollar rose by 30%. The combined rise of these last two variables, 48%, offset just less than half of the rise in the Mexican price level. By the end of 1994, U.S. goods looked 50% cheaper to Mexicans than they did at the beginning of the 1990s.[1] Mexicans responded to the relative cheapening of U.S. goods by going on a shopping spree in the United States.

How did Mexico maintain an overvalued exchange rate? Equivalently, how did it finance the associated trade deficit? In part, Mexico maintained the value of the peso by running down the reserves of its central bank. More important, over the years 1991 through 1993, Mexico benefited from heavy inflows of capital. The promise of a North American free trade zone plus low Mexican wages made Mexico an attractive place to invest. Troubles arose in January 1994 with the uprising in Chiapas and assassination in March of Luis Donaldo Colosio, a presidential candidate and secretary-general of the Institutional Revolutionary Party (PRI). Thereafter, foreign investors became increasingly concerned about the stability of the peso.

The government could have let the peso depreciate, but depreciation beyond a minimum amount would have violated the pacto (a wage agreement with the unions).[2] It did not want wage negotiations reopened before the August elections. Helped by the Fed and the U.S. Treasury, which offered loans to Mexico in the form of swaps, Mexico restricted the depreciation of the peso to the amounts agreed upon in the pacto. It did so by offering insurance to investors against exchange rate risk. Much of the investment from the United States had been in short-term financial instruments, rather than in equity or long-term bonds. Mutual funds in particular sold shares to investors lured by the high rates of return earned in many emerging markets. Initially, these funds put money into cetes (peso-denominated government debt). In early 1994, in order to retain this source of capital inflows, the Mexican government switched its debt issue from cetes to Tesobonos, which were indexed to the dollar.

Investors then remained willing to hold Mexican debt. From 1988 to 1994, Mexican banks raised short-term dollar borrowing from $8.6 billion to $24.8 billion (Auerbach 1997, 3). In 1994, Mexico issued $28 billion in Tesobonos to finance its trade deficit and avoid a preelection peso depreciation. By keeping the peso overvalued, it made inevitable a large, discrete fall. (A remark made at the time was that the central bank won the election but lost the peso.) In effect, investors exchanged exchange-rate risk for default risk. After the August 1994 elections, Mexico resisted devaluation to preserve the reputation of past president Raul Salinas, who was campaigning for first head of the new World Trade Organization.

When the inevitability of default became obvious, investors fled, and the peso collapsed in December 1994.[3] Swap lines arranged with the Fed and the treasury helped some investors get their money out of Mexico. The large amount of dollar-denominated debt, however, swamped the swap lines. The administration and the Fed then tried to put together a huge international loan.

The issue was who would pay for the shopping spree the Mexicans went on while the peso was overvalued? Initially, short-term capital inflows had financed the imports from the United States. That "hot money" wanted out. There were two alternatives. One was a partial default on the Tesobonos. It would occur in the form of a forced exchange of the short-term Tesobono debt for long-term, peso-denominated debt paying a low interest rate. The investors who financed the import surge would pay. The alternative was for Mexican taxpayers to pay. If Mexico, helped by U.S. guarantees, borrowed to pay off the Tesobonos, then its taxpayers would pay.

Many of Mexico's banks had issued liabilities denominated in dollars. The devaluation, by lowering the dollar value of their assets, left many insolvent. A rapid fall in real estate prices also hurt bank solvency. There was a fear of a flight of deposits from banks and a collapse of the banking system. The specter of a Venezuelan-style bailout emerged where the government, by printing money to bail out depositors, would set off inflation.

The United States, aided by the IMF and other wealthy countries, put together a rescue package to bail out holders of dollar-denominated Mexican debt. Given the significant bargaining power possessed by Mexico, that result was no surprise. Mexico could threaten the United States with domestic instability, political and economic, that would create large-scale emigration to the United States and also unleash its drug lords. President Clinton needed to prevent the North American Free Trade Agreement (NAFTA) from unraveling.

The treasury had already made contingency plans for emergency aid in October 1993 just before the November vote in Congress over NAFTA (*New York Times* December 12, 1994). It feared that defeat of NAFTA might precipitate a capital outflow from Mexico. The package involved a $12 billion credit line jointly financed by U.S. and European central banks. Half of the $6 billion U.S. commitment came from an increase in the Fed swap line to Mexico from $700 million to $3 billion.[4] NAFTA passed, and the arrangement lapsed.

Congress ratified NAFTA, and Mexico did not at that time draw upon the swap line. In March 1994, in response to the assassination of Colosio, the FOMC increased temporarily the size of the swap line to $6 billion. In August 1994, two weeks before the Mexican presidential election, the FOMC again approved a temporary increase in the swap line to $6 billion. This time, Japan joined. Mexico did not use the swap line. In December 1994, its foreign exchange reserve depleted by capital flight, Mexico abandoned the exchange rate peg and the peso plummeted.

On January 31, 1995, Clinton and congressional leaders announced a $47.8 billion Mexican aid package. It included $20 billion from the United States, $17.8 billion from the IMF, and $10 billion from the central banks of G-10 countries lending through the BIS.[5] The FOMC positioned itself to make up to $26 billion available to Mexico. The FOMC raised its Mexican swap line back to $6 billion and raised to $20 billion the amount of yen and deutsche marks it stood ready to warehouse for the ESF. Mexico drew on the swap lines and the ESF at various times.[6] Although the Fed had lent funds to Mexico in the past via swap lines, for example, after the 1988 presidential election, the 1995 arrangement was unprecedented in size and in potential duration. Past loans did not exceed $1 billion, and Mexico repaid them within six months.

The Mexican bailout allowed foreign investors holding short-term, dollar-denominated Mexican debt to escape unscathed. That escape had two consequences. First, it saddled Mexican taxpayers with the cost of bailing out the Mexican banking system – $60 billion as of December 1998 (15% of GDP). Second, it set the precedent that the United States would not allow the banking systems of its strategic allies to default on foreign debt.[7]

II. Moral Hazard

On July 2, 1997, Thailand devalued its currency, the baht. A cascade of events followed that shook the international financial system. Seemingly prosperous economies in Asia collapsed with little obvious warning. Popular commentary attributed the crisis to the herd behavior of investors. But bankers are in the business of assessing risk. Why would they have lent in the first place on the basis of minimal information about the health of Asian banking systems? And then why would they flee en masse? Moral hazard created by the IMF offers answers.

The IMF bailed out international investors in Mexico in early February 1995, the year that bank flows to Asia rose dramatically. Large money center banks believed that the United States and the other G-7 countries would use the IMF to prevent the financial collapse of strategically important countries. At a conference on Asia sponsored by the IMF and the Federal Reserve Bank of Chicago in Chicago October 8–10, 1998, a director of the Deutsche Bundesbank, Helmut Schieber, said in comments that the Bundesbank had asked German banks why they had lent so heavily to Pacific Rim banks. According to him, they replied that they believed the IMF would bail them out in case of trouble (author's notes).

Led by the United States, the G-7 countries concluded from the Mexican experience that the IMF needed more resources. At the 1995 and 1996 G-7 summits, participants agreed on funding increases and an expedited decision-making process for emergency lending. They agreed upon a 45% increase in member quotas to raise IMF capital to $285 billion. They also agreed to create a new lending facility called the New Arrangements to Borrow with $21 billion in addition to the General Arrangements to Borrow. The U.S. share amounted respectively to $14.4 billion and $3.5 billion for each part. The amounts involved in subsequent IMF bailouts rose dramatically. During the Asia crisis, in billions, South Korea got a $58.2 package, Indonesia $47.7, Brazil $41, Russia $22.6, and Thailand $17.2.

From 1977 through 1989, capital flows to the emerging markets of Asia averaged about $16 billion per year. From 1990 to 1994, they rose to $40 billion. Then in 1995 and 1996, they surged to $103 billion annually, before falling to only $13.9 billion in 1997 (see IMF 1995, 33; 1998, 13). Large banks generated the sharp swings in capital flows. Over the period 1993 through 1997, portfolio investment by institutional investors and foreign direct investment remained steady at about $15 billion and $10 billion per year, respectively. Capital inflows from foreign banks to Indonesia, Korea, Malaysia, the Philippines, and Thailand averaged $16 billion per year from 1990 to 1994. Foreign bank lending then rose to $58 billion for most of 1995 and 1996. It fell to an annual rate of $22 billion in 1996Q4 and most of 1997. In 1997Q4 and 1998Q1, banks withdrew over $75 billion in funds.[8] For example, in Thailand, short-term credit extended by foreign banks grew by 35% from December 1995 through June 1996. From June 1997 through December 1997, it fell almost 35% (World Bank 1998, 161).[9]

The IMF characterized its assistance to Mexico as responding to a financial panic. In Mexico, as in Asia, its strategy was to put together an aid package with an enormous headline amount to convince investors that they could again invest safely in the country. To reassure investors, the IMF prevented foreign banks from losing money. The IMF pressures debtor countries not to default by never lending into arrears. (The IMF does not lend to a country if it is in default on its foreign debts.) As a result, banks had good reason to believe that they would be bailed out in the case of debt defaults.[10] Krueger (1998, 2014) wrote: "It seems plausible that, especially after Mexico, bankers came to believe that the IMF would always bail them out and therefore they did not feel the need to concern themselves greatly with individual countries' economic policies." Greenspan (May 7, 1998, 4) said: "I pointed earlier to cross-border interbank funding as potentially the Achilles' heel of the international financial system. Creditor banks expect claims on banks, especially in emerging economies, to be protected by a safety net and, consequently, consider them essentially sovereign claims."

Furthermore, banks are in a strong position to ask their governments to pressure debtor countries to guarantee loans against default. The IMF must keep them in countries it is assisting; otherwise, newspapers will characterize IMF lending as a large bank bailout. In the case of Korea, government officials and regulators urged banks not to withdraw. The *New York Times* (January 2, 1998) reported: "Treasury Secretary Robert E. Rubin has also played a forceful role with the banks, personally calling chief executives at some of the largest banks to make them aware of America's interest in seeing South Korea through its economic crisis." Bank regulators in other countries followed suit (*Wall Street Journal* December 31, 1997).

III. The Asian Crisis

The Asian Tigers had oriented their economies toward exporting to the West. Powered by exports, they had grown phenomenally. By opening their economies to trade, they had traveled part way to a free market economy. However, they had yet to adopt competitive capital markets and financial systems.

A. The No-Fail Policy

Most Pacific Rim countries followed the Japanese "main bank" system. In the postwar period, Japanese bureaucrats in the Ministry of International Trade and Industry (MITI) and the Finance Ministry allocated credit to corporations that promoted national objectives, especially by exporting. The absence of domestic capital markets that could compete for savings meant that governments could keep bank deposit rates low and subsidize favored corporations with cheap credit. Also, the "convoy system" meant that banks kept afloat troubled corporations until the government and other corporations in its group could organize a rescue that did not involve bankruptcy and layoffs. Banks existed to channel cheap funds to favored industries, not to winnow the weak from the strong. This system encouraged debt rather than equity financing. Because governments kept large conglomerates from failing, conglomerates could finance themselves with debt rather than equity. In 1996, Korean manufacturing companies had debt–equity ratios of more than 300% – three times the U.S. average.

The system bred corruption. For example, in Korea in 1997, when Hanbo Iron and Steel went bankrupt, its chairman paid several hundred million dollars to bribe officials to continue to authorize cheap bank loans (*New York Times* January 4, 1998). The system also favored an oversupply of large-scale manufacturing facilities. The financial system lacked the ability to reallocate resources in response to changes in international comparative advantage. Banks could not foreclose on loans and force customers into bankruptcy because of the social stigma of creating unemployment. The financial system worked to preserve the status quo when it should have promoted a shift from manufacturing to a service economy. By encouraging growth without requiring profitability, the Asian financial system became an engine for disaster.

B. Overvalued Exchange Rates Collapse

The breakdown in Asia of currency pegs to the dollar precipitated the crisis. A combination of factors rendered the currencies of the Asian Tigers overvalued. The demand for their exports to Japan faltered, especially after Japan entered into recession in summer 1997. For the first part of the 1990s, the depreciation of the dollar had made the exports of the Tigers more competitive. However, in 1995 the dollar began to appreciate, and their exports became less competitive. China challenged the industrial dominance of the Tigers. Slow growth in Europe reduced the demand for consumer electronics.

Rather than disinflate to prevent their currencies from becoming overvalued, the central banks of the Tigers ran down their foreign exchange reserves. Central bank secrecy kept knowledge of the loss of reserves from the market until their virtual depletion. Markets then forced sudden depreciations. When Thailand allowed its currency to float, its central bank had spent $60 billion to maintain a pegged rate to the dollar. The devaluations came as a shock. Taking advantage of lower dollar-denominated interest rates, Asian businesses and banks had borrowed heavily in dollars without hedging. Devaluation made many of them insolvent. Financial and economic collapse then spread.

The crisis revealed a pattern of credit allocation on the basis of personal relations. The banking system could not put borrowers out of business by pulling the plug on companies that did not generate the cash flow to pay their loans. The rapid growth associated with the adoption by Asia of Western technology had made this triage function unnecessary. But, inevitably Asian economies had to adjust to a reduction in rapid growth and make a transition away from heavy industry to a service-oriented economy. The low profitability of the existing system, its corruption, and its inability to reallocate resources from less productive to more productive activities produced a calamitous collapse.

Initially, none of the Asian governments could put together a political consensus to submit to an IMF program of structural reform and fiscal austerity. It also became evident that the cost of bailing out banks would amount to a large fraction of GDP. The implicit government guarantees that had made investors willing to tolerate high debt levels for conglomerates appeared problematic. Investors feared the disappearance of the safety net, so they fled. Their flight turned a moderate into a huge depreciation, which exposed the unhedged dollar debt of banks and businesses.

Both fixed exchange rates and IMF funded bank bailouts created the same perverse incentives. Each created one-way bets for investors and rewards for being first out in the event of trouble. Each of the large banks lent on the assumption that it could be the first out. However, when one jumped, they all jumped. The popular press talked of "herd behavior," but investors behaved rationally faced with socially perverse incentives.

C. Conditional IMF Lending

In Manila in November 1997, Treasury Deputy Secretary Lawrence Summers outlined the U.S.–IMF strategy to deal with the Asia crisis: The IMF would require a rigorous reform program in return for loans (*Financial Times* January 2, 1998). A strong reform program would persuade investors to remain in troubled countries so that IMF and G-7 money would not simply serve to bail out fleeing investors. The IMF model of reassuring investors with promises of future reforms did not work in Asia where reform required not so much fiscal discipline as the replacement of political favoritism with market discipline. Fears of social instability and street violence overwhelmed the promise of future reform. Economic disruption then highlighted the absence of bankruptcy laws and independent court systems willing to deliver assets to foreign investors.

The IMF strategy fell apart immediately in Korea. South Korea did not agree to the $57 billion IMF package announced December 3, and the won continued to fall. Nevertheless, the IMF delivered its loans up front without tying them to implementation of reform. In doing so, it avoided blame for default by Korean commercial banks. However, the priority attached to averting private-sector bank losses meant that the IMF could not make its lending conditional. And it could not exercise leverage to compel the foreign creditors of Korean banks to work out a debt rescheduling that would impose losses on those foreign creditors.

On October 8, 1997, the IMF, the Asian Development Bank, and the World Bank offered Indonesia a $37 billion aid package. Indonesia provided a test of the assumption that the IMF can restore investor confidence by obtaining credible promises of reform in return for aid. "IMF and World Bank officials acknowledge that they were hoping investors would stampede back into the rupiah following the announcement of the reform package" (*Washington Post* January 17, 1998). However, the bargaining power of the IMF is limited when the aid recipient is a strategic ally of the West. In explaining the U.S. contribution of $3 billion to Indonesia,

Treasury Secretary Rubin (*New York Times* November 1, 1997) stated: "Financial stability around the world is critical to the national security and economic interests of the United States." Indonesia not only controls the strategic Straits of Molucca but also has a history of unrest. An estimated half million Indonesians perished in the unrest in 1965 following the fall of Suharto's predecessor Sukarno.[11]

Moreover, economic reform in Indonesia undermined the political system. "Nor did the IMF seem to fully appreciate the extent to which bank closures and the removal of monopolies would undermine former president Suharto's political base and, consequently, how unlikely it would be that he and his allies would ever really adhere to the three successive programs imposed on the regime in return for financial assistance" (Muehring 1998, 86). In dealing with American allies in a crisis, the IMF cannot credibly commit either to withholding aid or to making foreign investors take losses. The *Wall Street Journal* (September 19, 1997) explained the Thai rescue package, the first to follow Mexico:

One government expert compared the situation to the dilemma presented by a kidnapper's demand for ransom.... It may... be best to have a firm policy of never paying ransom. But once someone is kidnapped, it isn't a good time to... enforce such a policy. The need to rescue Mexico and Thailand, Treasury officials reason, outweighed the virtue of punishing investors.

IV. The Russian Crisis

In late May 1998, against a background of crisis in Asia, investors became reluctant to buy Russian debt. Russian Prime Minister Kiriyenko lacked the political clout to pressure the Duma into balancing the budget. Russia had achieved budget balance only by not paying wages to workers of state-owned enterprises. However, strikes by coal miners forced the government into promising to pay back wages. The Duma, dominated by the oligarchs who controlled Russian industry, refused to force companies to pay taxes. A decline in oil prices pushed Russia over the brink.

On July 10, 1998, Russian President Boris Yeltsin called President Clinton for assistance. Treasury Deputy Secretary Larry Summers and Undersecretary David Lipton worked with the G-7 to put together an additional aid package for Russia (Muehring 1998, 90). On July 20, the IMF approved $11.2 billion in aid in addition to the $14.3 billion already outstanding. In the statement announcing the additional aid, the IMF noted: "Unfortunately, parliamentary backing has not been forthcoming for needed actions relating to the personal income tax" (IMF August 3, 1998, 1).

Foreign investors, attracted by Russian bill yields of 90%, continued to finance government deficits. They assumed that the West would not let Russia default on its foreign debt ("too nuclear to fail"). However, Russia immediately ran through an initial $5 billion in IMF funds. When Russia asked for more funds without undertaking reforms, the West refused. On August 13, George Soros called for ruble devaluation, and Russian stocks and bonds plummeted. On August 17, the Russian central bank devalued the ruble and decreed a moratorium of 90 days on payments by Russian banks, including some $50 billion due on forward contracts. On August 23, Yeltsin fired his reformist prime minister and reappointed Viktor Chernomyrdin, who had dithered for years instead of reforming as prime minister in the early 1990s. On August 26, Russia suspended foreign exchange trading.

The fall in the ruble's value following the end of central bank intervention in foreign exchange markets made clear that Russian banks could not pay their dollar-denominated debts. Also, the Russian government changed the rules of the game so that investors could not seize the assets of defaulting banks (*Euromoney* 1998, 58; *Financial Times* August 28, 1998, 3). The central bank allowed Russian banks to reduce their capital so that there would be no assets left to seize in default. The Russian debt moratorium set off a worldwide shock in financial markets. By August 31, the DJIA had fallen 20% from its July 17 peak. The MSCI Index, a world stock market index, fell 13.4% in August. In September, the Nikkei hit a 12-year low. A flight-to-quality pushed the 30-year treasury bond yield down to a low of 4.7% in October.

Suddenly, the world appeared to be a much riskier place for investors. "The speed at which the hundreds of billions of dollars that flowed into emerging economies in the 1990s have flowed out was ... unprecedented. The inflow occurred, [Treasury Secretary] said, because 'investors got progressively less rigorous about risk.' Now they see risk everywhere, Rubin and other Treasury officials note" (*Richmond Times Dispatch* September 6, 1998). Investors began to shun risk, most especially in emerging markets. Lending to emerging markets had amounted to $63 billion from January through July 1998 but then virtually ceased in August. It fell from $11 billion in August 1997 to $2.6 billion in August 1998 (*Wall Street Journal* September 8, 1998).

Given the trivial size of the Russian economy relative to the world economy, the reaction of world markets appeared irrational. Its economy was the size of the Netherlands and accounted for less than 1% of U.S. exports. Foreign holdings of Russian assets were large only in absolute terms. The Institute of International Finance estimated outside debt and equity holdings at $200 billion (*Financial Times* August 28, 1998, 3). Markets reacted to the Russian debt default because suddenly the world appeared riskier.

The wealthy countries of the world became unable to provide the financial aid necessary to keep afloat the economies of other countries strategic to world security. Their inability reflected the absence of leadership. Polls showed in Germany that Gerhard Schroeder would defeat Chancellor Kohl in fall elections. Prime Minister Yeltsin of Russia disappeared into the countryside whenever there was a crisis. The Japanese Prime Minister Keizo Obuchi was an aging Liberal Democratic Party (LDP) dealmaker with no expertise in finance and whose tenure at the time was widely acknowledged as temporary. The world looked to the United States, but found a weak president. Clinton had been unable to persuade Congress and his own party to give him fast-track trade negotiating authority or to fund the UN and was mired in the Monica Lewinsky scandal.

Clinton's weakness hindered administration efforts to persuade the Republican Congress to provide increased capital for the IMF. The IMF lacked the resources to counter the huge swings in capital flows in 1998. Furthermore, Japan, which had offered in fall 1997 to replace IMF lending to Asian countries like Thailand, became immobilized by the looming necessity of recapitalizing its banking system. The German government had provided considerable aid to Russia by guaranteeing $30 billion in loans by its banks since 1991. However, further support became impossible when the opposition Social Democrats made the guarantees a political issue.

Investors had bought Russian government debt only because of Western guarantees. The abrupt end of those guarantees produced the Russian shock that threw world financial markets into turmoil. With no IMF, there would have been no shock.

V. Concluding Comment

With the fall of the Berlin Wall in 1989, a belief in free markets and the free flow of capital triumphed. However, by 1998, talk of protectionism and capital controls proliferated. Discourse emphasized the supposed irrationality of investor behavior. Supporters of market irrationality pointed to three phenomena. First, they stressed the sudden, cataclysmic decline in asset values in Asian financial markets. For example, at one point, the Indonesian rupiah lost 80% of its value. Second, they stressed overshooting, like the large declines in Asian stock markets followed by recoveries. Third, they pointed to contagion. Starting from weakness in Thailand, like dominoes, markets collapsed in Thailand, Indonesia, Malaysia, Korea, and Russia.

However, market irrationality was not the source of the financial crisis that began in 1997. The fundamental source was the moral hazard created by the investor safety net put together by the no-fail policies of governments in emerging-market economies for their financial sectors and underwritten by IMF credit lines. The Fed response to the Asia crisis would propagate asset market volatility by exacerbating a rise in U.S. equity markets.

APPENDIX: SEIGNIORAGE AND CREDIT ALLOCATION

Central banks can engage in fiscal policy (off-budget taxing and spending) through seigniorage (Hetzel 1996). Seigniorage is the transfer of resources to government for issuing money. To understand how the government records seigniorage, consider the following example: The Fed purchases a government security from the public, and simultaneously the treasury sells a government security to the public. The debt outstanding in the hands of the public does not change. However, the treasury now has additional funds in its checking account at the Fed. The treasury then spends those funds. The *actual gain* from seigniorage to the government occurs with this transaction. The government has gained real resources in return for issuing paper money, or its electronic equivalent of bank reserves. As a consequence of this transaction, the Fed holds additional government securities. Over time, it returns the interest on those securities to the government. The *public record* of seigniorage occurs when the government records those transfers from the Fed as part of its receipts.

The way the government records the gains from seigniorage is a bookkeeping convention, but an important one. The Fed records as its income the interest on the government securities it holds. As a result, it does not have to depend upon appropriations from the government for its operation. Also, the revenue from seigniorage appears explicitly as a receipt of the government. Because Congress decides how to spend these receipts as part of its appropriations process, there is democratic oversight.

As part of the bookkeeping arrangements that buttress Fed independence, government accounts treat the Fed as a member of the public. In order to measure accurately the fiscal policy actions of the government, however, the balance sheets of both the treasury and the Fed should be consolidated. The reason is that the Fed turns over to the treasury the interest it receives on the government securities it holds (above its costs). As far as the government is concerned, interest paid on securities held by the Fed is a wash. For the purposes of fiscal policy, the key implication is that it makes no difference whether the treasury or the Fed sells a security to the public. Either way, there is an increase in the debt on which the federal government must pay interest financed by some future increase in taxes or reduction in expenditure. In short, the Fed, like the treasury can take fiscal policy actions. Consider the following examples.

The Fed can make a discount window loan to an insolvent bank. For example, in 1984 it lent Continental Illinois Bank somewhat more than $7 billion, 85% of the bank's uninsured deposits. In conjunction with such lending, the Fed sold government securities from its portfolio to keep bank reserves unchanged. That is, it engaged in a pure fiscal policy action with no consequences for monetary policy. Government debt in the hands of the (non-Fed) public rose. Control over the composition of its asset portfolio gives the Fed the ability to engage in fiscal policy; in this case, it is in the form of credit allocation.[12]

Consider next the direct monetization of treasury assets that occurs when the Fed acquires assets from the treasury's Exchange Stabilization Fund (ESF). These assets take the form either of SDRs or foreign exchange.[13] When the Fed acquires assets from the ESF, it credits the treasury's deposit account at the New York Fed. When the treasury draws down its newly acquired deposits, the reserves of the banking system increase. The Fed then sells treasury securities out of its portfolio to offset that increase. The net result is to substitute either an SDR or an asset denominated in foreign exchange for a treasury security in the Fed's portfolio.[14] Government securities held by the (non-Fed) public rise, and the Fed finances the activities of ESF foreign exchange intervention.

Seigniorage allows the Fed to engage in lending to foreign countries. Consider a swap between the Fed and a foreign central bank. In a swap with Mexico's central bank, the Fed accepts peso deposits in exchange for dollar deposits. The Fed invests the pesos in a peso-denominated security. When Mexico spends the dollars it receives, bank reserves in the United States increase. The Fed then sells a treasury security to offset that increase. The net result is to substitute a peso-denominated security for a treasury security in the Fed's portfolio. Government securities held by the (non-Fed) public rise.[15]

The Fed established swap lines with foreign central banks in 1962 to defend the fixed exchange rate system without raising interest rates (Hetzel 1996). The collapse of the fixed rate system in 1973 eliminated the rationale for swaps. The Fed, however, put them to another use. For instance, in 1973, the administration asked the Fed to help Italy deal with the increase in its balance of payments deficit in the aftermath of the large rise in oil prices. "The Federal Reserve … came to the aid of Italy, whose chronic political instability prevented rapid response to the energy crisis. The central bank expanded its swap line with the Bank of Italy from $2 billion to $3 billion to help that country finance imports in the short run" (Wells 1994, 125).

The use of swaps to provide short-term assistance to foreign countries has prompted debate within the FOMC. In response to a question from a governor about whether the Fed might provide long-term assistance to Italy, Burns (Board of Governors *Minutes* July 16, 1974, 783) responded:

If the Federal Reserve were to abandon the principle that the swap lines were available only to meet short-term needs, there would be a natural tendency for other agencies of Government to look to the System, rather than to Congress, for the resources to deal with a broad variety of international financial and political problems. If the System were to provide those resources it would, in effect, be substituting its own authority for that of the Congress. A decisive case could then be made in support of the charge that the System was using Federal moneys without regard to the intent of the Congress.

Congress delegated to the Fed the monopoly on the creation of the monetary base. Money creation allows the Fed to undertake fiscal policy independent of Congress. Such operations are not subject to the open debate generated by congressional actions. Therefore, they limit the accountability provided for in the provision of the Constitution that "[n]o money shall be drawn from the Treasury, but in consequence of appropriations made by law." The use of seigniorage revenues by the central bank for purposes other than financing its own operation reduces the public's ability to monitor government activities and erodes constitutional safeguards.[16]

SEVENTEEN

Monetary Policy Becomes Expansionary

Credibility allowed the FOMC to run an expansionary monetary policy in response to the international economic crises that started in summer 1997. Expansionary policy appeared initially as strong real growth not inflation.

I. The Fed's Response to Asia

In 1997, the FOMC debated how to reconcile strength in the economy and a falling unemployment rate with low inflation. At his July 1997 Humphrey–Hawkins testimony, Greenspan talked of a "new paradigm" where technological growth would keep capacity in line with increased demand. However, he added that growth in employment could not indefinitely exceed growth of the labor force. By fall, the unemployment rate had fallen to 4.8%. In October 1997, a hawkish Greenspan (December 1997, 965) warned Congress: "The law of supply and demand has not been repealed.... Short of a marked slowing in the demand for goods and services...the imbalance between the growth in labor demand and expansion of potential labor supply...must eventually erode the current state of inflation quiescence."

Markets assumed that the FOMC was ready to raise the funds rate. Subsequently, the Asia crisis emerged. Although a rate hike had appeared likely at the November FOMC meeting, stock market volatility intervened. Concern over weakness in Asian equity markets produced a fall of 554 points in the DJIA on October 27, 1997. Added to the declines of the two prior days, the index fell 10.9%. Asia then came to dominate policy.

At its November meeting, the FOMC refrained from raising rates to avoid strengthening the dollar. A rise in the foreign exchange value of the dollar would have made it harder for Asian countries to repay their dollar-denominated debts. The *Minutes* (Board of Governors, *Minutes of FOMC Meetings, Annual Report 1997*, 166) of the meeting stated that "While developments in Southeast Asia were not expected to have much effect on the U.S. economy, global financial markets had not yet settled down.... [A] tightening of U.S. monetary policy risked an oversized reaction." Greenspan (U.S. Cong. July 21, 1998, 32) later acknowledged the constraint on FOMC actions in 1997 and 1998 from fear of dollar appreciation. "[W]e need to be aware that monetary policy tightening actions in the United States could have outsized effects on very sensitive financial markets in Asia." Stanley Fischer, first managing IMF director, warned developed countries not to raise interest rates as they were "the prime determinant of capital flows to the developing countries" (*Financial Times* May 6, 1998).

In fall 1997 the FOMC suspended its practice of raising the funds rate in response to strength in economic activity. For the next year and a half, it relied on forecasts that economic weakness in Asia would slow unsustainably high domestic growth. Net exports would fall due to a widening of current account surpluses of Asian countries. Deterioration in corporate profits would reduce corporate investment. And deteriorating profits would weaken consumption by inducing a fall in the stock market. The December 16, 1997, Greenbook stated: "Virtually all signs point to a continuation this quarter of the economic pattern we have been witnessing for some time: strong growth of real GDP, huge gains in jobs.... We are predicting a marked deceleration [in real GDP growth] in the near term."

Incoming data contradicted the forecast of economic slowing, and the FOMC waited in vain for the economy to slow (Figure 13.2).

II. Russian Default, LTCM, and Capital Flight from Emerging Markets

In August 1998, Russia defaulted on its debt. Prior to the Russian crisis, the Greenbook had assumed that the economy would slow to a sustainable growth rate without a rise in the funds rate. After the Russian crisis, the FOMC actively lowered the funds rate both to prevent a possible future decline in economic activity and to counter a market psychology of risk aversion. After Russia, forecasters talked of world recession and deflation with spillover effects that could tip the United States into recession.

On September 4, Greenspan (September 4, 1998) delivered a speech intended to calm financial markets. He disregarded the emphasis on labor market tightness of the prior July Humphrey–Hawkins testimony and went on to say that foreign developments not only would continue to restrain inflation in the United States but also would impact U.S. prosperity negatively. The DJIA rose 387 points on September 8, the first day of trading after the Labor Day weekend. The dollar also fell against other currencies.

Greenspan and Rubin testified before the House Banking Committee on September 16. There, Greenspan repeated the statement in his earlier speech that "it is not credible to perceive that we can remain an oasis of prosperity ... with the rest of the world under increasing stress." However, market observers interpreted Greenspan's reassuring words about the U.S. economy as indicating that the FOMC might not reduce rates at its September meeting. To correct that misimpression, on September 23, Greenspan (November 1998) testified before the Senate Budget Committee and repeated the "oasis" statement. Market observers concluded the Fed would ease, and the DJIA rose 257 points by the end of the day.

Uncertainty in financial markets peaked with the near collapse of the hedge fund Long-Term Capital Management (LTCM) and with the associated heavy losses announced at large money center banks. John Meriwether, a former bond trader at Salomon Brothers, created LTCM in 1993 along with two academic Nobel Prize winners, Myron Scholes and Robert Merton, and former Board of Governors vice chairman David Mullins, Jr. LTCM made bets that unusually wide interest rate spreads between risky and safe securities would revert to normal values.

The company used high amounts of leverage to increase the profits derived from the arbitrage of yield differences slightly out of line with historical differences. It would borrow from banks to purchase securities, which then served as collateral for the loan. Next it would create a derivative the value of which would be tied to a security whose yield appeared out of line with the purchased security. The resulting bet would not be directional. That is, LTCM would neither win nor lose if the level of market interest rates changed without affecting the yield spread between the two instruments. It would win if the yield spread narrowed, but lose if it widened.

Early in 1998, LTCM made two fatal mistakes. It returned capital to its owners so as to increase its debt leverage to a ratio of more than 35 to 1. Also, it began to take "directional" trades by moving into emerging-market debt. The effective default by Russia on its debt raised risk premia on emerging-market debt. It also set off a flight to quality that depressed yields on U.S. bonds. LTCM's market convergence and directional bets soured. At the end of August, as their equity vanished, the partners of LTCM attempted unsuccessfully to raise new capital.

In late September, the New York Fed helped facilitate a bailout to keep LTCM afloat. On September 22, Peter Fisher, senior vice president at the New York Fed, called a meeting at the Fed with Goldman Sachs, J. P. Morgan, the Swiss bank UBS, and Merrill Lynch. That group then held a meeting with LTCM's other large creditors. Fisher told the group "that a collapse of the investment partnership could be chaotic for markets and that there was a public interest in a collective industry option to keep Long-Term Capital afloat" (*New York Times* November 2, 1998). He said: "[T]he systemic market risk posed by LTCM going into default was very real" (*Wall Street Journal* November 16, 1998).

The next day New York Fed President William McDonough adjourned the meeting to consider a bid to buy LTCM by Warren Buffet. Goldman Sachs would manage LTCM and Meriwether would have to leave. However, Meriwether turned down the offer. McDonough then returned to the group, which organized a consortium to keep LTCM afloat. Its members agreed to inject $3.6 billion in capital.

The members of the consortium had a self-interest in keeping LTCM afloat. The pre-August perception that the IMF, backed by the G-7, would prevent the collapse of the financial systems of strategic emerging-market countries created an incentive for all the large bond houses and money center banks to take the same bets as LTCM. If LTCM failed, it would have to liquidate its securities positions, which were large and of unknown size. In a buyers market, the price of the dumped securities might have fallen drastically. Bond houses and large money center banks would have suffered additional losses. Even without the failure of LTCM, large money center banks suffered heavy losses. Bank of Boston, J. P. Morgan, and Citigroup all reported heavy third-quarter trading losses. The Bank of America, recently merged with Nationsbank, lost the $1.7 billion it had loaned to D. E. Shaw, a hedge fund that made bets similar to LTCM.

Greenspan (U.S. Cong. June 17, 1999, 9) testified that the FOMC lowered the funds rate to ensure that markets would clear:

[A] benign economic environment can induce investors to take on more risk and drive asset prices to unsustainable levels. . . . The Asian crisis, and especially the Russian devaluation and debt moratorium of August 1998, brought the inevitable rude awakening. In the ensuing weeks, financial markets in the United States virtually seized up, risk premiums soared, and for a period sellers of even investment-grade bonds had difficulty finding buyers. The Federal Reserve responded with a three-step reduction in the federal funds rate totaling 75 basis points.

Did markets really stop clearing ("seized up") as Greenspan contended? Risk premia charged for lending to emerging markets rose dramatically, but did a "contagion" spread to the rest of the money market? The *New York Times* (September 17, 1998, C1) wrote that "sales of risky over-the-counter bonds such as junk bonds and convertible bonds tied to small stocks dried up in the fall as investors reassessed their risk exposure." Issuance of commercial mortgage-backed securities dried up. However, intermediation that had gone through the money market then went through banks, which were well capitalized and capable of handling a surge in credit demand. Businesses with low credit ratings drew on lines of credit. Bank credit, which had grown at an annualized rate of 5.5% in the first half of 1998, rose at annualized rates of 18.7, 16.6, and 28.4% in August, September, and October, respectively (Board of Governors release H.8). Also, the Fed's funds rate peg made it possible for banks to create money in response to increased liquidity demand. From August through November, M2 growth averaged an annualized 12.3%.

Business remained largely unaffected by the market's increased aversion to risk. Risk premia rose only moderately for most private lending. Spreads on junk (high-yield) bonds over that of comparable treasury securities (seven-year notes) rose from an average of somewhat more than 3 percentage points in 1997 and the first half of 1998 to a peak of almost 7 percentage points in October. (The spread averaged 4.9 for 1980 to 1997.) Moody's composite yield spread for Baa less Aaa corporate bonds rose to 0.9 percentage points in November from an average of 0.6 in the first half of 1998. However, the spread had averaged 1.2 in the period 1980 to 1997.

The real problem was the market for emerging-market debt not domestic debt. Risk premia (measured by the spread between the J. P. Morgan Emerging-Market Bond Index of stripped Brady bonds and comparable treasury yields) on such debt had been rising all year due to the fall in commodity prices produced by the Asian recession, and they soared after the Russian default. Early in 1997, they had averaged around 3 percentage points. The Asia crisis pushed the spread up to 6 percentage points. Then from July to September, it rose from 6 to 16 percentage points.

At the time, it was possible to imagine a sequence of events leading to world recession. During the LTCM crisis, the treasury and IMF were involved in negotiations with Brazil. Brazil, with both a large internal and external deficit, could have suffered financial collapse. Such a collapse could have precipitated another series of foreign exchange crises in emerging markets. In the first half of 1998, the world economy had ceased growing. Moderate growth in Canada, Europe, and Latin America just offset negative growth in Asia including Japan. World recession not only would have reduced U.S. growth through a fall in its exports but also would have created additional protectionist pressures arising from the widening U.S. current account deficit.

At its September meeting, the FOMC lowered the funds rate based on a forecast of slowing. Governor Meyer (October 5, 1998) said, "[T]the current move can be justified in a forward-looking variant of the Taylor Rule, where today's policy depends on the forecast of future output gaps and inflation." On October 15, in a telephone conference, the FOMC lowered the funds rate another 0.25 percentage point to 5%. The surprise move began a rally in world financial markets. The FOMC had received little new information about the economy since its last meeting. The easing could only have reflected continuing concern with financial markets. The FOMC issued the statement that "Growing caution by lenders and unsettled conditions in financial markets more generally are likely to be restraining aggregate demand in the future." Greenspan (September 4, 1998) talked of a vicious cycle: "Our experiences with those vicious cycles in Asia emphasize the key role in a market economy of a critical human attribute: confidence or trust in the functioning of a market system. . . . A key characteristic, perhaps the fundamental cause of a vicious cycle, is the loss of trust." Other central banks reduced their discount rates.

In October, the bad news turned into an uninterrupted string of good news. On October 7, the Japanese government announced a bank recapitalization bill to provide up to $500 billion (12% of GDP) in aid for its banks. Brazil stabilized after Secretary Rubin's speech on September 11 in which he stated that "[t]he financial stability and prosperity of Brazil is of vital importance to the U.S." (*New York Times* September 24, 1998). This speech plus a speech by President Clinton in which he mentioned IMF and G-7 emergency aid to Brazil convinced investors that a devaluation of the Brazilian real was unlikely.

In congressional testimony on September 23, 1998, Greenspan (November 1998) provided the rationale for an international effort to prevent a Brazilian debt default and devaluation. He used the word "contagion" repeatedly and warned: "There is little evidence to suggest that the contagion has subsided." Greenspan explained that the Fed and the United States, along with other G-7 countries, would act to counteract the capital flight from emerging markets. The Republican Congress, not wanting to give Clinton a campaign issue that would distract from the Lewinsky affair, authorized an $18 billion funding increase for the IMF. The IMF and G-7 countries then put together a $41.5 billion aid package for Brazil.

An unexpectedly strong showing by Democrats in the November 3 elections removed the uncertainty of a presidential impeachment. Happy with the economy, voters were not in the angry mood that would have supported impeachment of President Clinton. An Election Day poll in The *New York Times* revealed that only 12% of voters said that their financial situation was worse "today" than two years ago. Only 21% thought the economy would worsen in 1999. Markets turned optimistic, and the S&P 500 Index climbed to a new record with a P/E ratio around 28 at year-end, a postwar record. The DJIA reached a record 9374 on November 23. Asian stock markets surged.

The economy looked strong at the time of the November 16 FOMC meeting. Available data showed third-quarter real GDP growing at an annualized 3.6%. Consumption was growing strongly at 3.9%, and residential investment, at 7.7%. Nevertheless, the FOMC lowered the funds rate to 4.75%. The FOMC consensus emphasized the problems created by capital flight.

New York Fed President McDonough (Board of Governors *Transcripts* November 17, 1998, 77) warned that large money center banks faced funding problems. An *American Banker* (September 22, 1998) article noted that "Spreads [over treasury securities] on Chase Manhattan Corp., Citicorp, and other money-center banks' bonds ballooned by as much as 15 basis points." Money center banks would have funding problems at year-end when institutional investors want their portfolios to look clean. Keeping money center banks in emerging-market debt required changing market psychology to make investors less risk averse.

As the *New York Times* (November 18, 1998, A1) reported:

Had the Fed been looking strictly at recent economic data, it would almost certainly not have cut rates. "Where is the slowdown?" asked Peter Canelo, United States investment strategist at Morgan Stanley Dean Witter. "What they did today was unnecessary...." Indeed, with gross domestic product growing at more than a 3 percent clip, there is a boom in housing demand, and sales of both automobiles and smaller-ticket consumer goods are strong.

However, as headlined in the *New York Times* (November 18, 1998), the FOMC's rate reductions were "Part of the Game Plan in a World Economic Defense:"

The Federal Reserve's decision to cut interest rates again marks the completion of a three-part strategy, put together over the last seven weeks by the Clinton Administration and Alan Greenspan.... "We had to deal first with rebuilding confidence, so that capital would stop flowing out of countries," Treasury Secretary Robert E. Rubin told a group of business executives.... Washington's strategy, which appeared to have been carefully coordinated, was laid out in pieces, first in speeches by President Clinton and Mr. Greenspan and then fleshed out by Mr. Rubin and his aides. While the Fed remains independent, Mr. Rubin and Mr. Greenspan have discussed the global crisis frequently and conducted some key discussions with allies together. They have often used similar language in describing America's objectives in calming the turmoil. Part 1 was to cut interest rates.... Part 2 was to stabilize Brazil, with a $41.5 billion bailout package.

In fall 1998, the FOMC departed from procedures calling for rate increases with above-trend growth flagged by declines in unemployment. "[T]o counter a seizing-up of financial markets" (Greenspan in U.S. Cong. July 28, 1999, 8), it reduced the funds rate despite strong employment growth (Figure 14.7). In 1998 and 1999, real GDP grew in excess of 4%, and the unemployment rate fell from 4.9% in 1997 to 4% in 2000. While output grew strongly and equity prices surged, the real short-term interest rate remained stable (Figure 8.3). The one-year real rate averaged 3.4% from January 1997 through September 1998 (Figure 14.2). It then fell to 2.8% from October 1998 through February 1999. Over the subsequent period March 1999 through October 1999, at 3.6%, it basically returned to the earlier level.

Expected inflation declined starting in summer 1998. Measured by the yield spread between nominal treasuries and TIPS (treasury inflation-protected securities), 10-year expected inflation fell from 2% in the first part of 1998 to just over 1% in early December (Figure 17.1). Given the bias in measured price indices of somewhat less than 1%, that expectation was consistent with near-price stability. Expected inflation then rose sharply in early 1999 as growth surged and returned to 2% in May 1999.

With both actual inflation (Figure 14.1) and expected inflation near 1% by yearend 1998 (Figure 17.1), the FOMC could have attempted to lock in price stability. Neither its actions nor communications, however, suggested the desirability of preserving price stability. The FOMC began to undo the funds rate decreases of fall 1998 only at its June 30, 1999, meeting. Only in November 1999 did it return the funds rate to its summer 1998 level.

With no inflation target to make the public's expectation of inflation consistent with the FOMC's (chairman's) intentions, expected inflation first fell and then rose significantly in 1998 and 1999. The 10-year nominal-TIPS spread had fallen from 3.25% in early 1997 to 0.75% in late 1998. It then rose to 2% by mid 1999 and to almost 2.5% by early 2000. Inflation (core PCE), which had fallen to 1.25% in 1998, rose above 2% by yearend 2001.

III. Concluding Comment

Later, critics contended that the FOMC should have raised rates to avert an unsustainable rise in equity prices. However, the problem was not that it failed to pop a market bubble but rather that expansionary policy exacerbated an unsustainable

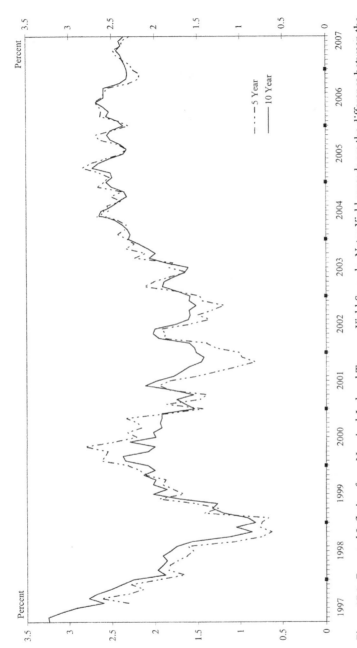

Figure 17.1. Expected Inflation from Nominal-Indexed Treasury Yield Spreads. *Notes:* Yield spreads are the difference between the yields on nominal and inflation-indexed securities of similar maturity. Data are monthly averages of daily data. *Source:* Haver Analytics.

rise in equity prices. Why did the FOMC allow policy to become expansionary in the Asia crisis after a decade of caution? The perils of the combined crises in Asia, Russia, and Latin American seemed to require expansionary policy. Credibility appeared to permit it without a rise in inflation. Despite strong job creation (Figure 14.7), in the absence of inflation, policymakers were reluctant to raise interest rates. It is hard to appear to be the spoiler of an economy creating jobs without inflation.

EIGHTEEN

Departing from the Standard Procedures

From mid 1997 through mid 1999, the FOMC departed from its standard procedures by not raising the funds rate in response to increases in resource utilization rates, particularly as measured by increased labor market tightness. Greenspan's conception of policy explains this departure. Greenspan viewed policy as a forecasting exercise based on reduced-form relationships for predicting inflation, especially between unit labor costs and prices. However, these relationships changed unpredictably over time. As a result, policy had to be discretionary. This discretion took the form of "risk management." Especially, Greenspan believed that monetary policy should counter the irrational expectations of investors, as long as actual and forecasted inflation were benign. Expectations were always central, but because they are not disciplined by a monetary policy rule, policy is necessarily discretionary.

In *Measuring Business Cycles*, Burns and Mitchell (1946) pioneered the atheoretical approach to forecasting used by business economists. They searched over the business cycle for empirical regularities, which they used to classify economic indicators as leading, contemporaneous, and lagging. Greenspan came out of this school. For him, monetary policy involved using empirically derived forecasting relationships in a way that allowed the FOMC's response to change when those forecasting relationships changed.

Greenspan (June 15, 2004, 11) wrote: "Policymakers have needed to reach beyond models to broader – though less mathematically precise – hypotheses about how the world works."[1] Greenspan (March 1997, 196) summarized his views:

There are . . . certain empirical regularities . . . that we can follow with some degree of confidence. . . . Many of these relationships are embedded in the traditional notion of the business cycle developed by Wesley Clair Mitchell three–quarters of a century ago and worked out with Arthur F. Burns. . . . Even so, each cycle tends to have its own identifying characteristic. For example, in the late 1980s . . . the economy was dominated by the sharp fall in the market value of commercial real estate.

With regard to this fall in commercial real estate values, the *Financial Times* (October 15, 1992) and *New York Times* (October 15, 1992) reported, respectively, extemporaneous comments by Greenspan:

[T]he US ... [was] confronting asset deflation which policymakers had little experience in predicting. ... "A number of the old rules of thumb that policymakers used are inoperative."

No models can explain the types of patterns we are having. ... We are being forced to look at different structures.

I. Risk Management as Discretion

As with Volcker, the signature characteristic of the Greenspan regime was the emphasis on inflationary expectations. When combined with the desire to restore stability to expectations that had become unmoored in the era of stop–go policy, that emphasis created the rule-like behavior of the Volcker–Greenspan era. However, Greenspan never expressed the idea that expectational stability depends upon a monetary policy rule. His opposition to an inflation target manifested a more general opposition to the idea of conducting policy by a rule.

Greenspan's opposition to a rule encompassed three specific themes. First, the evolving character of the economy changes the character of desirable monetary policy in unpredictable ways. Second, the lowest politically feasible inflation rate depends upon variable factors beyond the Fed's control. Third, an inflation target could force a uniformity of behavior on policy that would constrain the use of monetary policy to counter investor herd behavior.

The first theme expresses the idea that uncertainty renders a rule impractical because the policymaker cannot specify in advance all the contingencies to which he of she will need to respond. Greenspan (May 2004, 39) wrote:

[N]o *simple* rule could possibly describe the policy action to be taken in every contingency and thus provide a satisfactory substitute for an approach based on the principles of risk management. ... Our problem is ... the ... complexity of the world economy whose underlying linkages appear to be continuously evolving. ... The success of monetary policy depends importantly on the quality of forecasting. ... The first signs that a relationship may have changed is usually the emergence of events that seem inconsistent with our hypotheses of the way the economic world is supposed to behave. (italics in original)

Because Greenspan viewed policy as a forecasting exercise subject to the vagaries of changing empirical relationships, he believed that policymakers must identify those changes in an ongoing way.[2] Greenspan (U.S. Cong. February 26, 1997, 9) testified: "[T]he circumstances that have been associated with increasing inflation in the past have not followed a single pattern. The processes have differed from cycle to cycle, and what may have been a useful leading indicator in one instance has given off misleading signals in another."

Greenspan then referred to how job insecurity restrained inflation by restraining real wage growth. More generally, Greenspan (U.S. Cong. June 17, 1999, 8 and 17) wrote: "[A]n impressive proliferation of new technologies is inducing major shifts in the underlying structure of the American economy. . . . As a consequence, many of the empirical regularities depicting the complex economic relationships on which policymakers rely have been markedly altered. . . . [W]e need a degree of flexibility to address things."

Second, Greenspan believed that the political feasibility of price stability depended upon whether it would raise productivity growth. Productivity needed to increase enough to offset the wage compression that would occur from the inability of firms to lower real wages by cutting nominal wages rather than by raising them less than inflation. He opposed an explicit inflation target for this reason (FOMC *Transcripts* July 2, 1996, 67). Even after achievement of near-price stability, Greenspan still opposed an inflation target. He attributed low inflation not to monetary policy but rather to a conjunction of nonmonetary forces. "The size and geographic extent of the decline in inflation" meant that nonmonetary forces had been at work. He mentioned "political support for stable prices," "globalization," and "an acceleration of productivity" (Greenspan May 2004, 33).[3]

Third, Greenspan believed that countering cyclical instability required judgment about when to use policy to counter excessive investor pessimism.[4] Like Burns (Hetzel 1998, 28), Greenspan believed that alternating waves of optimism and pessimism drove economic cycles. Greenspan (U.S. Cong. February 20, 1996, 22; February 26, 1997, 10; July 18, 2001, 55–6) testified:

[Because] people get excessively exuberant on occasion and inordinately depressed on occasion, you get a cycle.

Excessive optimism sows the seeds of its own reversal in the form of imbalances. . . . When unwarranted expectations ultimately are not realized, the unwinding of these financial excesses can . . . amplify a downturn.

Can fiscal and monetary policy . . . eliminate the business cycle? . . . The answer . . . is no because there is no tool to change human nature. Too often people are prone to recurring bouts of optimism and pessimism that manifest themselves . . . in the build up or cessation of speculative excesses. . . . [O]ur only realistic response to a speculative bubble is to lean against the economic pressures that may accompany a rise in asset prices . . . and address forcefully the consequences of a sharp deflation of asset prices.

Or more simply, "The business cycle is essentially a function of human nature" (Greenspan in U.S. Cong. February 22, 1995, 23).

When to intervene to prop up falling asset prices was a matter of judgment. Greenspan (September 27, 2007, 2) stated:[5]

In perhaps . . . the greatest irony of economic policymaking, success at stabilization carries its own risks. . . . A decline in perceived risk is often self-reinforcing. . . . But . . . risk premiums cannot decline indefinitely. . . . [H]istory cautions that extended periods of low concern about credit risk have invariably been followed by reversal, with an attendant fall in the prices of risky assets. Such developments . . . reflect . . . the all-too-evident alternating and infectious bouts of human euphoria and distress and the instability they engender. . . . A highly flexible system needs to be in place to rebalance an economy in which psychology and asset prices could change rapidly.

According to Greenspan (May 24, 2001, 6), booms reflect a self-reinforcing process whereby investor optimism lowers risk premia and encourages investment. At some point, inevitably, investors realize that asset prices are unrealistically high. "A bursting speculative bubble has historically too often been the end result" (Greenspan May 24, 2001). Greenspan then turned this real bills view on its head.[6] Although monetary policy cannot reliably identify and prick a speculative bubble as it occurs, it can "address forcefully the consequences of a sharp deflation of asset prices" (Greenspan May 24, 2001). Although the FOMC could not recognize a speculative bubble as it occurred, Greenspan (November 16, 1995, 5; U.S. Cong. June 17, 1999, 9) believed that the FOMC needed to counter market failure caused by collective investor withdrawal. Greenspan (U.S. Cong. February 13, 2001, 55) testified about the stock market decline in 2000:

While technology has quickened production adjustments, human nature remains unaltered. We respond to a heightened pace of change and its associated uncertainty in the same way we always have. We withdraw from action, postpone decisions, and generally hunker down until a renewed, more comprehensible basis for acting emerges. In its extreme manifestation, many economic decisionmakers not only become risk averse but attempt to disengage from all risk. This precludes taking any initiative, because risk is inherent in every action.

Greenspan (August 27, 2005, 2) understood the consistency in policy: "[T]he Federal Reserve and most other central banks generally pursue price stability and, consistent with that goal, ease when economic conditions soften and tighten when they firm." However, he opposed a rule. When inflation is not a problem, Greenspan (U.S. Cong. June 17, 1999, 10) believed the FOMC should use policy to rectify financial market instability.[7] In commenting on a congressional directive to maintain price stability, Greenspan (U.S. Cong. June 17, 1999, 17) asked that it give to the FOMC "the degree of flexibility when the economy is somewhat slack to recognize that we would not be jeopardizing our long-term goal of price stability by taking actions which may not . . . be fully directed at creating stable prices."

Because a rule must be simple, the dependence of policy on the behavior of asset prices renders a rule infeasible. The complexity of financial markets and the difficulty of differentiating between herd behavior and rational adjustment to adverse news mean that policy predicated on the behavior of asset prices cannot be simple.[8] If the judgment of the policymaker can at times reliably supplant that of the market and supersede the working of the price system, then discretion is desirable.

II. Greenspan and the New Paradigm

The FOMC raised the funds rate to 5.5% in March 1997. Despite the steady fall in the unemployment rate from 5.2% in March 1997 to 4.0% by end 1999, it did not raise the funds rate above 5.5% until February 2000. Why did it depart from the pattern that had characterized its earlier policy? Greenspan did not consider inflation a threat because he believed that productivity growth was restraining inflation. The FOMC could then concentrate on the financial volatility engendered by the Asia crisis.

Why did Greenspan believe that inflation was not an immediate threat even though the unemployment rate was falling? Unemployment and inflation fell together after 1995. To explain this apparent anomaly, Greenspan looked to resurgent productivity growth. Greenspan had long watched for signs of a pickup in productivity growth because of his belief that restoration of the expectation of price stability that had existed in the first part of the 1960s would restore the high productivity growth of that period.[9] Greenspan (April 19, 1993, 5; U.S. Cong. February 22, 1994, 46) stated:

[T]he lack of pricing leverage has once again concentrated the minds of business people on the need to increase productivity.... [E]conomic experience appears to be running full circle, back to the early 1960s: a period of low-inflation and strong productivity growth.... [L]ower inflation historically has been associated...with faster growth of productivity.... Lower inflation and inflation expectations reduce uncertainty in economic planning and diminish risk premiums for capital investment.

As a business economist who predicted inflation based on wage pressures, Greenspan argued that productivity was restraining inflation by lessening growth in unit labor costs. Greenspan first offered a "numerator" (wage rate) explanation and then a "denominator" (output per hour) explanation of the effect of productivity on unit labor costs. In his July 1996 Humphrey–Hawkins testimony, he conjectured that a rapid rate of technological process had created fears of skill obsolescence among workers (U.S. Cong. July 18, 1996, 37; July 22, 1997, 20). The resulting worker insecurity moderated wage demands.

However, when strong job creation lessened job insecurity, Greenspan then turned to a denominator explanation of the moderation in inflation.[10] Accordingly, a rise in productivity growth had depressed growth in unit labor costs and inflation. The fall in inflation initiated a "virtuous" cycle by changing the psychology of businesspeople (U.S. Cong. July 21, 1998, 30). Because they believed that raising prices was not an option for coping with higher wages, they concentrated on raising productivity. The availability of new technologies made such productivity enhancements possible (Greenspan May 6, 1999, 4; U.S. Cong. June 14, 1999, 16). Also, the fall in inflation made businesspeople more willing to invest by decreasing uncertainty (U.S. Cong. June 17, 1999, 16). Greenspan (U.S. Cong. February 24, 1999, 61–2) testified:

[R]ecent restrained inflation may be emanating more from employers than from employees. . . . [B]usinesses . . . have lost pricing power. . . . Price relief evidently has not been available in recent years. But relief from cost pressures has. The newer technologies have made capital investment distinctly more profitable. . . . Since neither firms nor their competitors can count any longer on a general inflationary tendency to validate decisions to raise their own prices, each company feels compelled to concentrate on efforts to hold down costs. The availability of new technology to each company and its rivals affords both the opportunity and the competitive necessity of taking steps to boost productivity.

From mid 1997 through mid 1999, the apparently lessened inflation threat meant that Greenspan could practice "risk management" by focusing on the undesired strength in the dollar and capital flight from emerging-market economies.

For Greenspan, inflationary expectations were central. However, like Burns, they were the expectations of businesspeople and investors unconstrained by a monetary policy rule. Greenspan (1967; September 1, 1981; Chapter 10) believed that the gold standard had provided a nominal anchor because of the discipline it imposed on government deficit spending. In the absence of that discipline, the strains on financial markets created by deficits led central banks to monetize those deficits and create inflation. He could not articulate how the current monetary regime provides a nominal anchor because he did not consider that rule-like behavior by the FOMC would trump all other factors influencing the public's expectations.[11] As a result, and in accord with the perspective derived from his life-long profession as a business forecaster, Greenspan turned to real factors, especially productivity growth, to explain the low inflation and falling unemployment that coexisted at the end of the 1990s.[12]

For Burns in 1970, stagflation (high and rising unemployment in conjunction with high inflation) arose from the influence of unit labor costs pushed up by wage-push pressures. For Greenspan after 1997, boomdisflation (low and falling unemployment in conjunction with disinflation) arose from the influence of unit labor costs restrained by high productivity growth. Both looked to a special factor rather than to a change in the credibility of monetary policy to explain these apparent anomalies.

III. Concluding Comment

Because central bankers operate in the money market, they naturally seek expectational stability. However, is the central bank responsible for the expectational stability of asset prices or of goods prices? By choosing the latter, Martin moved the Fed away from real bills. Burns placed great weight on inflationary expectations, but he wanted fiscal policy and incomes policies to control them. Volcker brought the Fed back to Martin's choice, although at the end he attempted to influence the expectations of the foreign exchange value of the dollar as well.

The desire to restore nominal expectational stability imposed discipline on monetary policy for most of Greenspan's tenure. However, Greenspan believed that nonmonetary forces affected actual and expected inflation. To lower inflation, the central bank needed to weigh in to either accommodate disinflationary forces or offset inflationary forces. Policymakers had to conduct policy discretionarily in a way that depended upon the ongoing evolution of those forces. During the Asia crisis, Greenspan believed that real disinflationary forces permitted an expansionary policy. However, that policy exacerbated the rise in equity prices. As a result, it contributed to the severity of their subsequent fall and to the resulting recession. The FOMC was ill-served by discretion.

NINETEEN

Boom and Bust

1997 to 2001

The Asia crisis made raising the funds rate difficult because a stronger dollar would have put additional pressure on Asian currencies already weakened by capital outflows. In the absence of rising inflation, nothing offset the pressure to keep interest rates down. From fall 1997 through the first half of 1999, the FOMC departed from its policy rule of raising the funds rate when output growth above trend tightened labor markets. Commentators applauded Greenspan for allowing job creation. However, bust followed boom, and job destruction followed job creation.

I. A Nonmonetary Explanation of Inflation

Until 1999, the forecasting consensus held that the economy could grow at 2.5% per year due to 1% labor force growth and 1.5% productivity growth. However, the economy grew somewhat above 4% in 1996, 1997, and 1998 and at 5% in 1999 and the first half of 2000. Furthermore, that growth occurred with minimal inflation. Figure 19.1 shows a measure of the output gap based on data available contemporaneously. The positive gap that prevailed from 1994 on was associated with moderately declining inflation. The Board of Governors staff, which relied on a Phillips curve to forecast inflation, overestimated inflation (Figure 8.4).

The fall in the unemployment rate associated with this high real growth did raise the real wage rate (Figure 19.2), but until 1999 unit labor costs accelerated without a rise in inflation (Figure 19.3). Rather than look to credibility for an explanation of this lack of "pricing power," Greenspan looked to the computer–IT revolution. Greenspan (FOMC Board of Governors *Transcripts* February 3, 1999, 104–10) told the FOMC:

[T]he economy has been exhibiting substantial . . . strength. . . . Price pressures should be mounting . . . but instead they are going in the other direction. . . . [I]nterpreting these results requires a fundamental reassessment of how we look at the world. . . . [T]he acceleration in the downward adjustment of prices suggests that we have a very large backlog of unexploited investments that . . . are displacing labor. . . . Our . . . models that

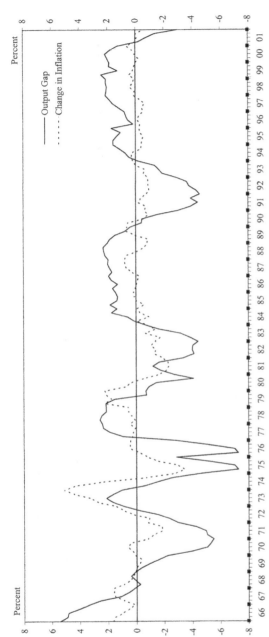

Figure 19.1. The Output Gap and the Change in Inflation. *Notes:* The output gap (solid line) is the percentage difference between "current" real output and trend real output (real GNP before 1992 and real GDP thereafter) calculated as of FOMC meetings using the figures contained in the Greenbook. If the FOMC meeting was in the first or second month of the quarter, the value of current real output used to calculate the output gap is the Greenbook value predicted for the contemporaneous quarter. If the FOMC meeting was in the last month of the quarter, the value of current real output used to calculate the output gap is the Greenbook value predicted for the succeeding quarter. Trend real output is the value (for the same quarter as current real output) of a trend line fitted through the 40 quarters of data ending with current observation for real output. The last two or three quarterly figures of output used in the calculation of the trend line are predicted values from the Greenbook. The prior figures are the contemporaneously available figures taken from the Federal Reserve Bank of Philadelphia Real Time Data Set. Observations in the figure are the quarterly averages of the output gap series. The change in inflation (dashed line) is the difference between subsequently realized four-quarter inflation (the average of the four quarterly future inflation rates starting with the succeeding quarter) and the prior four-quarter inflation rate (the average of the four quarterly past inflation rates starting with the contemporaneous quarter). Inflation is calculated using the personal consumption expenditures (excluding food and energy) price index. Negative values indicate that the inflation rate is falling. Heavy tick marks indicate the fourth quarter.

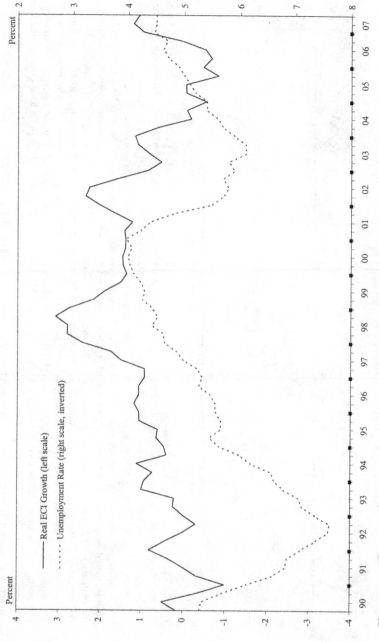

Figure 19.2. The Unemployment Rate and Lagged Real Wage Growth. *Notes:* Quarterly observations of four-quarter percentage changes in the employment cost index (ECI) for wages and salaries deflated by the personal consumption expenditures (PCE) deflator. Heavy tick marks indicate the fourth quarter of the year.

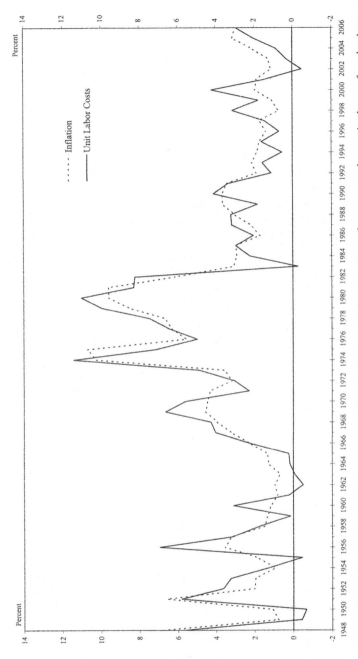

Figure 19.3. Inflation and Growth of Unit Labor Costs. *Notes*: Annual observations of percentage changes in the nonfarm business sector deflator and unit labor costs (nonfarm business sector. BLS data).

237

are projecting... price acceleration are not properly specified... unless some means are found to capture the technologically driven price-capping variable.... [I]f nominal wage increases pick up, there is clear evidence in recent years that producers will endeavor to dip into that untapped pool of technological capital projects.

Productivity growth did rise as inflation fell. After 1996, growth of output per worker rose fast enough so that by 2003 it had made up for the post-1973 shortfall (Figure 19.4).[1] A number of factors pointed to an increase in trend rather than cyclical productivity. The increase in productivity came long after the economic recovery phase of the business cycle. Atypically, productivity surged with high rates of utilization of the labor force. Also, the decade of the 1990s experienced an investment boom.[2] A fall in the price of computing power unrelated to the cyclical behavior of the economy could explain the investment boom. Indirect evidence for a continued rise in productivity came from persistent high corporate earnings growth despite a high level of investment. Surveys of institutional analysts conducted by Primark (I/B/E/S) showed that the median estimate of growth in corporate earnings rose from 11% per year in 1995 to 16% in 2000.

Greenspan became the apostle of the new economy. He even provided a date for the start of the productivity revolution – 1993 when orders for high-tech equipment rose (Greenspan June 13, 2000, 4). The title of a *BusinessWeek* article by Dean Foust (August 31, 1998) read, "Visionary Alan Greenspan: An Unlikely Guru: The Fed chairman sees a high-tech economy as a natural inflation fighter." A later article (*BusinessWeek* May 3, 1999) bore the title, "The Fed's New Rule Book: The premise for now: productivity is curbing inflation." The message that productivity would restrain inflation carried the optimistic message to investors discounting future stock returns that the economy could grow rapidly with low interest rates.[3]

II. Stock Market Bust and Recession

After the Asia crisis, with the June 1999 meeting, the FOMC began to raise the funds rate. However, it did so cautiously in the absence of evidence of rising inflation and in the belief that high productivity growth was restraining inflation.[4] The economy continued to surge. For the four quarters ending 2000Q2, annualized quarterly real GDP growth averaged 6.1%. The accompanying rapid productivity growth and moderate inflation made believable the new paradigm. Rapid productivity growth promised the indefinite continuation of double-digit earnings growth. The future seemed to belong to the computer and communications industries.[5]

Equity markets soared. Figure 19.5 exhibits the ratio of stock market capitalization to GDP. The equity market began its phenomenal rise in 1995 after investors realized that the Fed's 1994 tightening would not initiate recession. From 1994 through 1998, the ratio of forecast earnings to price for the S&P 500 followed the bond rate (Figure 14.5). However, for 1999 and 2000, the S&P 500 rose in excess of the capitalized value of earnings forecasts. In that sense, market valuations could

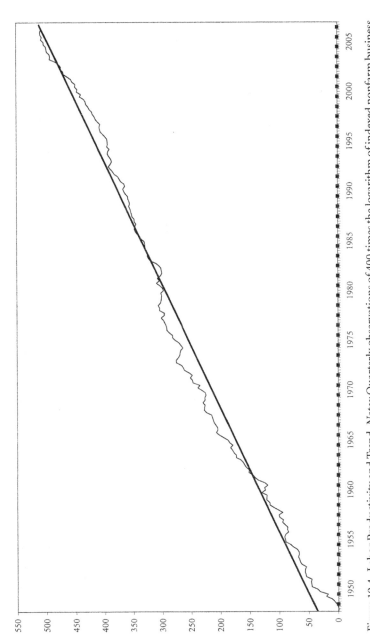

Figure 19.4. Labor Productivity and Trend. *Notes*: Quarterly observations of 400 times the logarithm of indexed nonfarm business labor productivity, where the first quarter of 1948 equals 1. The slope of the trend line equals 2.2. Data are from the BLS. Heavy tick marks indicate the fourth quarter of each year.

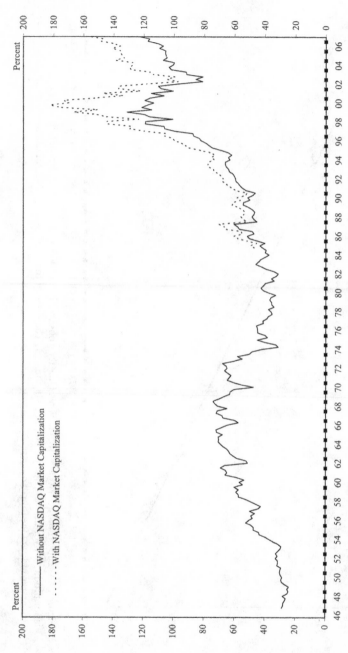

Figure 19.5. Ratio of Equity Wealth to GDP. *Notes:* The solid line is the ratio of market capitalization of stocks traded on the New York Stock Exchange and the American Stock Exchange to GDP. The dotted line adds the market capitalization of the NASDAQ. The data represent the market capitalization on the last day of the quarter. The market capitalization data for NYSE and Amex series after 1995 and the entire NASDAQ series are obtained from Haver Analytics. Heavy tick marks indicate the fourth quarter of each year.

240

have represented an unjustifiable euphoria. The rise in financial wealth stimulated consumption. Through the first half of 1997, real consumption growth averaged around 3%. It then rose and peaked at over 6% in early 2000.

Incoming economic data did not support investor optimism. From 1991 through 1997, productivity gains had outpaced increases in labor costs, and after-tax corporate profits grew. However, from 1998 through 2001, increases in labor costs outpaced productivity gains and profits fell. Accumulating evidence pointed to moderate economic growth, which could not sustain the double-digit growth in earnings that powered the elevated P/E ratios of high-tech firms. In 1999, annualized three-month payroll employment numbers regularly came in at two to three times the growth rate of the labor force. The number released on June 2, 2000, showed annualized three-month growth at 3.6%. In contrast, the number released September 1, 2000, showed three-month growth at −0.3%. The NASDAQ peaked at 5,049 on March 10 and began a prolonged fall in September 2000. The *Wall Street Journal* (March 5, 2001) reported: "[B]ecause the Nasdaq grew so much in the past decade, and became the place to be for many new investors, the loss in sheer wealth exceeds anything previously witnessed. Investors in the Nasdaq have lost more than $3.6 trillion since the March high of last year, more than the entire stock market was worth at the beginning of 1981."

Was the rise and fall of NASDAQ a bubble? Proponents of discretionary policy like the idea of market irrationality because it presupposes a need for "rational" policymakers who periodically must intervene to prevent market excesses. Certainly, the strength in NASDAQ drew in the greedy. The *Wall Street Journal* (March 5, 2001) quoted a lawyer, "It was amazing. It seemed there were endless buying opportunities.... You felt like an idiot if you weren't investing in the NASDAQ."

The fall in wealth reduced spending, and economic activity peaked in March 2001. Growth rates of real consumption fell from an annualized average of 5.3% over 1997Q3 through 2000Q1 to 2.4% over the succeeding six quarters. The most dramatic declines in spending occurred in real nonresidential fixed investment. From an annualized average growth rate of 14.6% over the first two quarters of 2000, it fell to −10.1% in 2001. From 2000Q3 through 2001Q3, the economy hardly grew averaging only .2% per quarter.

Already in August 2000, incoming data showed a moderation in growth. The three-month average of payroll employment growth through July (reported on August 4) fell to near zero (Figure 14.7). Initially, the board staff did not forecast weakness (Figure 13.2), and the FOMC was slow to respond to weakness when it developed (Figure 21.5). Prior expansionary monetary policy made easing difficult. With the unemployment rate at 4% in 2000, tightness in the labor market militated against easing. Although the FOMC did lower the funds rate beginning in 2001, the sharp falloff in nominal GDP growth in the last half of 2000 suggests that monetary policy was contractionary after mid-2000 (Figure 14.6).

At its December 19, 2000, meeting, the FOMC maintained the funds rate at the 6.5% established at the May 2000 meeting. However, in a telephone conference on January 3, 2001, it reduced the funds rate by 0.5 a percentage points. From January 2001 to June 2003, the FOMC moved the funds rate down from 6.5 to 1%. Although the short-term real interest rate fell from 5% in mid 2000 to zero in mid 2002, the fall may not have been rapid enough to prevent monetary policy from being contractionary (Figure 14.2).

The key to understanding the low real rate in this period is the interaction between productivity growth and the public's degree of optimism about the future. The real interest rate is the price of current resources in terms of future resources. When productivity growth is high and the public extrapolates that high growth to the future, people feel wealthy. The real rate must be high to constrain contemporaneous aggregate demand to available supply.

In contrast, when productivity growth is high and the public is pessimistic about the future, the real rate must be low to raise aggregate demand sufficiently to meet supply. After the collapse in equity wealth, the terrorist attack in September 2001, the corrosive corporate governance scandals that unfolded in 2002, and the Iraq War in 2003, pessimism and uncertainty about the future prevailed.[6] Despite the recession, productivity growth remained at a high level. From 1995Q4 through 2001Q4, growth in labor productivity (nonfarm business) averaged 2.7%, the same value as in the 1948Q4 to 1973Q4 period. Productivity growth then surged, averaging 4.3% over the 2001Q4 to 2004Q2 period.

III. Dealing with a Poor Hand

The title comes from Velde (2004), "Poor Hand or Poor Play." Velde asked whether the benign combination of low, stable inflation and of low output variability in the V–G era relative to the stop–go era came from a reduction in exogenous shocks (poor hand) or the elimination of bad policy (poor play). Starting with the Asia crisis, a succession of shocks has dealt policymakers a poor hand. Following the real shocks of the Asia crisis, a drastic decline in equity wealth, the terrorist attack of 9/11, corporate governance scandals, and Middle Eastern geopolitical tensions came an inflation shock from a huge rise in the price of oil. Despite a recession, the U.S. economy performed well. Although inflation rose from 2004 to 2006, it remained moderate. How does one account for these benign results given these malign shocks? How did good play overcome a poor hand?

The issue reverts to the old one of rules versus discretion. As illustrated by Greenspan's concern in early 2001 (U.S. Cong. February 28, 2001, 60ff) that a snowballing pessimism could drag down the economy, Greenspan believed that good play requires policymaker discretion to counter volatile market sentiment.

It is difficult for economic policy to deal with the abruptness of a break in confidence.... This unpredictable rending of confidence is one reason that recessions are so difficult to forecast. They may not be just changes in degree from a period of economic expansion, but different processes engendered by fear. Our economic models have never been particularly successful in capturing a process driven in large part by nonrational behavior.

A *Wall Street Journal* (February 1, 2001) article by Fed watcher Greg Ip and Greenspan confidante (Meyer 2004, 98) carried headlines: "Latest Fed Rate Cut Takes on a Contagion of Low Confidence; Amid New Signs of Gloom, Anxiety about Recession Could be Self-Fulfilling."

Alternatively, the view here is that good play came from a rule that maintained a nominal anchor in the form of the expectation of low, stable inflation and that moved the funds rate in a way that allowed the price system to work. At issue are the nature of inflation, the ability of the price system to equilibrate shocks, and the nature of the monetary standard.

TWENTY

Backing Off from Price Stability

The characterization here of policy in the final Greenspan years is that the FOMC pursued its basic expected inflation/growth gap procedures but raised its implicit inflation target from price stability to low inflation. If that characterization is correct, the issue arises of whether there is a conflict between the twin objectives of "price stability" and "maximum employment" legislated in the Federal Reserve Act. Does achievement of "maximum employment" require secular depreciation of the currency, albeit at a low level? Does positive inflation "buy" stability of real output?

I. Raising the Implicit Inflation Objective

After the Asia crisis, the FOMC replaced its implicit long-run objective for price stability with an objective of low inflation (Chapter 17). Henceforth, the FOMC demonstrated an aversion to inflation as low as 1%. Figure 20.1 shows inflation compensation inferred from the difference in nominal and TIPS yields for the five-year interval, five years in the future. It measures the market's expectation of trend CPI inflation.[1] Markets expected near-price stability in fall 1998. Over 1999, expected trend CPI inflation rose to 2.5%. The FOMC conveyed no message that this level of expected inflation exceeded its desired level for actual inflation.

Over 2000, expected trend CPI inflation drifted down and at year end reached 1.75%. In 2001, policy followed the basic lean-against-the-wind pattern. In 2001 as the recession became evident, the FOMC lowered the funds rate in an amount commensurate with its past responses to weakness (Figure 21.5).[2] By emphasizing the danger of deflation rather than the preservation of price stability, it packaged its funds rate decisions in a way that made expected inflation jump (Figure 20.1). By the last half of February 2001, expected inflation had jumped to above 2% and by May to above 2.5%.

In 2003, the FOMC again reversed a decline in expected trend inflation toward price stability (Figure 20.1). In the last half of 2002, inflation began to decline. The

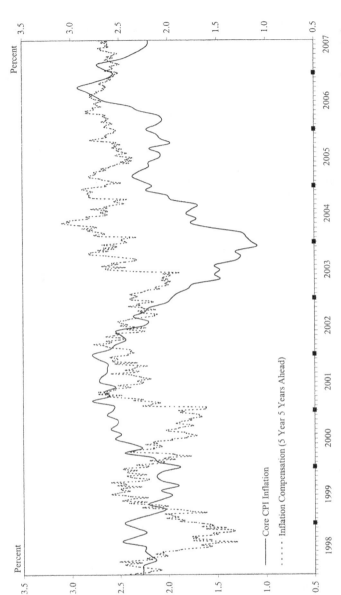

Figure 20.1. Core CPI Inflation and Inflation Compensation (Five-Year, Five-Years Ahead). *Notes:* Core CPI inflation is the annualized 12-month percentage change in the core CPI price index. The CPI data are from Haver Analytics. The five-year five-years-ahead inflation compensation observations are implied by the five-year and ten-year inflation compensation numbers. The latter are the differences between the yield on nominal off-the-run treasury securities and TIPS securities of the same maturity. Nominal yields are obtained from the Federal Reserve Board Division of Monetary Affairs, and TIPS yields are from Bloomberg. Heavy tick marks indicate December.

high value of the real rate reached in August 2000 and the slowness with which it fell are consistent with the hypothesis that restrictive monetary policy produced the decline. Despite reductions in the funds rate, not until November 2001 did short-term real interest rates fall to cyclically low levels (Figure 8.3). In March 2003, core CPI inflation fell to just below 1%.

In 2003, the combination of disinflation and a negative output gap combined to make the FOMC concerned that disinflation could become deflation. Greenspan (August 26, 2005, 5) recounted: "In the summer of 2003 . . . the FOMC viewed as a very small probability that the then gradual decline in inflation would accelerate into a more consequential deflation. But because the implications for the economy were so dire should that scenario play out, we chose to counter it with unusually low interest rates."

Strong productivity growth rather than employment growth powered GDP growth after the November 2001 cyclical trough. As of February 2004, nonfarm payroll employment remained 2.35 million below the March 2001 peak. Comparisons with the recovery in the early 1990s, itself termed the "jobless recovery," led to talk of a shortfall of 3 million jobs. Declining growth in unit labor costs reinforced disinflation fears (Figure 19.3).

With the funds rate at 1.25% since the November 2002 meeting, the FOMC became concerned with the zero-bound problem: How does it lower the real interest rate with a nominal interest rate of zero? In 2003, Governor Bernanke (2003, 7) noted, "[E]ven if the economy recovers smartly for the rest of this year and next, the ongoing slack in the economy may still lead to continuing disinflation." Bernanke (2003, 3–4) expressed concern for a situation

[i]n which aggregate demand is insufficient to sustain strong growth, even when the short-term real interest rate is zero or negative. . . . [D]eflation places a lower limit on the real short-term interest rate . . . [as] a consequence of the well-known zero-lower-bound constraint on nominal interest rates.

[D]eflation might grow worse as economic slack led to more aggressive wage- and price-cutting. Because the short-term nominal interest rate cannot be reduced further, worsening deflation would raise the real short-term interest rate. . . . The higher real interest rate might further reduce aggregate demand, exacerbating the deflation and continuing the downward spiral.

Greenspan (U.S. Cong. July 16, 2003, 49) outlined "an especially pernicious . . . scenario in which inflation turns negative . . . engendering a corrosive deflationary spiral."[3] Greenspan (U.S. Cong. February 25, 2004, 28) repeated, "[W]ere it [deflation] to happen, the consequences would be extraordinarily negative." Japanese deflation provided the backdrop. Greenspan (U.S. Cong. May 21, 2003, 21) testified: "The notion that deflation would emerge just never entered our heads until the Japanese demonstrated to us otherwise. . . . [N]ot having had any experience in the modern world with dealing with deflation and fiat currencies, our knowledge base was virtually nonexistent." President Yellen (2005; 2006) said:

We know from history that such an outcome [deflation] can be extremely damaging to the economy. Perhaps the most unsettling aspect of the experience of Japan over the past decade is how difficult it can be to extract oneself from deflation.... [E]xperience of... deflation here in Japan ... has heightened my concern relating to the zero lower bound on the policy interest-rate.

The possibility that the funds rate could drop to zero appeared real. The November 6, 2002, FOMC statement referred to the "uncertainty ... attributable to heightened geopolitical risks." Such risks concerned in part resumption of nuclear weapons production by North Korea but mainly the possibility of war with Iraq. The Iraq invasion, which did occur on March 20, 2003, could have destabilized parts of the world and induced terrorist attacks. Another 9/11 attack could have made the natural (full employment) interest rate negative. The statement issued by the FOMC at its June 24–25, 2003, meeting read:

With the economy thought likely to continue to operate below its potential for an extended period and productivity growth expected to remain robust ... some further disinflation could be in store.... [T]here was concern that inflation could be approaching a level that would begin to complicate the implementation of monetary policy if economic weakness unexpectedly persisted or the economy was subjected to another negative demand shock.

In the statement for the May 6, 2003, meeting, the FOMC altered the risk assessment to deal separately with inflation and growth: "[T]he Committee perceives that ... upside and downside risks to the attainment of sustainable growth are roughly equal. [T]he probability of an unwelcome substantial fall in inflation, though minor, exceeds that of a pickup in inflation."

In the absence of an inflation target, this language allowed the FOMC to signal an unwillingness to let inflation fall further. Also, the language allowed it to bend down the yield curve without further funds rate reductions. A funds rate near zero would have encouraged a public debate over the zero-bound problem, which was theoretically contentious and unfamiliar ground for the FOMC. Also, a further rate reduction would have sent a pessimistic signal about the economy that could have derailed a fragile economic recovery.

After the May FOMC meeting, Greenspan (*New York Times* June 4, 2003) commented that the minimal likelihood of a revival of inflation permitted the FOMC to take out "insurance against economic weakness." Along with the May FOMC statement, this language produced a sharp decline in bond rates. The 10-year treasury yield declined from 3.89% before the May meeting to 3.25% before the June meeting. However, at the latter meeting, the reduction of the funds rate by 0.25 percentage point instead of one half caused the yield to rebound.[4]

At its June meeting, the FOMC discussed ways of conducting policy with a funds rate at zero, but reached no consensus.[5] What emerged was an attempt to lower the yield curve without reducing the funds rate. To this end, the FOMC made public statements that the funds rate was likely to remain low for an extended period. At its August 12, 2003 meeting, the FOMC issued a statement containing the phrase "policy accommodation can be maintained for a considerable period." The longer-lasting consequence of this episode was a desire to maintain some inflation in excess of price stability. Greenspan (Meyer 2004, 193) talked about a "firebreak," and Bernanke (2002, 4) said "the Fed should try to preserve a buffer zone for the inflation rate."

In 2004, a small inflation scare replaced the 2003 deflation scare. Based on available data, core PCE inflation had averaged an annualized 0.8% over the first eight months of 2003. Over the six months from October 2003 through March 2004, it jumped to 2.1%. This episode confirmed the problematic character of inflation forecasts based on an output gap.[6] What made the 2003 episode into an "experiment" were the contrasting implications for inflation of inflationary expectations and the output gap.[7] The 10-year nominal TIPS yield gap, which had been as low as 1.6% in June 2003, began to rise and reached 2.6% by May 2004 (Figure 17.1). Rising inflationary expectations contrasted with a negative output gap, and expectations trumped the output gap in forecasting inflation. The predictive ability of a Phillips curve with forward-looking expectations outperformed one with backward-looking expectations.

The appropriate conclusion is not to dismiss the possibility of the zero-bound problem. What is important is to realize that it would only create a problem if associated with a mutually reinforcing downward spiral between actual and expected deflation. However, monetary policy can discipline expectations through implementation of a rule. A rule that created the expectation of price stability would cause the public to associate deflation with a rise in inflation and, as a result, lower the real rate even with a zero nominal rate.[8] The FOMC can handle the zero-bound problem better through such a rule than through ad hoc attempts to influence the yield curve through public statements. Positive inflation is no substitute for an explicit, credible rule. What makes a rule a bulwark against deflation is the unlimited ability of central banks to create dollars through "a printing press (or, its electronic equivalent) . . . at essentially no cost" (Bernanke 2002, 5).[9]

After mid 1999, the FOMC adhered to its basic expected-inflation/growth-gap procedures. Within that framework, the FOMC demonstrated a commitment not to allow inflation to rise above a moderate level, presumably 2% based on frequent reference by FOMC participants to a "comfort zone" of 1 to 2%. Real GDP grew strongly over the last half of 2003, and the FOMC raised the funds rate when employment growth exceeded labor force growth in June 2004. At its June 2004 meeting, the FOMC raised the funds rate, which had been at 1% for a year.[10]

At the time, evidence that recovery had taken hold was still tentative. Over the interval October 2003 through February 2004, contemporaneously available three-month payroll employment growth had averaged only 0.65%. In March 2004 at 5.7%, the unemployment rate was still near its cyclical peak of 6%. At the June meeting, the FOMC only had figures available for two months, April and May, showing three-month payroll employment growth above 2%. Despite the uncertainty over whether a recovery had taken hold sufficient to reduce unemployment, the FOMC initiated funds rate increases.

In fact, three-month annualized growth rates of payroll employment for July, August, and September fell back below 1%. Also, throughout 2004, growth in unit labor costs was negative (Figure 19.3). Nevertheless, the FOMC persisted with 0.25 percentage point increases in the funds rate. The FOMC advertised its commitment to control inflation by the initial promptness with which it began to increase the funds rate and by the persistence of those increases through June 2006 despite occasional evidence of a faltering recovery. That commitment provided continuity with the overall Volcker–Greenspan monetary era (Hetzel 2006).

The success of the rule-like behavior of policy in the V–G era in disciplining expected and actual inflation appeared in the failure of an inflation shock of the magnitude of that of 1973 and 1979 to raise trend inflation. The price of a barrel of oil rose from $30 at the end of 2003 to a peak of $74 in summer 2006. Despite the impact of this price rise on headline inflation, expected trend CPI inflation remained steady from mid 2003 onward at about 2.5% (Figure 20.1). Consistent with this level of expected trend inflation, core PCE inflation remained steady just above 2%.

II. Inflation Control: Opportunistic or Systematic?

Greenspan (U.S. Cong. July 22, 1999, 19) described the basic lean-against-the-wind pattern of policy that makes persistent change in resource utilization the indicator for funds rate changes. "We cannot tell . . . what the actual potential [growth rate] is. . . . But it shouldn't be our concern. Our concern should be the imbalances that emerge." Greenspan (U.S. Cong. February 23, 2000, 14) later amplified this statement in response to a question about whether the Fed limited growth by raising interest rates:

Senator, I do understand where you are coming from because I have been in the same place. . . . The question of how fast this economy grows is not something the central bank should be involved in. . . . What we are looking at is basically the indications that demand chronically exceeds supply. . . . The best way to measure that is to look at what is happening to the total number of people who . . . are unemployed. . . . [W]hat . . . we are concerned about is not the rate of increase in demand or the rate of increase in supply, but only the difference between the two. . . . [W]e don't know whether the potential growth rate is 4, 5, 6, or 8 percent. What we need to focus on . . . is solely the difference between the two.

The issue is whether the real and nominal stability of the V–G era resulted from a discipline on these lean-against-the-wind changes that provided a nominal anchor and allowed the price system to work. Alternatively, did it result from discretionary behavior that allowed inflation to drift downward in response to benign real forces and that in crises superseded the working of markets and the price system? Greenspan, as a student of Burns's NBER methodology, did not believe in rules. He did not emphasize the consistency with which the price system provides for macroeconomic stability in response to shocks, but rather he emphasized the unreliability of rules of thumb such as NAIRU rules for forecasting inflation. The task remains for the FOMC to articulate the nature of the monetary standard.

The view here is that by yearend 1999, the FOMC returned to the basic expected inflation/growth gap targeting characteristic of the V–G era. With these procedures, the FOMC allows the price system to work but manages inflationary expectations. By moving the funds rate in a persistent way in response to sustained growth gaps, it causes the real funds rate to track the natural interest rate. The nominal anchor derives from a credible commitment that funds rate changes will cumulate to whatever extent necessary to maintain trend inflation invariant to shocks. Trend inflation is always and everywhere a nominal expectational phenomenon controlled by the central bank (Hetzel 2006).

APPENDIX: JAPANESE DEFLATION AND CENTRAL BANK MONEY CREATION

Japan's experience with deflation made the zero-bound problem seem real (Gramlich 2005, 23; Meyer 2004, 190, 202). That experience revived much of the monetary mythology that had surrounded the Great Depression. (For an expression of these views, see Posen 2006.) Accordingly, the Bank of Japan should have prevented emergence of the "bubble" in land and equity prices that arose at the end of the 1980s. Once the bubble burst, powerful nonmonetary forces overwhelmed monetary policy. With its overnight rate at zero, the BoJ became impotent to stimulate the economy. Its "quantitative easing" policy demonstrated the inability of money creation to stimulate aggregate demand. A Keynesian liquidity trap frustrated monetary stimulus.

Hetzel (1999; 2003; 2004b) challenged these views. Historically low M2 growth in Japan after 1990 meant that monetary policy was deflationary. Confusion arose from the BoJ's labeling of its post-March 2001 policy as "quantitative easing." In February 1999, the BoJ had introduced the zero interest rate policy of encouraging the call (funds) rate to fall below 0.15%. In August 2000, it abandoned the policy and increased the call rate. In fall 2000, Japan went into recession. In March 2001, the BoJ returned to the policy of zero interest rate targeting. However, because the Policy Board governor did not want to appear to be returning to a policy that the BoJ had abandoned prematurely, he labeled the policy change "quantitative easing" (author's interview with former Policy Board member Nobuyuki Nakahara, October 2, 2003).

With this policy, the BoJ kept the short-term section of the yield curve flat at zero and kept excess reserves at a level consistent with this interest rate objective (Hetzel 2004b). The BoJ accommodated the demand for excess reserves that a troubled banking system desired at a near-zero overnight rate. At no time did it use the monetary base as an instrument to stimulate aggregate nominal demand and raise the price level. Friedman (2005) showed that only stock market declines accompanied by monetary contraction lead to deflation. Nothing in Japanese experience demonstrates that deflation renders ineffective monetary stimulus from open-market purchases of illiquid assets.

The fundamental source of confusion arises from the use by central banks of the interest rate as their policy instrument. As a result, there is a bias toward thinking of central banks as masters of the price system rather than as creators of money. It is true that, at a zero short-term interest rate, the central bank cannot lower the real interest rate by reducing its policy instrument; however, it can always create liquidity that forces portfolio rebalancing through the purchase of illiquid assets.

The Fed could more clearly communicate the fundamental nature of a central bank by using bank reserves rather than the funds rate as a policy instrument. Specifically, it could revive the reserves procedures adopted by the FOMC in early 1972, but vitiated by Burns (Chapter 8, Appendix: "Monetary Policy Procedures under Burns"). For a specific proposal to replace funds rate targeting with reserves targeting, see Hetzel (2004a, Section 4).

TWENTY-ONE

The Volcker–Greenspan Regime

The lean-against-the-wind (LAW) character of policy whereby the FOMC raises (lowers) the funds rate in a persistent, measured way if the economy grows above (below) trend is the foundation of FOMC procedures. That fact, however, leaves two issues unsettled. First, how does the FOMC impose discipline on these changes to ensure that trend inflation remains unchanged? Second, how much knowledge does it possess about the real economy? Does it possess reliable knowledge of excess capacity or instead the lesser amount of knowledge of how the rate of resource utilization is changing?

The "expected-inflation/growth-gap" label used here to characterize monetary policy in the V–G era suggests the answers supplied in Sections I and II of this chapter. First, although the FOMC abandoned money targets in October 1982, its compass remained the desire to reanchor inflationary expectations unmoored by stop–go monetary policy. The FOMC monitored bond markets as the "canary in the coal mine" for expected inflation. It varied the frequency and magnitude of its routine LAW funds rate changes to the extent necessary to convince the market that those changes would cumulate to whatever extent required to maintain low, stable trend inflation. Second, the routine "housekeeping" funds rate changes that constitute LAW are a measured, persistent response to sustained changes in resource utilization (a growth gap). The Taylor Rule makes the more demanding (and unrealistic) assumption that the FOMC possesses reliable knowledge of excess capacity (an output or unemployment gap).

Sections III and IV explain why characterization of the monetary standard is so contentious. Section V evaluates whether the V–G experiment supports the rational expectations hypothesis. The Appendix provides an empirical overview of the V–G regime.

I. Keeping Trend Inflation Unchanged

Formula (1) summarizes the consistent part of V–G policy:

$$i_t = i_{t-1} + \alpha\left(\pi_t^e - \pi^*\right) + \beta\Delta R_t^{RU} \qquad \alpha, \beta > 0 \tag{1}$$

where i is the funds rate, π_t^e is expected inflation, π^* is an implicit inflation target, and ΔR_t^{RU} is an estimate of the persistent change in resource utilization. The variable ΔR_t^{RU} measures the extent to which output is growing faster (slower) than potential output, that is, $(\Delta y_t^s - \Delta y_t^P) \neq 0$, where (the log of) real output is y_t. The superscript s indicates smoothed real output, that is, output purged of transitory factors. The superscript p indicates potential output and the first-difference operator is Δ.[1]

The V–G objective of low, stable expected trend inflation required consistent policy to shape expectations. First, the FOMC had to reduce expected trend inflation. Second, it had to remove the expectation of a positive correlation between trend inflation and positive real shocks (divergences of output growth relative to potential) and between trend inflation and inflation shocks (changes in relative prices that pass through to the price level). The resulting discipline meant that the FOMC could no longer supplant the working of the price system as it had attempted with stop–go policy. That attempt had created the monetary emissions that forced changes in prices. The imperative of nominal expectational stability disciplined LAW and gave it a rule-like character that allowed the price system to work.

Consider a real shock that causes real growth to exceed potential (causes the rate of resource utilization to rise in a sustained way). With credibility, markets believe that funds rate increases will cumulate to whatever extent necessary to prevent a change in trend inflation.[2] The entire rise in the yield curve reflects the expectation of higher future real rates, not inflation. In effect, the market continually assesses the level of the real yield curve necessary to return output to trend, but in an environment of nominal expectational stability (Hetzel 2006).

The driving force behind the V–G monetary policy was the desire for credibility. Policymakers understood their responsibility for making the public's expectation of inflation conform to a low, stable target for trend inflation. When Representative Neal asked Volcker (U.S. Cong. July 21, 1987, 21) "how inflation has been brought under control," he replied: "[T]he inflationary process can develop a momentum of its own. It . . . proceeds from lack of confidence about whether measures will be taken to deal with inflation. . . . [A] lot depends upon whether there is, indeed, confidence that an environment will be maintained where you don't have to worry about inflation." The bedrock of credibility is the market's belief that the FOMC possesses instrument independence: It will move the funds rate by whatever amount required to preserve low, stable inflation.

Under Volcker and Greenspan, the FOMC measured its credibility by the behavior of the long-term bond rate.[3] Greenspan (U.S. Cong. February 19, 1993, 55–6) explained the new expectational monetary standard:

[T]he [Humphrey–Hawkins] Act . . . requires the Federal Reserve "to promote effectively the goals of maximum employment, stable prices, and moderate long-term interest rates." The goal of moderate long-term interest rates is particularly relevant.... Lower intermediate- and long-term interest rates and inflation are essential to the structural adjustments in our economy and monetary policy thus has given considerable weight to helping such rates move lower.

Inflation scares were times of drama because of the fear that a rise in the public's inflationary expectations might force an accommodative policy (Goodfriend 1993). During an inflation scare, to maintain credibility, the FOMC had to raise the real interest rate and risk imposing output losses. It could not use the funds rate both to track the natural rate and to control inflationary expectations.[4] As Governor Mitchell said in 1974: "The Committee had one problem with respect to its public image and credibility and another problem with respect to the effects of monetary policy on real economic activity" (cited in Mayer 1999, 49).

Even with credibility, the concern that bond holders price the future dollars for which they contract without incorporating an inflation premium imposes discipline on the period-by-period setting of funds rate changes. Markets understand the systematic procedure the central bank uses to respond to sustained changes in resource utilization. Over a long horizon, the uncertainties of forecasting mean that policymakers and markets will often disagree over the funds rate path required to keep real output at potential (and inflation unchanged). However, policymakers are reluctant to surprise markets with an unanticipated funds rate move or a failure to move as anticipated. A reluctance to depart from the common understanding of the rule imposes commitment to the rule.[5]

II. Implementing Lean-against-the-Wind

The FOMC did not attempt to reach consensus on numerical estimates of growth gaps but rather looked for evidence of sustained changes in resource utilization. Although macroeconomic shocks cause changes in the optimal degree of resource utilization, the working assumption was that resource utilization rates cannot rise or fall indefinitely. With Formula (1), the FOMC moved the funds rate away from its prevailing value in response to sustained changes in resource utilization.

According to the Taylor Rule, the FOMC used an output gap to set the funds rate. However, even in the pre-1979 period, there is no evidence in FOMC *Minutes* that the FOMC used the output gap. Probably, its impreciseness of measurement limited the ability of FOMC members to use it in internal debate. However, in the earlier period, it influenced policy through the assumption that inflation occurring with a negative output gap (measured by unemployment in excess of 4%) had to be cost-push rather than aggregate-demand inflation. Phillips curve estimates of inflation based on overly pessimistic estimates of the output gap produced inflation forecasts that were too low (Figure 8.4; Mayer 1999; Orphanides 2003b; 2003c; Orphanides and van Norden 2002).

In the 1980s, policymakers became willing to move the funds when the *growth* gap became positive rather than when a negative *output* (unemployment) gap neared zero.[6] The use of a growth gap as opposed to an output gap eliminated the need to estimate the level of the path of potential output (or the unemployment rate associated with full employment).[7] Policymakers only needed to know that a persistently falling unemployment rate indicates unsustainably high growth. In the 1980s, FOMC concern for inflationary expectations imposed use of a growth gap indicator because "bond market vigilantes" forced bond rates up whenever real output grew strongly.[8]

A growth gap indicator does not require the FOMC to reach agreement over its constituent elements – actual and trend real output growth.[9] Instead, it requires only consensus on the sustainability of real growth through agreement over the change in resource utilization. Greenspan (U.S. Cong. February 20, 1996, 8) testified:

[P]ersistent deviations of actual growth from that of capacity potential will soon send signals that a policy adjustment is needed. . . . Through the four quarters of 1994, for example, real GDP . . . rose $3\frac{1}{2}$ percent. If that were the true rate of increase in the economy's long-run potential, then we would have expected no change in rates of resource utilization. Instead, industrial capacity utilization rose nearly 3 percentage points, and the unemployment rate dropped 1 percentage point. Moreover, we began to see signs of strain on facilities: deliveries of materials slowed appreciably, and factory overtime rose sharply.

FOMC discussion centered on indirect evidence for a growth gap (see Greenspan in U.S. Cong. January 25, 1995, 4). Greenspan (U.S. Cong. July 20, 1994, 54–5) summarized the variety of indirect evidence the FOMC examined in evaluating the existence of a positive growth gap:

[P]olicymakers need to look . . . for evidence of tightness that might indicate whether inflationary pressures are indeed building. . . . Reports of shortages of skilled labor, strikes, and instances of difficulties in finding workers in specific regions all would be more likely. To attract additional workers, employers would presumably step up their use of wants-ads. . . . Firms might choose to bring on less skilled workers and train them on the job. . . . As firms experienced difficulty in expanding production to meet rising demand, we would also expect to see increasing signs of shortages of goods as well as labor. Businesses might have difficulty in obtaining certain materials. Vendor performance would deteriorate, and lead times on deliveries of new orders would increase. Pressures on supplies of materials and commodities would be reflected in rising prices of these items.

The most important evidence of increased resource utilization came from a tightening labor market. Figure 21.1 plots real GDP growth versus the change in the unemployment rate (Rudebusch 2000). Above-trend growth accompanies falling unemployment.[10] The unemployment rate can mislead because a tightening labor market increases labor force participation rates and restrains declines in unemployment. FOMC members therefore also looked at payroll employment

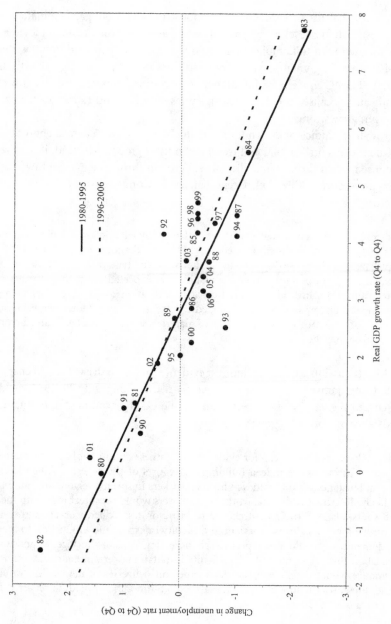

Figure 21.1. Real GDP Growth Rate versus Change in Unemployment Rate.

growth relative to growth in the working-age population. Greenspan (U.S. Cong. July 28, 1999, 44) testified:

[S]urges in economic growth are not necessarily unsustainable – provided they do not exceed the sum of the rate of growth in the labor force and productivity for a protracted period. However, when productivity is accelerating, it is very difficult to gauge when an economy is in the process of overheating. In such circumstances, assessing conditions in labor markets can be helpful in forming those judgments. Employment growth has exceeded the growth in working-age population this past year by almost $\frac{1}{2}$ percentage point.... It implies that real GDP is growing faster than its potential.... There can be little doubt that, if the pool of job seekers shrinks sufficiently, upward pressures on wage costs are inevitable, short ... of a repeal of the law of supply and demand.

Before 1980, the unemployment rate was a target. Afterward, it became an indicator variable. Greenspan (U.S. Cong. July 28, 1999, 16) commented:

Focusing on a specific unemployment rate as an economic goal ... is very shortsighted. I think what you try to do is to get maximum sustainable growth.... What unemployment rate falls out as a consequence of that policy ... would be the appropriate unemployment rate.

III. Conceptualizing the Monetary Standard

A conceptualization of the monetary regime emerges from the way that theory intermediates between the empirical regularities observed in the policy process and those observed in macroeconomic variables. The empirical regularities of the policy process begin with lean-againsts-the-wind. The FOMC raises the funds rate when growth is "strong" – that is when growth exceeds potential and the unemployment rate falls – and conversely when growth is "weak." (See Appendix, "An Empirical Overview of the V–G Regime.") Theory defines the monetary regime through the way that it guides understanding of the discipline imposed on these period-by-period LAW funds rate changes. An implication of the quantity theory is that the central bank must provide a nominal anchor (i.e., give money a well-defined value). This implication highlights the discipline imposed by the effort of Volcker and Greenspan to reestablish the nominal expectational stability lost in the stop–go era. Accordingly, I emphasize the rule-like character of the policy process imposed by the desire to maintain unchanged the expectation of low inflation.

An alternative characterization of monetary policy is that the FOMC conducts policy discretionarily to allow itself "flexibility" to choose in an ongoing manner the trade-off between inflation and unemployment given by the Phillips curve. Former Governor Blinder (Blinder and Reis 2005, 14–16) wrote: "Federal Reserve policy under his [Greenspan's] chairmanship has been characterized by the exercise of pure, period-by-period discretion, with minimal strategic constraints of any kind, maximal tactical flexibility at all times, and not much in the way of explanation."

The reason for the disparate interpretation of the same LAW policy actions is that different theories of price-level determination suggest different empirical regularities to characterize FOMC policy actions.[11] With the quantity theory assumption used here, the character of the nominal anchor determines the behavior of inflation. The alternative assumption is that there is a hard-wired (intrinsic) persistence to inflation.[12] That is, in the absence of an FOMC engineered increase in unemployment, the inflation produced today by an inflation shock propagates into tomorrow. The latter assumption highlights "smoothing" regularities imposed by the FOMC on its LAW funds rate changes. The issue is whether they are core regularities that make a "policy" out of LAW or whether they are simply smoothing that the yield curve ignores in setting longer term rates.

The first of these smoothing regularities is that the FOMC only infrequently reverses the sign of funds rate changes (Goodfriend 1991). This behavior is evident in Figure 21.2 from the paucity of turning points (marked by diamonds) in the funds rate. Over the interval from 1971, when the FOMC began to set a funds rate target, through 2006, there were only 32 turning points. The FOMC makes funds rate changes unidirectional for long periods by reversing a run of decreases only after incipient economic strength becomes clearly persistent, and conversely for runs of increases.[13]

Second, the FOMC avoids association between increases in the funds rate and in the unemployment rate. From January 1983 through 2006, there are 10 exceptions out of 176 observations to this generalization; however, all but 3 of them fall into 2 intervals.[14] The first interval is the deliberate disinflation begun in 1988, and the second interval is the uninterrupted quarter point increments begun in June 2004 when the funds rate started at the unsustainably low 1% level. In both intervals, there is a clear overall cyclical decline in the unemployment rate. The other 3 exceptions occur during inflation scares, that is, instances of significant increases in bond rates or in nominal-TIPS measures of expected inflation (Figure 17.1). They occur on August 15, 1984, after the unemployment rate went from 7.1 to 7.5%; August 16, 1994, when the unemployment rate went from 6.0 to 6.1%; and March 21, 2000, when the unemployment rate went from 4.0 to 4.1%.

Because both of these constraints address the employment concerns of the political system, I refer to them as the dual-mandate constraints. The first avoids the situation during economic recovery where the FOMC raises the funds rate in response to an incipient recovery only to have the recovery falter. A subsequent reduction in the funds rate would then incur accusations that the Fed had "aborted the recovery." This smoothing constraint appears in the unwillingness of the FOMC to raise the funds rate until recovery is firmly established.

The second constraint avoids the accusation that the Fed is controlling inflation "on the backs of working people." In general, it does not bind because an increase in unemployment is an indicator of a sustained fall in the resource utilization rate and calls for a funds rate reduction.[15] However, the dual-mandate sensitivity comes to the fore when expected inflation exceeds the FOMC's implicit inflation target

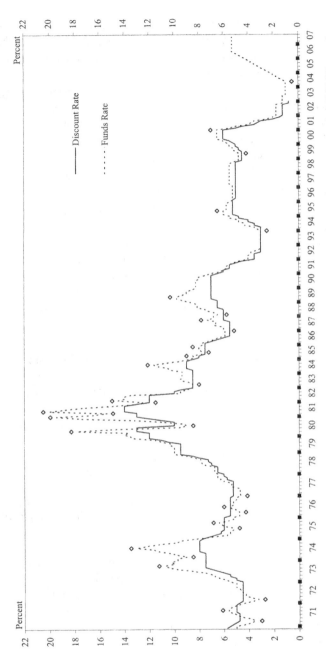

Figure 21.2. The Funds Rate Peg, Its Turning Points, and the Discount Rate. *Notes:* Observations correspond to FOMC meetings: monthly through 1978 and 8 per year thereafter (11 in 1980). *See* Appendix, "FOMC Data," for description of the funds rate series. Diamonds mark turning points. Turning points that would be created by a change in the funds rate target of 0.125 percentage point are ignored. The discount rate for adjustment credit is the value in effect at the New York Fed on the day of the FOMC meeting. Adjustment credit borrowing ended January 9, 2003, and was replaced by primary credit borrowing at a rate tied to the funds rate. Heavy tick marks indicate December FOMC meetings.

and the unemployment rate is rising, perhaps during an inflation scare. The lack of an explicit inflation target gives the FOMC flexibility as to whether to address the lack of credibility by not committing it to procedures that could entail an increase in the funds rate when the unemployment rate is rising.

Are these two constraints on the funds rate innocuous, potentially destabilizing, or the heart of an activist policy? The view here is that they are innocuous provided that the FOMC has established credibility for an inflation target that never drifts. The timing of funds rate changes over short intervals then does not affect the more distant forward rates that shape the yield curve. However, in the past, the FOMC has allowed actual and expected inflation to drift. As a result, funds rate smoothing became the funds rate inertia that produced stop–go cycles.

At stake is how the central bank keeps trend inflation on target when it has established credibility for the target.[16] In 1981–2 and 1990, the FOMC did put inertia into the funds rate at cyclical peaks to lower inflation. However, with credibility does the control of inflation in a way that respects dual-mandate sensitivities require this sort of interest rate inertia? Is the world characterized by inflation shocks propagated by hard-wired inflation persistence so that a politically feasible strategy for correcting inflation overshoots requires waiting opportunistically for periods of economic weakness in which to lower the funds rate in a grudging manner that maintains excess unemployment?

An affirmative answer implies the desirability of strategies for dealing with inflation overshoots labeled at different times as gradualism, flexible inflation targeting, and opportunistic disinflation.[17] Kohn (Board of Governors *Transcripts* December 19, 1995, 30), FOMC secretary and economist, in response to a question by President Jordan (Cleveland), characterized opportunistic disinflation as follows:

[T]he economy is constantly being hit by shocks, and it is not a question of deliberately putting slack in the economy to bring inflation down. It is a question of taking those shocks, whether they are on inflation expectations, demand, supply, or whatnot, and using them to bring inflation down. Over time, if you react asymmetrically to shocks, strongly to upward shocks and less strongly to downward shocks, the inflation rate will work its way lower.

How did this strategy of opportunistic disinflation work in practice? It appeared most clearly in the stop–go period. During the initial expansion phase of rising inflation when the economy grows strongly and the unemployment rate falls, the FOMC raises the funds rate in a persistent way. Eventually, the real funds rate rises enough to weaken the economy. Subsequently, the FOMC lowers the funds rate, but belatedly and then only cautiously. The intention is to lower inflation in a gradual, prolonged way by maintaining a moderately high real funds rate and a moderate amount of excess unemployment.

During the disinflation phase, without explicit guidance from the Fed, expected inflation and, as a consequence, actual inflation fall only slowly. The public only learns that the Fed is enforcing a new, lower trend inflation rate through the brute force of excess unemployment. The experience with 1970s stagflation revealed how expectations gaps (the lack of credibility) trump output gaps for considerable periods in maintaining inflation. Axilrod (1971, 27) pointed out how the slow adjustment of inflationary expectations can create pressures on the FOMC to prolong monetary restriction:[18] "When combating inflationary psychology is taken as a primary goal of policy..., it becomes difficult to permit an easing in money market conditions because this might be taken as signaling an unwillingness of the System to persist in its efforts to reduce inflationary expectations."

These policy-induced cycles of expansion and disinflation put persistence into inflation. Inflation shocks add to that persistence. However, the persistence is not hard-wired in the sense that inflation propagates itself independently of the character of the monetary regime.[19] It does not follow that inflation persistence allows the FOMC to control real variables by manipulating aggregate nominal demand. Similarly, it does not follow that the Fed must periodically pay a high price in terms of unemployment, given by a fixed sacrifice ratio, to suppress inflation. The inference that because of inflation persistence, the FOMC must follow a policy of opportunistic disinflation in order to limit the rise in unemployment necessary to control inflation is circular.

Moreover, the policy can destabilize output. Friedman (1968) and Lucas (1972) argued that the Phillips curve is not "exploitable." If the inverse unemployment–inflation correlations in the data are generated by unanticipated fluctuations in aggregate nominal demand, an attempt to control unemployment by manipulating inflation will cause the inverse relationship between the two variables to disappear. The converse also holds. If Friedman and Lucas are correct, then an attempt to create and sustain a moderate amount of unemployment to work inflation down in a gradual, prolonged manner will fail. The behavior of unemployment shown in Figure 21.3 is consistent with this implication. When the four-quarter growth rate of unemployment reaches a threshold of 0.3 percentage point, it continues upward rather than falling back.

IV. The V–G Era: Discretion or Rules?

Different characterizations of monetary policy coexist because of different assumptions about the nature of inflation and its interaction with the real economy. Does monetary policy condition the behavior of actual and expected inflation or is there a hard-wired persistence that propagates whatever inflation occurs today into the future? The latter assumption implies that the FOMC can choose discretionarily the trade-off between inflation and unemployment on an ongoing basis. The intertemporal constraint on funds rate changes that defines policy is not the desire to achieve nominal expectational stability but rather the dual-mandate imperative to balance inflation and unemployment. Different assumptions about inflation

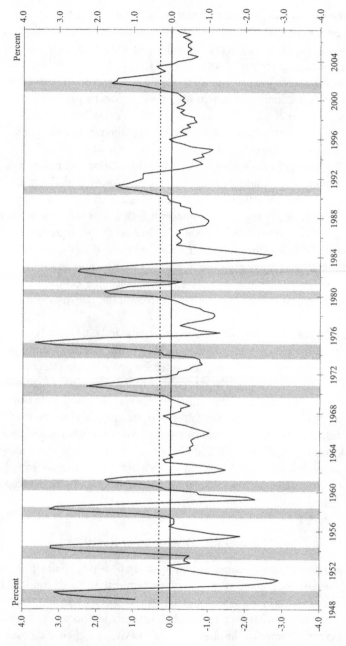

Figure 21.3. Unemployment Growth Rate. *Notes:* Four-quarter percentage change in the unemployment rate. The dashed line lies 0.3 percentage point above the zero axis.

aid in distinguishing these contrasting characterizations of policy as rule-like or discretionary.

In the V–G era, the public changed the way that it forecast inflation compared to the end of the stop–go period. By the end of the V–G era, real shocks and relative price shocks ceased to alter expected trend inflation. The years 2004 to 2006, which display such shocks, offer evidence that the public predicts trend inflation based on the nature of monetary policy rather than on extrapolation of observed inflation. From 2004 through early 2006, expected trend inflation remained stable despite a conjunction of three shocks that had raised expected inflation in the past.

First, real GDP grew above trend. Over the quarters 2003Q2 through 2006Q1, it grew on average at 3.9%, above the 3% consistent with potential growth.[20] Second, energy and commodity prices rose rapidly. The price of oil rose from $34 per barrel in early 2004 to $70 per barrel in September 2005 (a relative price rise comparable to the 1973–4 and 1979–80 oil price increases). Metals prices like copper also rose rapidly. Third, the dollar depreciated.[21] Evidence for the importance of nominal expectational stability is the stability of core PCE inflation relative to PCE inflation (Figure 14.1). In sum, expectations are not invariant to the character of the monetary regime.

Reaching a consensus about the monetary regime and articulating that consensus to the public is unfinished business for the FOMC. Volcker committed the Fed to controlling inflation, initially through low money growth. When money turned out to be an unsatisfactory predictor of nominal demand, the nominal anchor changed from money to nominal expectational stability. Greenspan continued the Volcker policy, although concentrating more on the level of bond rates than on discrete increases. Neither, however, articulated the new monetary standard they had created.

The choice among empirical regularities and their organization into a coherent characterization of the monetary regime requires a model that characterizes the nature of inflation. The challenge is formidable. The FOMC packages funds rate changes for the public as optimal based entirely on the contemporaneous behavior of the economy. Although the resulting impression is one of discretionary management of the real economy, that impression reflects only the correlation between real economic activity and the funds rate not any deep causation. The FOMC cannot explain the restoration of near price stability except as an uninterrupted succession of good luck. The FOMC cannot discuss causation until it replaces the language of business economics, which is descriptive, with the language of economics which identifies cause and effect.

The absence of FOMC discussion using the language of economics also means the FOMC possesses no systematic way to learn from experience. As long as there is no intellectual consensus over the nature of the monetary regime, the regime will remain fragile.[22] Public ignorance and the vagaries of the political appointments process could again combine to make monetary policy a source of instability.

V. Overview

The defining characteristic of the V–G era was rule-like behavior to restore nominal expectational stability. The resulting discipline constrained the FOMC to allow the price system to work. To prevent expected inflation from rising during economic recovery, the FOMC raised the funds rate whenever the economy grew faster than potential as indicated by increasing rates of resource utilization. As a result, it removed cyclical inertia in the funds rate. The unemployment rate ceased being a target and became only an indicator of the change in resource utilization. The FOMC turned determination of the level of unemployment over to the price system. By no longer trying to supersede the working of the price system, the FOMC ended the alternation of periods of expansionary and contractionary monetary policy.

The revolution in the intellectual environment at the end of the 1970s, which relocated responsibility for inflation from market forces to monetary policy, allowed the Volcker revolution. As much as the idea that inflation is a monetary phenomenon, the rational expectations idea that the central bank can discipline expected inflation has changed the intellectual environment. To institutionalize the V–G standard, the FOMC would have to accept responsibility for expected inflation by disciplining its policy actions with a rule. The first step would be an explicit, numerical inflation target that commits the FOMC not to allow inflation to drift. Such a target would encourage the FOMC to explain funds rate changes not as individual events taken in light of the contemporaneous behavior of the economy but rather as part of an ongoing strategy for controlling inflation and allowing the price system to work.

Such a change would require the FOMC to replace the language of discretion with the language of rules. To do that, it would have to confront the issue of the dual mandate. Does the dual-mandate rule out locking into a set of procedures that could force the FOMC into associating an increase in the funds rate with an increase in the unemployment rate? Can the FOMC disavow opportunistic disinflation?

To master inflationary expectations, Volcker (September 20, 2006, 9) accorded priority to credibility:

[W]e had a problem in expectations and inflation is a good part of expectations.... Gradualism...gave you this feeling that we could deal with this problem gently, and that [if] we just go about it in this sophisticated way we can do it with relatively little pain. [This] never seemed realistic to me. It sent the wrong message.... [In] the stuff that the staff was preparing for congressional testimony...the word "gradual" kept appearing. I used to cross it out every time because I wanted to get the message through that once we'd started the process we wanted to finish it.

Volcker had the political acumen to realize that the public would endure short-term pain to master inflation. Future FOMC chairmen could argue that with low inflation there is no such support. Limiting in any way the chairman's discretionary control over the funds rate could endanger the Fed's independence by forcing it to inflict short-term pain in a visible way.

Table 21.1. *Funds Rate Correlations*

$$\Delta FR = 0.15\ GG + 0.016\ MISSI + 0.32\ \Delta BR + 0.15\ \Delta\ BRL1 + \hat{u}$$
$$\qquad\ (8.0)\qquad\ (0.42)\qquad\quad (5.2)\qquad\quad (2.5)$$

$CRSQ = 0.45, SEE = 0.26, DW = 1.6, DF = 148$, date: February 1983 to December 2001

Notes: ΔFR is the change in the funds rate following FOMC meetings. GG is the growth gap: the difference between actual and sustainable real output growth. MISSI is the difference between actual and targeted inflation. ΔBR is the change in the bond rate the day prior to FOMC meetings (30-year through 1999 and 10-year thereafter) and is set equal to zero after 1995. $\Delta BRL1$ is the lagged value of the change in the bond rate.

See Appendix, "FOMC Data" for explanation of the funds rate series. Inflation predictions are for the implicit GNP deflator prior to 1988, CPI ex food and energy from 1989 through May 2000, and PCE ex food and energy chain-weighted price index thereafter.

CRSQ is the corrected R-squared; SEE is the standard error of estimate; DW is the Durbin-Watson statistic; and DF is degrees of freedom. The absolute value of t-statistics is in parentheses.

What is at stake is articulation of the essential nature of a modern central bank. If the price system works poorly to achieve macroeconomic stability and there is intrinsic inflation persistence, then the central bank should and can choose discretionarily each period how to balance off inflation and unemployment. Mystique (secrecy) is essential to keeping that trade-off out of the political system. In contrast, if the price system works well and there is no intrinsic inflation persistence, the central bank should commit to an explicit rule to maintain price stability. With price stability, a change in a dollar price unambiguously conveys information about a change in a relative price.[23] Explicitness allows the central bank to take its place among the institutions that make it possible for free, competitive markets to allocate resources.

APPENDIX: AN EMPIRICAL OVERVIEW OF THE V–G REGIME

The policy process summarized in Formula (1) implies a positive correlation between changes in the funds rate and both a growth gap (the difference between actual and sustainable real growth) and a credibility gap (the difference between expected inflation and the FOMC's implicit inflation target). The regression of Table 21.1, which tests for these correlations, used the following proxies.

The "actual" part of the growth gap proxy used Greenbook real output forecasts. If an FOMC meeting was in the first or second month of the quarter, I used the forecast of growth for the contemporaneous quarter. If the meeting was in the last month of the quarter, I used the forecast for the succeeding quarter. For the "sustainable" part of the growth gap proxy, I tried three proxies. Specifically, I constructed three proxies for the path for real growth that the FOMC believed would bring actual growth in line with trend real growth.

First, I tried the midpoint of the "central tendency" range of forecasts of real output growth that the FOMC chairman presents in biannual congressional oversight hearings (see Appendix, "FOMC Data").[24] FOMC members make these forecasts based on an assumption of "appropriate" monetary policy.[25] In making them, they therefore assume a funds rate path estimated to discipline output to grow in line with trend real output. The resulting forecasts can thus proxy for the growth considered compatible with moving growth to trend.[26] For the FOMC meetings in the first three months of the year, I used the central tendency range from the February oversight hearings. For the remainder of the meetings, the range came from the July oversight hearings.[27]

As a second proxy, I used longer run Greenbook forecasts for real output growth. For FOMC meetings in the first five months of the year, I used the forecasted value in the January Greenbook for growth between the fourth quarters of the prior and contemporaneous years. For the remainder of the meetings, I used the annualized two-quarter growth rate in the June Greenbook for growth between the second and fourth quarters of the contemporaneous year. Although these figures are forecasts, they are contingent on a funds rate path consistent with maintaining the staff's best guess of the inflation rate the FOMC considers acceptable.[28] As a third proxy for near-term growth compatible with sustainable growth, for each FOMC meeting, I averaged the succeeding five quarters of Greenbook forecasts for real growth.

For the growth gap, I used the second proxy for sustainable growth.[29] For each FOMC meeting, Figure 21.4 plots this series and the proxy for actual output growth. Figure 21.5 plots the growth gap (the difference between the actual and sustainable growth proxies) and changes in the funds rate. Diamonds mark episodes of rate increases not associated with positive growth gaps. Examination of Figure 14.3 shows that they correspond to increases in bond rates–inflation scares. As a proxy for the behavior of the credibility gap, the regression uses changes in bond rates.

The Taylor Rule, which assumes that the FOMC controlled inflation in the V–G era through a willingness to increase the funds rate more than increases in inflation, provides an alternative to Formula (1) as a summary of policy. According to the view here, the Taylor Rule fails to capture the preemptive character of policy, which involved raising the funds rate in response to increases in expected inflation even when actual inflation remained quiescent. To test the Taylor Rule, I included a proxy for the gap between actual inflation and the FOMC's implicit "interim" target for inflation, where "interim" is analogous to sustainable real growth. The interim target keeps inflation on a path consistent with a longer-run target of price stability.

For FOMC members, forecasting inflation is not like forecasting the weather. Apart from transitory fluctuations, they control inflation. A forecast of a high or rising inflation rate would constitute an admission by the policymaker that he or she will not perform his or her job responsibly. In oversight testimony, Greenspan (U.S. Cong. February 24, 1998, 266) commented: "[T]he policymakers' forecasts also reflect their determination to hold the line on inflation."[30] I constructed proxies for actual and interim inflation in a way analogous to the second proxy discussed previously for actual and sustainable real output growth.[31]

Table 21.1 shows a regression of changes in the funds rate on proxies for the growth gap, credibility gap, and inflation gap.[32] The regression includes

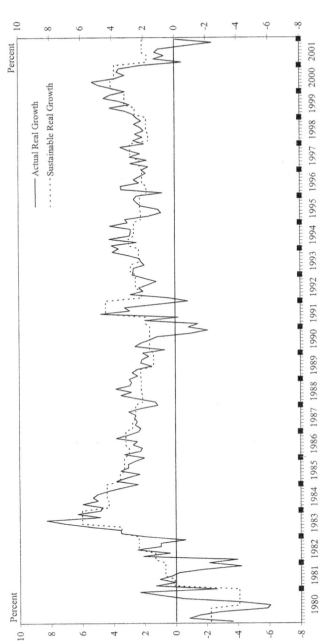

Figure 21.4. Actual and Sustainable Real Output Growth. *Notes:* Actual real output growth is an estimate of the annualized quarterly rate of growth of real output (GNP before 1992, GDP thereafter) available at FOMC meetings. If an FOMC meeting is in one of the first two months of a quarter, it is for the contemporaneous quarter. If the meeting is in the last month of a quarter, it is for the succeeding quarter. Sustainable growth is a longer run forecast of real output growth from the Greenbook. For the first three FOMC meetings in a year, it is the real output growth predicted to occur over the four-quarter period ending in the fourth quarter found in the January Greenbook. For the remainder of the meetings, it is the two-quarter annualized growth rate ending in the fourth quarter found in the June Greenbook. Observations correspond to FOMC meetings. Heavy tick marks indicate a December FOMC meeting.

267

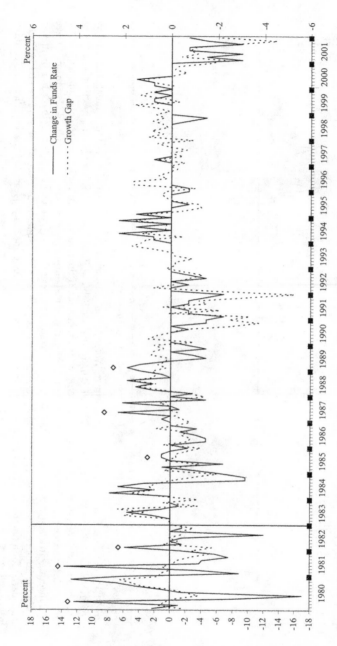

Figure 21.5. Growth Gap and Funds Rate Changes. *Notes*: The growth gap is the difference between the actual and sustainable values shown in Figure 21.4. The left scale is for the 1980–2 period. The right scale is for the subsequent period. The funds rate is the target set at FOMC meetings. (See Appendix: "FOMC Data.") Changes in the funds rate are multiplied by three. Diamonds mark the following dates: (1) March 1980, (2) May 1981, (3) February 1982, (4) August 1985, (5) May 1987, (6) February 1989. Heavy tick marks indicate December FOMC meetings.

268

intermeeting changes in the bond rate recorded the day before the FOMC meeting as a measure of the change in inflationary expectations. The bond rate variable is set to zero after 1995. Credibility in the recent period apparently causes the bond rate to lose its explanatory power. The regression runs from February 1983 through December 2001.[33] A positive correlation exists between changes in the funds rate target and the two independent variables: the growth gap and bond rate changes. The statistically insignificant coefficient on the inflation gap contradicts the Taylor Rule assumption that the FOMC responded directly to observed inflation.

Figure 21.6 shows actual and simulated funds rate changes. A number of factors lower the correlation between changes in the funds rate and the growth gap proxy. (1) The Greenbook forecast of growth used for actual growth may incorporate transitory factors that the FOMC ignores. (2) The regression does not capture the inertia in funds rate changes around cyclical turning points (Figure 21.2). (3) The FOMC need not accept the board staff forecast. (4) The relevant policy variable is the revision to the funds rate path the FOMC believes will achieve sustainable growth and keep inflation on target, not changes in the funds rate.[34]

Factors 1 and 2 highlight the need for judgment in implementing the assumed V–G rule, which calls for raising the funds rate in response to persistent above-trend growth in real output, and conversely for below-trend growth. The need to make decisions contemporaneously renders difficult identification of persistent as opposed to transitory strength (weakness). At cyclical turning points, the problem is especially acute. The year 2006 illustrates the pervasiveness of the difficulty.

The United States had experienced a sustained housing boom. From 1995 through 2005, home ownership rose 5 percentage points. The low real rates experienced during the recovery from the 2001 recession spurred housing. In 2006, a sharp fall in home sales and construction left housing with a large inventory overhang. A fall in residential construction combined with weak demand for domestic vehicles, especially SUVs made less attractive by the rise in gas prices, to cause real GDP to grow below trend in 2006. The fact that the FOMC did not lower the funds rate is consistent with the inference that it considered below-trend growth to be transitory, in addition to actual and expected inflation being too high.

APPENDIX: FOMC DATA

This appendix discusses the data used in Figures 21.2 through 21.4 and in the regression of Table 21.1.

The observations in the figures and regressions correspond to FOMC meeting dates. Starting in 1981, there have been eight FOMC meetings a year. Forecasts of growth rates for real output and inflation are from the Greenbook ("Current Economic and Financial Conditions"), which is prepared by the staff of the Board of Governors and circulated to FOMC participants before meetings. Part 1, "Summary and Outlook," contains quarterly forecasts for nominal and real output

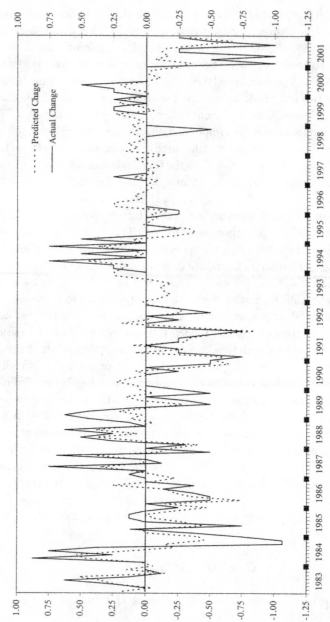

Figure 21.6. Actual and Simulated Funds Rate Changes. *Notes:* Simulated values are within sample simulated values from the regression in Table 21.1. Heavy tick marks indicate December FOMC meetings.

(GNP before 1992, GDP thereafter). Greenbooks remain confidential for five full calendar years after the year in which they were constructed.

At FOMC meetings from June 1988 through March 1989, the FOMC looked at forecasts of GNP growth adjusted for the effects of the 1988 drought. The details of the drought adjustment are found in the Greenbooks. The Commerce Department estimates of the differences between drought-adjusted GNP growth and actual GNP growth are 0.7 (1988Q2), 0.5 (1988Q3), 1.0 (1988Q4), and −2.2 (1989Q1) percentage points. For these meetings, to obtain predictions of drought-adjusted levels of GNP, drought-adjusted growth rates are applied to the initial 1988Q1 GNP figure, which was unaffected by the subsequent drought.

For the November 1970 through September 1979 FOMC meetings, the funds rate is the initial value set by the FOMC as reported in the Board of Governors staff document called the Bluebook ("Monetary Policy Alternatives"). For the last two meetings in 1979, in 1980, 1981, and the first half of 1982, the funds rate is the actual funds rate prevailing in the first full statement week. (For January 1980, May 1980, May and July 1981, and November 1981, it is possible to obtain a value expected to prevail by the Desk.) From the last half of 1982 through 1993, the funds rate is the value the New York Desk expected to prevail in the first full statement week after an FOMC meeting as reported in "Open Market Operations and Securities Market Developments" published biweekly by the New York Fed. Starting in 1994, the funds rate is the target the FOMC announced after its meetings.

TWENTY-TWO

The Fed

Inflation Fighter or Inflation Creator?

After 1983, high, variable inflation gave way to low, stable inflation while real output became less variable. Section I advances the "inflation-fighter" explanation of this result. Inflation arose in the 1970s because the FOMC responded only halfheartedly to inflation shocks. The subsequent decline in real variability arose from a decline in inflation shocks.

Section II advances the "inflation-creator" view, which emphasizes how discretion in the 1970s destroyed nominal expectational stability. Subsequent rule-like behavior restored it. The resulting discipline imposed on funds rate changes caused the yield curve to move in a way that replaced the alternation of periods of contractionary and expansionary monetary policy with a neutral policy that turned economic stabilization over to the price system (Hetzel 2006). An appendix argues that the Taylor Rule fails to offer a useful framework for understanding monetary policy.

I. The Fed as Inflation Fighter

The inflation-fighter view is in a traditional Keynesian spirit, which emphasizes a Phillips curve with inertia in inflationary expectations that exists independently of monetary policy. This inertia, reflected in expectations based on realized inflation, propagates inflation shocks. Consistent with the belief that the FOMC can predictably manipulate real variables, inflation arises when the central bank fails to raise the real interest rate and the unemployment rate sufficiently to offset such shocks.

Blinder and Reis (2005, 16) exposit this view:

[T]he expected inflation rate . . . is a slow-moving state variable rather than a fast-moving "jump" variable. So when the FOMC sets the *nominal* federal funds rate . . . , it . . . also sets the *real* federal funds rate. . . . And if the *neutral* real rate . . . is pretty stable over time, it also sets the deviation of the real funds rate from the neutral value. (italics in original)

The FOMC manipulates the amount of monetary stimulus "to penalize *both* inflation *and* deviations of output from its full-employment level" (Blinder and Reis

272

2005, 21). The dual mandate of the Federal Reserve Act ("to promote effectively the goals of maximum employment [and] stable prices") requires trading off between inflation and employment variability.

The Fed-as-inflation-fighter view makes inflation shocks the initiating factor in inflation.[1] Blinder (1982, 261) attributes the 1970s inflation to cost-push shocks: "[D]uring the 1970s . . . large unavoidable adjustments in relative prices bred inflation." Implicit in these explanations is the assumption that reversal of such price increases would have required unacceptably large increases in unemployment. In the language of the Phillips curve, the sacrifice ratio is high.[2] Blinder (1981, 71) wrote: "Because prices and wages are unresponsive to changes in demand in the short run, the massive realignments of *relative* prices required by poor agricultural harvests, OPEC, and the end of wage–price controls caused most of the great inflation of 1973–1974 and most of the great recession of 1973–1975" (italics in original). Ball (1991, 439) offers a similar characterization: "Mishaps including the Vietnam War and the rise of OPEC produced several episodes of high inflation. . . . And once inflation arises, it proves stubbornly persistent. . . . Inflation continues until the Fed becomes sufficiently unhappy to tighten policy. At that point inflation falls, but at the cost of a recession." Because inflation-fighter explanations of inflation stress FOMC failure to respond aggressively to realized inflation, they possess implications for the temporal relationship between money and prices. Counterfactually to these cost-push theories of inflation, as shown in Chapters 23–25, higher money growth preceded higher inflation rather than followed it.

A recent variation of this "cruel dilemma" view emphasizes price-level indeterminacy. Chari, Christiano, and Eichenbaum (1998, 466) presented a model of how a "transitory real shock can lead to increased expectations of inflation, which are validated by the monetary authority." Christiano and Gust (2000) and Leduc (2003) attributed inflation to "expectations traps," where inflation arises from increases in expected inflation not necessarily related to monetary policy. To avoid recession, they argued, the FOMC validated such inflation with higher money growth.

Clarida, Gali, and Gertler (2000) also argue that a failure by the FOMC to respond strongly to realized inflation led to an indeterminacy of inflation. Self-fulfilling revisions in expectations drove fluctuations in inflation. However, the data contradict theories implying that increases in inflationary expectations preceded increases in inflation. Expected inflation lagged rather than led actual inflation (Figure 4.4). Inflation produced a loss of the credibility carried over from the gold standard instead of a loss of credibility producing inflation.

II. The Fed as Inflation Creator

The inflation-creator view is in the quantity theory tradition (Hetzel 2008a; 2008b). To give the price level a well-defined value, the central bank must control some nominal variable – money, the exchange rate, the price of gold. With the V–G monetary standard, that nominal variable became the public's expectation of the future price level. Stability in the contemporaneous value of the price level requires the central bank to follow consistent behavior that creates stability in the expected future value of the price level. As expressed in New Neoclassical Synthesis (NNS or New Keynesian) models, trend inflation derives from a monetary rule that controls expected inflation (Goodfriend 2004a; Goodfriend and King 1997; Rotemberg and Woodford 1997; Woodford 2003, 187). Because there is no intrinsic inertia in expected inflation, as long as the central bank possesses credibility, inflation shocks do not propagate.

According to the inflation-creator view, in the V–G era, the Fed followed rule-like behavior that made it responsible for the control of inflation and that turned over to the price system control of the real economy. During stop–go, the FOMC turned this policy on its head. The belief that it carried the weight of sustaining real growth and low unemployment on its shoulders made the FOMC reluctant to raise short-term interest rates. At the same time, the belief that inflation arose from cost-push pressures made it tolerant of inflation.[3]

Following the Keynesian consensus, in the 1970s, the FOMC believed that it had to choose between inflation and low unemployment.[4] In their overview of the monetarist–Keynesian debate, Hafer and Wheelock (2001, 4) cite Perry (1966):

[A] fairly general consensus exists among economists . . . [that] successively higher levels of activity are associated . . . with correspondingly larger rates of price increase. [T]he more traditional problem of adjusting aggregate demand so as to reach full employment without overshooting into the area of inflation must be replaced with the dual problems of deciding what combination of unemployment and inflation to aim at and then adjusting aggregate demand to reach this point.

The Great Depression produced a consensus that the price system works poorly to maintain aggregate demand at a level consistent with full employment. It followed that government had a responsibility to maintain aggregate real demand at a level sufficient to ensure a high level of employment, subject to the amount of inflation it was willing to accept. DeLong (1997) argued that the experience of the Depression caused policymakers to focus on maintaining full employment while dismissing the costs of the inflation presumed to be associated with full employment. Mayer (1999, 77), who concluded that the most important reason for the Great Inflation was acceptance of the menu interpretation of the Phillips curve, cited the 1977 Report of the JEC:

At present the bulk of the burden of inflation control falls on production and unemployment. . . . To make willing, but marginal workers the principal victims of what amounts to a national disease is cruel and primitive. . . . It is also exceedingly costly and inefficient. The "side effects" of inflation control by means of fiscal and monetary restrictions are too enormous to be tolerated. If we are to refuse to accept continued sluggish growth and excessive unemployment we will either have to learn to control inflation by means that do not cause unemployment, or we will have to learn to be more tolerant of inflation.

Paul Samuelson expressed the same view to the FOMC. After the surge in inflation that began in early 1973, he told the FOMC that "cost-push inflation is not something that the monetary authorities can or ought to do a lot about."[5]

As embodied in NNS models, three abstractions explain why the rule-like behavior of the FOMC in the V–G era provided both nominal and real stability (Hetzel 2005). First, the price system works. The story of the last century is how monetary policy that did not respect the role played by the real interest rate in the price system produced instability rather than how policymakers learned to manage the economy. There is a real business cycle core to the economy with a stationary representation of real variables. The price system works (the real interest rate and real wage vary) to counteract shocks and return real variables to a balanced growth path. The expectation that variables will return to this path after shocks imposes stability on their contemporaneous value. Although obscured by the unpredictability of shocks, continuity in the self-equilibrating operation of the price system requires continuity in the procedures the FOMC uses to vary the funds rate.

The central bank requires procedures that allow it to track the natural rate – the real interest rate consistent with the real business cycle core of the economy. The FOMC raises the funds rate in a measured, persistent way in response to sustained increases in resource utilization, and conversely. Such increases in resource utilization produce markup compression (reductions in the ratio of price to marginal cost). Because increases in the real interest rate restrain real aggregate demand, FOMC procedures keep the markup fluctuating around its profit-maximizing level. Although positive real shocks produce markup compression, the assumption by price setters that the compression is transitory prevents the coordination among them necessary to allow a collective, sustained price rise (inflation) (Goodfriend 2004a; Broaddus and Goodfriend 2004).

Second, the price level is a monetary phenomenon. The arrangements the central bank puts into place for creating and destroying the monetary base determine the equilibrating role played by the price level. With fixed exchange rates, the price level varies to equilibrate the balance of payments. With floating rates, it varies to endow the nominal quantity of money with the purchasing power the public desires. Because the public cares only about real variables, control over money creation (a nominal variable) endows the central bank with control over actual inflation through its control over expected inflation.

Third, price setters learn to form their expectation of inflation in a way that conforms to the systematic behavior of the central bank (rational expectations). When combined with the forward-looking behavior of price setters, a monetary policy rule allows a credible central bank to control trend inflation without shocking the real economy. Stability in the expectation of future prices creates stability in contemporaneous prices.

Credibility explains how the rule-like behavior of the FOMC in the V–G era created both nominal and real stability. In response to a shock, markets believe that the FOMC will persist with measured changes in the funds rate until they cumulate to the extent necessary to prevent a change in trend inflation. In the case of a positive real shock, the yield curve will rise, and the increase in forward rates will be entirely real. The market continually moves the yield curve in a way that returns output to its balanced growth path. This rule-like behavior stabilizes real output by allowing the price system to work and stabilizes trend inflation by controlling expected inflation (Hetzel 2006).

In the absence of credibility, in contrast, a positive real shock will produce a rise in the yield curve from an increase in forward rates due both to an increase in real rates and inflation premia. Firms must guess how much they need to raise their dollar prices to preserve relative prices. Because they must do so in an uncoordinated way, relative prices change capriciously. If the central bank does put inertia into funds rate changes that allows shocks to alter trend inflation, monetary nonneutrality renders the expected values of real variables less certain and that instability feeds back into contemporaneous real instability. Instability in inflation and real output go together. The discretionary aggregate demand policies of stop–go destabilized output and inflation, while the rule-like behavior of the V–G era stabilized them.

These three abstractions imply that the central bank cannot exploit the real–nominal correlations of the Phillips curve. It cannot control inflation through manipulation of unemployment. Instead, it must use a rule that provides for monetary control. Because use of an interest rate instrument makes the monetary base endogenous, monetary control requires that the central bank discipline the public's nominal money demand to grow in line with its inflation target.[6] It does so by getting "right" the prices that determine nominal and real money demand.

First, the central bank must follow a rule (behave consistently) that causes the public to expect an inflation rate consistent with the bank's target for inflation. Second, it must possess a procedure for varying the funds rate in a way that discovers the natural interest rate (Hetzel 2004a; 2005; 2006). With the real rate equal to the natural rate, real output grows in line with the dynamics of the real business cycle. Given the funds rate target, the central bank accommodates the resulting changes in real money demand plus random fluctuations. Nominal money then grows in line with nominal money demand, which is given by this change in real money demand and by expected inflation (equal to the inflation target). As a result, inflation need not deviate from target to bring the purchasing power of nominal money into line with real money demand. Actual and expected inflation are always and everywhere a monetary phenomenon.

APPENDIX: TAYLOR RULE ESTIMATION

Taylor Rule regressions explain the funds rate by the behavior of inflation and of cyclical movements in output (Taylor 1993). By making the funds rate depend upon realized inflation, the Taylor Rule incorporates the inflation-fighter view. That is, the FOMC controlled inflation by vigorously responding to its appearance rather than by preventing its appearance through rule-like behavior that created low expected inflation. Taylor (1999) contended that the increase over time to a value greater than one in the estimated coefficient on inflation in Taylor Rule regressions accounted for the FOMC's success in controlling inflation in the V–G era.

Because of the failure to address the identification problem that arises in a regression of one endogenous variable on another, the ability of Taylor Rules to capture FOMC behavior is doubtful. To begin, there is no effort to justify the functional form. The use of the output gap appears appropriate for the stop–go period when policymakers believed that they knew the level of potential output because of its assumed association with a 4% unemployment rate. However, in the later period, there is no evidence that the FOMC reached a consensus over the magnitude of an output gap as a prerequisite for changing the funds rate. The output gap is so imprecisely measured that it lacks operational significance (Chapter 21). Furthermore, even though the use of inflation is appropriate in the stop–go period, its use in the later period appears less so. The focus in the V–G era on expected inflation is more appropriate for capturing the preemptive character policy. Finally, the assumption of a fixed inflation target is inappropriate for the stop–go period when the Fed let inflation drift upward.

Simultaneous equations bias arises because both the dependent variable (the funds rate) and an independent variable (inflation) depend upon a third variable (expected inflation). Because the FOMC is sensitive to inflationary expectations, the funds rate depends upon expected inflation. Assuming the validity of the New Keynesian Phillips curve, which makes current inflation depend upon expected inflation, inflation also depends upon expected inflation.[7] The resulting difficulty in knowing whether Taylor Rule regressions capture the behavior of the FOMC or of the public appears in the interpretation of the increase over time in the estimated coefficient on inflation.

The interpretation of this coefficient depends upon the nature of inflationary expectations (Sargent 1971). As the repeated underprediction of inflation made evident, until the end of the 1970s, markets retained a residual belief that inflation was a stationary process (Figure 4.4). In the 1960s and 1970s, because of the autoregressive nature of inflationary expectations, increases in inflation produced proportionately smaller increases in expected inflation than later. The increase over time in the estimated coefficient on the inflation term may only reflect the change from regressive to extrapolative inflationary expectations. As a result of this change, the constraint imposed on policy by a rise in inflation was greater in the 1980s than in the 1970s.

To solve the problem of simultaneous equations bias, Clarida, Gali, and Gertler (CGG, 2000) use rational expectations identifying restrictions, which assume certainty by the public about a monetary policy rule. However, in the postwar period, the public and the Fed itself had difficulty learning about a monetary standard that evolved unpredictably. CGG posit a policy rule according to which the FOMC responded to deviations between forecasted and targeted inflation and to the forecasted output gap (the percentage difference between actual and potential output). In their regression, the error term includes errors made in forecasting inflation and the output gap. Because the estimation procedure uses lagged values of inflation and the output gap as instruments, these errors must be uncorrelated with the realized values of inflation and the output gap.

For example, even though a positive forecast error for inflation last period might be associated with a positive forecast error in the current period, a positive forecast error should not be predictably associated with a high value of inflation. However, in the postwar period, forecast errors for inflation were positively correlated with inflation. Neither the public nor the Fed understood the inflation-generating process, and both made persistent forecasting errors (Figures 4.4 and 8.4). Figure 13.2, which shows board staff forecasts of real growth, also suggests that forecast errors of the output gap were serially correlated.

Another problem is that the correlation between the funds rate and inflation in Taylor Rule regressions may arise primarily from a common trend rather than from the reaction of the FOMC to realized inflation. Figure 13.3 shows the common movement between the funds rate and inflation.[8] That is, the apparent fit of Taylor Rule regressions may arise from the Granger–Newbold (1974) spurious regression phenomenon. If the estimated regressions embody a behavioral relationship, they should survive estimation in first differences, which removes common trends. In fact, as shown later, estimated coefficients in Taylor Rule regressions fall significantly upon first differencing.

The observations used in the following regressions begin with Greenspan's chairmanship and use contemporaneously available data (Hetzel 2000). The funds rate i_t^* is the value targeted by the FOMC at the conclusion of its meetings. The output gap x_t is the percentage deviation of current output from a trendline fitted through the 40 prior quarters. Output is real GDP (GNP before 1992) spliced together from Greenbook data and the Federal Reserve Bank of Philadelphia Real Time Data Set (Croushore and Stark 1999). If the FOMC meeting was in the first or second month of the quarter, current output is for the quarter prior to the quarter in which the FOMC meeting occurred. If it was in the last month of the quarter, current output is for the contemporaneous quarter.

π_t is a four-quarter average of annualized quarterly percentage changes in the implicit nominal output deflator through 1988, the CPI ex food and energy from 1990 until mid 2000, and the core PCE thereafter. If the FOMC meeting was in the first or second month of the quarter, the four lagged inflation values averaged to calculate π_t begin with the quarter prior to the quarter of the FOMC meeting. If the FOMC meeting was in the last month of the quarter, the four lagged values begin with the contemporaneous quarter. I also experimented with "predicted" values of inflation and the output gap that relied more heavily on forecasts of the future made by the board staff. However, none of the estimated regressions fit better than those reported here. I also estimated regressions for the Volcker period August

1979 through July 1987, and for the pre-Volcker period November 1965 through July 1979. These regressions "survived" first differencing even more poorly than the ones reported here.

Equation (2) is the first-differenced form of (1). Regression (3) adds the lagged funds rate to (1), and (4) is the first-differenced form of (3).[9] The fall in the estimated values of the coefficients in the regressions going from level to first-differenced form casts doubt on whether the regressions capture FOMC behavior. From (1) to (2), the estimated coefficients on inflation fall from 1.54 to 0.4 and on the output gap from 0.81 to 0.14. From (3) to (4), the long-run coefficients (the estimated coefficient divided by 1 minus the estimated coefficient on the lagged term) fall from 1.57 to 0.78 for inflation and from 1.14 to 0.1 for the output gap. Neither of the differenced equations fit well. The first-differenced regressions exhibit low R-squares and the standard error of estimates are about equal to the average magnitude of a funds rate change.

$$i_t^* = 0.48 + 1.54\pi_t + 0.81x_t + \hat{\mu}_t \tag{1}$$
$$(2.5) \quad (25.0) \quad\;\; (22.3)$$

Date August 1987 to March 2003: R-Bar $= 0.87$, SEE $= 0.8$, DW $= 0.33$, DF $= 131$

$$\Delta i_t^* = 0.4\Delta\pi_t + 0.14\Delta x_t + \hat{\mu}_t \tag{2}$$
$$(3.2) \quad\;\; (2.3)$$

Date August 1987 to March 2003: R-Bar $= 0.07$, SEE $= 0.29$, DW $= 1.5$, DF $= 132$

$$i_t^* = 0.03 + 0.22\pi_t + 0.16x_t + 0.86i_{t-1}^* + \hat{\mu}_t \tag{3}$$
$$(0.5) \quad (4.8) \quad\;\; (6.9) \quad\;\; (32.6)$$

Date August 1987 to March 2003: R-Bar $= 0.99$, SEE $= 0.26$, DW $= 1.5$, DF $= 130$

$$\Delta i_t^* = 0.32\Delta\pi_t + 0.04\Delta x_t + 0.39\Delta i_{t-1}^* + \hat{\mu}_t \tag{4}$$
$$(2.8) \quad\quad\;\; (.7) \quad\quad\;\; (4.7)$$

Date August 1987 to March 2003: R-Bar $= 0.20$, SEE $= 0.27$, DW $= 1.5$, DF $= 131$

The absolute value of the t-statistic is in parentheses, R-Bar is the corrected R-squared, SEE is the standard error of estimate, DW is the Durbin-Watson statistic, and DF is degrees of freedom.

TWENTY-THREE

The Stop–Go Laboratory

The Woodrow Wilson Presidential Library in Staunton, VA, contains an exhibit entitled "The Federal Reserve: Wilson's Enduring Legacy: A modern industrial nation must have a money supply that can expand and contract with the economic cycle." There is a quotation from a 1913 address by Wilson to Congress: "We must have a currency, not rigid as now, but readily, *elastically responsive to sound credit....* And the control of the system of banking must be public, not private, must be vested in the government itself" [italics added]. The aggregate demand management of stop–go imparted the same procyclical bias to money that had existed under the real bills doctrine.[1] However, it did so with an inflationary bias.

Chapters 23–5 identify the empirical regularities that characterize the almost 20-year stop–go period following 1964. The Fed, not private markets, produced "inflation shocks." Inflation is a monetary phenomenon in that high rates of money growth *preceded* increases in inflation. Contrary to Taylor (1999), the inertia in the interest rate that made monetary policy inflationary preceded inflation rather than followed it.

To use historical experience to decide between the competing hypotheses of Fed as inflation creator and inflation fighter (Chapter 22), one needs to understand how the monetary regime affects the predictive relationship between money and prices. In case 1, the central bank accepts responsibility for inflation, possesses credibility for its inflation target, and pursues a strategy consistent with achieving the target. It maintains the real interest rate equal to the natural rate, and its inflation target determines expected inflation. Because expected inflation controls the behavior of money and prices, money possesses no predictive power for prices.[2] In case 2, the stop–go regime, the central bank does not consistently maintain the real interest rate equal to the natural rate. As a result, it creates monetary emissions that force changes in prices. If the money demand function is stable, money predicts prices.[3]

If case 2, one can use the temporal relationships between money and prices to distinguish between competing hypotheses.[4] According to the inflation-fighter view, inflation shocks initiated the inflation of the 1960s and 1970s and money growth followed inflation. According to the inflation-creator view, excess money creation preceded inflation. McCallum (2002, 83) argued that models of price-level determination need not include money so long as the central bank uses the interest rate as an operating instrument and empirically the real balance effect is minimal. In case 1 where the central bank is not a source of independent disturbances, the argument is unobjectionable. However, in case 1, one cannot test the quantity theory. One needs a case 2 world where the central bank has performed the "experiment" of attempting to control systematically the behavior of real variables. Then the behavior of money is informative.

Another reason the stop–go period is an extraordinary laboratory is the existence of a monetary aggregate (M1) with a demand function that was both stable and interest inelastic (Hetzel and Mehra 1989). Consequently, M1 growth rates measured the degree of monetary stimulus. Through 1980, quantity changes in M1 conveyed information about aggregate nominal demand. The nationwide introduction of NOW accounts in January 1981 made real M1 demand interest sensitive.[5]

A problem for the inflation-fighter view, which attributes the origin of inflation to inflation shocks, is the paucity of inflation shocks. The 1973 and 1978–9 oil price shocks occur well after the onset of an expansionary monetary policy and after inflation begins to rise (Chapters 8 and 11). In the postwar period, there are four other candidates for an inflation shock. The first is the removal of World War II price controls in October 1946. Suppressed inflation initially caused measured inflation to soar. However, after August 1948, inflation fell off rapidly.

The next inflation shock occurred during the Korean War in November 1950 when the Chinese invasion of North Korea threatened to ignite World War III (Hetzel and Leach 2001a, 40).[6] Fearing the reimposition of price controls and the reappearance of shortages, consumers rushed to buy consumer durables. Annualized CPI inflation, which had been running around 5%, jumped to 21% in December 1950 and January and February 1951. In early 1951, Congress raised taxes to pay for the war, and the Fed regained its independence to raise interest rates. Near-price stability then replaced inflation. Over the 12-month intervals March 1951 through March 1952 and March 1952 through March 1953, CPI inflation was, respectively, 1.9 and 1.1%.[7] Neither of these inflation shocks exhibited significant persistence. Inflation persistence does not appear to be hard-wired into the Phillips curve, but rather depends upon how the monetary regime has conditioned expectations.

A third candidate for an inflation shock occurs with the final removal of price controls in April 1974. Although there was a surge in inflation, the FOMC responded and the real rate rose rather than fell (Figure 8.3). The final candidate is the oil price shock from 2005–6. By summer 2006, this inflation shock had only barely passed into core inflation, which remained near 2%. The longer that the current near-price stability persists without a breakout of inflation put down by the purposeful creation of unemployment, the less plausible is the idea that inflation shocks cause inflation.

Table 23.1. *M1 Steps, Nominal Output Growth, and Funds Rate*

	Nominal GDP peak, trough	Funds rate peak, trough	Lag in quarters	Change in M1 step
P	1966 Q1 (12.8%)	1966 Q4 (5.6%)	3	−5.2
T	1967 Q2 (3.1%)	1967 Q4 (4.2%)	2	5.2
P	1969 Q1 (10.7%)	1969 Q4 (8.9%)	3	−4.2
T	1970 Q4 (1.4%)	1972 Q1 (3.5%)	5	5.3[a]
P	1973 Q4 (13.2%)	1974 Q3 (12.1%)	3	−3.7[b]
T	1975 Q1 (2.4%)	1977 Q1 (4.7%)	8	4.5[c]
P	1980 Q1 (11.5%)	1981 Q3 (17.6%)	6	−5.6[d]

[a] From 1969Q2–1970Q2 step to 1972Q1–1973Q1 step
[b] From 1972Q1–1973Q1 step to 1974Q2–1975Q1 step
[c] From 1974Q2–1975Q1 step to 1976Q4–1978Q4 step
[d] From 1976Q4–1978Q4 step to 1981Q1–1981Q4 step
Notes: The dates correspond to the turning points in the series shown in Figure 23.1. The numbers in parentheses are the values at turning points. The lags show the quarters elapsed from turning points in nominal GDP growth and the funds rate. The "Change in M1 step" refers to the difference between the M1 steps in Figure 23.1.

The stop–go period may forever remain the best laboratory for tests of monetary nonneutrality. Such tests require identification of monetary policy shocks. Such identification requires monetary policy actions that are adventitious to the working of the price system. A key characteristic of policy in the stop–go period was cyclical inertia in the funds rate. That inertia created monetary accelerations and decelerations, which with a lag affected growth in real output and prices.[8] Before 1979, after troughs in economic activity, the FOMC began to raise the funds rate only tardily because of a desire to eliminate a negative output gap. After peaks in economic activity, it began to lower the funds rate only tardily because of a desire to lower inflation.

Figure 23.1 and Table 23.1 document the lag in turning points of the funds rate behind cyclical turning points in nominal output growth. Figure 23.1 graphs nominal output growth, the funds rate, and an M1 step function.[9] The arrows connect dates when nominal output growth began to fall (rise) with subsequent dates when the funds rate began to fall (rise). The low M1 steps are 1966Q2 to 1967Q1, 1969Q2 to 1970Q2, 1973Q2 to 1975Q1, and 1981Q1 to 1981Q4. As shown by the arrows, the beginning of these steps is associated with falling nominal output growth and a rising funds rate.[10] The high M1 steps are 1967Q2 to 1969Q1, 1970Q3 to 1973Q1, 1976Q4 to 1978Q4. As shown by the arrows, the beginning of these steps is associated with rising nominal output growth followed belatedly by a rising funds rate.[11]

Table 23.1 shows the lag in turning points of the funds rate behind nominal output growth. It also shows the monetary decelerations and accelerations associated

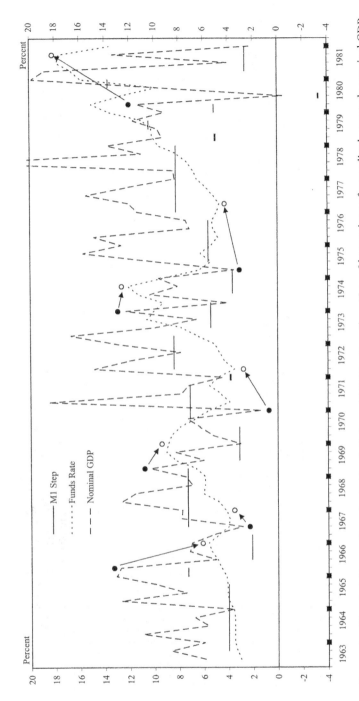

Figure 23.1. Nominal Output Growth, the Funds Rate, and M1 Step Function. *Notes*: Observations of annualized, quarterly nominal GDP growth and the funds rate. The M1 steps are an average of the annualized quarterly M1 growth rates. In 1981, M1 is "shift adjusted" (Bennett 1982). Dark circles mark changes in nominal output growth. Light circles mark significant turning points in the funds rate. Heavy tick marks indicate the fourth quarter.

283

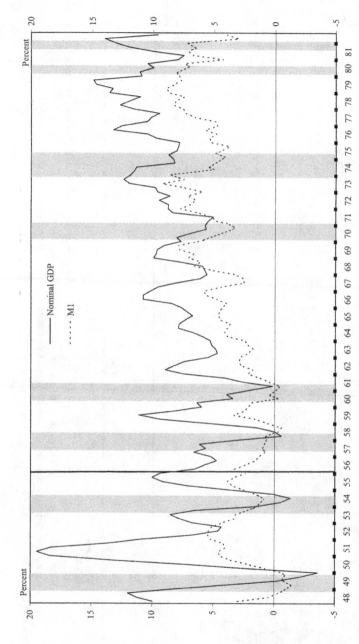

Figure 23.2. Growth of Nominal Output and Lagged Money. *Notes:* Quarterly observations of four-quarter moving averages of nominal GDP and M1. Beginning in 1956, M1 is lagged two quarters. The vertical line separates lagged and unlagged M1 growth. In 1981, M1 is shift-adjusted M1 (Bennett 1982). Shaded areas indicate recession. Heavy tick marks indicate the fourth quarter of the year.

284

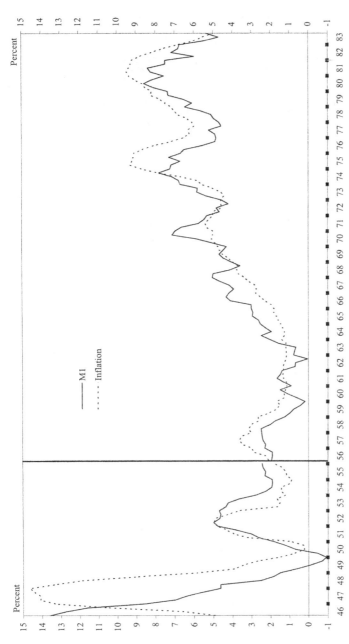

Figure 23.3. Inflation and Lagged Money Growth. *Notes:* Inflation is the annualized percentage change in the fixed-weight GDP deflator over an eight-quarter period. The GNP deflator from Balke and Gordon (1986) is used before 1947. Money growth is the annualized percentage change in M1 over an eight-quarter period. Beginning in 1956, M1 is lagged seven quarters. The vertical line separates lagged and unlagged M1 growth. In 1981, M1 is shift-adjusted" (Bennett 1982). Heavy tick marks indicate the fourth quarter of the year.

285

with that lag. Figure 23.2 shows the common cyclical movements in nominal output and money growth.[12] Beginning in 1956, money is lagged two quarters. Chapters 4 and 5 explain the beginning of the lagged relationship through the start of the lean-against-the-wind procedures following the 1953–6 recession. Figure 23.3 shows the positive relationship between trend inflation and trend money growth.[13] Money growth and inflation display similar trends.[14] The seven-quarter lag in money growth supports Friedman's (1989, 30–1) empirical generalization about the length of time required for a change in money growth to produce a change in inflation.

In the post-1982 period, the FOMC moved the funds rate promptly in response to changes in nominal output growth. The relative stability of inflation and economic activity in the latter period is evidence that the funds rate inertia of the earlier period caused the FOMC to fail to track the natural interest rate. The association of cyclical inertia in interest rates with monetary accelerations and decelerations is evidence that the money creation occurred prior to a change in real money demand. Nominal expenditure and prices then had to adjust. The price level is a monetary phenomenon: Prices adjust to endow nominal money with the real purchasing power desired by the public.

TWENTY-FOUR

Stop–Go and Interest Rate Inertia

The Great Inflation stretched from 1965 through 1981. No one has provided a comprehensive empirical characterization of the go–stop character of policy in this period, which included four cycles of expansionary and contractionary policy. The characterization here highlights the monetary accelerations and decelerations that accompanied cyclical interest rate smoothing and the temporal antecedence of money with respect to inflation.

According to Taylor (1999), inflation appeared and then policy became expansionary because the FOMC raised the funds rate only timidly. In fact, monetary policy became expansionary and then inflation rose. As documented in the Appendix, "A Taxonomy of Stop–Go," in this period, funds rate inertia is more aptly characterized as occurring relative to changes in nominal output growth rather than relative to changes in inflation. Finally, characterizations of monetary policy that omit money inadequately summarize the temporal relationships between variables produced by monetary shocks.

The following summarizes the empirical regularities of this period for economists who want to test models with monetary shocks. Figures 24.1 through 24.3 plot data available to the FOMC at its meetings. (Data are in Appendix: Data Seen by FOMC for Stop–Go Period.) The data continue on Figures 24.1A through 24.3A, which use a larger scale because of the increased volatility in the early Volcker period. I divide the graphs into four cycles of go–stop policy with three phases in each cycle. One should examine the four phase 1 intervals across the three graphs and then the phase 1a intervals and finally the phase 2 intervals. Reading across the rows of Table 24.1 summarizes the regularities apparent from this examination.

In phases 1, the FOMC either maintained the funds rate at a low level or lowered it out of concern for real economic activity. Initially, the growth rate of industrial production was negative or falling. The unemployment rate was "high" judged by the full-employment benchmark of 4% (apart from the second cycle). Inflation was either low or falling. A monetary acceleration occurred in phase 1.

In phases 1a, FOMC priorities changed as the unemployment rate fell while inflation rose. (In the third phase 1a, price controls depressed the rise in inflation.)

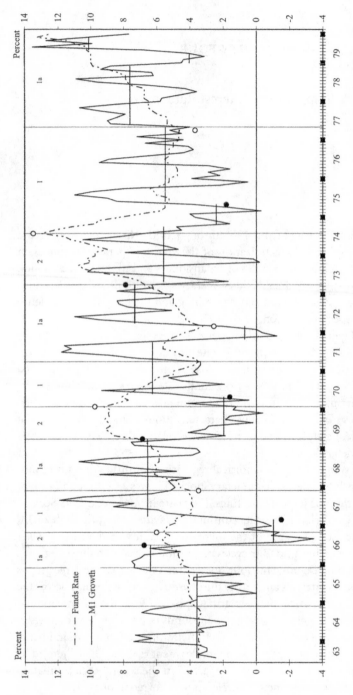

Figure 24.1. M1 Growth, M1 Step Function, and the Funds Rate as Seen by the FOMC. *Notes:* Data correspond to monthly FOMC meetings. M1 growth is the three-month annualized growth rate ending in the month prior to an FOMC meeting available to the FOMC at the time of its meetings. The M1 step function is fitted to this series. For the dates July 30, 1963, through October 20, 1970, and for November 20, 1979, the funds rate is the actual average value in the first full statement week following an FOMC meeting. Otherwise, it is the value set by the FOMC at its meeting. Dark circles mark changes in M1 steps. Hollow circles mark significant turning points in funds rate series. If two FOMC meetings occur in a month, the first is used. For 1979, the observations correspond to the nine FOMC meetings. Heavy tick marks indicate last FOMC meeting of the year.

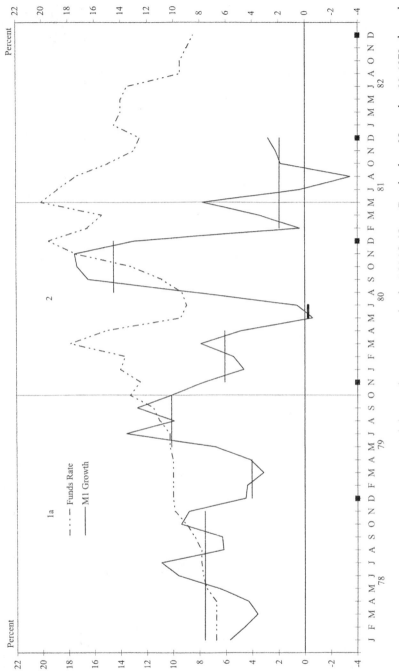

Figure 24.1A. M1 Growth, M1 Step Function, and the Funds Rate as Seen by the FOMC. *Notes:* For the dates November 20, 1979, through October 6, 1981, the funds rate is the actual average value in the first full statement week following an FOMC meeting. Otherwise, it is the value set by the FOMC at its meeting. In 1981, M1 is shift-adjusted M1 (Bennett 1982). Otherwise, see notes to Figure 24.1.

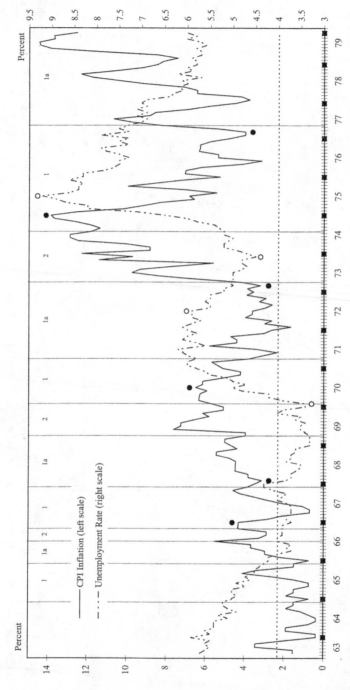

Figure 24.2. Inflation and the Unemployment Rate as Seen by the FOMC. *Notes*: Data correspond to monthly FOMC meetings. Inflation is the most recent three-month annualized growth rate of the CPI (generally ending in the month two-months prior to an FOMC meeting) available to the FOMC at the time of its meeting. The unemployment rate is the most recent rate (generally in the month prior to an FOMC meeting) available to the FOMC at the time of its meetings. Dark circles mark significant turning points in the CPI series; hollow circles in unemployment series. The dashed line is at 4%. If two FOMC meetings occur in a month, the first one is used. For 1979, observations correspond to the nine FOMC meetings. Heavy tick marks indicate last FOMC meeting of the year.

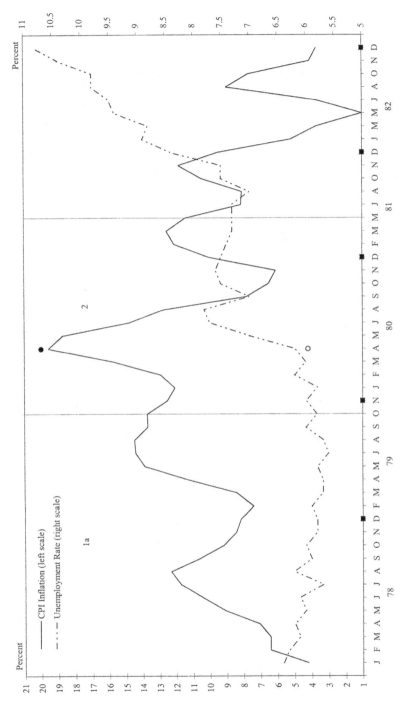

Figure 24.2A. Inflation and the Unemployment Rate as Seen by the FOMC. *Notes:* Data correspond to FOMC meetings. See notes to Figure 24.2.

291

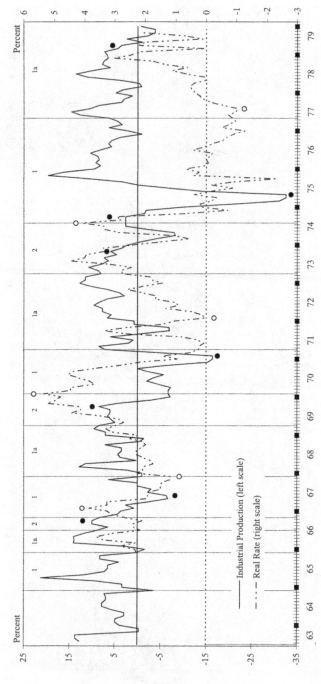

Figure 24.3. Growth in Industrial Production and the Real Rate of Interest as Seen by the FOMC. *Notes:* Data correspond to monthly FOMC meetings. Growth in industrial production is the most recent three-month annualized growth rate (generally ending in the month prior to an FOMC meeting) available to the FOMC at the time of its meetings. The real rate of interest is the commercial paper rate minus Board of Governors staff forecasts of inflation contained in the Greenbook (Figure 8.3). If two FOMC meetings occur in a month, the first is used. For 1979, the observations correspond to the nine FOMC meetings. Dark circles mark significant turning points in industrial production series; hollow circles in real rate series. Heavy tick marks indicate the last FOMC meeting of the year.

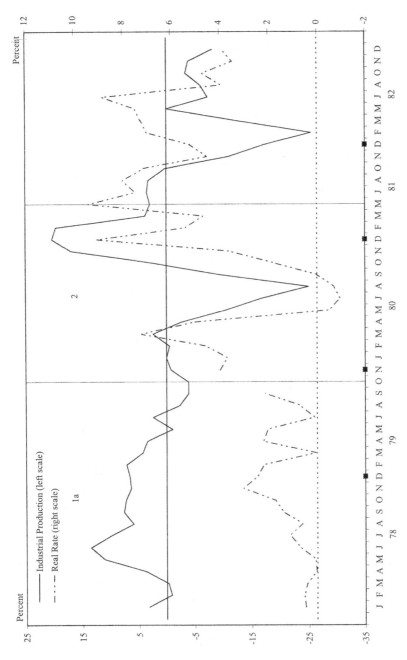

Figure 24.3A. Growth in Industrial Production and Real Rate of Interest as Seen by the FOMC. *Notes:* October 1979 real rate observation is missing as there was no Greeenbook (board staff inflation forecast) for that FOMC meeting. Otherwise, see notes to Figure 24.3.

Table 24.1. *The Funds Rate Target and Data Seen by the FOMC at Its Meetings*

	(1) FR	(2) ΔFR	(3) Int ΔFR	(4) RR	(5) ΔRR	(6) IP	(7) ΔIP	(8) CPI	(9) ΔCPI	(10) U	(11) ΔU	(12) ΔM1 step	(13) M1 step date
PHASE 1													
Cycle 1 (12/64–11/65)	4.1		.1			7.5		1.8		4.7		2.8	10/65
Cycle 2 (11/66–11/67)	4.4	−1.1	−1.5	2.3	−0.1	−0.3	−9.0	2.9	−0.4	3.9	0	7.5	2/67
Cycle 3 (2/70–3/71)	6.2	−2.7	−5.0	3.0	−1.2	−6.0	−8.5	5.5	−0.5	5.1	1.5	5.3	4/70
Cycle 4 (8/74–4/77)	6.0	−3.9	−7.5	−0.1	−3.0	0.3	−2.2	7.6	−2.3	7.6	−2.7	5.2	4/75
PHASE 1a													
Cycle 1 (12/65–6/66)	4.8	0.7	0.7	2.8		9.1	1.6	3.1	1.3	3.9	−0.8		
Cycle 2 (12/67–3/69)	5.9	1.5	2.5	2.3	0	4.9	5.2	4.4	1.5	3.6	−0.3		
Cycle 3 (4/71–3/73)	4.9	−1.3	3.0	1.4	−1.6	5.2	11.2	3.5	−2.0	5.7	0.6		
Cycle 4 (5/78–10/79)	8.2	2.2	7.9	0.7	.8	5.0	4.7	9.3	1.7	6.2	−1.4		
PHASE 2													
Cycle 1 (7/66–10/66)	5.5	0.7	0	2.4	−0.4	8.7	−0.4	3.3	0.2	3.9	0	−7.4	6/66
Cycle 2 (4/69–1/70)	8.9	3.0	.6	4.2	1.9	2.5	−2.4	6.0	1.6	3.6	0	−4.6	3/69
Cycle 3 (4/73–7/74)	9.9	5.0	6.0	2.9	1.5	2.5	−2.7	9.9	6.4	4.9	−0.8	−4.9	3/73
Cycle 4 (11/79–5/81)	14.2	6.0	7.5	3.7	3.0	0.2	−4.8	12.4	3.1	7.0	0.8	−8.2	10/79

Notes: Observations are averages across phases of the data used in Figures 24.1 through 24.3, that is, data available to the FOMC at the time of its meetings. FR is the funds rate; RR the real interest rate; IP is the growth rate of industrial production; U is the employment rate; and M1 is the monetary aggregate M1. CPI measures CPI inflation. Δ indicates the change from one phase to the next. Int Δ FR is the change in the funds rate from the first to last date of the phases. M1 step date is the date of the last observation of the preceding step. The Δ M1 step dated 4/70 is the rise from the 4/69–4/70 step to the 3/72–3/73 step. The Δ M1 step dated 3/73 is the fall from the 3/72–3/73 step to the 10/74–4/75 step. The M1 step dated 4/75 is the rise from the 10/74–4/75 step to the 5/77–11/78 step. The Δ M1 step dated 10/79 is the fall from the 5/79–10/79 step to the 2/81–12/81 step.

Although the FOMC began to raise the funds rate, the real interest rate failed to rise significantly. The monetary acceleration (the rise in the M1 step function) that began in phase 1 continued.

In phase 2, the FOMC concentrated on reducing inflation. The funds rate moved up to its cyclical peak. Monetary deceleration began in phase 2 as indicated by a fall in the M1 step function. (The end of the March 1980 credit controls introduced a brief monetary acceleration in the fourth phase 2.)

The key characteristic of monetary policy was the cyclical interest rate smoothing by the FOMC. That smoothing was the counterpart of an activist policy of manipulating nominal expenditure. During economic recovery, through the monetary acceleration produced by restrained funds rate increases, the FOMC engendered relatively high growth rates of nominal expenditure to stimulate real output growth. Subsequently, through the monetary deceleration produced by restrained funds rate declines, the FOMC engendered relatively low growth rates of nominal expenditure to lower inflation.

Table 24.2 summarizes the temporal relationships that emerged from the monetary shocks of the stop–go period. One should read across the rows of Table 24.2. For example, the third row begins with the cyclical peak in money associated with the second go–stop cycle. The end date of the preceding high M1 step is March 1969. The M1 growth step falls from 6.5 to 2.0% (row 4). The growth rate of industrial production peaks in September 1969 at 8.4% – a lag of 6 months (column 7). The funds rate peaks in January 1970 at 9.2% (the same time as the real rate) – a lag of 10 months behind the M1 peak (column 8). The unemployment rate reaches a trough in January 1970 at 3.4%. Inflation peaks in June 1970 at 6.5% – a lag of 15 months behind the M1 peak (column 9). Finally, the cyclical peak in the real rate of 5.3% occurs in January 1970 – 4 months after the peak in the growth rate of industrial production. The other rows reveal similar lags. The funds rate lags the cycle. A monetary shock impacts real variables initially and then inflation. The Appendix provides a detailed overview of the data summarized in the figures and tables.

APPENDIX: A TAXONOMY OF STOP–GO

Figure 24.1 plots the most recent annualized three-month M1 growth rate available to the FOMC at the time of its meetings and fits a step function to it. It also plots the funds rate immediately following FOMC meetings. Figure 24.2 plots the most recently available figure for the annualized three-month rate of CPI inflation and the unemployment rate. Figure 24.3 plots the most recently available figure for the three-month growth rate of industrial production and the real interest rate. The latter is calculated as the commercial paper rate minus the inflation rate predicted in the Greenbook. The real rate series starts in November 1965 when Greenbook forecasts begin. (See Appendix, "Series on the Real Interest Rate" in Chapter 4.)

Table 24.2. *Turning Points and Lags in Data Seen by the FOMC*

	(1)	(2)	(3)	(4)	(5)	(6)	(7)	(8)	(9)	(10)
							Lags in months			
Peaks troughs	M1 step	Ind prod	Funds rate	Real rate	U rate	Inflation	M1-IP	M1-FR	MI-CPI	IP-RR
P (1)	6/66 (6.4)	9/66 (10.0)	10/66 (5.6)	1/67 (3.8)		12/66 (4.3)	3			4
T (2)	2/67 (−1.0)	5/67 (−6.4)	11/67 (4.0)	11/67 (1.2)		1/68 (3.1)	3	9	11	6
P (2)	3/69 (6.5)	9/69 (8.4)	1/70 (9.2)	1/70 (5.3)	1/70 (3.4)	6/70 (6.5)	6	10	15	4
T (3)	4/70 (2.0)	1/71 (−16.4)	2/72 (3.3)	1/72 (0)	6/72 (5.9)	2/73 (3.2)	9	22	34	12
P (3)	3/73 (7.3)	10/73 (5.9)	7/74 (13)	7/74 (4.1)	11/73 (4.5)	12/74 (13.9)	7	16	7	9
		9/74 (2.6)					18			
T (4)	4/75 (2.4)	4/75 (−32.5)	3/77 (4.6)	7/77 (−1)	6/75 (9.2)	2/77 (4.0)	0	23	22	27
P (4)	11/78 (7.6)	4/79 (3.5)	5/81 (20.0)	5/81 (9.4)	4/80 (6.2)	4/80 (19.6)	5	31	18	25
	10/79 (10.1)	3/80 (2.4)					5			

Notes: The dates (month/year) correspond to significant turning points in the series shown in Figures 24.1 through 24.3, that is, in data available to the FOMC at the time of its meetings. After Ps and Ts, the numbers in parentheses show the go–stop cycle number. Thereafter, the numbers in parentheses are the values at those turning points. For each of the four cycles shown in Figures 24.1 through 24.3, the "Lags in months" observations show the lags, respectively, between turning points in M1 growth and industrial production growth (IP), in M1 growth and the funds rate (FR), in M1 growth and inflation (CPI), and growth in industrial production and in the real interest rate (RR). On row 6, the Ind prod entry, 9/74 (2.6), is an alternative cycle peak. Similarly, in the last row, the entries under M1 step – 10/79 (10.1) – and Ind prod give alternative cycle peaks.

296

These figures divide the four go–stop cycles of the period from 1965 through 1981 into three phases. Phase 1 demarcates those intervals over which the FOMC placed a higher priority on encouraging real growth than on controlling inflation. The FOMC kept its funds rate peg at a level that produced a monetary acceleration. Phase 1 became phase 1a when the FOMC became willing to raise its rate peg. In phase 1a, strengthening real growth and rising inflation caused the FOMC to raise the funds rate peg, but not by enough to prevent continued high money growth.

By the end of phase 1a intervals, inflation had become the predominant concern of the FOMC. Phase 1a became phase 2 when M1 growth began to fall. In phase 2, the FOMC initially maintained a high funds rate peg despite monetary deceleration and a decline in economic activity. By the end of phase 2, the FOMC had become more concerned with deteriorating real growth than inflation. Phase 2 became a new phase 1 when the FOMC began to lower the funds rate.

Table 24.1 summarizes the information contained in Figures 24.1 through 24.3. In all phase 1 intervals except the second, where growth of industrial production fell sharply, the unemployment rate was at a level considered unacceptable (column 10). Growth of industrial production fell from the preceding phase (column 7). The inflation rate either remained low or declined until well into the phase (columns 8 and 9).

In phase 1, the FOMC kept the funds rate at a level that produced a monetary acceleration. The funds rate fell over the duration of phase 1 except in the first phase, which is anomalous as the first phase of the four go–stop cycles (column 3). The average funds rate also fell relative to the prior phase 2 (column 2), as did the real rate of interest (column 5). During phase 1, M1 growth, expressed as a step function, rose (column 12). Over the four phases, it rose on average by 5.2 percentage points.

Phase 1a started when the FOMC became willing to let the funds rate rise. It marked a transitional phase in FOMC priorities away from stimulating real growth and toward restraining inflation. The unemployment rate either reached or moved toward cyclical lows (column 11). Industrial production grew strongly and growth rates rose relative to phase 1 (columns 6 and 7). Over the course of phase 1a intervals, inflation rose (column 9). (The exception is the third phase 1a, April 1971 to March 1973, in which price controls constrained the rise in inflation until the end. In April 1973, the FOMC saw inflation soar.) During phases 1a, the FOMC began to let the funds rate rise, but not by enough to let the real interest rate rise appreciably (column 5). Nor did the funds rate rise enough to constrain the monetary acceleration begun in phase 1.

In phase 2 intervals, the FOMC concentrated on reducing inflation. These intervals started when M1 growth began to fall. The unemployment rate remained low in phase 2 (columns 10 and 11). Industrial production grew strongly at the beginning, but declined as the phase progressed and fell relative to phase 1a (column 7). Inflation rose in phase 2 (columns 8 and 9). (In the fourth phase 2, it declined after rising sharply, but remained high.)

The funds rate and real rate rose in phase 2 (columns 2, 3, and 5). (The exception was the short phase 2 from July 1966 to October 1966, where the Board of Governors pressured banks into rationing credit quantitatively rather than through a rise in interest rates.) The M1 step function fell strongly at the beginning of all phase 2 intervals (column 12). The decline in economic activity toward the end of phase 2 caused the FOMC's priority to shift away from inflation. The stop phase then became the next go phase 1 when the FOMC began to lower the funds rate.

Table 24.2 shows the lags in the significant turning points in the series, marked by the dots on the figures. Across the four cycles, first, the rate of growth of M1 peaked, then the rate of growth of industrial production, and then the funds rate and the real rate. Finally, the rate of inflation peaked. The lags of the second cycle are typical. On March 1969, starting phase 2, the FOMC saw the three-month M1 growth rate decline, and the M1 step function moved down from 6.5 to 2%. The FOMC then saw three-month growth rates of industrial production turn down in September 1969 and become negative in November. The funds rate did not peak until January 1970, and the real rate peaked the same month. Note also that the real rate reached its peak four months after the peak in growth of industrial production. The inflation rate peaked only in June 1970. The lags just detailed are evidence of a monetary policy that imparted considerable inertia over the business cycle to the short-term rate of interest.

The following provides a detailed chronology of the four go–stop cycles. Each cycle divides into a go phase (divided into phases 1 and 1a), over which money growth rises, and a stop phase, over which money growth falls (phase 2). Phase 1 starts when the FOMC begins to lower its funds rate peg as real growth replaces inflation as its main priority. Phase 1 becomes phase 1a when the FOMC begins to raise its rate peg as inflation as well as real growth becomes a concern. However, in phase 1a, it is unwilling to raise its rate peg sufficiently to stop the monetary acceleration. Phase 1a becomes phase 2 when money growth begins to fall.

In the paragraphs labeled "Phase 1," "Phase 1a," and "Phase 2," the data cited are from the corresponding figures. The observations in these figures correspond to the months of FOMC meetings and are the most recent data actually available to the FOMC at the time of its meetings. The paragraph labeled "Nominal Output Growth, the Funds Rate, and M1" documents for the go phases 1 and 1a the lag in increases in the funds rate behind increases in nominal output growth during economic recoveries and the associated monetary acceleration. For the stop phase 2, it documents the lag in decreases in the funds rate behind decreases in nominal output growth and the associated monetary deceleration.

Cycle 1: December 1964 to November 1966

Phase 1: During phase 1 of the first cycle (December 1964 to November 1965), the unemployment rate remained above 4%. It fell steadily from 5% in December 1963 to 4.3% in November 1965. CPI inflation generally remained below 1.5%.

The funds rate was steady at 4%. Toward the end of phase 1, the M1 step function rose from 3.6 to 6.4%.

Phase 1a: During phase 1a of the first cycle (December 1965 to June 1966), the unemployment rate fell to a low of 3.7%, and industrial production grew strongly. Three-month CPI inflation rose strongly from less than 1 to 5.5%. The funds rate rose steadily to 5.2%.

Phase 2: During phase 2 of the first cycle (July 1966 through October 1966), the unemployment rate remained near 4%. However, growth of industrial production, after reaching 10% in September 1966, declined sharply. Inflation, which had averaged 1.8% in phase 1, rose to an average of 3.3%. The funds rate peaked at about 5.7%, while the M1 step function fell from 6.4 to −1%.

Nominal Output Growth, the Funds Rate, and M1: From 1964 to 1965, nominal output growth rose 4.1 percentage points, from 6.7 to 10.8%, while the funds rate rose only about 0.5 percentage point, from about 3.5% to a little more than 4%. In 1965Q4, the M1 step function rose from 3.6 to 6.4%. Nominal GDP growth peaked at about 13% in 1966Q1. The funds rate peaked three quarters later at 5.6%. In 1966Q3, the M1 step function fell from 6.4 to −1.0%.

Cycle 2: December 1966 to January 1970

Phase 1: During phase 1 of the second cycle (November 1966 to November 1967), the unemployment rate remained near 4%, but the rate of growth of industrial production fell and became negative. CPI inflation fell initially to almost zero but then rose to almost 4%, back to where it started the phase. The funds rate declined throughout, falling from 5.5 to 4%, while the real rate fell from over 3 percentage points to about 1%. M1 growth rose sharply. From negative values in the prior phase 2, it peaked at almost 12%.

Phase 1a: During phase 1a of the second cycle (December 1968 through March 1969), the unemployment rate fell to a low of 3.3%. Inflation rose, peaking at about 5.5%. The funds rate rose about 2.5 percentage points to just over 7%, while the M1 step function remained at a relatively high 6.5%.

Phase 2: During phase 2 of the second cycle (April 1969 through January 1970), the unemployment rate remained low, dropping to 3.4%. Growth of industrial production began strongly, peaked in September 1969 at 9.1%, and then became negative. Inflation rose early in the interval to 7.6% and then declined to 5.5%. The funds rate remained high at about 9%, and the real rate climbed to above 5% in January 1970. The M1 step function fell from 6.5 to 2%.

Nominal Output Growth, the Funds Rate, and M1: During the go phase of the second cycle, in 1967Q2, nominal GDP growth fell to 3.1% and then began to rise. Two quarters later in 1967Q4, the funds rate began to rise, but only modestly from its cyclical low of 4.0%. In 1968Q1, it began to rise more strongly, from 4.2 to 4.8%. The M1 step function rose from −1 to 6.5%. During the stop phase, nominal GDP peaked at 10.7% in 1969Q1. The funds rate continued rising and reached 9% in

1969Q3 and was essentially unchanged in 1969Q4. It fell moderately to 8.6% in 1970Q1 and 7.9% in 1970Q2. The M1 step function fell from 6.5 to 2.0%.

Cycle 3: February 1970 to July 1974

Phase 1: During phase 1 of the third cycle (February 1970 through March 1971), the unemployment rate rose sharply from its January 1970 low of 3.4% to a high of 6%. Growth of industrial production remained negative throughout. CPI inflation fell irregularly from over 6% at the beginning to somewhat less than 4% at the end. The funds rate declined from over 9% going into the period to 3.5% by the end, while the real interest rate fell from over 5% in January 1970 to almost zero. M1 growth rose moderately, but irregularly from 1% at the beginning to about 3.5% at the end.

Phase 1a: During phase 1a of the third cycle (April 1971 through March 1973), the unemployment rate fell a percentage point from 6 to 5.1%. Industrial production rose strongly, peaking at 12.7% near the end of the interval. Price controls suppressed inflation for most of the interval, but it began to rise by March 1973. In fall 1971, the FOMC pushed down the funds rate, which reached a low of 3.25% after the February 1972 meeting. The real rate rose after the imposition of controls as a consequence of a reduction in expected inflation but then fell to zero at the January 1972 FOMC meeting as the FOMC reduced the funds rate. By the end of the interval, March 1973, the funds rate had risen to 6.75%, and the real rate, to 2.75%. The M1 step function fell sharply in October 1971, along with the rise in the real rate produced by the controls, but then jumped up to 7.3% in March 1972.

Phase 2: During phase 2 of the third cycle (April 1973 through July 1974), the unemployment rate remained relatively low at about 4.9%. Growth of industrial production fell, became negative, but then recovered by summer 1974. Inflation rose throughout, reaching almost 13% by the end. The funds rate rose and peaked at 13% in July 1974. The M1 step function fell moderately from 7.3 to 5.6%.

Nominal Output Growth, the Funds Rate, and M1: In the go phase, in 1970Q4, nominal GDP growth fell to 1.4% and then began to rise vigorously. The funds rate reached a trough only in 1972Q1 at 3.5%. The M1 step function rose from 2.0, to 6.25%, and finally to 7.3%. In the stop phase, nominal GDP peaked at 13.2% in 1973Q4, while the funds rate peaked later in 1974Q3 at 13%.

Cycle 4: August 1974 to May 1981

Phase 1: During phase 1 of the fourth cycle (August 1974 through April 1977), the unemployment rate rose strongly, from 5.3% at the beginning to a peak of 9.2% in June 1975. By the end of the period, it had fallen to 7.3%. CPI inflation fell from low double digits to 4% in January 1977. The funds rate fell sharply at first, from 13% in July 1974 to 5.25% in May 1975. (The short-lived rise in the funds rate in June 1975 followed a transitory surge in M1 growth resulting from one-time tax rebates made to stimulate the economy.) The funds rate ended the period at 4.75%. Over the entire interval, the real interest rate averaged −1%. M1 growth rose over the period as a whole, with the M1 step function rising from 2.4 to 5.5%.

Phase 1a: During phase 1a of the fourth cycle (May 1977 through October 1979), the unemployment rate fell to a low of 5.6% in July 1979. Inflation cycled upward, reaching a peak of 14.5% in August 1979. The funds rate rose steadily, reaching 13.25% toward the end of the period. The M1 step function, after a brief fall following the fall of 1978 tightening, surged to 10.1% by the end.

Phase 2: Figures 24.1A through 24.3A depict the final stop phase – the Volcker disinflation. Toward the end of the 1970s, it becomes less clear how to date phases. One could date the beginning of monetary tightness in December 1978, rather than in November 1979 as previously. Inflation rose in 1978, from a low near 4% in the beginning of the year to 12% in July. The foreign exchange value of the dollar also fell. In response, the FOMC raised the funds rate from 6.75% in January to almost 10% in November 1978.

The M1 step function fell from 7.6 to 4% starting December 1978. Growth in industrial production began to fall in February 1979. Early in 1979, the Board of Governors staff predicted a recession, and the FOMC then backed off from further funds rate increases. M1 growth then revived. The FOMC began to push the funds rate up again in August when Volcker replaced G. William Miller as FOMC chairman. One could then argue that tightness began in December 1978, followed by a short-lived relapse. Moreover, the Carter credit controls, imposed in March 1980 and abandoned in July 1980, add a short-lived bust-boom cycle that obscured the longer phase of disinflation.

The figures date the final phase 2 to October 1979 with the fall in the M1 step function from 10.1 to 6.1%. The unemployment rate fluctuates around 6% until May 1980. It then fluctuates around 7.5%, before rising sharply again in December 1981. Industrial production grows strongly through April 1979. It then falls to moderately negative values for the remainder of 1979, but revives in early 1980 and becomes positive again by March 1980.

Growth rates of industrial production decline and then rise with the imposition and lifting of the credit controls. They turn sharply negative again in the last two months of 1981. Three-month CPI inflation rises to a peak of 19.6% in April 1980. It then falls, but rebounds twice to low double-digit figures again, first in early 1981 and then again in late 1981.

In March 15, 1980, the Fed implemented the credit control program. The funds rate jumped to 17.8% following the March 18 FOMC meeting. At its May and July meetings, the FOMC saw three-month M1 growth rates fall to zero, and the funds rate fell to 9% following the July meeting. The abandonment of the controls in July then led to a resurgence of the M1 step function to 14.5% over the August to December 1980 period, and the funds rate following the December 1980 meeting reached 19.4%. The funds rate remained high in 1981, but began to decline with the October meeting. The M1 step function (with the shift-adjusted

M1 data used at the time by the FOMC) fell to 1.9% from February through December 1981.

Nominal Output Growth, the Funds Rate, and M1: During the go phase of the fourth cycle, nominal output growth reached a trough of 2.4% in 1975Q1. It then rebounded strongly, growing at an average, annualized rate of 13.5% over the next four quarters. The funds rate, however, reached its trough of 4.7% only in 1977Q1, two years after the trough in nominal output growth. The M1 step function rose from 2.4 to 5.5% in 1975Q2 and then rose again to 7.6% in 1977Q2. Over the period 1975Q2 through 1980Q1, nominal output growth fluctuated around an average of 11.4%. The funds rate climbed steadily from its trough in 1977Q1 and reached 17.8% in March 1980. M1 growth fell in 1979Q1, surged in 1979Q2 and 1979Q3, fell in 1979Q4 and 1980Q1, became negative in 1980Q2, surged in 1980Q3 and 1980Q4, and then fell sharply in 1981. Over the period 1979Q4 through 1981Q4, M1 growth averaged 5%, down from the prior step of 7.6%.

APPENDIX: DATA SEEN BY FOMC FOR STOP–GO PERIOD

The funds rate is for the first full statement week (Thursday to Wednesday) following the FOMC meeting. The other series are the figures available to the FOMC at the time of their FOMC meetings and are from the Greenbook. Release dates of the statistical series were examined to identify instances when data were released after the publication of the Greenbook but before the FOMC meeting. In this case, data are from the statistical releases.

The nominal GNP (labeled "Nominal Output Growth" in the prior Appendix: A Taxonomy of Stop–Go) series is from predictions in the Greenbook available to the FOMC at the time of FOMC meetings. The predictions are annualized quarterly growth rates for the contemporaneous quarter if the FOMC meeting was in the first or second month of the quarter and for the succeeding quarter if the FOMC meeting was in the last month of the quarter.

The M1 growth rate is the annualized three-month growth rate ending in the month preceding the FOMC meeting as predicted in documents available to the FOMC at the time of its meeting. Figures from 1963 through April 1972 are from the Bluebook (or its predecessor). From May 1972 through 1979, figures are from the Greenbook. For the CPI and industrial production series, the base figures used in calculating growth rates are not in the Greenbook, but are taken from the *Federal Reserve Bulletin* released just prior to the FOMC meeting. If there were two FOMC meetings in a month, the first one is used.

TWENTY-FIVE

Monetary Nonneutrality in the Stop–Go Era

The overview of stop–go in Chapters 23 and 24 identified monetary shocks with the monetary accelerations and decelerations associated with cyclical interest rate smoothing. Chapter 24 examined the timing relationships between these shocks and macroeconomic variables. This chapter uses a narrative overview to trace out the relationship between monetary disturbances, the real interest rate, and real output (hours worked).

I. A Narrative Overview

Starting in late 1968, the FOMC decided to lower inflation, which had risen from just over 1% in the years from 1960 through 1965 to 5% in the last half of 1968. It raised the funds rate and kept it at a cyclically high level even when weakness appeared in nominal output growth. M1 growth peaked in January 1969, growth in hours worked peaked six months later in July 1969, and the real rate peaked even later in July 1970 (row 3, Table 25.1).[1] An empirical regularity is the lag in turning points in the real rate behind hours worked. In Table 25.1, column 7 shows the lag in turning points of hours worked behind M1, and column 8 shows the lag in turning points of the real rate behind hours worked.

In March 1971, the FOMC pushed the funds rate down to 3.5% (Figure 8.2). From February through June 1971, the real commercial paper rate averaged only .3% (Figure 8.3). M1 growth surged into low double-digits (Figure 8.2). Over the longer period from November 1965 through January 1971, the real interest rate had averaged 2.9%. The only previous period of comparably low real rates had been July to November 1967, when real rates had averaged 1.4%.

A brief low M1 step from October 1971 to February 1972 broke the pattern of monetary acceleration.[2] It arose as a by-product of Nixon's surprise announcement on August 15, 1971, of price controls. The FOMC, concerned that it not appear to undercut the controls through easy monetary policy, initially kept the funds rate basically unchanged. In the week of the announcement, the funds rate was 5.6%. In November, the funds rate averaged only somewhat lower, 4.9%. Expectations

Table 25.1. *Cyclical Timing Relationships between Money, Hours, Real Interest Rate*

Character of M1 growth step (1)	Level of M1 growth (2)	Start date of M1 (3)	Change in step level (4)	Hours peak/ trough date (value) (5)	Real rate peak/ trough date (value) (6)	M1–Hours lag (7)	Hours – real rate lag (8)	M1 – real rate lag (9)
high	7.6							
(1) low	0.0	4/66	−7.6	6/66 (7.5)	1/67 (3.8) p	2	7	9
(2) high	7.5	1/67	7.5	2/67 (−11.0)	11/67 (1.2) t	1	9	10
(3) low	3.2	1/69	−4.3	7/69 (7.1)	7/70 (4.5) p	6	12	18
(4) high #1	8.1	7/70	4.9	9/70 (−9.3)	5/71 (0.1) t	2	8	10
(5) mini-low	3.8	7/71	−4.4		9/71 (3.3) p	—		2
(6) high #2	9.5	12/71	5.8		1/72 (0.03) t			
(7) low #1	5.2	1/73	−4.3	2/73 (12.5)	7/73 (4.5) p	1	5	6
(8) low #2	3.2	3/74	−2.0	5/74 (10.8)	7/74 (4.1) p[1]	2		4
(9) high #1	5.9	4/75	2.7	2/75 (−17.2)	9/75 (−2.3) t	−2	7	5
(10) high #2	8.6	9/76	2.7	1/77 (2.6)	7/77 (−1.0) t[1]	4	6	10
(11) mini-low	4.7	9/78	−3.9		1/79 (3.1) p			4
(12) mini-high	11.6	2/79	6.9		6/79 (1.1) t			4
(13) low #1	6.2	7/79	−5.4	12/79 (3.5)	11/79 (5.4) p	5	−1	4
(14) low #2	−6.5	2/80	−12.7		4/80 (5.0) p[1]			2
(15) high	10.5	5/80	17.0	5/80 (−11.0)	6/80 (−9) t	0	3	3
(16) low	0	4/81	−10.5	7/81 (3.5)	9/81 (8.0) p	3	2	5

Notes for columns: (2) The level of the step function is the annualized rate of growth of M1 from the final month of the preceding step to the final month of the contemporaneous step. In 1981, M1 is the shift-adjusted M1 used by the FOMC (Bennett 1982). (4) Change in the level from the preceding to contemporaneous step. (5) Month and year at which growth in hours worked begins a sustained decline (peak) or rise (trough). The figure in parentheses is the annualized one-month rate of growth of hours worked on this date. Hours worked is from the BLS establishment survey of civilian, nonsupervisory employees on nonagricultural payrolls. (6) Month and year at which the real rate of interest begins a sustained decline (peak) or rise (trough). The real rate is the six-month commercial paper rate minus predicted inflation from the staff of the Board of Governors through 1978 and from DRI (now Global Insight) thereafter. (7) Difference in months between turning points in M1 (column 3) and hours worked (column 5). (8) Difference in months between turning points in hours worked (column 5) and the real rate (column 6). (9) Difference in months between turning points in M1 (column 3) and the real rate (column 6).

of inflation, however, fell sharply after the announcement. Between the July 27 and September 21, 1971, FOMC meetings, the Greenbook predictions of inflation (implicit GNP deflator) for 1971Q4 fell 3.1 percentage points.

In July, the real rate had been 0.5%; in September it was 2.3% (Figure 25.1). A decline in M1 growth validated the rise in the real rate. The FOMC lowered the funds rate until in February 1972 it reached a cyclical low of 3.3%. The period of reduced money growth in fall 1971 separated two periods of monetary expansion. Each is associated with a low in the real rate. The first low was 0.1% in May 1971, and the second low was zero in January 1972.

Starting in early 1973, M1 growth moved down in two steps. The M1 step function fell 4.3 percentage points after January 1973, and another 1.9 percentage points after March 1974. Each decline preceded a peak in hours worked and in the real rate. (Real rate peaks were 4.5% in July 1973 and 4.1% in July 1974.) This pattern of monetary deceleration can explain the recession that began in November 1973 and, in combination with the surge in inflation that accompanied the end of price controls in April 1974, its intensification in fall 1974.[3]

Starting in 1975, M1 growth moved up in two steps. The M1 step function rose 2.7 percentage points after April 1975 and another 2.7 percentage points after September 1976. Each rise preceded a trough in the real rate (−2.3% in September 1975 and −1% in July 1977). Real economic activity picked up strongly in summer 1975. In June 1975, the FOMC raised the funds rate briefly in response to high M1 growth produced by the one-time tax rebates. Overall, however, the funds rate drifted lower and reached a trough only in March 1977. The FOMC did not raise the funds rate in a sustained way until almost two years of vigorous real growth. By then, it had seen inflation rise since May 1976.

Starting in the late 1970s, shifts in monetary policy became more frequent. Inflation rose rapidly in 1978, from a low near 4% in the beginning of the year to 12% in July. The foreign exchange value of the dollar fell sharply. In response, the FOMC raised its rate peg from 6.75% in January 1978 to almost 10% in November 1978. The real rate rose from zero in April and May to 2.5% by December 1978. M1 growth fell from 9% over the period January through September 1978 to less than 5% from October 1978 through February 1979. Starting in 1979, the trend real interest rate rose. Through the first half of the 1980s, it averaged about 5%.

Early in 1979, the board staff predicted a recession, and the FOMC retreated from further funds rate increases. As inflation rose again in 1979, expected inflation rose. With an unchanged funds rate, the real interest rate fell to zero in April 1979, and M1 growth rose back to double digits. The M1 step function rose 6.9 percentage points. The FOMC began to push the funds rate up again in August 1979 when Volcker became FOMC chairman.

In fall 1979, the M1 step function fell 5.4 percentage points, and the real rate rose to 5.4% in November 1979. On March 15, 1980, the Fed implemented the credit control program, and the funds rate rose to 17.8%. With the imposition and lifting of the controls, M1 growth and output plunged and then surged

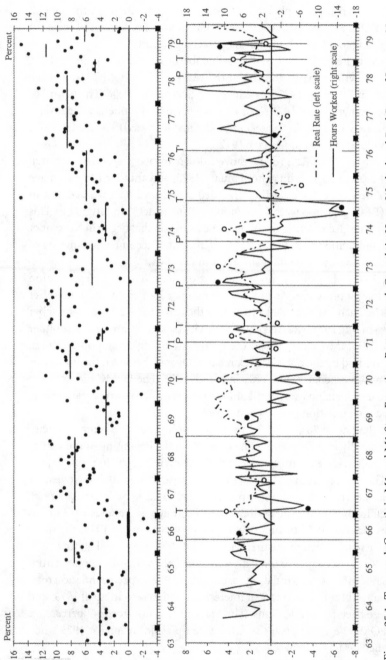

Figure 25.1. Top panel: Growth in M1 and M1 Step Function; Bottom panel: Growth in Hours Worked and Real Rate of Interest. *Notes:* The top panel shows annualized two-month M1 growth rates (dots) and a step function with step heights equal to the average annualized monthly growth rates of M1. The bottom panel shows annualized two-month growth in hours worked from the Bureau of Labor Statistics establishment survey and the short-term real rate of interest (commercial paper rate minus inflation forecasts initially from the staff of the Board of Governors, then from DRI starting in 1979. See Appendix, "Series on the Real Interest Rate," in Chapter 4). Vertical lines are placed at the last observation of the M1 step in the top graph. Ps mark the end of high steps and Ts the end of low steps. Dark circles mark significant turning points in hours worked series; hollow circles in real rate series. Heavy tick marks indicate December.

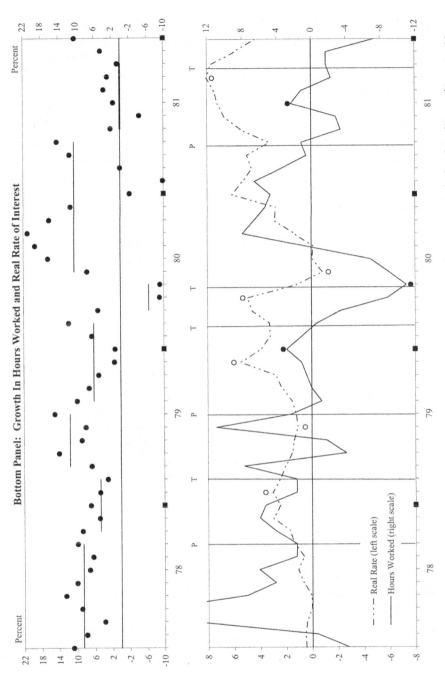

Figure 25.1A. Top panel: Growth in M1 and M1 Step Function; Bottom panel: Growth in Hours Worked and Real Rate of Interest. *Notes:* M1 is shift-adjusted M1 in 1981 (Bennett 1982). Otherwise, see notes to Figure 25.1.

(Figures 24.1A, and 24.3A). At its May and July meetings, the FOMC observed three-month M1 growth rates of zero. A high M1 step (10.5%) then began with the phasing out of the credit control program. The funds rate fell to 9% following the July meeting, and the real rate reached a low of -0.9% in June 1980.

FOMC procedures pushed the funds rate up to almost 20% in December 1980, and M1 growth fell sharply. M1 appeared to revive by the April 1981 meeting, but it remained at the bottom of the Humphrey–Hawkins target range (Figure 13.1). The funds rate fell to 15.4% in March 1981, but then rose and peaked at 20% in May 1981 (Figure 24.1A). In 1981, the funds rate exhibited the inertia relative to real output associated with earlier recessions. Although the FOMC saw the three-month growth rate of industrial production fall at its March meeting, it implemented its nonborrowed-reserves procedures in a way that raised the funds rate (Chapter 13). It did not begin to lower the funds rate significantly until the October meeting. The three-month shift-adjusted M1 growth rate seen by the FOMC reached a low of −3.5% in July 1981. By December, it was still only at 2.8%. Despite the sharp reduction in money growth, the FOMC maintained the funds rate at around 18% through the summer. The peak in the real rate, 8.0%, occurred on September 1981. July 1981 was the peak in the business cycle.

Why did the FOMC raise the funds rate in 1981 despite weakness in growth of output and M1? The FOMC saw inflation peak at 19.6% in April 1980 and then fall sharply to 6.1% in November (Figure 24.2A). By spring 1981, however, it saw inflation begin to rise again, climbing back to 12.6% in March 1981. Bond rates rose sharply. The driving force behind FOMC actions throughout this period was concern for the inflationary psychology of financial markets (Chapter 13). Volcker feared that it would spread to wage setting behavior and make the reduction in inflation unacceptably costly (Lindsey et al. 2005). He therefore manipulated the nonborrowed-reserves operating procedures to produce a high enough funds rate to break the back of inflationary expectations. It was not until June 1982 that the FOMC felt that expectations had abated to the point where it could begin to lessen significantly the restrictive stance of monetary policy.

II. A Liquidity Effect

For the stop–go period, a negative correlation exists between changes in growth rates of money and the real interest rate. Figure 25.1 displays money growth and the real interest rate.[4] The top panel plots an M1 step function fitted to annualized monthly M1 growth rates. (The dots are monthly observations of annualized two-month M1 growth rates.) The vertical lines in the bottom panel correspond to the end of the steps, with Ps and Ts indicating, respectively, the final dates of high and low M1 steps. The bottom panel plots monthly observations of the real interest rate, measured as the commercial paper rate minus board staff Greenbook inflation predictions through 1978 and by DRI (Global Insight) thereafter.[5] The bottom panel also plots monthly observations of annualized two-month growth

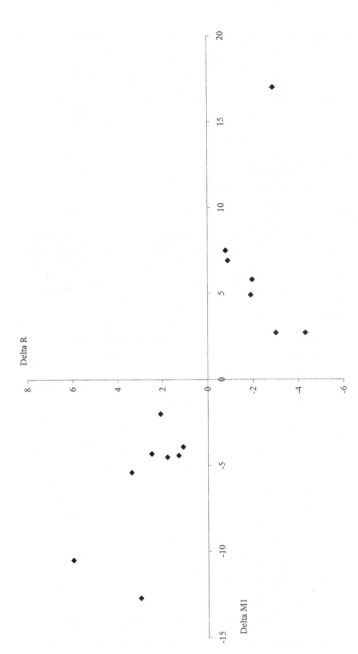

Figure 25.2. Scatter Diagram of Changes in M1 Step Function and Subsequent Peaks or Troughs in the Real Interest Rate. *Notes:* Paired observations are the change in the M1 step function (top panel in Figures 25.1 and 25.1A and column 4 of Table 25.1) and the subsequent peak/trough values of the real rate of interest (bottom panel in Figures 25.1 and 25.1A and column 6 of Table 25.1) minus 2.

rates of hours worked. Dots mark the beginning of sustained rises or falls in these series.[6]

Declines in the M1 step precede peaks in the real rate. Similarly, increases in the M1 step precede troughs in the real rate (Ps and Ts precede the hollow circles on the real rate dashed line in the bottom panel). Table 25.1 records this inverse relationship between shifts in the M1 steps (column 4) and subsequent turning points in the real interest rate (column 6). For example, as shown in row 3, the M1 step falls 4.3 percentage points after January 1969, and the real rate peaks subsequently at 4.5% on July 1970. For the entire period November 1965 through December 1981, the real rate averaged 2.0%. The July 1970 real rate peak is, then, 2.5 percentage points above the average.

The correlation between changes in the M1 step function and the subsequent value of the real interest rate at its turning point is −0.8. Figure 25.2 is a scatter diagram of changes in the M1 step function and the subsequent deviation of the real rate from its mean: the value in column 6 minus 2.0. Consistent with a liquidity effect, the observations lie in the second quadrant (prior decreases in M1 and increases in the real rate) and fourth quadrant (prior increases in M1 and decreases in the real rate).

In a straightforward way, monetary shocks and nonneutrality explain the ordering of turning points shown in Table 25.1, which runs from money, to hours worked, to the real rate. When the FOMC pursued a contractionary policy to lower inflation, it raised the nominal and real funds rate through monetary deceleration. Monetary deceleration produced a rise in the real rate, a downturn in economic activity and then a reduction in inflation.[7]

TWENTY-SIX

A Century of Monetary Experiments

Deflation or inflation prevailed during most of the 65 years following the establishment of the Fed. Instability in the real economy accompanied monetary instability. In contrast, starting after the Volcker disinflation, low, stable inflation accompanied considerable real stability. An understanding of these outcomes requires a combination of knowledge about the way that monetary policy evolved and of theory. The evolution of monetary policy reflects an increased assumption over time by the Fed of a responsibility for actual and expected inflation. The theory assumes that actual and expected inflation are monetary phenomena shaped by the systematic part of central bank procedures. Also, in the absence of central bank behavior that makes the price level evolve unpredictably, the price system works well to maintain macroeconomic equilibrium.

Three lessons emerge: (1) Inflation is a monetary phenomenon whose behavior is determined by the central bank. (2) Central bank credibility evidenced by stability in expected inflation is central to inflation stability. (3) The central bank must allow the price system to work. These lessons provide the foundation for understanding monetary policy in the V–G era as rule-like behavior that disciplined the lean-against-the-wind character of funds rate changes to ensure that macroeconomic shocks left actual and expected trend inflation unchanged.

I. A Nominal Anchor Lost and Regained

For the founders of the Fed, who took the gold standard for granted without understanding it, the marketplace determined the price level. They did not understand that their ability to create paper gold (the monetary base) required them to adhere to gold standard rules if market forces were to anchor the price level. The new Fed's purpose was to prevent the speculation that led to financial collapse and economic distress. By restricting credit to productive uses, real bills criteria for discount window lending would prevent speculative excess and the financial boom–bust cycle. In the lobby of the Board of Governor's Eccles building, there is a bas-relief figure of Carter Glass with an inscription stating the Fed's mission as the prevention of financial "debauches." Ironically, the Fed viewed the Depression as the fulfillment of its founders' fears not the result of its own flawed policy.

After March 1933, by freezing the size of its asset portfolio, the Fed ceded control over monetary policy to the treasury. In 1936–7, it attempted to regain control by reviving the free-reserves operating procedures of the 1920s. By immobilizing the greater part of banks' excess reserves through increased required reserves, the Fed intended to force banks back into the discount window when they extended loans. The Fed would then regain leverage over market rates through the discount rate. Chastened by the end of vigorous economic recovery, the Fed again withdrew. The wartime interest rate peg rate, which lasted until March 1951, continued the Fed's monetary policy exile.

Martin created the modern Fed with the inauguration of lean-against-the-wind monetary policy in the 1953 recession. The Fed began to move money market rates (proxied for by free reserves) in response to macroeconomic conditions rather than in response to asset prices. Real bills practitioners had focused on expectations, and Martin did likewise. However, by looking for speculative psychology in bond markets as a precursor not to unsustainable asset price inflation but rather to price-level inflation, Martin departed from real bills in a way that allowed the recreation of a nominal anchor. For Martin, the Fed could control inflationary expectations by raising money market rates early on in an economic recovery.

Because the Eisenhower administration's philosophical opposition to government intervention in markets ruled out wage and price controls, Martin could experiment with creation of a monetary policy that would both stabilize economic activity and prices. However, both he and the treasury interpreted the gold outflows in 1959 as evidence of a lack of confidence in the dollar. In 1959, the Fed induced monetary contraction through rate increases. The 1960 recession, which followed closely after the 1957 one, produced an environment of expected price stability.

In the Kennedy administration, the Fed, the treasury, and the White House shared a common concern for the stability of the dollar. Martin at the Fed and Dillon at treasury gave credibility to the administration's commitment to defend the dollar price of gold. The nominal anchor provided by this convertibility ended in November 1964 when the political system reacted negatively to a discount rate increase made in response to balance of payments outflows. The United States then turned to capital controls to deal with payments outflows.

When Martin raised the discount rate in December 1965, President Johnson called him publicly to his ranch. Internal divisions due to Democratic appointments to the board put Martin in an untenable situation. After a brief attempt at restriction in 1966, he chose to use the threat of high interest rates as a lever to get a tax increase. An end to the deficit spending produced by a fiscal policy of "guns and butter" would hopefully reduce the need for rate increases by reducing credit demand. Martin misjudged. Money growth and inflation rose. In 1969, Martin pursued a restrictive policy, but with his term ending in January 1970, he lacked time to restore price stability. Martin left the Fed with the first instance of expansionary–contractionary policy termed stop–go but more aptly characterized as go–stop.

After Burns became FOMC chairman in 1970, the combination of unemployment above 4% and inflation convinced him that wage-push pressures drove inflation. For Burns, wage controls became more important than monetary policy in ending inflation. Although Burns focused on expectations, he saw them as unmoored by monetary policy. Instead, labor union militancy conditioned the expectations of businesspeople. By assuaging their fears of wage inflation through incomes policy, the Fed could simultaneously reduce inflation and create an investment boom. However, in the Ford administration, with controls ruled out, Burns had to rely on monetary policy to control inflation.

Although not a Keynesian, Burns's views and those of Keynesians accorded during go phases. Keynesians believed that a failure of the price system produced a chronic shortfall of the aggregate demand required to maintain full employment. They also believed that nonmonetary forces drove inflation. When the unemployment rate exceeded the full employment 4% level, policy should be stimulative. Because high unemployment signaled idle resources, stimulative monetary policy would put those resources to work instead of increasing inflation. The existence of idle resources meant that the inflation that did arise had to derive from cost-push inflation. Incomes policies (government intervention in wage and price setting) would allow the control of inflation without recourse to high unemployment.

Keynesian influence on monetary policy reached its apogee in the Carter administration. The numerous forms of incomes policies advanced in public debate attested to the prevalent view that the primary goal of monetary policy should be low, stable unemployment not price stability. The absence of discipline imposed by an imperative to stabilize the behavior of some nominal variable meant that policy could be discretionary. Starting in late 1978, an increase in oil prices produced an inflation shock. In spring 1979, the Board of Governors staff predicted a recession. FOMC chairman Miller followed the conventional wisdom in leaving the funds rate unchanged to accommodate the oil-induced surge in prices.

However, the prior experience with discretion during which the FOMC had allowed inflation to drift upward had unmoored inflationary expectations. When inflation surged in 1979, the residual expectation in financial markets that inflation was a stationary process with a low mean value disappeared. Volcker and later Greenspan assigned priority to reestablishing expectational stability for inflation. Worldwide, following repeated failed attempts to use incomes policies to control inflation, governments turned to central banks. Margaret Thatcher (1993, 33), writing in April 1979, expressed the new consensus: "There would also have to be a fundamental overhaul of the way in which prices were controlled by such interventionist measures as the Price Commission, government pressure, and subsidy. We were under no illusion. . . . Inflation was a monetary phenomenon which . . . would require monetary discipline to curb."

Initially, central banks turned to money targets. Volcker (January 2, 1980, 3) told the National Press Club: "Our policy... rests on a simple premise – one documented by centuries of experience – that the inflationary process is ultimately related to excessive growth in money and credit.... [M]oderate, non-inflationary growth in money and credit, sustained over a period of time, is an absolute prerequisite for dealing with... inflation."

The V–G monetary standard emerged in the white-hot crucible of the effort to anchor inflationary expectations unmoored by stop–go. To establish credibility, Volcker made an explicit commitment to low money growth. Money proved an inadequate indicator for moving the policy instrument (borrowed reserves and, at one remove, the funds rate) in a way that stabilized the real economy. Volcker then focused on reversing sharp increases in bond rates taken as a proxy for deteriorating inflationary expectations. He dealt decisively with the inflationary scare of 1983–4 and later Greenspan did likewise with the inflationary scare of 1994.

Already in 1978, Volcker (1978, 58, 61) had written:

[T]he reactions of... interest rates to increases in the money supply seemed to be becoming almost perverse.... [T]he anticipation of more inflation would tend to offset or reduce the effects of more liquidity.... Wider recognition of the limits on the ability of demand management to keep the economy at a steady full employment path, especially when expectations are hypersensitive to the threat of more inflation, provides a more realistic starting point for policy formulation.

In 1979, while New York Fed president, Volcker emphasized the volatility in inflationary expectations. At the February 6, 1979, FOMC meeting, Volcker (Board of Governors *Transcripts* February 6, 1979, 10) commented: "The greatest risk to the economy, as well as [to actual] inflation, is people having the feeling that prices are getting out of control." At the specially convened October 6, 1979, meeting, Volcker (Board of Governors *Transcripts* October 6, 1979, 6) commented: "[W]e are not dealing with a stable... expectational situation.... [O]n the inflation front we're probably losing ground. In an expectational sense, I think we certainly are, and that is being reflected in extremely volatile financial markets."

The attempt in early 1979 to prevent the oil price shock from initiating a recession became a turning point when heightened inflationary expectations neutralized the impact of expansionary monetary policy. Volcker (U.S. Cong. February 19, 1980, 3) concluded: "[S]timulative policies could well be misdirected in the short run.... [F]ar from assuring more growth over time, by aggravating the inflationary process and psychology, they would threaten more instability and unemployment."

Creation of a new monetary standard based on nominal expectational stability required rule-like behavior imposed by a consistent focus on shaping expectations. The FOMC had to earn credibility through its response to inflation scares, through a willingness to raise rates at the beginning of economic recovery, and through the soft-landing strategy of lowering rates slowly during economic recovery from the 1990 recession to work down bond rates. The FOMC had to possess courage to give priority to maintaining expectational stability for inflation rather than to maintaining real growth.

The juxtaposition of the monetary policies of stop–go and nominal expectational stability altered the intellectual environment. Samuelson and Solow (1960) had defined the central question for activist monetary policy given its goal of low, stable unemployment. How much inflation is required to purchase low, stable unemployment? The newly invented Phillips curve appeared to provide an answer. The question became paramount when the Kennedy administration adopted a 4% unemployment rate as a national goal and the Johnson administration vetoed monetary policy as a tool for dealing with the balance of payments.

Later, Friedman (1977) and Lucas (1972) claimed that the question was a false one. In their terminology, the Phillips curve was not "exploitable." Policymakers could not "purchase" low unemployment with high inflation. The prediction that low unemployment would accompany high inflation failed in the stagflation of the 1970s. Just as important was the failure of the Keynesian diagnosis of stagflation as evidence of cost-push inflation with its policy prescription of price controls. The massive Keynesian consensus gave way to intellectual ferment.

In what became known as the NAIRU model, Modigliani and Papademos (1975) redefined the Samuelson–Solow question as: How much variability in inflation is required to produce low variability in unemployment? With the replacement of G. William Miller by Volcker, the goal of low, stable inflation replaced the goal of low, stable unemployment. That new goal reversed the Modigliani–Papademos question, which then became: How much variability in unemployment is required to maintain price stability? The results provided by the V–G experiment were as dramatic as the stagflation of the 1970s. When the variability of inflation *decreased*, the variability of unemployment *decreased* rather than *increased*. Economists then became receptive to the rule-based policy prescriptions of modern macroeconomics (Kydland and Prescott 1977; Lucas 1976; 1980). However, the Fed has yet to make the transition to communication with the language of rules rather than discretion.

II. The Experiment with Discretion

Monetary policy can seem indecipherable because of the difficulty of seeing beyond the incessant stream of data that policymakers synthesize to read the economy. The Rosetta stone for deciphering policy is the importance that policymakers assign to credibility for controlling inflationary expectations. Under the classical gold standard, the credibility attached to the expectation of a fixed nominal price of gold was paramount.

The great modern heresy of monetary policy has been discretion. In addition to wartime, the interregnum of discretion appeared with real bills and stop–go. With real bills, policymakers cared about expectations, but in the form of speculative psychology that raised asset prices unsustainably. They wanted to control those expectations through the allocation of credit away from financial markets and toward short-term commercial lending. Failing in that goal, periodic recourse to restrictive monetary policy created a deflationary bias. With stop–go, policymakers also cared about expectations, but they wanted to control them through incomes policies so that monetary policy was free to lower unemployment.

Martin (when unconstrained by the populist politics of LBJ), Volcker, and Greenspan made nominal expectational stability the centerpiece of policy. For Volcker and Greenspan, credibility meant not only the expectation of low inflation, but also the invariance of expected trend inflation to relative-price (inflation) shocks and to above-trend real growth in economic recovery. In the V–G era, discretion ceded to rule-like behavior.

III. Institutionalizing the New Regime

The FOMC succeeded in controlling inflation by behaving consistently. It raised the funds rate in a persistent, measured way as long as real output was growing above trend in a sustained way. Above-trend growth appears in sustained changes in resource utilization rates. "Measured" means 0.25 percentage point per meeting, but more if expected trend inflation rises above the FOMC's implicit inflation target. With credibility, markets extrapolate changes in the funds rate in a stabilizing way. The key to credibility is the belief by markets that in response to macroeconomic shocks the FOMC will ultimately move the funds rate by whatever amount required to maintain trend inflation unchanged.

In the case of above-trend growth, forward rates rise, and the entire rise is real. Markets set the yield curve at the level expected to return real growth to trend. In general, the real funds rate may be too low or too high, but the system is forgiving because the real yield curve continuously adjusts in response to new information in a way that moves real output growth toward trend. With stop–go, in contrast, the FOMC held the funds rate at a low or high level for long periods in an attempt to make monetary policy stimulative or restrictive (to keep real growth above trend or below trend). Now, the funds rate moves whenever the FOMC believes that output is growing unsustainably fast or slow so that the yield curve moves in a way that keeps policy neutral.

Institutionalization of the V–G regime would start with adoption of an explicit inflation target. Much has had to happen to make that feasible. First, the Fed had to disinflate and survive as an institution. That survival depended in part on the good luck of having a president, Ronald Reagan, with a visceral dislike of inflation. Good luck also accompanied the 1984 and 1994 episodes in which the FOMC raised the funds rate sharply in response to an increase in inflationary expectations. Unlike the tightening in 1981 and early 1982, when the Fed could rally public support from high inflation, inflation was falling. The FOMC raised rates in response to a rise in expected, not actual inflation. After a moderation in growth, strong real growth, not recession, followed. Volcker and Greenspan demonstrated that the Fed possessed instrument independence by raising the funds rate without the ready rationale of rising inflation.

The feasibility of an inflation target also required a change in the intellectual environment produced by the Volcker disinflation. According to the 1970s consensus, powerful nonmonetary forces drove inflation. The combination in the 1970s of high money growth and inflation weakened that consensus, and the combination after 1983 of low inflation and low unemployment destroyed it. In the 1970s, the idea that central bank credibility for low inflation would permit low inflation without sustained, or at least periodic, recourse to high unemployment appeared implausible. That changed when the Fed not only brought inflation down but also kept it down without high unemployment.

Failure to communicate using a policy rule creates a paradox for the Fed. Ambiguity about goals and strategy renders political attack more difficult. However, in a constitutional democracy, support for institutions derives from widespread public knowledge about them. An explicit inflation target accompanied by an explicit strategy for achieving it would enhance public understanding of the Fed and support for its independence.

Appendix: Data Seen by FOMC for the Stop–Go Period Shown in Figures 24.1, 24.2, and 24.3

		FOMC date	M1 3-m % ch	M1 step function	Industrial production 3-m % ch	Funds rate target	Real rate of interest	Unemployment rate	CPI 3-m % ch
	1963	30-Jul	2.44	3.59	12.77	3.49		5.7	1.52
		20-Aug	3.53	3.59	13.71	3.49		5.6	1.52
		10-Sep	2.98	3.59	13.71	3.48		5.5	3.43
		22-Oct	2.97	3.59	−0.32	3.49		5.6	3.43
		12-Nov	3.5	3.59	−0.32	3.33		5.5	1.89
		3-Dec	7.37	3.59	3.87	3.48		5.9	0.37
	1964	28-Jan	6.24	3.59	4.86	3.5		5.5	0.37
		11-Feb	7.29	3.59	4.86	3.44		5.6	1.88
		24-Mar	3.17	3.59	2.87	3.48		5.4	1.88
		14-Apr	3.43	3.59	2.87	3.48		5.4	0.75
		26-May	1.82	3.59	5.77	3.5		5.4	0.37
		16-Jun	1.83	3.59	7.72	3.44		5.1	0.37
		7-Jul	3.42	3.59	7.72	3.5		5.3	0.75
		18-Aug	5.27	3.59	6.92	3.46		4.9	1.12
		29-Sep	6.9	3.59	6.87	3.3		5.1	1.87
		20-Oct	6.31	3.59	7.18	3.48		5.2	1.49
		10-Nov	4.94	3.59	−3.56	3.7		5.2	1.49
Cycle 1		15-Dec	4.13	3.59	3.33	4		5	0.74
	1965	12-Jan	3.59	3.59	3.33	3.86		4.9	1.86
		2-Feb	3.58	3.59	9.26	4.02		5	1.48
		2-Mar	0	3.59	21.34	4.09		5	1.48
		13-Apr	1.01	3.59	11.74	4.08		4.7	0.74
Phase 1		11-May	1.76	3.59	7.16	4.12		4.9	0.74
		15-Jun	0.76	3.59	6.48	4.04		4.6	1.48
		13-Jul	3.8	3.59	6.48	4.1		4.7	2.6
		10-Aug	3.78	3.59	4.05	4.02		4.5	4.1
		28-Sep	1	3.59	8.15	4.11		4.5	3.33
		12-Oct	6.35	6.37	8.15	4.08		4.4	1.47
		2-Nov	7.37	6.37	0.28	4.1	2.27	4.3	1.47
		14-Dec	7.33	6.37	−1.65	4.57	2.34	4.2	0.73
	1966	11-Jan	7.5	6.37	2.8	4.4	2.82	4.2	2.2
		8-Feb	6.97	6.37	14.07	4.63	2.32	4	2.94

(*continued*)

	FOMC date	M1 3-m % ch	M1 step function	Industrial production 3-m % ch	Funds rate target	Real rate of interest	Unemploy- ment rate	CPI 3-m % ch
Phase 1a	1-Mar	6.73	6.37	13.9	4.71	3.38	3.7	2.94
	12-Apr	4.57	6.37	14.08	4.69	3.59	3.8	3.67
	10-May	6.4	6.37	11.79	5.08	3.07	3.7	3.65
	7-Jun	4.1	6.37 P(1)	8.8	5.24	2.16	4	5.52
	26-Jul	−2.07	−1.02	6.41	5.61	2.36	4	3.25
	23-Aug	−3.47	−1.02	9.98	5.68	2.38	3.9	2.87
Phase 2	13-Sep	−0.9	−1.02	9.98 P(1)	5.22	2.1	3.9	2.87
	4-Oct	−1.37	−1.02	8.23	5.62 P(1)	2.67	3.9	4.33
Cycle 2	1-Nov	0.75	−1.02	4.42	5.48	3.1	3.9	4.32
	13-Dec	−0.9	−1.02	3.61	5.34	3.23	3.7	4.30 P(1)
1967	10-Jan	−0.43	−1.02	0.76	4.79	3.84 P(1)	3.8	2.84
	7-Feb	0.27	−1.02 T(2)	2.56	4.94	3.24	3.8	2.12
	7-Mar	3.33	6.54	−2.49	4.51	3.25	3.7	0.7
	4-Apr	5.43	6.54	−6.64	3.95	1.95	3.7	0.7
Phase 1	2-May	5.9	6.54	−6.38 T(2)	3.97	1.9	3.7	1.05
	20-Jun	8.63	6.54	−2.28	3.83	1.89	3.8	2.11
	18-Jul	7.37	6.54	−3.03	3.94	1.48	4	2.82
	15-Aug	11.93	6.54	0	3.89	1.5	3.9	3.52
	12-Sep	10.47	6.54	0	3.92	1.45	3.8	4.23
	3-Oct	6.33	6.54	6.31	4.06	1.19	4.1	4.57
	14-Nov	5.17	6.54	−1.02	4.02 T(2)	1.18 T(2)	4.3	3.85
	12-Dec	4.9	6.54	−1.02	4.57	2.24	4.3	3.48
1968	9-Jan	5.1	6.54	2.3	4.66	2.08	3.9	3.12 T (2)
	6-Feb	5.3	6.54	12.82	4.73	2.04	3.7	3.81
	5-Mar	3.97	6.54	11.42	5.6	1.73	3.7	3.81
	30-Apr	9.45	6.54	0.25	6.12	1.81	3.6	4.47
	28-May	4.8	6.54	3.77	6.1	2.1	3.5	4.46
Phase 1a	18-Jun	7.4	6.54	4.26	5.99	2.29	3.5	4.46
	16-Jul	8.43	6.54	3.48	6.09	2.28	3.8	4.44
	13-Aug	10.73	6.54	3.48	5.86	2.14	3.7	4.77
	10-Sep	8.77	6.54	7.07	5.85	1.98	3.7	5.45
	8-Oct	3.87	6.54	−0.49	5.81	2.09	3.6	5.43
	26-Nov	3.4	6.54	−1.44	5.85	2.49	3.6	4.37
	17-Dec	3.6	6.54	6.98	6.25	2.25	3.3	4.69
1969	14-Jan	7.33	6.54	6.98	6.35	3.1	3.3	5.01
	4-Feb	7.53	6.54	9.53	6.68	3.27	3.3	5
	4-Mar	4.37	6.54 P(2)	8.45	7.13	2.96	3.3	3.96
	1-Apr	1.87	1.97	4.86	8.59	2.71	3.4	3.95
	27-May	4.1	1.97	5.8	8.8	2.85	3.5	7.62
	24-Jun	3.07	1.97	6.5	9.1	3.43	3.5	7.25
	15-Jul	2.87	1.97	5.96	8.83	4.41	3.4	7.25
Phase 2	12-Aug	0.2	1.97	5.96	8.94	4.12	3.6	6.52
	9-Sep	1.87	1.97	8.41P(2)	9.14	4.19	3.5	5.82
	7-Oct	1.6	1.97	4.24	8.88	5.23	4	6.13
	25-Nov	−0.4	1.97	−2.95	8.93	4.96	3.9	5.09
	16-Dec	1.4	1.97	−7.14	8.83	4.79	3.4	5.09
1970	15-Jan	1.2	1.97	−6.72	9.18P(2)	5.34P(2)	3.4T(2)	5.71

		FOMC date	M1 3-m % ch	M1 step function	Industrial production 3-m % ch	Funds rate target	Real rate of interest	Unemploy- ment rate	CPI 3-m % ch
Cycle 3		10-Feb	4.2	1.97	−6.72	8.46	4.47	3.9	6.33
		10-Mar	0.43	1.97	−7.19	7.72	4.45	4.2	6.31
		7-Apr	3.23	1.97 T(3)	−4.59	8.08	3.66	4.2	6.27
		5-May	5.2	6.25	−2.09	7.73	3.83	4.8	5.92
		23-Jun	9.33	6.25	−3.47	7.33	4.19	5	6.49 P(2)
		21-Jul	4.33	6.25	−5.72	6.82	4.53	4.7	6.14
Phase 1		18-Aug	1.93	6.25	−2.33	6.48	4.37	5	6.14
		15-Sep	4.5	6.25	0	6.13	3.7	5.1	5.17
		20-Oct	5.27	6.25	−6.47	5.92	2.83	5.5	4.23
		17-Nov	3.53	6.25	−15.34	5	2.18	5.6	4.21
		15-Dec	3.77	6.25	−16.42	5	0.96	5.8	5.11
	1971	12-Jan	3.53	6.25	−16.42 T(3)	4.25	1.41	6	5.4
		9-Feb	3.37	6.25	−4.51	3.75	0.52	6	5.68
		9-Mar	3.37	6.25	7.08	3.5	0.26	5.8	3.78
		6-Apr	7.1	6.25	8.43	3.75	0.22	6	3.07
		11-May	8.9	6.25	1.96	4.5	0.08	6.1	2.37
		8-Jun	11.8	6.25	0.97	4.875	0.26	6.2	3.4
		27-Jul	11.2	6.25	5.93	5.625	0.81	5.6	5.8
		24-Aug	11.63	6.25	−0.75	5.625	2.62	5.8	4.4
		21-Sep	7.47	6.25	−6.92	5.5	3.32	6.1	4.4
		19-Oct	3	0.7	−6.9	5.25	2.59	6	4.72
		16-Nov	−1.23	0.7	0.76	4.75	1.42	5.8	3
		14-Dec	−0.37	0.7	0.76	4.3125	1.05	6	2.65
	1972	11-Jan	0	0.7	6.62	3.625	0.03 T(3)	6.1	1.65
		15-Feb	2.1	0.7	5.76	3.25 T(3)	0.14	5.9	2.98
Phase 1a		21-Mar	6.47	7.33	7.69	3.875	0.49	5.7	2.64
		17-Apr	9.43	7.33	7.64	4.25	1.31	5.9	3.97
		23-May	11	7.33	9.55	4.25	0.92	5.9	3.62
		19-Jun	7.8	7.33	8.29	4.5	1.05	5.9 P(3)	3.62
		18-Jul	5.1	7.33	6.65	4.625	1.66	5.5	2.94
		15-Aug	7.7	7.33	2.87	4.75	1.63	5.5	2.61
		19-Sep	8.3	7.33	3.94	5	2.09	5.6	3.26
		17-Oct	8.4	7.33	6.5	5	2.57	5.5	2.92
		21-Nov	5.2	7.33	10.2	5	2.1	5.5	3.9
		19-Dec	5	7.33	12.74	5.5	1.44	5.2	3.55
	1973	16-Jan	8.4	7.33	11.49	5.8125	1.75	5.2	3.87
		13-Feb	6.2	7.33	11.49	6.375	1.84	5	3.21 T(3)
		20-Mar	6.3	7.33 P(3)	7.99	6.75	2.73	5.1	4.17
		17-Apr	1.7	5.59	8.66	7	2.79	5	6.45
		15-May	4.1	5.59	10.75	7.5	2.46	5	8.42
		19-Jun	5.9	5.59	7.82	8.5	3.16	5	9.73
		17-Jul	10.2	5.59	6.38	9.75	4.46	4.8	9.33
		21-Aug	9.9	5.59	7.28	10.5	4.01	4.7	7.6
		18-Sep	5.2	5.59	4.56	10.75	3.94	4.8	5.62
		16-Oct	−0.2	5.59	5.86 P(3)	10	3.33	4.8	11.41
Phase 2		20-Nov	0.2	5.59	3.52	10.25	3.37	4.5 T(3)	9.7
		18-Dec	4.2	5.59	2.23	9.75	2.43	4.7	12.28
	1974	22-Jan	7.9	5.59	−0.63	9.75	1.51	4.9	8.84
		20-Feb	4.7	5.59	−4.03	9	0.55	5.2	8.84
		19-Mar	5.5	5.59	−8.21	9.75	1.08	5.2	10.02

(*continued*)

		FOMC date	M1 3-m % ch	M1 step function	Industrial production 3-m % ch	Funds rate target	Real rate of interest	Unemployment rate	CPI 3-m % ch
		16-Apr	6.5	5.59	−7.97	10.375	2.87	5.1	12.46
		21-May	10.5	5.59	−2.21	11.25	3.32	5	12.89
		18-Jun	8.3	5.59	2.59	11.625	3.36	5.2	12.89
		16-Jul	6.7	5.59	2.59	13 P(3)	4.05 P(3)	5.2	11.8
Cycle 4		20-Aug	4.5	5.59	2.59	12.25	2.78	5.3	11.36
		10-Sep	4.8	5.59	2.59 P(3)	11.25	2.92	5.4	11.88
		15-Oct	1.6	2.41	−1.58	9.75	0.65	5.8	12.65
		19-Nov	2.6	2.41	−1.9	9.5	−0.71	6	13.71
		17-Dec	3.7	2.41	−9.84	8.25	0.13	6.5	13.89 P(3)
	1975	21-Jan	4	2.41	−21.3	7	0.2	7.1	12.56
		19-Feb	−0.3	2.41	−31.11	5.75	−0.2	8.2	10.12
		18-Mar	1.5	2.41	−32.53	5.5	−0.33	8.2	9.19
		15-Apr	3.8	2.41 T(4)	−32.53 T(4)	5.5	0.39	8.7	8.28
		20-May	8.4	5.49	−14.29	5.25	−0.17	8.9	6.59
		17-Jun	9	5.49	−7	5.25	−0.87	9.2 P(4)	6.83
		15-Jul	11	5.49	0	6	−0.18	8.6	5.45
		19-Aug	9.9	5.49	3.32	6.1875	−0.91	8.4	7.02
		16-Sep	7.9	5.49	10.57	6.375	−2.32	8.4	9.93
		21-Oct	2.2	5.49	19.67	5.625	0.41	8.3	8.55
		18-Nov	0.5	5.49	16.23	5.25	0.24	8.6	7.16
Phase 1		16-Dec	3.9	5.49	9.42	5.25	0.65	8.3	5.28
	1976	20-Jan	2.2	5.49	8.16	4.75	0.05	8.3	7.06
		18-Feb	2.9	5.49	9.21	4.75	−0.06	7.8	7.02
		16-Mar	1.6	5.49	8.42	4.75	0.01	7.6	6.22
		20-Apr	2.9	5.49	8.72	4.875	−0.09	7.5	4.17
		18-May	9.5	5.49	10.43	5.375	−0.2	7.5	3.16
		22-Jun	8.9	5.49	8.19	5.5	0.42	7.3	5.37
		20-Jul	6.7	5.49	5.74	5.25	0.06	7.5	5.37
		17-Aug	4.4	5.49	6.38	5.25	−0.21	7.8	6.36
		21-Sep	3.8	5.49	5.67	5.25	−0.55	7.9	6.29
		19-Oct	4.1	5.49	3.74	5	−0.67	7.3	6.29
		16-Nov	6.7	5.49	−0.91	5	−0.91	7.5	5.76
		21-Dec	4.4	5.49	2.15	4.625	−1.26	7.3	4.76
	1977	18-Jan	7.2	5.49	6.26	4.6875	−0.54	7.9	4.01
		15-Feb	4.5	5.49	3.42	4.6875	−0.73	7.3	4.00 T(4)
		15-Mar	5.2	5.49	4.32	4.625 T(4)	−0.96	7.5	5.42
		19-Apr	4	5.49	6.15	4.75	−0.85	7.3	8.3
		17-May	8.8	7.61	12.67	5.375	−0.74	7	9.75
		21-Jun	9	7.61	14.55	5.375	−0.97	6.9	10.67
		19-Jul	8.4	7.61	10.45	5.375	−1.03 T(4)	7.1	8.86
		16-Aug	7.9	7.61	8.48	6	−0.55	6.9	8.57
		20-Sep	9.5	7.61	3.55	6.25	−0.13	7.1	6.85
		18-Oct	10.7	7.61	2.93	6.5	0.09	6.9	5.88
		15-Nov	8.6	7.61	1.16	6.5	0.21	7	4.47
		20-Dec	5.8	7.61	4.72	6.5	0.36	6.9	3.78
	1978	17-Jan	5.7	7.61	3.21	6.75	0.47	6.4	4.21
		28-Feb	4.6	7.61	−0.86	6.75	0.53	6.3	6.44
		21-Mar	3.6	7.61	−0.29	6.75	0.41	6.1	6.44
		18-Apr	4.3	7.61	3.77	6.75	0.03	6.2	7.08
		16-May	6.5	7.61	11.1	7.5	0.07	6	9.11

		FOMC date	M1 3-m % ch	M1 step function	Industrial production 3-m % ch	Funds rate target	Real rate of interest	Unemploy-ment rate	CPI 3-m % ch
Phase 1a		20-Jun	9.6	7.61	13.57	7.75	0.67	6.1	10.43
		18-Jul	10.9	7.61	10.01	7.875	1.11	5.7	11.74
		15-Aug	6.2	7.61	6	7.875	0.62	6.2	12.33
		19-Sep	6.3	7.61	7.72	8.375	1.37	5.9	10.63
		17-Oct	9.4	7.61	7.37	9	1.73	6	9.2
		21-Nov	8.8	7.61 P(4)	6.45	9.875	3	5.8	8.45
		19-Dec	4.5	4.04	6.69	10	2.45	5.8	8.17
	1979	6-Feb	4.38	4.04	7.22	10	2.17	5.9	7.42
		20-Mar	3.13	4.04	4.35	10	0.05	5.7	8.42
		17-Apr	4.15	4.04	3.49 P(4)	10	2.2	5.7	11.34
		22-May	6.8	10.13	−1.06	10.25	2.01	5.8	13.88
		11-Jul	13.54	10.13	2.4	10.25	0.12	5.6	14.43
		14-Aug	9.92	10.13	−2.34	11	0.7	5.7	14.5
		18-Sep	12.72	10.13	−3.88	11.5	2.11	6	13.7
		6-Oct	10.11	10.13 P(4)	−3.88	13.25		5.8	13.73
		20-Nov	7.67	6.09	−0.78	12.5	3.98	6	12.55
	1980	8-Jan	4.63	6.09	0	14	3.67	5.8	12.09
		4-Feb	5.42	6.09	−0.52	13.64	4.53	6.2	12.94
		18-Mar	7.91	6.09	2.39 P(4)	17.78	7.21	6	15.76
		22-Apr	4.83	6.09	−2.6	15.12	5.05	6.2 T(4)	19.56 P(4)
		20-May	−0.62	−0.01	−10.32	9.46	−0.5	7	18.73
		9-Jul	0.61	−0.01	−16.7	8.98	−0.96	7.7	14.8
Phase 2		12-Aug	8.43	14.52	−24.94	9.35	−0.69	7.8	12.74
		16-Sep	16.46	14.52	−9.37	10.85	0	7	7.81
		21-Oct	17.29	14.52	2.57	13.17	1.78	7.5	6.52
		18-Nov	17.47	14.52	16.93	17.43	3.6	7.6	6.11
		18-Dec	12.93	14.52	20.28	19.44	9.04	7.5	10.04
	1981	2-Feb	0.39	1.92	19.62	16.51	5.36	7.4	12.12
		31-Mar	3.44	1.92	3.8	15.43	4.67	7.3	12.57
		18-May	7.78	1.92	2.93	20.0 P(4)	9.39 P(4)	7.3	11.45
		6-Jul	0.38	1.92	3.48	18.76	7.48	7.3	8.14
		18-Aug	−3.45	1.92	3.19	17.41	7.97	7	8.08
		5-Oct	1.83	1.92	0.26	14.93	7.13	7.5	10.5
		17-Nov	2.21	1.92	−10.95	13	4.51	7.5	11.85
		21-Dec	2.78	1.92	−17.25	12.54	5.2	8.4	9.5
	1982	2-Feb			−25.4	14.5	6.97	8.9	5.2
		30-Mar			−12.3	14	7.23	8.8	3.7
		18-May			0	14	7.49	9.4	1
		1-Jul			−7.3	13.5	8.82	9.5	3.7
		24-Aug			−6	9.5	3.95	9.8	9
		5-Oct			−3.4	9.5	4.67	9.8	7.7
		6-Nov			−3.9	9	3.45	10.4	4.1
		21-Dec			−8.1	8.5	3.9	10.8	3.7

Notes

Chapter 1. The Pragmatic Evolution of the Monetary Standard

1. The expectational nature of the nominal anchor springs from the nature of fiat money. One gives up goods, which satisfy real wants, today for paper money, which is intrinsically worthless, because of the *belief* that others will exchange goods for money tomorrow.
2. I reserve the term "rule" for an announced strategy to achieve explicit objectives. The strategy appears in the form of state-contingent language explaining the consistent way in which the central bank varies its instrument, the funds rate, in response to new information. Credible commitment to the rule allows the central bank to shape the way that the public forms its expectations in response to shocks (Hetzel 2006).
3. Greenspan (U.S. Cong. July 20, 2005, 33) testified: "[S]ince the late 1970s, central bankers generally have behaved as though we were on a gold standard. . . . So that the question is, 'Would there be any advantage . . . in going back to the gold standard?" And the answer is, "I don't think so because we're acting as though we were there.'" Ironically, perhaps because Greenspan viewed monetary policy from the perspective of the business economist, that is, as an exercise in forecasting the near-term behavior of the economy, he could never articulate this behavior.
4. Paul Samuelson expressed the prevailing Keynesian view. U.S. inflation was of the cost-push variety (Samuelson 1974, 802). To avoid high unemployment, the Fed had to accommodate this cost-push inflation (Samuelson 1977, 58; 1979, 972). See also Burns (1979).
5. According to Barro and Gordon, the central bank also dislikes inflation. The public understands the bank's incentives and expects a level of inflation above the bank's preferred level. The central bank must accommodate this level of expected inflation to avoid raising unemployment. Inflation ends up at a level high enough to cause the central bank to accept the sustainable unemployment rate even though that level exceeds its target.

Chapter 3. From Gold to Fiat Money

1. Bordo and Schwartz (1999) provide a review of monetary debates and summarize the most important contributions in the literature for the period 1880–1995. For a

discussion of the gold standard, see Bordo (1999), Wood (2005), and Yeager (1976; 1998).

2. The United States went onto the gold standard as opposed to a bimetallic standard in 1873.

3. Bureau of the Census, 1975, Series Y 335–8.

4. Central bank assets are monetary gold holdings and Federal Reserve credit, which includes loans to member banks (discounts) and holdings of private and government securities. Fed liabilities (the monetary base) are notes (currency) in circulation and member bank deposits.

5. Bureau of the Census, 1975, Series E 135–66.

6. All figures on money are from Friedman and Schwartz (1970).

7. Bureau of the Census, 1975, Series E 135–66 and E 23–39.

8. Like other countries on the gold standard, the United States had to back its currency with gold – the gold cover. The Fed had to maintain an amount of gold equal to a fixed percentage of its note liabilities and member bank deposits. Free gold was the excess beyond the statutory requirements for backing the currency.

9. Board of Governors 1921, 676.

10. Board of Governors 1920, 219.

11. Board of Governors 1921, 678.

12. Board of Governors 1930, 655.

13. See speeches of Governor Seay (1928).

14. Chandler (1958, Chapter 12), Friedman and Schwartz (1963a, 254ff), Meltzer (2003, Chapter 4). In general, on monetary policy in the Depression, see Bordo, Choudhri, and Schwartz (2002), Bordo, Erceg, and Evans (2000), Romer and Romer (2004), and Wood (2005).

15. Warburton (1966, 339) wrote: "In the early 1930's the Federal Reserve Banks virtually stopped rediscounting or otherwise acquiring 'eligible' paper" (cited in Timberlake 2005).

16. Beyond the quotation, see also Harrison's comments on pages 490–1, 495, 506, 508, and 517. Harrison did not argue that the Fed had been constrained by insufficient gold reserves. Representative Goldsborough (U.S. Cong. 1932, 488) pointed out that members of the Banking Committee had for a long time urged passage of legislation that would allow the collateralization of Federal Reserve notes with government securities. However, such legislation required the support of the Federal Reserve Board, which it had been unwilling to provide.

    The Board of Governors (1937, 828) opposed legislation requiring the Fed to "maintain a specified domestic price level": "The Federal Reserve System can regulate within limits the supply of money but there are other factors affecting prices and business activity fully as powerful as the money supply. Many of these factors are non-monetary and cannot be controlled by monetary action."

17. Section IV highlights the contrast with 1938–9 when the monetary base was exogenously determined by gold flows.

18. Strong was a forceful individual who might well have responded forcefully to bank runs. In contrast, Hetzel (2002a) shows George Harrison, Strong's successor, as a weak individual apparently unable to undertake decisive action.

19. Even today, the Fed's use of an interest rate instrument creates the perception of the central bank as a regulator of the price system not a creator of money.

20. Goldenweiser joined the Fed as an associate statistician in 1921. In 1925, he became associate director and in 1927 Director of Research and Statistics at the Board of Governors. He held the last post through 1944.

21. Board of Governors 1931, 437.
22. These figures come from the graph "Federal Reserve Bank Credit" in various issues of the *Federal Reserve Bulletin*. See also the table "Monetary Gold Stock of the United States."
23. Gold reserves of the world's central banks amounted to $11.3 billion in September 1931 (Board of Governors 1943, Table No. 165).
24. Board of Governors (1943, Table No. 172).
25. Board of Governors (1943, Table No. 160).
26. Dollar depreciation earned the appellation "beggar thy neighbor" because it produced gold outflows and deflation in countries that remained on the gold standard. U.S. dollar depreciation later gave flexible exchange rates a bad reputation. However, that assumption derived from confusion between pegged exchange rates that were periodically manipulated and freely floating exchange rates.
27. Balke and Gordon (1986, Appendix B).
28. Board of Governors (1943, Table No. 102).
29. A variety of evidence signals this change. From early 1934 to the middle of 1937, the Fed did not change the discount rate. Also, because borrowed-reserves procedures set money market rates, they automatically take the seasonal out of interest rates by putting a seasonal into Federal Reserve credit. Starting in 1933, seasonality reappeared in interest rates and disappeared in Federal Reserve credit. In addition, borrowed-reserves procedures create an inverse relationship between Federal Reserve credit and changes in factors affecting reserves like gold flows and changes in treasury deposits at the Fed. This inverse relationship disappeared after 1933. (See Friedman and Schwartz 1963a, 504–5.)
30. Starting at the end of 1931, both velocity series exhibit a decline unexplained by this opportunity cost, but they bounce back in 1933. The interval of unusual strength in money demand coincides with uncertainty over the maintenance of the gold standard and with bank runs. The resulting uncertainty about the net worth of individuals and many smaller banks would have made transactions effected with money rather than credit relatively more attractive and would have increased the demand for money.
31. The Board of Governors (1937, 377) wrote: "Through the elimination of about $3,000,000,000 of excess reserves, the Federal Reserve System was brought into closer contact with the market and was placed in a position where sales or purchases in the open market could ease or tighten credit conditions in accordance with the public interest."
32. Friedman and Schwartz (1963a, 522, fn. 21) quote George Harrison, president of the New York Fed: "If we increase reserve requirements, we shall put the Reserve Banks in the position where they will have a chance to control the situation by open market operations and changes in discount rates."
33. The quotes are from Sproul (1951, 299).
34. Summers (1991) argued for positive trend inflation as a buffer against the zero-bound problem. Apparently, the FOMC abandoned its longer run objective of price stability for this reason (Chapter 20). Keynes used the idea of a floor under the interest rate (a liquidity trap) to argue that the price system could fail to produce full employment. Pigou (1947) challenged Keynes by pointing out that the resulting deflation would stimulate spending by increasing the real value of money. The current debate echoes the previous debate. Those who argue that the zero lower-bound problem could result in a deflationary spiral implicitly argue that the central bank cannot follow a rule that stabilizes the price level by creating the expectation

of price stability. Given a fall in the price level, the expectation of price stability
would create expected inflation, which would lower the real interest rate (Wolman
1998).

35. Board of Governors (1943).

36. For documentation of Fed operating procedures in the twenties, see Chandler (1958,
Chapter 6), Meltzer (2003, Chapter 4), and Wheelock (1991).

37. Later, the Fed used the term "free reserves" to describe these operating procedures.
Free reserves are excess reserves minus borrowed reserves.

Chapter 4. From World War II to the Accord

1. Bureau of the Census (1975, Series D 85–6).

2. See history of Fed–treasury relations in U.S. Treasury (*1951 Annual Report*, 258ff).

3. There are two sources of information on the inflation expected by the public at
this time. One is the Board of Governors's Survey of Consumer Finances, which is
a survey of households conducted annually beginning in early 1946. The other is
the Livingston Survey, which is a survey of business economists conducted twice a
year since late 1946. This survey records expectations for CPI inflation for future
6-month and 12-month intervals.

4. Over the four-quarter periods ending 1945Q3, 1946Q3, and 1947Q3, M1 grew,
respectively, at the declining rates of 16.2, 7.1, and 4.1%. Over the four-quarter
period ending 1947Q3, real GNP fell 2% (Balke and Gordon 1986, Appendix B).
Postwar demobilization makes it difficult to isolate the effect of monetary contraction on output, however.

   The impact of the monetary deceleration depends upon how the public adjusted
its real money balances. M1 velocity fell from 2.5 in 1944 to 2.1 and to 2.0 in 1945
and 1946, respectively. Presumably, the increased demand for money reflected the
expectation of postwar depression. Its failure to materialize reversed this increase
in real money demand. M1 velocity rose to 2.1 in 1947 and to 2.3 in 1948 and
1949.

   After 1946, real money fell as a result of inflation and a decline in money growth.
(Given its interest rate peg, the Fed accommodated reductions in the public's
demand for real money.) After the surge in the price level following the end of
controls, inflation settled down approximately to 6% (Figure 4.3). Friedman and
Schwartz (1963, 561) argue that during the war consumers held cash in their portfolios in place of then unavailable consumer durables. After the war as consumer
durables became available, they reduced their holdings of cash with consumer
durables. Plausibly, August 1948 marks the end of the postwar adjustment to the
unusually high level of wartime cash balances.

5. This deceleration reflected the Fed's accommodation, at a pegged interest rate, of
an ongoing reduction in the public's desired real money balances. An argument
that a monetary deceleration produced the November 1948 peak in the business
cycle requires the assumption that the rise in the real interest rate that preceded
the peak produced a monetary deceleration greater than that desired by the public.
That explanation is possible given that M1 velocity did not rise between 1948 and
1949.

6. See Hetzel and Leach (2001a) for an account of the accord. See Bremner (2004)
and Hetzel and Leach (2001b) for an account of how Martin created the modern
Fed.

Chapter 5. Martin and Lean-against-the-Wind

1. See Saulnier interview in Hargrove and Morley (1984, 150–1), Martin (U.S. Cong. February 6, 1959, 462 and 482), and Stein (1990, 344).
2. Compare this statement to the Volcker quotations in Chapter 13.
3. A later expression of this view comes from a 1963 FOMC meeting (Board of Governors FOMC *Minutes* December 17, 1963, 1129). Martin told the FOMC, "The whole western world was again faced with the specter of inflation . . . and he was opposed to inflation because it led to deflation."
4. The ideas in the remainder of the sections come from Martin (April 13, 1953; May 6, 1953; April 8, 1954; October 19, 1955; January 12, 1956; 1957; January 9, 1958; December 12, 1958). On Martin, see Bremner (2004) and Wood (2006).
5. Along with Alvin Hansen, Seymour Harris at Harvard was the dean of Keynesian economics. Harris (U.S. Cong. February 6, 1959, 498) expressed this view in hearings before the Joint Economic Committee: "[T]he crucial point is, in the face of these cost pushes, whether it is the responsibility of the Federal Reserve to offset these by restrictive monetary policies and thus bring on unemployment."
6. Romer and Romer (2002; 2004) express a similar view of Martin.
7. Martin (U.S. Cong. February 6, 1958, 384) took responsibility for the inflation of 1956 and 1957 by allowing "inflationary excesses."

Chapter 6. Inflation Is a Nonmonetary Phenomenon

1. The term "nonmonetary" refers to theories that explain inflation without any necessary reference to monetary policy. Another term would be "eclectic factors." Through most of the 1960s, Keynesians assumed that a high elasticity of money demand (in the limit a liquidity trap) implied that changes in money demand accommodated whatever inflation real forces produced.
2. *Report* refers to the *Economic Report of the President* and the *Annual Report of the Council of Economic Advisers* transmitted annually to Congress by the administration.
3. Kennedy also set a target for long-term growth of 4.5%. In the 1960s, most economists believed that government policy could alter the trend growth rate of real output. If government ran a "tight" fiscal policy of surpluses, then the central bank could run an "easy" policy of "low" interest rates, which would spur investment and growth. For example, Seymour Harris (1964, Chapter 16), urged an objective for real growth of 4 to 5%. He stressed that a failure to grow at least that fast would allow the economy of the USSR to surpass that of the United States by the end of the millennium.
4. Their paper reads like a position paper prepared in the event that Kennedy would win the 1960 presidential election.
5. The Phillips curve appeared to capture the need for a "high" unemployment rate to restrain the inflationary wage and price setting of large corporations and unions. In general, Keynesian economics with its assumptions that markets do not work because they were no longer competitive and that powerful nonmonetary forces drove inflation represented a triumph of descriptive reality over optimizing behavior.
6. Nonmonetary theories of inflation lead to a taxonomy of inflation classified by cause. For a more detailed taxonomy, see Ackley (1961, Chapter XVI) and Bronfenbrenner and Holtzman (1963).
7. Milton Friedman disassociated himself from this recommendation.

Chapter 7. The Start of the Great Inflation

1. Martin's view that a "high" rate of interest should accompany a high rate of growth now appears modern. The Keynesian thinking of the Heller CEA appeared in an anecdote told by Heller (Hargrove and Morley 1984, 173) about his first meeting with presidential candidate Kennedy. [Kennedy said,] "Seymour Harris tells me that we can't grow all that fast with high interest rates. But then I'm told that Germany has been growing very fast with a 5% interest rate. How about that?"

2. The discussion of the relationship between the Fed and the administration under different presidents comes from Hargrove and Morley (1984), which is a collection of interviews with CEA chairmen under the presidents from Truman through Carter. Bremner (2004) is a thorough account of Martin's entire career. Bach (1971) covers the 1960s.

3. At the hearings, members of the House Banking Committee introduced legislation to erode the institutional underpinnings of Fed independence. They introduced legislation that would have made the Fed subject to a Government Accounting Office (GAO) audit and submitted legislation that would have put the Fed on budget by not allowing it to finance its activities through retention of interest payments on its government securities. They also attempted to remove the presidents of the regional Federal Reserve Banks as voting members of the FOMC, which would have destroyed the federal character of the Fed.

4. Woolley (1984), Kettl (1986), and Bremner deal with this period.

5. If Congress had rebuffed the pleas of the housing industry for aid, it would have forced the S&Ls to adjust the maturity of their liabilities to that of their assets, either by giving up the small savers market and funding long-term in the capital market or by issuing variable rate mortgages. Instead, through its attempt to allocate credit, the political system started the nation down the road to the S&L debacle of the 1980s. Congress extended to the S&Ls the Reg Q ceilings on interest rates, which since the Depression had limited the rates banks could pay on time deposits. Furthermore, the regulatory agencies (the Fed, the FDIC, and the Federal Home Loan Bank Board) favored the S&Ls by setting their ceilings half a percentage point higher than banks. Low Reg Q ceilings promised cheap credit to S&Ls, and the interest difference promised a ready supply. In the 1980s, the high inflation of the 1970s brought down the scheme for allocating credit to housing.

6. Memo Ackley to President, November 8, 1966, LBJ Library, WHCF, FI.

7. Letter from Martin to Johnson, December 13, 1966, LBJ Library, WHCF, FI4.

8. M1, which had grown at a 5.75% annualized rate in the first half of 1966, ceased growing in the second half. Annualized real GNP growth went from 3.75% in 1966Q3 to 2.2% over the three quarters 1966Q4 to 1967Q2. CPI inflation remained near 3.5% through the end of 1966, but then fell to 1.75% in the first half of 1967.

9. Memo Okun to President, "Suggested Agenda for Quadriad Meeting," June 24, 1968, LBJ Library, WHCF, FI.

10. From 1953 through 1963, annualized M1 growth had averaged 1.7%. From 1963Q4 through 1966Q4, it increased to 3.8% and then to 6.9% from 1966Q4 through 1969Q1.

11. See also Martin (May 22, 1969).

Chapter 8. Arthur Burns and Richard Nixon

1. CPI inflation rose from 1.3% in 1964 to 5.8% in 1969 while the unemployment rate fell from 5.5 to 3.5%.
2. The loss of manufacturing supremacy that the United States had enjoyed after World War II created protectionist pressures in the early 1970s. The *1979 Economic Report* (p. 161) illustrated this loss with a graph ("U.S. Share of Fifteen Industrial Countries' Exports of Manufactured Goods," Chart 13). From 1968 to 1972, the U.S. share of manufactured goods in world exports fell from 24 to 19%. Manufacturing employment, which had risen in the 1960s, stopped rising in the 1970s.
3. "Memo for the President's file, 11/20/70, meeting of Shultz, McCracken, Stein, Ehrlichman, Flanigan, and the President," [WHSF]BE, NA. See other memos such as Stein Memo, November 27, 1970, Stein Box 1, NA; Memo McCracken to Shultz, December 12, 1970, McCracken Box 52, NA; Memo McCracken to Ehrlichman, December 14, 1970, McCracken Box 47, NA.
4. He did so based on econometric work of Arthur Laffer, who had been an assistant professor at the University of Chicago's business school. Laffer found a strong contemporaneous relationship between M1 and GNP, which he used to derive the 6% M1 figure. Use of seasonally unadjusted data rendered the results doubtful.
5. Gyohten and Volcker (1992, 76) and Haldeman (1994), August 12, 1971 Diary entry.
6. See testimony of Paul McCracken (U.S. Cong. July 8, 1971, 33–4) and Charls Walker (U.S. Cong. November 1, 1971, 36).
7. See Burns letter to Nixon, June 22, 1971 [WHSF]BE5, NA.
8. For the 1972 election, Connally put together a set of villains different from those against whom Nixon had run in 1968. The program announced on August 15, 1971, would have an import surcharge to satisfy American workers who believed unfair competition from Japan stole their jobs. It would have wage controls to satisfy businesspeople who believed that labor militancy pushed up wages. To be politically palatable, wage controls required price controls. Price controls appealed to consumers who believed that greedy corporations forced up prices through price gouging. See Safire (1975, 588), Shultz and Dam (1978, 113), Forbord (1980, Chapters VI and VII), and especially Haldeman (1994), Diary entries for June 27 and July 21, 1971, and various entries for August 1971.
9. JEC testimony, August 19, 1971, in *Congressional Quarterly* (August 28, 1971, 1827).
10. See the December 25, 1971, and May 20, 1972, issues of *Congressional Quarterly* for summaries of the controls.
11. Gordon (1997) estimated the natural rate of unemployment for this period as 6–6.5%.
12. Nixon wrote Burns (Letter Nixon to Burns, December 4, 1971, n. 1, Burns Papers, FL): "[T]his ['the Fed's policy of holding the money supply down for too long a period'] is exactly what happened in 1959 and 1960, when as you recall, you came into the office and criticized McChesney Martin for keeping the lid on too tight and, thereby, helping to trigger the unemployment increase which was probably the decisive factor in our defeat in November of 1960.... Many elections in this country have been determined because of an increase in unemployment which resulted in the voters turning out the party in power. I cannot think of one election where inflation had any effect whatever in determining the result."

13. Memo, January 4, 1972, "To the Presidents of all Federal Reserve Banks," Burns Meeting Papers, FL.

14. The Bluebook, which is circulated to FOMC members prior to their meetings, suggests alternative language for the directive. It contained forecasts of money growth consistent with different choices for the funds rate.

15. Because of the later public dispute over Burns's actions before the November 1972 election, I have included in the Appendix ("Monetary Policy Procedures under Burns") an overview of operating procedures and how the FOMC implemented them in this period.

16. The most controversial accusation of political partisanship by Burns came in a July 1974 *Fortune* magazine by Sanford Rose. Rose claimed that shortly before the election Burns left a deadlocked FOMC meeting to call the White House. Intimidated, the FOMC agreed not to raise rates. However, this assertion is implausible. Because an FOMC chairman derives his prestige from Fed independence, no chairman is ever going to suggest anything other than his complete independence. The story is most likely an exaggerated account of an attendee upset by Burns's statements that the FOMC needed to support Burns's decisions because of the need to support government policy.

17. The public saw Phase III as a weakening of controls, especially because of the initial absence of a wage guideline. To demonstrate toughness, the administration imposed controls on the oil industry and crude oil (Congressional Quarterly *Weekly* March 10, 1973, 493).

18. See Chapter 21, Appendix: FOMC Data for reference to the Greenbook.

19. Table C-33, *1974 Economic Report of the President.*

20. Minutes of CID, February 14, 1973, Burns Papers, FL.

21. Letter to the President, June 1, 1973, Burns Papers, Nixon File, FL.

22. FOMC *Minutes* April 15–16, 1974, 508.

23. Patinkin (1981, 34) wrote that "the formal theory of inflation has drawn much closer to the folk wisdom of inflation." One reason is "the increasing popularity of talking about 'supply shocks' and, more generally cost inflation. A prime example of this is the . . . increase in OPEC oil prices on the inflationary process. The man in the street . . . was always ready to describe inflation as the consequence of increases in specific prices." In "Supply-Shock Staginflation," Blinder (1981, 65) wrote, "The simple story of stagflation caused by supply shocks provides an excellent explanation of what actually happened during the sorry seventies." However, Blinder and Newton (1981, 1) conclude, "The dismantling of controls can thus account for most of the burst of 'double digit' inflation in non-food and non-energy prices during 1974."

24. Burns (1973, 796) listed M1 growth by country for the period 1971Q4 through 1972Q4: United States (7.4%), United Kingdom (14.1%), Germany (14.3%), France (15.4%), and Japan (23.1%).

    With the second oil price shock in 1979–80, Japan allows one to distinguish between monetary policy and the oil price shock as a source of inflation because the Bank of Japan continued its policy of disinflation. Because of its dependence on imported energy, Japan should have been more affected than the United States by the rise in energy prices. In fact, Japan experienced only a short-lived, moderate rise in inflation and no recession (Hetzel 1999, 8).

25. The figures in this and the following paragraph are from Hutchison (1991, 20–32), who summarizes the economic environment existing in the major industrialized

countries at the time of the 1973, 1978, and 1990 oil price increases. The G-7 countries are the United States, Japan, Germany, France, the United Kingdom, Canada, and Italy. The series Hutchison uses for money are for the United States, (M2), Japan (M2+CDs), Germany (M3), France (M2), and the United Kingdom (M0).

26. Governor Brimmer (FOMC *Minutes* April 18, 1972, 448) supported Burns: "The significant point was that the Administration had decided at that time [August 15, 1971] – with the support of the Congress and the Federal Reserve – that the way to solve the problem of inflation was to apply direct controls rather than to slow the rate of economic growth and increase excess capacity. If more effective means of fighting inflation were needed, they should be sought in tighter controls . . . and not through monetary policy."

27. Board of Governors, *Record of Policy Actions Board, Annual Report 1972*, 98.

28. Hayes letter to Burns, February 19, 1971, Burns Papers, d4, FL.

29. FOMC *Minutes* February 14–15, 1972, 144.

30. FOMC *Minutes* February 14–15, 1972, 149.

31. FOMC *Minutes* September 19, 1972, 871.

32. FOMC *Minutes* September 19, 1972, 879.

33. FOMC *Minutes* September 19, 1972, 921–3.

34. "Report of Open Market Operations and Money Market Conditions for the Week Ended September 20, 1972," 3.

35. FOMC *Minutes* September 19, 1972, 926.

36. Letter Board of Governors to Alfred B. Hayes, October 10, 1972, Bernard, b25, Burns Papers, FL.

Chapter 9. Bretton Woods

1. For an overview of the Bretton Woods system, see Bordo (1993), Solomon (1982), and Yeager (1976; 1998).

2. Yeager's (1976, 429) summary of the Bretton Woods era is a chronicle of crises and ad hoc protectionist measures. "The Italian lira is rescued . . . from a crisis that began the year before. Sterling suffers a severe crisis but is rescued; Britain imposes an import surcharge. . . . Calm prevails before the storm. . . . Crises occur in the spring in midsummer, with flights from the dollar." International monetary relations appeared to require management by treasury and central bank professionals. The market, in the form of speculators, became the villain in times of crisis. Yeager (1976, 406) comments: "As for episodes of bold, large-scale, and successful IMF activity in times of crisis, these hardly serve as evidence for the success of the system if the system itself tends to breed in the opportunities for display of such heroism."

3. "At the end of 1948, the US held 71% of the free world's monetary gold stock; by June 1962, the US share had fallen to 40%. During the same period, Western Europe's share grew from 15% to 44%" (*1963 Economic Report*, 95).

4. Since 1960, "the dollar has contributed most of the increase in the total stock of monetary reserves. Gold has made very little contribution in the 1960s, and none at all in the past two years" (*1968 Economic Report*, 179).

5. "In recent years, about one-fourth to one-half of our over-all deficit has been settled in gold. . . . The rise in dollar holdings . . . makes the dollar peculiarly vulnerable. A decline of confidence in the dollar, resulting from widespread conversion of dollars

into gold, would create a serious problem for the international payments system" (*1963 Economic Report*, 95).

6. Various issues of the *Economic Report of the President* contain these quarterly figures.
7. At the end of 1969, U.S. liabilities to foreign central banks amounted to $16 billion. By the end of 1971, they amounted to $50.65 billion.
8. Vice President Bodner (FOMC *Minutes* September 21, 1971, 946) of the New York Fed reported to the FOMC in September 1971: "The initial reaction of the Japanese to the President's address had been to tighten exchange controls sharply.... Their attempt to keep themselves from being flooded with dollars, however, had resulted in the complete disruption of their payments mechanism, so that they were forced to relax the regulations. As soon as they did so, however, they were flooded with $1.7 billion in two days." One reason that Japan was determined not to revalue the yen was that the Ministry of Finance had compelled Japanese banks to hold the dollars they purchased rather than turn them into the Bank of Japan for yen. After Nixon's August 15 speech, called the "Nixon Shock" in Japan, the Bank of Japan bought dollars at the existing exchange rate of 360 yen to the dollar to prevent the banks from incurring losses on their dollar holdings. Later, it turned out that Japanese banks were also arbitraging exchange rates by borrowing dollars abroad and then reselling them to the Bank of Japan (Volcker and Gyohten 1992, 93–4).

Chapter 10. Policy in the Ford Administration

1. Greenspan (Hargrove and Morley 1984, 432) recounted that Burns exercised significant influence within the administration: "He [Burns] had a great deal of weight in the Ford administration.... I would say that the Fed had very considerable input into the administration's policies."
2. This memo and the ones cited in this chapter are from the Alan Greenspan Files, 1974–76, FL, Ann Arbor, MI.
3. See also the A. James Reichley interview with Alan Greenspan (January 28, 1978), FL.
4. See Greenspan (U.S. Cong. September 25, 1974, 85–6; U.S. Cong. September 26, 1974, 19) testimony. Greenspan attributed recession and high unemployment to increased uncertainty (U.S. Cong. January 6, 1975, 9). Because policies that increased longer-term inflation created uncertainty, Greenspan (U.S. Cong. May 2, 1975, 23) prescribed "a sustainable noninflationary type of system." Greenspan (U.S. Cong. September 25, 1974, 111) stated: "[O]ne of the advantages of having a credible long term policy in place is that . . . things happen to the way people behave." Greenspan (U.S. Cong. November 3, 2005, 6) commented later, "We began to recognize [from observing the 1970s] that, indeed, rising inflation causes unemployment." These views led to a concern for eliminating the inflation premia in bond rates that characterized Greenspan's tenure as FOMC chairman.
5. Letter December 14, 1974, Alan Greenspan Files, FL.
6. Darryl Francis (St. Louis Fed president) parted ranks and accused the Fed of causing inflation by monetizing the federal deficit.
7. Greenspan offers insight into his thinking with his critique of econometric models (Hargrove and Morley 1984, 441). In econometric models, monetary policy appeared to explain the 1974–75 recession. However, monetary policy, that is, the sharp rise in interest rates, picked up the effect of inflation, the true cause of recession. The usefulness of econometric models was limited because they only explained past

experience, and past experience had not included such a surge in inflation. Ongoing changes in the structure of the world render models useless for predicting.

8. In early 1975, the EPB (memo March 24, 1975, Alan Greenspan Files, FL) told Ford that the recession was "a short-term contraction, caused largely by a massive liquidation of inventories rather than a cumulative erosion of final demand."

9. From December 1972 through February 1973, the FOMC used a range for M1 with a midpoint of 5.5%. Thereafter, it specified a single number. Through summer 1974, the target remained close to 5.5%.

10. The FOMC set a range for the funds rate. Based on forecasts for money growth, the Desk moved the funds rate within this range between meetings.

Chapter 11. Carter, Burns, and Miller

1. See Congressional Quarterly *Almanac* 1976, 371–2.

2. One consequence is that FOMC discussions concentrate on the immediate policy action with only implicit understanding of the objectives and strategy of policy. An amusing illustration of the way this restriction limits FOMC discussion appears in a question posed by Burns (FOMC *Minutes* April 20, 1976, tape 3, 4): "I would like to ask one question [of Peter Sternlight]. If you had operated on nonborrowed reserves, do you think that considering the objectives of our monetary policy, which I am not going to define at the moment, but I'll let you define it in your own way, (Don't do it out loud please), do you think that you would have done better than we have done during the past month?" The reference to "tape" after *Minutes* is to the transcripts that Burns deposited in the Ford Library for the period after March 1976, when the FOMC stopped publishing the *Memorandum of Discussion*, until the end of his tenure in March 1978.

3. The first two citations in this paragraph are from Biven (2002, 31, 36).

4. Majority sentiment among the Board of Governors staff and FOMC members was Keynesian. Accordingly, the belief in the existence of excess capacity implied that monetary stimulus would not exacerbate inflation. At the February 15, 1977, FOMC meeting, the board staff expressed the view that because of excess capacity, "[t]here will be little upward pressure on inflation." Governor Partee commented that "[i]t will take a long time to hit capacity problems." At the April 19, 1977, meeting, the board staff explained its inflation forecast for mid 1978 of 5.5%. It equaled the difference between nominal wage growth of 8% and productivity growth of 2.5%. Predicted nominal wage growth came from a Phillips curve relationship. A negative output gap would prevent any further rise in inflation.

5. The Appendix ("Did the FOMC Target Money in the 1970s?") explains FOMC operating procedures in the last half of the 1970s. The FOMC used the tolerance ranges it set for money growth primarily to control the timing of funds rate changes.

6. Stephen Axilrod, staff director for monetary policy, told the FOMC that M1 had increased at an annualized rate of 6% over the last 6 months. The FOMC was aware that changes in the payments system were reducing the public's demand for M1 through a shifting of business deposits from demand to savings deposits. The resulting reduction in M1 demand made M1 growth even more stimulative.

7. Information on FOMC discussions for 1976 and 1977 are from notes taken by Michael Keran, who was director of research at the San Francisco Fed. For 1977, quotations are from his notes not the *Transcripts*, which were not available at the time of writing. The notes are in the personal collection of Keran and myself.

8. In a public relations gesture, Burns recommended lowering the top of the target ranges for M2 and M3. He noted that as market rates rose during the recovery, disintermediation would reduce their growth. Because Reg Q kept banks from raising the rates on time and savings deposits, higher market rates made these M2 deposits less attractive.

9. Richmond Fed archives for the April 19, 1977, FOMC meeting.

10. Greenbook forecasts did not reflect Burns's pessimism about the effects of energy policy. The May 1977 Greenbook, which incorporated the effects of the energy program, forecast the same real GNP growth as the April Greenbook, 5.9% from 1977Q2 through 1978Q2. The tone of the April 1977 Greenbook was optimistic. It reported that "[e]conomic activity has strengthened considerably in recent months.... Industrial production is estimated to have risen nearly $1\frac{1}{2}$ percent in March.... Consumer spending rose strongly further in March." The Greenbook also reported that "In February, the consumer price index rose 1 percent."

11. Burns (Board of Governors *Transcript* January 17, 1978, 5) later explained the "fundamental corrective actions" he wanted from the administration to limit the dollar's depreciation: "One is the passage of an energy bill, which would assure the world that we will be conserving oil on some scale and more important that we will be stimulating the development of new sources of energy supply. Second, I think we need an anti-inflation policy on the part of the Administration, something we don't have at the present time."

12. "Carter's economic advisors ... were continually concerned that the Federal Reserve would offset the fiscal stimulus with monetary restraint" (Biven 2002, 89).

13. The document "Current Economic Comment by District" circulated prior to FOMC meetings and was the predecessor of the Beigebook. First District comments included advice offered by economists.

14. One consequence of attributing inflation to expectational inertia unrelated to monetary policy was the extreme pessimism about the value of the sacrifice ratio – the amount of unemployment required to lower inflation. For example, the January 4, 1980, Bluebook listed alternative multiyear strategies for discussion by the FOMC. Strategy I assumed 6% M1 growth for the years 1980, 1981, and 1982, while strategy II assumed 4.5% M1 growth. After 3 years of 4.5% as opposed to 6% M1 growth, predicted inflation was only 0.9% lower. However, predicted real growth was only 0.5% as opposed to 2.3%. Also at the end of 3 years, the unemployment rate was 11.6% as opposed to 9.3%. See also Okun (1978).

15. President Volcker (New York) commented: "Europe sees a decline in the dollar value as a free ride for U.S. exports.... We must consider the exchange value of the dollar as one of our major objectives in policy discussions." However, he was not yet the Volcker of October 1979. At the February 1978 FOMC meeting, Volcker (Board of Governors *Transcript* February 28, 1978, 24) commented: "I myself do not think it [inflation] is something that monetary policy can very adequately handle by itself, unaided by new policies elsewhere in the government."

16. On June 30, 1978, the Board of Governors approved the recommendation of nine regional Banks for a discount rate increase. The fact that so many banks were in for an increase showed dissatisfaction among the regional Banks with monetary policy. Even then, Chairman Miller and Gov. Partee dissented. Financial markets reacted negatively to the unprecedented situation in which the Board outvoted its own chairman (Kettl 1986, 170).

17. *Record* is the *Record of Policy Actions*, a summary of FOMC discussion, which became the *Minutes* in February 1993.
18. Governor Partee (Board of Governors *Transcripts* April 18, 1978, 21) stated: "[A]n unemployment rate leveling off at 5.8 and tending to drift up . . . is unacceptable to most people in Congress. It is unacceptable . . . to the Administration. It is unacceptable to the drafters of the Humphrey–Hawkins bill and it is probably unacceptable to large segments of the population."
19. The material in this paragraph comes from Biven (2002, 140–1, 199–200).
20. For an account of this period, see Mayer (1980), Solomon (1982), and Biven (2002).
21. By distorting the behavior of the monetary aggregates, the rise in interest rates in fall 1978 increased the difficulty of formulating policy. The rise created an incentive for banks to circumvent the controls restricting their ability to pay interest on deposits. As seen contemporaneously, M1 growth declined from fall 1978 through March 1979 before surging in April. Weakness in the measured monetary aggregates undercut the position of the hawks on the FOMC, who had pointed out the inflationary consequences of high money growth. However, they were a small group. They included Robert Black (Richmond), John Balles (San Francisco), Larry Roos (St. Louis), Phillip Coldwell (Texas), and Governor Wallich. Not until Volcker moved from Bank president to FOMC chairman in August 1979 was there a significant hawkish element on the FOMC.
22. The price of a barrel of oil jumped from $12.80 in 1978Q3 to $40 in 1979Q4. Price controls and federal allocation rules produced long lines at gas stations in 1979.
23. This material summarizes Hetzel (1981).

Chapter 13. The Volcker Disinflation

1. See Goodfriend (1997; 2004b; 2005), Goodfriend and King (2005), and Hetzel (1986).
2. See the Appendix, "October 6, 1979, Operating Procedures."
3. Quoted in Lindsey, Orphanides, and Rasche (2005), which is the definitive account of this period.
4. Uncertainty over the level of the real interest rate necessary to restrain inflation limited the ability of the FOMC to lower bond rates through a rise in the funds rate. Because the bond markets watched the funds rate for information on the FOMC's judgment of what interest rate would suffice to control inflation, increases in the funds rate increased the entire maturity spectrum of rates.
5. See Schreft (1990) for a comprehensive discussion of the 1980 credit controls.
6. The quotations are from notes furnished by Michael Keran ("Meeting with Member Banks," March 17, 1980). The quotations, therefore, are Keran's paraphrases, not an actual transcription.
7. See the interviews in Greider (1987).
8. It required banks to hold loan growth to within 6 to 9%. Also, for large banks, it increased the reserve requirement to 10% on managed liabilities exceeding a base level. The board imposed a special surcharge on the discount rate of 3 percentage points for borrowing by large banks. It also imposed a special deposit requirement of 15% on increases in covered types of credit such as credit card lending. Lenders had to hold noninterest-bearing deposits with the Fed equal to 15% of credit extended in excess of the amount outstanding on March 14, 1980.

Finally, the SCRP subjected increases in assets of money market mutual funds to a reserve requirement of 15%.

9. The NBER date for the start of recession, January 1980, probably reflected the price rises produced in 1980 by the oil price shock (similarly to the way that the end of price controls in 1974 exacerbated the then existing recession).

10. The SCRP pulled M1 down below its target range. From March through May, annualized M1B growth was −7.4%. The FOMC did not realize initially that its targets for bank credit and money would conflict. At its March and April meetings, it extended the target for M1B in line with the targets of previous meetings. Maintenance of the targets for nonborrowed reserves, in combination with the fall in demand for total reserves associated with the fall in money, produced a sharp decline in borrowed reserves and the funds rate. The funds rate dropped about 10 percentage points from early April to late May.

 The FOMC modified its definition of M1 to account for the relabeling of demand deposits as savings deposits undertaken to evade the prohibition of payment on demand deposits. M1B added the checking-type deposits (like the NOW accounts offered in Massachusetts) at all depository institutions including S&Ls to the checking accounts at commercial banks and currency.

11. The New York Fed *Quarterly Review* reported on Desk actions.

12. The implicit GNP deflator rose by 8.9% from 1980Q4 to 1981Q4, a slowing of only 1 percentage point from the previous year. The rise in the CPI moderated in 1981Q1 and 1981Q2, but rose more strongly in the third quarter.

13. In 1981, the FOMC targeted shift-adjusted M1B. The introduction nationwide in 1981 of the new interest-bearing checkable deposits (NOW accounts) imparted a one-time fall to the income velocity of M1 to the extent that deposit inflows into M1 came from nonmonetary deposits. The same Reg Q ceiling on savings and NOW accounts encouraged movement into the latter because they offered transactions services not offered by the former. Shift-adjusted M1 represented an attempt by the board staff to construct a money series comparable to the old M1 series by removing increments to NOW accounts originating from non-M1 sources such as savings deposits (Bennett 1982; Simpson and Williams 1981).

 NOWs made the newly defined M1 highly interest sensitive (Hetzel and Mehra 1989). As a result, cyclical changes in market interest rates relative to the (relatively steady) rate that banks paid on NOWs introduced procyclical changes in M1 velocity. M1 growth fell (velocity increased) with strength in economic activity and increases in interest rates. Quantity changes in M1 then lost usefulness as a predictor of nominal demand. By using this shift-adjusted measure, growth rates of M1 can summarize through 1981 the impact of Fed policy actions on the growth of nominal demand.

14. When M1 fell after the May FOMC meeting, the Desk reduced the path for total reserves derived from the M1 target in line with reductions in actual total reserves in order to keep borrowed reserves and the funds rate from falling. At the end of June, the Desk ceased lowering the M1 target in line with realized M1. Weakness in M1 then caused borrowed reserves to fall. However, the normal effect of this fall in producing a lower funds rate did not appear. The extended period during which banks had been in the discount window had increased Fed administrative pressure for them to turn to the funds market. That pressure widened the spread between the funds rate and the discount rate.

Only in September did the fall in borrowed reserves depress the funds rate significantly. By early October, the shortfall of total reserves from path had reached an unprecedented level. A 1 percentage point reduction in the discount rate on November 2 was the first significant discretionary action taken in response to this shortfall.

15. See comments by Volcker at the August 1981 FOMC meeting (Board of Governors *Transcripts* August 18, 1981, 39).

16. The dates when the funds rate fell (first date) and then the bond rate rose (second date) were late 1979 and early 1980, spring 1980 and summer 1980, early 1981 and spring 1981, and late 1981 and early 1982.

17. Disagreement over the value of explicit objectives appeared in the following exchange (Board of Governors *Transcripts* February 4, 1997, 74–5):

"Pres. Melzer (St. Louis): [T]here are some economic costs associated with our not being more explicit. There is a tradeoff between the political risk on the one hand and on the other perhaps some real economic costs associated with the uncertainty we may cause by not being explicit.

"Greenspan: I think that monetary policy action is what does it. There is no evidence in my experience that words have had the slightest effect.... It is what we do, not what we say, that is going to matter."

18. This issue surfaces occasionally in FOMC debate over whether the effect on expectations of a credibly announced inflation target would lower the sacrifice ratio (the excess-unemployment cost of reducing inflation). Governor Meyer (Board of Governors *Transcripts* July 2, 1996, 57) argued the Keynesian case for hard-wired expectations invariant to the character of monetary policy:

"[T]here is clearly a sizable one-time cost associated with disinflation and absolutely not a shred of evidence that enhanced credibility of the Fed from announced or legislated inflation targets reduces that cost."

19. Greider (1987, 680–1) expressed the populist political pressures that such explicitness would have engendered: "Volcker was guided by an anxiety rarely mentioned.... If the Fed eased money, it was supposed that the bond investors would feel threatened by inflation and would react by pushing long-term rates even higher.... [T]he sensibilities of the money market, thus, were ultimately guiding the U.S. government's economic policy. The general desire for a healthier economy was stymied by the particular fears of a particular interest group. When the psychology of investors improved and long rates declined ..., then the Fed would move too."

Chapter 14. Monetary Policy after the Disinflation

1. Figure 4.5 shows similarly high real rates prior to 1950 during instances of deflation scares.

2. The FOMC targeted the funds rate indirectly by setting a target for borrowed reserves. Volcker then had some discretion over the resulting funds rate. President Solomon, New York (Board of Governors *Transcripts* December 17, 1984, 9) told the FOMC, "In practice, there is a modest range of flexibility [for the funds rate] based on consultation ... [with] the Chairman." In reference to the high level of the funds rate in summer 1984, President Morris, Boston (Board of Governors *Transcripts* November 7, 1984, 30) suggested that the FOMC have a way of addressing

situations where "the borrowing level is producing a significantly different level of rates than the Committee expected." Volcker conceded that the funds rate was higher than had been expected given the target for borrowed reserves, but that the outcome was desirable given rapid money growth and "ebullient forecasts" of the economy.

3. Although the transcript makes clear that FOMC members focused on the behavior of the funds rate, Volcker was unwilling to admit that it was the de facto policy instrument. Although he made clear his conviction that the markets should see the Fed tightening, he was in an awkward position and let others make the case for tightening.

4. His speeches indicated that Volcker viewed disinflation as working through reductions in credit creation. The high Reagan deficits would increase the cost of disinflation by raising interest rates. Without knowing in advance the cost of disinflation, the Fed could not publicly commit to an explicit rule.

5. Volcker (April 30, 1984, 2) later explained the title of the speech ("We Can Survive Prosperity"): "It's a legitimate question to ask – what will happen when the recovery proceeds? We haven't passed the test of maintaining control over inflation during a period of prosperity. Can we live with prosperity in that sense?"

6. Because of the need to sell treasuries out of its portfolio to offset the increase in the monetary base, the FOMC worried about whether it would have sufficient collateral to back outstanding Federal Reserve notes. The FOMC also worried about whether it would have to use discount window lending to backstop lending by the Home Loan Banks to insolvent thrifts (Board of Governors *Transcripts* August 21, 1984, 3–4).

7. A miniinflation scare occurred in August 1985. As growth moderated in 1985, the FOMC lowered the funds rate to about 7.75% after its July 1985 meeting. Bond yields, which had fallen from a peak of about 14% in 1984, reached a trough in mid June and early July at 10.25%. They then rose and reached 10.75% in early September. In response, the FOMC raised the funds rate half a percentage point to 8% between its August and October meetings.

8. This stability compared to the rise following the troughs of the recessions in 1960, 1970, and 1975 is striking.

9. With trend output growth of 2.25% due to productivity growth of 1.25% and labor force growth of 1%, this growth of nominal demand pushed inflation above 4%.

10. Japan's current account went from a deficit of 2% of GDP in 1980 to a surplus of 4% in 1986, while the U.S. current account went from a small surplus to a deficit of 3.4% of GDP in those years.

11. Volcker (February 2, 1983) itemized claims of U.S. banks on the LDCs. Non-OPEC developing countries owed $60.3 billion to the nine largest U.S. banks, half of which was owed by Argentina, Brazil, and Mexico. Their total indebtedness constituted 222% of their capital.

12. Volcker retained a life-long predisposition to thinking of monetary stability in terms of exchange rate stability. Volcker (1994, 150) said that before the Plaza Agreement he "had pleaded many times . . . for agreement on coordinated intervention."

13. For the political economy of this period, see Funabashi (1988), Volcker and Gyohten (1992, 248–58), James (1986, 433–53), Ueda (1993, 264–5, 207–9), Sawamoto and Ichikawa (1994, 94–6), and Solomon (1999, 21–9).

14. Gyohten (Volcker and Gyohten 1992, 251) wrote: "[A]fter discovering that a weaker dollar . . . did not produce the quick adjustment in the balance of payments that

they [U.S. policymakers] desired, they shifted the focus to macroeconomic policy at the Tokyo Summit in May 1986 and then at the Louvre meeting in February 1987."

15. See, for example, Volcker (U.S. Cong. July 17, 1985, 54).

16. Supply-siders would have gone one step further and tied the dollar to gold.

17. Volcker (Volcker and Gyohten 1992, 231) talked about "expectational and 'band-wagon' effects that occur when traders try to ride out a trend" and about the market having "lost any real sense of what exchange rates were appropriate." When Representative Leach asked Volcker at the latter's last oversight hearing if he would favor "some kind of formula for the conduct of monetary policy to assure noninflationary growth," Volcker responded he would have "sympathy" for a system "that put a good deal more weight on stability of exchange rates internationally" [U.S. Cong. July 21, 1987, 32]. Later, Volcker (2003, 35) expressed the importance he attached to exchange rate stability: [P]olicy makers ought to be able to arrive at some conclusion about what constituted 'a reasonable range of exchange rates. . . . [W]ithout any sense of what the right exchange rate is . . . the market just carried it to extremes. That is the way markets go. I would think if Governments were able to give some reasonable indication of what they thought was a kind of central tendency, the market would give some weight to that.'"

18. Later, Volcker (Volcker and Gyohten 1992, 283) questioned Treasury Secretary Baker's "candor" in making such a pledge.

19. Gyohten (Volcker and Gyohten 1992, 271) wrote: "[American policymakers] used the blackmail of dollar depreciation and the threat of protectionism, while ignoring that part of the problem resided in the failure of the United States . . . to correct its own fiscal excesses. . . . [That pressure] has generated an ugly mood of frustration and distrust."

20. Commentary like the following was frequent (*Wall Street Journal* April 6, 1987): "Investment managers fear that a lower dollar would mean higher inflation in the U.S. as prices of imports rise. . . . Also . . . foreign investors may shun U.S. securities."

21. A *Wall Street Journal* (October 26, 1987) article quoted the editor of Standard & Poor's *Outlook* as having said before the stock market decline that foreign buying is "the tail that's wagging the dog. It's been responsible for big gains this year and has made US investors confident that the market will keep moving up." The article quoted statistics from the Flow of Funds Accounts on acquisition of stocks by foreigners. "Investors abroad made a record $18.9 billion of net purchases of US stocks last year, more than tripling the previous annual record set in 1981. The 1986 total was surpassed in this year's first half alone, as foreigner's purchases minus their sales jumped to nearly $20 billion."

22. Volcker coordinated the funds rate increase with the Bank of Japan. "Volcker and his colleagues believe that the best solution to the dollar's woes is not for the Fed to tighten but for America's major trading partners . . . to *cut* their interest rates. . . . That was the idea behind the interest-rate reduction announced by Japanese Prime Minister Yasuhiro Nakasone announced on April 30, the same day that Mr. Volcker disclosed the Fed's move to tighten up. . . . To prod Tokyo and Bonn, the Fed is willing . . . to play 'chicken' with the dollar. The Fed knows if the dollar falls, the export-oriented economies of Japan and West Germany would be hurt" (*Wall Street Journal* May 19, 1987). On May 1, 1987, Japan and the United States made coordinated public announcements designed to halt the slide of the dollar.

23. New York Fed President Gerald Corrigan (Board of Governors *Transcripts* May 19, 1987, 20) said, "[E]ither actual or forecast rates of inflation have stepped up by . . . a half point and maybe even as much as a point."

24. To avoid dollar depreciation, in 1986, the Board had coordinated discount rate reductions with the Bundesbank (Volcker in U.S. Cong. February 26, 1987, 83).

25. Budget Director "James Miller said he was 'worried' . . . that an overreaction by the Fed could cause a recession. . . . [I]t's clear they [U.S. officials] are anxious to avoid achieving that goal [currency market stability] with a substantial rise in U.S. interest rates. Rather, they . . . expect that Japan and West Germany will step in . . . to lower rates. . . . The U.S. has been arguing . . . that the best way to bolster the dollar and resolve global trade imbalances is for Bonn and Tokyo to adopt stimulative policies and import more goods" (*Wall Street Journal* April 17, 1987). "The Federal Reserve is refraining from nudging U.S. interest rates higher because it doesn't want to take pressure off the Bank of Japan to ease credit, according to a senior U.S. official" (*Wall Street Journal* April 22, 1987).

26. An August 18, 1987, *Wall Street Journal* headline read, "Bond Prices Tumble as Dollar's Plunge Prompts Additional Fears of Inflation." The *New York Times* (September 3, 1987) reported: "Bond prices plunged again yesterday in waves of nervous, heavy selling. . . . Traders kept talking about a growing fear among investors of holding dollar – denominated assets. In his FOMC briefing, Donald Kohn (Board of Governers *Transcripts* September 22, 1987, 1–3) suggested that the dollar depreciation caused bond rates to rise because of a rise in inflationary expectations and because dollar depreciation would increase aggregate demand in an already strong economy. He pointed out the contrast with 1986 when declines "occurred against the backdrop of a weaker economy, higher unemployment rate, and continuing disinflation."

27. Baker also spiked hopes for a deficit-cutting package. When asked "whether any of the provisions in the roughly $12 billion congressional tax-increase package might be acceptable to President Reagan," he responded, "Absolutely, completely, unalterably, and unconditionally, the answer is no" (*Wall Street Journal* October 19, 1987).

28. This section comes from a conversation with Anne-Marie Meulendyke, December 18, 1999, who was an officer at the Desk in 1987.

29. Under the assumption of a positive correlation between actual and expected real growth and between actual and expected inflation, the nominal interest rate consistent with monetary control (the natural rate plus expected inflation) will vary positively with nominal output growth.

30. Over the period from 1983 through the end of the century, CPI inflation (ex F&E) remained mostly within a range of 5 to 3%. The standard deviation of annualized quarterly real GDP growth rates fell from 4.3% from 1964Q1 to 1982Q4 to 2.3% from 1983Q1 to 1999Q4.

31. See Cook and Hahn (1988) for the different effect on market interest rates produced by different packaging of discount rate announcements.

32. As recorded in "Open Market Operations and Securities Market Developments" published biweekly by the New York Fed, the Desk always began the period after FOMC meetings with a clear understanding of where the funds rate should be.

33. The Board abandoned lagged reserves accounting (LRA) for contemporaneous reserves accounting (CRA) in 1984 and then readopted lagged reserves accounting in 1998. With the funds rate as the instrument, the reserves accounting regime is

irrelevant. The reason is that if the FOMC sets a funds rate target, it will supply whatever reserves banks demand. CRA is only important if the FOMC wants to supply a given amount of total reserves to banks and let the marketplace determine short-term interest rates.

34. The new Board appointees were Preston Martin, Manley Johnson, Wayne Angell, and Martha Seger. Wags called them the gang of four.

Chapter 15. Greenspan's Move to Price Stability

1. For a description of FOMC meetings, see former governor Meyer (2004, Chapter 2). Meyer (2004, 47) wrote: "[FOMC] members sometimes got giddy with the prospect of actually having an opportunity to debate some aspect of the policy decision at the meeting and decide on it, as opposed to accepting the Chairman's recommendation." To start the policy go-around, Greenspan spoke at length. Everyone else then had only a minute or so to respond. Even if someone were quick enough to counter the chairman, there was minimal time for discussion. Without an interactive discussion, there was no way to challenge the chairman's logic. Basically, one either agreed or disagreed with the funds rate recommendation. The hurdle to disagreeing was high in that dissents by more than one or two members would advertise a split in the FOMC.

2. Greenspan believed that price stability was politically feasible only if it increased productivity sufficiently to cause real wages to rise at a rate sufficient to prevent wage compression (Chapter 18).

3. The discussion was necessitated by the need for the chairman to present an FOMC view on proposed legislation by Senator Mack mandating the FOMC to achieve price stability. Greenspan (Board of Governors *Transcripts* July 2, 1996, 72) warned the FOMC: "[I]f the 2 percent inflation figure gets out of this room, it is going to create more problems for us than I think any of you might anticipate." Greenspan himself did not sign on to a number.

4. Greenspan (1989, 798) had endorsed this expectational definition of price stability during the hearings in 1989 on Representative Neal's (D. NC) resolution (H.J. Res. 409) requiring the Fed to achieve zero inflation within five years of the resolution's enactment. Greenspan supported the resolution conditional on the language that "inflation be deemed to be eliminated when the expected rate of change of prices ceases to be a factor in individual and business decision making." The language is in *Congressional Record*, 101st Cong., 1st sess., vol. 135, no. 106, August 1, 1989. The statement here about the provenance of the language comes from a conversation of the author with Governor Martha Seger at the July 1991 Western Economics International Association meeting in Seattle.

5. Greenspan (U.S. Cong. February 25, 2004, 29) testified: "We know there are significant biases remaining in the price indexes we use so that true price stability would be reflected in price indexes which are positive, probably somewhere between .5 percent and a little under a full percentage point." In the January 28, 2000, Bluebook (p. 11), the Board staff performed a simulation with its FRB/US model, which it characterized as a "price stability scenario [which] brings core PCE inflation down to 3/4 percent – close to the estimated measurement bias in this price index."

6. The February 1988 Greenbook permits an inference of the board staff's estimate of trend growth. Because the staff forecast an unchanged unemployment rate of

5.8%, the associated forecast of real GNP growth of 2.8% had to represent trend real growth.

7. The behavior of the FOMC in the 1991 recovery was similar to its behavior in the 1958 recovery when it was concerned that short-term rates not fall too low because of gold outflows. Progress in achieving credibility meant that the FOMC prevented a rise in inflationary expectations during the 1991 recovery without the funds rate increases required during the 1983–4 recovery.

8. This result relies on the forward-looking behavior embodied in New Keynesian models where the Phillips curve makes inflation depend upon expected not realized inflation.

9. Nonfarm business labor productivity averaged 1.4% per annum.

10. At the July 1996 FOMC meeting, Governor Yellen prodded Greenspan into allowing the FOMC to agree on 2% as an inflation target. See earlier discussion.

11. After the introduction of TIPS in 1997, the difference between nominal Treasury and TIPS real yields (inflation compensation) gradually became the most important measure of expected inflation for the FOMC.

12. The FOMC begins to increase the funds rate after a succession of decreases only after it decides that economic strength has become sustained so as to avoid the possibility of a return economic of weakness that would require a reversal of a prior rate increase. Such a reversal would prompt an outcry from critics that the Fed had thwarted recovery by prematurely raising rates.

13. The preemptive character of policy drew populist attacks. For example, the Joint Economic Committee (U.S Cong. *The 1994 Economic Report of the President*, p. 40) highlighted statistics like growth in unit labor costs of only 0.8% in 1993 and concluded that "[t]here is little in the recent evidence on inflation to support the Fed's . . . hike in interest rates."

14. The widening in the international trade balance on goods and services since 1991 kept real GDP growth below growth in real expenditure. In 1998, the former grew 3.9%, while the latter grew 5.1%.

15. The figures are annual averages of the twelve monthly forecasts in the Table "Quarterly Summary for the U.S. Economy, Control." Until January 1996, they are for the fixed-weight GDP deflator. Thereafter, they are for the chain-weighted GDP deflator. The Survey of Professional Forecasters also indicates a fall in expected inflation starting in mid 1995. For the years 1992, 1993, 1994 and the first half of 1995, these forecasts averaged 2.9%. For the last half of 1995 and 1996, they averaged 2.5%, and for 1997 and 1998, 2.3 and 1.9%, respectively.

Chapter 16. International Bailouts and Moral Hazard

1. The actual situation was even more unfavorable because the overvalued exchange rate held down Mexican prices. Mexican M1 rose by a factor of 4.4 over the period 1990Q1 through 1994Q3.

2. In 1992–3, the central bank kept the exchange rate pegged at 3.1 pesos to the dollar. In early 1994, it let the peso fall to the bottom of a band set by the pacto. The bottom of the band allowed for an annual depreciation of the peso of 4.6%. From the beginning of 1993 to the inauguration of Zedillo in December 1994, the peso depreciated by about 10%.

3. President Zedillo's first finance minister, Jaime Serra Puche, promised that there would be no change in the exchange-rate policy followed in the Salinas

administration. Shortly after making this promise, confronted by a failure of the Mexican government to sell the dollar-indexed Tesobonos, he devalued the peso by 13%. Two days latter, December 22, 1994, Mexico was forced to let the peso float. By early 1995, the peso had fallen another 40%.

4. The Fed had a history of lending to Mexico using swap lines with the Bank of Mexico. It also financed lending by the treasury through warehousing for the Exchange Stabilization Fund (ESF). (Warehousing is the arrangement whereby the Fed gives the treasury dollars in return for foreign currencies held by the ESF.) There was no explicit congressional authorization for those activities. Given the real-bills philosophy of the authors of the Federal Reserve Act, it is certain that these individuals did not intend for the Fed to extend credit either to foreign central banks or directly to the treasury. When warehousing began in 1962, Congress was unwilling to authorize it. The FOMC finessed the issue of its legal authority to engage in such lending by arguing that, for purposes of transactions in foreign exchange, foreign central banks and the treasury are no different from the other participants in the money markets with whom it transacts (Hetzel 1996).

5. The IMF's director, Michel Camdessus, committed the IMF to its share of the Mexican loan without obtaining the necessary approval of his board (*New York Times*, April 2, 1996). Anne Krueger (1998, 2014) wrote: "[T]he usual minimal notice to executive directors (so that they may consult with their governments before voting) was not given, and some European executive directors abstained in protest." The $17.8 billion loan far exceeded the amount permissible under fund guidelines. Given the IMF limit on a loan to 1.5 times the country's quota minus outstanding loans, Mexico was only eligible for somewhat more than $3 billion.

6. The figures are published in the New York Fed's quarterly *Public Policy Review*.

7. Calomiris (1998) points out the perverse incentives beyond moral hazard that a global no-fail policy creates. If lenders to emerging-market countries had to bear the risk of default, countries would have to compete for foreign funds by doing more than simply offering the highest interest rate. They would have to develop the protections for property rights that make possible line-of-credit arrangements in developed countries.

8. The figures are from Grenville (1998, Graphs 2 and 7).

9. Moreno, Pasadilla, and Remolona (1998, Table 2) document the sharp precrisis increase in short-term borrowing from foreign banks by the Asian Tigers. From midyear 1994 to midyear 1997, measured as a percentage of GDP, such borrowing rose from 9% to 16% in Korea, 19 to 29% in Thailand, 11 to 17% in Indonesia and Malaysia, and 4 to 10% in the Philippines. In Korea, at the end of November 1997, of total gross foreign debt of $156.9 billion, domestic banks owed $115.5 billion (73.6%). According to the Bank of Korea, foreign banks withdrew $13 billion in the first three weeks after the early December 1997 IMF bailout (Muehring 1998, 86). In contrast, in Taiwan, short-term bank borrowing edged up from only 7 to 8%. Taiwan is not a member of the IMF, and thus its banking system is not eligible for an international bailout. Taiwan, which grew at about 5% in 1998, weathered the storm.

10. Based on increased dispersion in spreads on emerging-market debt after the Russian debt default, Dell'Arricia et al. (2006, 1690) concluded: "[P]rior to 1998, official crisis lending must have mitigated the perceived risk of holding emerging market debt."

11. One small fact makes the point that reform does not necessarily come quickly. The IMF tried to persuade Indonesia to forsake the clove monopoly granted to one of Suharto's sons. More than 200 years earlier, Adam Smith in *The Wealth of Nations* (1937 Cannan edition, 600) had already criticized the Dutch East India companies for their Indonesian clove monopoly.

12. The credit allocation arises because of the nonmarket allocation of funds. In this example, the Fed also transfers the liability for the insolvency from the uninsured depositors to the FDIC. Because the premiums that banks pay to the FDIC go into general federal government revenues and because the disbursements of the FDIC are government expenditures, the Fed transfers the liability to the taxpayer.

13. The IMF periodically allocates to member countries special drawing rights, which the ESF carries as assets.

14. In 1988 and 1989, the U.S. Treasury and the Fed engaged in coordinated sterilized foreign exchange intervention with other central banks to counter strength in the dollar. In December 1987, the mark/dollar exchange rate was 1.6. In May 1988, the yen/dollar exchange rate was 125. By September 1989, the value of the dollar had risen so that 1.95 marks exchanged for one dollar and 145 yen for one dollar. The administration became concerned about the appreciation of the dollar given a large U.S. current account deficit. As a consequence, the administration and the Fed began sterilized purchases of marks and yen.

The Fed and the ESF divided their purchases. When the ESF ran out of dollars to sell, it obtained additional dollars from the Fed both through warehousing and through monetizing the SDRs it held. In 1989, the Fed's foreign-exchange-related transactions added about $23 billion to reserves. That was more than the additions to currency that year, and the Fed sold on net about $10 billion in government securities.

The SDRs on the books of the Fed increased from $5.0 billion at the end of 1988 to $8.5 billion at the end of 1989. In 1989, Fed warehousing of foreign currencies for the treasury rose from zero to $7 billion. Fed monetization of the SDRs held by the ESF increases the ESF's assets permanently as the ESF uses the dollars it acquires to acquire interest-bearing assets. (See Schwartz 1997, especially Table 1.)

Figures on SDRs are from the Fed's balance sheet reported in the *Federal Reserve Bulletin*. Figures on Fed warehousing are from quarterly reports, "Treasury and Federal Reserve Foreign Exchange Operations," in the Federal Reserve Bank of New York *Quarterly Review*.

Broaddus and Goodfriend (1995) criticized such interventions for sending contradictory signals about the stance of monetary policy. In this case, the dollar was strengthening because the FOMC had raised its funds rate peg to almost 10% in May 1989 to contain a rise in inflation. By selling dollars to weaken the foreign exchange value of the dollar, the FOMC was sending an opposite message about the desired stance of monetary policy from what it was sending domestically by raising the funds rate. Kaminsky and Lewis (1996) make the same point.

15. For example, in September 1989, Mexico drew on its swap line with the Fed for $784.1 million. At the same time, it drew on an ESF swap line for $384.1 million. Figures on swap line drawings are from quarterly reports, "Treasury and Federal Reserve Foreign Exchange Operations," in the Federal Reserve Bank of New York *Quarterly Review*.

The Fed does not lose interest on the assets in its portfolio because it receives interest on the peso-denominated assets. The basic point is that the Fed can engage in the loan transaction with Mexico because of its control over seigniorage.

16. See also Broaddus and Goodfriend (1995), Goodfriend (1994), Goodfriend and King (1988), Hetzel (1997), and Schwartz (1992).

Chapter 18. Departing from the Standard Procedures

1. Alternatively, Greenspan (September 24, 1990, 5) commented: "If the structure of the economy is more like a moving target than a sitting duck, we will rarely accumulate enough observations . . . to estimate accurately the parameters of our models."
2. On discretion, see Greenspan (May 2004; August 26, 2005, 3). On forecasting inflation, see Greenspan (U.S. Cong. March 20, 1997, 1).
3. Greenspan (November 3, 2005) testified: "[L]ow inflation . . . is attributable to the remarkable confluence of innovations . . . which . . . have elevated the growth of productivity, suppressed unit labor costs, and helped to contain inflationary pressures. The result has been a virtuous cycle of low prices and solid growth. Contributing to the disinflationary pressures . . . has been the integration [of the former Soviet Bloc and China in the world marketplace]. [T]he . . . assimilation of these new entrants . . . has restrained the rise of unit labor costs . . . and has helped to contain inflation." Kohn (2004, 180; 2005, 339) expressed the same views. Volcker, in contrast, attributed inflation to excessive growth in money, which the Fed could control.
4. More specifically, the issue is whether policymakers should respond directly to asset prices or only indirectly as they influence real output.
5. See also Greenspan (U.S. Cong. February 26, 1997, 10).
6. Greenspan (September 27, 2005, 5) stated: "By the late 1990s, it appeared to us that very aggressive action would have been required to counteract the euphoria that developed in the wake of extraordinary gains in productivity growth. . . . [W]e would have needed to risk precipitating a significant recession. . . . The alternative was to wait for the eventual exhaustion of the forces of boom. We concluded that the latter course was by far the safer."
7. Blinder and Reis (2005) amplify Greenspan's characterization of risk management. They present a table of four macroeconomic risks and five financial risks and argue that in an ongoing way the FOMC moves the funds rate judgmentally in a way that reflects a combination of the greatest risks.
8. Moral hazard also prevents a central bank from articulating a rule dependent upon the behavior of asset prices.
9. See also Greenspan's (U.S. Cong. January 31, 1994, 17) discussion of the "chronically high inflation" of the 1970s: "[I]nflation expectations are a critical variable with respect to the actual performance of the economy and . . . the rate of inflation is associated inversely with the rate of growth of productivity."
10. After 1994, both the mean duration of unemployment and the percentage of unemployed workers leaving their last job involuntarily declined steadily.
11. Greenspan (U.S. Cong. February 24, 1999, 61) testified: "[O]ur current discretionary monetary policy has difficulty anchoring the price level over time in the same way that the gold standard did in the last century."
12. Greenspan lacked a theoretical framework for relating real variables (unemployment and real wages) to nominal variables (nominal wages and inflation). Real variables possess no implications for nominal variables independent of monetary policy. As argued by Friedman (1968) and Lucas (1972), the real-nominal link depends upon the way that monetary policy conditions expectations.

Chapter 19. Boom and Bust: 1997 to 2001

1. A trendline fit through real output per capita over the period 1870 through 2002 (real GNP divided by the total U.S. population) rises at an annual rate of 2.1%, practically the same as the trend growth shown in Figure 19.2.
2. In 1999, real equipment investment as a percentage of GDP rose to over 10% from an average of 6% in the 1980s. The information processing and software component constituted 6% of GDP.
3. Theory suggests that increased real growth and optimism about the future expressed in lofty equity prices should have been associated with a rise in the real interest rate. At the May 1997 FOMC meeting, President Broaddus (Richmond) challenged the view that high productivity growth would obviate the need to raise the funds rate through its restraining effect on the growth rate of unit labor costs and inflation. He pointed out that the more optimistic individuals feel about the future the higher the real rate required to restrain aggregate demand to supply. (See also Broaddus 2004.)
4. See the press release issued by the FOMC following its June 28, 2000, meeting and Greenspan (May 6, 1999).
5. In 1995, newspapers regularly published jeremiads lamenting that for the first time children would not experience a higher living standard than their parents. Secular stagnation in real wage growth would create a permanently impoverished working underclass. Five years later, newspaper headlines proclaimed the birth of the new economy. The *Wall Street Journal* (January 1, 2000) talked about an unprecedented era of abundance in a world that had repealed the laws of scarcity.
6. This uncertainty about the future appears in the high S&P 500 E/P ratio relative to the 10-year treasury yield (Figure 14.5). I am indebted to my former colleague Marvin Goodfriend for these insights into the behavior of the real interest rate.

Chapter 20. Backing Off from Price Stability

1. Historically, because of differences in their construction, the CPI has risen 0.4 percentage point faster than the PCE deflator. For this reason, subtracting this amount from the nominal–TIPS inflation compensation numbers offers a measure of expected PCE inflation. By using the core PCE in the economic projections contained in the semiannual *Monetary Policy Report*, the FOMC expresses a preference for the PCE as a measure of inflation.
2. Because Greenspan understood economic stabilization in terms of managing swings in investor optimism and pessimism rather than in terms of allowing the price system to work, he packaged the funds rate reductions as if he were averting a crisis of confidence (Chapters 18 and 19).
3. These concerns implicitly assume that at a zero short-term interest rate a policy of money creation through open-market purchases of illiquid assets will be ineffective in stimulating aggregate nominal demand. The Appendix, "Japanese Deflation and Central Bank Money Creation," disputes the contention that deflation in Japan demonstrated the impotence of monetary policy at a funds rate of zero. See also Chapter 3, Section IV.
4. Although many Fed watchers had anticipated a half-point reduction given the FOMC's disquiet over disinflation, concern existed in the FOMC that such a large change would send an unduly pessimistic signal about the economy. "[S]ome members commented that a larger reduction might be misread as an indication of more

concern among policymakers about the economic outlook than was in fact the case" (Board of Governors, *Minutes FOMC* June 24–25, *Annual Report* 2003, 192, 186).

The FOMC's attempt to influence the yield curve without actually changing the funds rate produced large fluctuations in bond rates. The *Financial Times* (August 12, 2003) wrote, "[T]heir [10-year bond yields] recent gyrations have been extraordinary and have generated damaging uncertainty." The *Wall Street Journal* (July 24, 2003) wrote, "Bruised bond traders blamed the Fed for misleading them on how worried they were about deflation."

5. "The members did not see the need at this time to reach a consensus on the desirability of any specific nontraditional approach to the implementation of monetary policy" (Board of Governors FOMC *Minutes* June 24–25, 2003).

6. For example, while a measure of the output gap based on deviations of output from trend remained positive from 1994 through 2000, inflation declined moderately (Figure 19.1). The short-lived fall in inflation in 2003 probably reflected short-lived monetary restriction from mid 2000 to mid 2001 (Chapter 19).

7. Bernanke (2003, 5–7) listed four determinants of inflation: economic slack; inflation expectations; supply shocks, such as changes in energy prices, food prices, or import prices; and inflation persistence. He commented that "the degree of economic slack is the one currently providing the greatest impetus for further disinflation" and also warned that high productivity growth might imply that "the true level of slack in the economy is higher than conventional estimates suggest, implying that incipient disinflationary pressures may be more intense."

8. See the related discussion in Chapter 4, Section IV; Goodfriend (2000); and Wolman (1998).

9. Friedman and Schwartz (1963b) found that when money exercised an independent influence, monetary accelerations and decelerations appeared in nominal expenditure with a two- to three-quarter lag. The power of money creation to influence nominal expenditure appeared dramatically in the stop–go era. Money creation reliably predicted nominal expenditure (Figure 23.2).

10. The FOMC started moving away from its 1% funds rate target in May when it changed the statement language from "the Committee believes that it can be patient in removing its policy accommodation" to "the Committee believes that policy accommodation can be removed at a pace that is likely to be measured."

Chapter 21. The Volcker–Greenspan Regime

1. With credibility, inflationary expectations are fixed, but monetary policy must still provide a nominal anchor. The public must believe that the FOMC will respond if trend inflation deviates from target. Policy is evolving toward a credible rule like the following.

$$i_t = i_{t-1} + 0.125 \left(\pi_t^{TR} - \pi^* \right) + 0.25 I_t^{RU} \tag{1}$$

where trend inflation π_t^{TR} replaces expected inflation π_t^e in (1). If trend inflation differs from target, the public must believe that regularly the FOMC will raise (lower) the funds rate by some amount, say, 0.125 times the inflation miss, until trend inflation returns to target. Similarly, the public must anticipate that the FOMC will raise (lower) the funds rate in a persistent way as long as the rate of resource utilization is rising (falling). I_t^{RU} is an indicator variable showing whether resource utilization is increasing or decreasing in a sustained way. It takes on the value 1 if the resource utilization rate is increasing, −1 if it is decreasing, and 0 otherwise (Hetzel 2006).

2. As shown in (1) with the formulation of the growth gap as the difference between smoothed output growth and potential output growth, the FOMC attempted to respond only to persistent growth gaps. It thus avoided short-term reversals of the funds rate. However, by waiting at the onset of a recovery cycle to raise the funds rate until incipient economic strength was clearly persistent, the FOMC put inertia into the funds rate. Credibility is then essential because the term structure rises when the incipient strength first emerges, tempered by the probability that it is transitory.

3. For econometric evidence, see Mehra (1999; 2001).

4. The natural rate is, alternatively, the real interest rate consistent with perfect price flexibility and with the real business cycle core of the economy. It is the interest rate produced by a rule that allows the price system to work.

5. This characteristic is common across central banks. For example, Lambert (2005, 60–1), a member of the Bank of England Monetary Policy Committee (MPC), wrote: "[T]he MPC does seem to prefer small incremental moves in interest rates to larger, bolder steps.... On top of this, there is a quite strong feeling on the Committee that sharp movements which will surprise the public are to be avoided unless they are essential." For the FOMC, see Poole (2007) who stresses the desirability of aligning actual funds rate changes with the changes expected by futures markets.

6. For the period from 1982 on, Orphanides (2003c) finds that a growth gap does a better job than an output gap in explaining the behavior of the funds rate.

7. Economists have documented the impracticality of estimating a real-time measure for the output gap. For the United States, see Croushore and Stark (1999), Kozicki (1999), Orphanides (2002; 2003a; 2003b), Orphanides and van Norden (2002), and Runkle (1998). For Japan, see Kuttner and Posen (2004). For the United Kingdom, see Nelson and Nikolov (2003). For the Euro area, see Mitchell (2003). Staiger, Stock, and Watson (1995) and King, Stock, and Watson (1995) demonstrate the imprecision of NAIRU estimates. Chang (1997, 12) summarizes: "[I]n practice, the concept of a [NAIRU] noninflation accelerating rate of unemployment is not useful for policy purposes."

   Mehra and Minton (2007, Figure 1) provide evidence of the imprecision of contemporaneous estimates of the output gap. They plot estimates of the output gap from the Congressional Budget Office that were made in 2006 and contemporaneously. Over the two-year period of economic recovery, 1991–2, the magnitude of the contemporaneously estimated negative output gaps exceeded the vintage 2006 output gap by almost 2.5 percentage points. Assuming use of a Taylor Rule, with the latter more accurate figures and a coefficient on the output gap of 0.5 (Taylor 1993), the funds rate would have been 1.25 percentage points higher in this period known as the "jobless recovery" (Chapter 15).

8. A search of FOMC transcripts and staff materials circulated to the FOMC for the years 1983 through 2000 revealed only very infrequent mention of an output gap. The former date is the assumed date when the FOMC began to follow the current policy procedures and the latter date arises because FOMC materials are confidential for five full calendar years after FOMC meetings. There was a single reference in FOMC meetings in each of the years 1988, 1992, 1993, 1994 and three references

in 1995 and in 1996. Only in two instances do FOMC members refer to an output gap in discussions among themselves. Governor Yellen mentions it in a reference to the Taylor Rule (February 1, 1995 meeting) and President Moskow (Chicago) mentions it in one sentence of a long prepared statement. In 1999, there are several meetings that include reference to an output gap, but they always occur in the context of the way in which Phillips curves with positive output gaps were overpredicting inflation. Although the Board of Governors staff uses the output gap in its inflation forecasts, at no time in this period does it give an explicit numerical estimate of the output gap. In contrast, consistent with use of a growth gap indicator, the use of the term "sustainable" as a characterization of the desirable growth rate of output was ubiquitous. For example, the directive issued at the January 28, 2004, FOMC meeting stated: "The Federal Open Market Committee seeks monetary and financial conditions that will foster price stability and promote *sustainable growth in output*" (italics added).

9. That fact became especially important after 1996 when uncertainty over trend productivity growth eliminated reliable estimates of trend growth. Until the last half of the 1990s, agreement existed in the forecasting community on the value of trend real growth because of agreement over its components. Trends in growth of the working-age population and in labor force participation rates determined labor force growth. General agreement also existed over trend growth of output per worker. For example, Allen (1997, 1) commented: "The conventional wisdom is that the potential growth rate ... is between 2.0 and 2.5 percent annually. This range reflects a projected growth in the labor force of about 1 percent and a trend growth of 1.0 to 1.5 percent in labor productivity."

10. The dashed line shows how potential output growth increased after 1995. That is, output could grow faster without a fall in unemployment. (The intersection of the fitted line with the *x*-axis shifts to the right.)

11. The reason for the difficulty in achieving consensus over the nature of the monetary regime lies in the simultaneity problem. Theory guides the choice of empirical regularities, but empirical regularities guide the choice of theory. The criterion used here for breaking out of this circle is to ask how well does a theory continue to predict over changes in the policy process indicated by documentary evidence. Changes in policy include changes from the gold standard to real bills, to wartime rate pegging, to postwar macroeconomic stabilization with varying emphasis placed on controlling unemployment versus inflation.

12. See, for example, Svensson (1997).

13. For example, note the lag in response of the funds rate to economic strength in late 1993 and early 1994 (Chapter 15 and Figure 14.6).

14. Observations correspond to FOMC meetings. I used the Greenbook to identify the last change in the monthly unemployment rate available to the FOMC at its meetings. The funds rate series is the funds rate coming out of an FOMC meeting shown in Figure 21.2.

15. Even if the view here is correct that the FOMC implements a rule-like procedure that causes the real funds rate to track the natural rate and leaves determination of unemployment to the market, the correlation between funds rate changes and strength in economic activity conveys the impression that the FOMC manages the economy. It would appear heartless for a policymaker to say that the impersonal forces of the marketplace are responsible for determining employment. Similarly, to say that monetary policy responds to increases in bond rates that reflect increased

expected inflation would appear to put the interests of bond holders in not incurring capital losses ahead of America's working men and women.

16. Lowering inflation below a level firmly incorporated in expectations will create transitory excess unemployment. The rational-expectations view here is that the output effect is basically unpredictable because predictability of the public's response to central bank actions requires predictable behavior by the central bank (Lucas 1980). In contrast, the hard-wired inflation persistence view assumes a fixed known sacrifice ratio for eliminating inflation overshoots.

17. During Greenspan's tenure, the major example is the "jobless recovery" following the July 1990 business cycle peak.

18. Stephen Axilrod was associate director, Division of Research and Statistics, at the Board of Governors.

19. The test of the assumption of hard-wired inflation persistence is whether the character of the monetary regime shapes actual and expected inflation. Evidence against intrinsic persistence comes from England. In 1997, the Bank of England received independence to set the interbank rate to achieve a 2% inflation target. From 1997Q1 through 2005Q4, the quarterly autocorrelation in inflation (RPI) was −.34. The annual autocorrelation was −.1. Positive inflation persistence disappeared.

20. For example, the forecasters surveyed for the May 1, 2006, issue of *Blue Chip Financial Forecasts* anticipated that real GDP would grow at about 3% from 2006Q3 onward.

21. Over the interval from early 2002 through yearend 2005, the real trade-weighted exchange rate between the United States dollar and other major currencies (euro, Canadian dollar, Japanese yen, British pound, Swiss franc, Australian dollar, and Swedish kroner) fell about 20% (St. Louis *International Economic Trends*).

22. A better objective for policymakers than "transparency" would be "communication." How do policymakers understand the way in which they control inflation and the trade-offs involved with unemployment? The Congress delegated responsibility for the monetary regime to the Fed without giving it a substantive mandate. The Fed has a responsibility to explain the nature of the monetary standard that it has created. It cannot do that without using the language of neoclassical economics.

23. A willingness to depreciate the value of the dollar (raise the price level) in a continuous way undermines arguments for an independent central bank. Volcker (September 20, 2006, 12) argued: "It [inflation] corrodes trust...in government. It is a government responsibility to maintain the value of the currency." A constitutional reason for assigning monetary policy to Congress and for delegation of that responsibility to an independent central bank is to prevent seigniorage from being abused to raise revenue without explicit legislation (Hetzel 1997). Price stability is the clear line that demonstrates the depoliticization of money.

24. Prior to Chairman Bernanke, the chairman did not contribute to the forecasts presented at oversight hearings. Greenbook forecasts may offer a better proxy for his estimate of sustainable output growth. Greenspan (U.S. Cong. February 25, 1992, 23) commented on the Humphrey–Hawkins forecasts: "I'm not in those numbers. I tend to be pretty much in line with the staff estimate [of real output growth] since I contribute to that particular process."

25. The word is contained in the instructions sent by the FOMC secretary to FOMC members.

26. Volcker (U.S. Cong. July 28, 1983, 283) commented: "[T]hose projections reflect a view as to what outcome should be both feasible and acceptable...otherwise monetary policy targets would presumably be changed."

27. These predictions are for the calendar year. The proxy for sustainable growth for the last half of the year is the midpoint of the central tendency range for the year divided by the annualized growth rate predicted in the Greenbook for the first half.

28. In a telephone call prior to FOMC meetings, the board staff relayed the numerical value of this path to regional bank presidents. The Greenbook contains a brief description.

29. Hetzel (2006) uses the first proxy.

30. In 2000, the European Central Bank (ECB) debated public release of the inflation forecasts that its own and member bank staffs make biannually. That debate raised the obvious problem with a central bank making a "forecast" of inflation when inflation is the variable that it targets and controls. The central bank cannot forecast an inflation rate different from its target, explicit in the case of the ECB. A forecast of an inflation rate higher than the central bank's target could make labor unions or bond holders set prices inappropriately (*Financial Times*, October 3, 2000).

31. For the inflation gap, the actual and target values are calculated similarly to the growth gap. The actual values are the contemporaneous quarterly inflation forecasts from the Greenbook, and the target values are the longer run forecasts. Through 1988, the inflation measure is the implicit GNP deflator. From 1989 through May 2000, it is the CPI ex food and energy (F&E). Thereafter, it is the PCE deflator ex F&E.

32. Estimation using proxies for the growth gap and inflation gap using the three methods described previously yielded similar results.

33. The regression begins in 1983, the year in which the FOMC abandoned its nonborrowed-reserves procedures. It ends when Greenbook data become confidential.

34. For example, in early 2004, the FOMC believed that the real funds rate was unsustainably low. At its June 30 meeting, after the economy began to grow faster than potential (when employment growth exceeded growth in the working-age population), the FOMC put the funds rate on an upward track. At the July 2004 oversight hearings, as indicated by the midpoint of the central tendency range for real output growth of 4.5%, FOMC members forecast the above trend real growth (a falling unemployment rate) appropriate for economic recovery. As long as real output growth came in at about this figure, the FOMC continued to raise the funds rate. As measured here, the growth gap was zero, whereas in fact the assumed true growth gap was positive.

Chapter 22. The Fed: Inflation Fighter or Inflation Creator?

1. Velde (2004) reviews explanations for the Great Inflation in "Poor Hand or Poor Play?" His "poor hand" classification refers to the work of authors like Sims and Zha (2006) who argue that bad shocks rather than monetary policy initiated the 1970s inflation.

2. The sacrifice ratio is the number of years of unemployment in excess of full employment (the NAIRU) required to reduce the inflation rate by 1 percentage point.

3. Nelson (2005) documents the prevalence of these views in the 1970s.

4. Sargent (1999) assumes that the Volcker disinflation represented acceptance of the rational expectations–natural rate hypothesis for the Phillips curve. Cho, Sargent, and Williams (2002) assume that the Fed has remained committed to a Phillips curve that omits expected inflation as a variable. However, through learning, it

adapted the parameters of this misspecified Phillips curve sufficiently to avoid inflation.

5. The Boston Fed polled economists before FOMC meetings for their advice, which the board reported in the Redbook. Mayer (1999, 100) cited Governor Bucher's approving repetition of Samuelson's comment at an FOMC meeting.

6. Patinkin (1981, 31) states: "The real question is whether the quantity of money is an exogenous variable or an endogenous one. Does the monetary increase come from outside the system, or is it generated by the dynamics of the system itself? Is it the cause of the increase in the price level, or is it the result?" Patinkin misstates the issue. With an interest rate instrument, money is always endogenously determined. If monetary policy procedures for setting the interest rate do a poor job of tracking the natural rate, the price level must adjust to the resulting monetary emissions. (The nominal stability of the last part of the twentieth century implies that the FOMC has developed procedures for setting the funds rate that respect the working of the price system.) If these procedures do track the natural rate, expected inflation determines both the behavior of money and prices. However, the central bank controls expected inflation through its ability to control money creation.

7. In inflation scares, the FOMC raised the funds rate in response to a rise in expected inflation. The ultimate restoration of credibility meant that influence went not just from expected inflation to the funds rate but also from the funds rate to expected inflation. The funds rate then influenced inflation, the independent variable, through its influence on expected inflation.

8. Visual inspection indicates that the FOMC did raise the funds rate one-for-one with inflation before the Volcker era.

9. The rationale for a lagged term is that the FOMC decides on a desired funds rate and moves only slowly over time to this desired value. However, nothing in FOMC procedures corresponds to such an assumption. Perhaps the lagged term captures the FOMC's pragmatic search procedure of moving the funds rate away from its prevailing value rather than the formulaic procedure of the Taylor Rule.

Chapter 23. The Stop–Go Laboratory

1. Poole (1975, 128) wrote: "In U.S. business cycle experience, steady or accelerating money growth and rising short-term interest rates are generally associated with expanding economic activity; similarly, decelerating money growth and falling interest rates are standard recession phenomena."

2. Money remains the ultimate instrument in that the ability of the central bank to create monetary shocks through money creation or destruction is what gives the central bank the power to align expected inflation with its inflation target.

3. The international gold standard is a third case. For a small country, changes in the price level will predict changes in money.

4. Friedman and Schwartz (1963b) chronicled the temporal relationship of money with economic activity and inflation in the period prior to stop–go.

5. The board's shift-adjusted M1 continued M1's usefulness as a predictor of nominal demand through 1981 (Chapter 13, n. 13).

6. Note that in Figure 14.4, this rise in inflation is the only one not predicted by velocity-adjusted M2 growth.

7. The most numerous examples of inflation shocks are the price increases of imported goods that occur when a country devalues its exchange-rate. If a central bank replaces

an exchange-rate peg with a credible commitment to an inflation target, devaluation need not raise the inflation rate. For example, in September 1992, Britain and Italy left the European Monetary System (EMS) and allowed their currencies to depreciate by more than 20%. In both countries, CPI inflation fell. Burstein, Eichenbaum, and Rebelo (2003) document the fact that in nine large post-1990 devaluations, "inflation is low relative to the rate of devaluation." The failure of such instances of exchange-rate devaluations to induce a persistent increase in inflation is evidence against hard-wired inflation persistence.

8. I date the beginning of stop–go to 1965. How to date the end is less clear. The recession that began in July 1981 is the final stop phase of a succession of periods of expansionary and contractionary monetary policy. Although the accession of Volcker to FOMC chairman in August 1979 marks abandonment of stop–go, that fact was not evident until after it became clear that the Fed could put the economy through a recession and retain its independence.

9. Friedman and Schwartz (1963b) studied the cyclical behavior of money using step functions fitted to money growth.

10. The exception is the 1979Q4 to 1980Q2 period when the funds rate rose steadily with stable nominal output growth.

11. The monetary acceleration 1980Q3 to 1980Q4 is hard to characterize because of the way the imposition and removal of the credit controls impacted both spending and money growth. Because of the brevity of the period, the arrow does not show.

12. Procyclical money growth would have been stabilizing if the shocks that produced the business cycle had been real productivity shocks rather than monetary shocks and if money growth had merely accommodated changes in the demand for money produced by changes in real output. However, in this event, there would have been no relationship between money growth and inflation.

13. Before 1956, Figures 23.2 and 23.3 plot contemporaneous observations on money growth. In this period, expected inflation drove prices and money growth (Chapter 4). Inflation rose with the end of price controls following World War II and in anticipation of controls with intensification of the Korean War. Given the prior experience with a commodity standard, positive inflation produced an expectation of negative inflation. Although market rates remained stable, real rates rose. Higher real rates required monetary deceleration. Money growth then either occurred contemporaneously with inflation or lagged it. The moral is that lead-lag relationships change with the monetary regime.

   In the period from 1964 through 1972, money growth generally exceeded inflation because of the favorable breakdown of nominal output growth between real output growth and inflation. Initially, the public did not anticipate the rise in inflation. Also, after August 1971, price controls restrained inflation.

14. The emphasis on maintaining low unemployment at the expense of price stability produced no long-run benefits. The unemployment rate averaged 4.0% in the first five years of the 1950s and 7.0% in the last five years of the 1970s. Over these two intervals, inflation rose from 2.7 to 7.3%.

Chapter 25. Monetary Nonneutrality in the Stop–Go Era

1. The M1 steps shown in Table 25.1 differ from those shown in Table 24.2 because the former use the revised figures available years later not the contemporaneously

available figures and the data are more finely partitioned. Also, the calculation of the growth rate differs.

2. The dates correspond to the period over which the FOMC saw M1 growth as low (Figure 24.1). With revised data, the period of low M1 growth was from August 1971 to December 1971.

3. Blanchard (2001) asserted that monetary policy could not have produced the recession because the real rate was negative in 1974. The data presented here contradict his assertion.

4. It begins in November 1965 when the real rate series becomes available. See Figure 8.3, and Appendix, "Series on the Real Interest Rate," in Chapter 4.

5. The results are basically the same when the real rate is constructed using the treasury bill rate. Occasionally, capital flows distorted the usual relationship of t-bill rates with money market rates. For example, in 1974, flows of funds from OPEC countries into treasury bills caused an unusually wide difference between money market and bill rates.

6. The location of the dots is determined by the monthly growth rates. The two-month averaging in the plotted series occasionally causes the dots to precede the apparent turning points by a month.

7. In principle, real rather than monetary shocks could have generated the data. If causality runs from real shocks to nominal money growth, peaks in the real rate produced subsequent increases in M1 growth (instead of prior declines in M1 growth causing the peaks in the real rate). This relationship is hard to rationalize.

Bibliography

Abbreviations used in citations for presidential papers

BE – Business-Economics
FL – Gerald R. Ford Library, Ann Arbor, Michigan
LBJ Library – Lyndon B. Johnson Presidential Library, Austin, Texas
NA – National Archives, College Park, Maryland; repository of Nixon Presidential Materials
    Project
WHCF – White House Central Files
WHSF – White House Special Files

Ackley, Gardner. *Macroeconomic Theory*. New York: Macmillan, 1961.
Allen, Donald S. "What Determines Long-Run Growth?" *National Economic Trends*, September 1997.
American Banker. "Bank Bond Investors Flee from Foreign Exposure." September 22, 1998, 32.
Auerbach, Nancy Neiman. "The Mexican Peso Crisis: Constituent Pressure and Exchange Rate Policy." *Claremont Policy Briefs*, Issue No. 97–02, December 1997.
Axilrod, Stephen H. "The FOMC Directive as Structured in the Late 1960s: Theory and Appraisal." In Board of Governors of the Federal Reserve System, *Open Market Policies and Operating Procedures – Staff Studies*, July 1971, 3–36.
    "What Really Went on in the Temple." Conference Board *Across the Board*, March 9, 1988, 58–61.
Bach, G. L. *Making Monetary and Fiscal Policy*. Washington, DC: Brookings Institution, 1971.
Balke, Nathan S., and Robert J. Gordon. "Appendix B: Historical Data." In Robert J. Gordon, ed., *The American Business Cycle: Continuity and Change*. Chicago: University of Chicago Press, 1986, 781–810.
    "The Estimation of Prewar Gross National Product: Methodology and New Evidence." *Journal of Political Economy* 97 (February 1989), 38–92.
Ball, Laurence. "The Genesis of Inflation and the Costs of Disinflation." *Journal of Money, Credit and Banking* 23 (August 1991, part 2), 439–61.
Barber, William J. "The Kennedy Years: Purposeful Pedagogy." In Craufurd D. Goodwin, ed., *Exhortation & Controls*. Washington, DC: Brookings Institution, 1975, 135–91.
Barro, Robert J., and Gordon, David B. "A Positive Theory of Monetary Policy in a Natural Rate Model," *Journal of Political Economy* 91 (August 1983), 589–610.

357

Barsky, Robert B., and Lutz Kilian. "Do We Really Know that Oil Caused the Great Stagflation? A Monetary Alternative." NBER *Macroeconomics Annual* 16 (2001), 137–83.

Bennett, Barbara A. "'Shift Adjustments' to the Monetary Aggregates." Federal Reserve Bank of San Francisco *Economic Review* (Spring 1982), 6–18.

Bergsten, C. Fred. "The Threat from the Overhand." *The Dilemmas of the Dollar*. New York: New York University Press, 1975.

Bernanke, Ben S. "Nonmonetary Effects of the Financial Crisis in the Propagation of the Great Depression." *American Economic Review* 73 (June 1983), 257–76.

"Deflation: Making Sure 'It' Doesn't Happen Here." Remarks before the National Economics Club, Washington, DC, November 21, 2002.

"An Unwelcome Fall in Inflation?" Remarks before the Economics Roundtable, University of California, San Diego, La Jolla, July 23, 2003.

Biven, W. Carl. *Jimmy Carter's Economy: Policy in an Age of Limits*. Chapel Hill: University of North Carolina Press, 2002.

Blanchard, Olivier. "Comment." NBER *Macroeconomics Annual* 16 (2001), 183–95.

Blinder, Alan S. "Supply-Shock Stagflation: Money, Expectations and Accommodation." In J. Flanders and A. Razin, eds., *Development in an Inflationary World*. New York: Academic Press, 1981, 61–101.

"The Anatomy of Double-Digit Inflation in the 1970s." In Robert E. Hall, ed., *Inflation: Causes and Effects*. Chicago: University of Chicago Press, 1982, 261–82.

Blinder, Alan S., and William J. Newton. "The 1971–1974 Controls Program and the Price Level: An Econometric Post-Mortem." *Journal of Monetary Economics* 8 (July 1981), 1–23.

Blinder, Alan S., and Ricardo Reis. "Understanding the Greenspan Standard." Paper prepared for a symposium sponsored by the Federal Reserve Bank of Kansas City, Jackson Hole, WY, August 25–27, 2005.

Blue Chip Financial Forecasts, Aspen Publishers.

Board of Governors of the Federal Reserve System. *Banking and Monetary Statistics: 1914–1941*. Washington, DC: Board of Governors of the Federal Reserve System, 1943 and 1976.

Board *Minutes*, available at Board of Governors.

"Current Economic and Financial Conditions" (Greenbook), various issues.

Federal Open Market Committee. *Minutes*, 1936–March 1976.

Minutes of Federal Open Market Committee Meetings, 1993–, *Annual Report*, various issues.

"Monetary Policy Alternatives." (Bluebook), various issues.

Record of Policy Actions of the Board of Governors, Annual Report, 1935–, various issues.

Record of Policy Actions of the Federal Open Market Committee, Annual Report, 1935–1992, various issues.

"Selected Interest Rates." H.15, historical data, www.federalreserve.gov.

Transcripts of the Federal Open Market Committee, April 1976–.

"Review of the Month." *Federal Reserve Bulletin* 6 (March 1920), 213–14.

"The Gold Situation." *Federal Reserve Bulletin* 7 (June 1921), 676–81.

"Review of the Month." *Federal Reserve Bulletin* 16 (November 1930), 655–8.

"Review of the Month." *Federal Reserve Bulletin* 17 (August 1931), 435–8.

"Review of the Month." *Federal Reserve Bulletin* 23 (May 1937), 377–9.

"Proposals to Maintain Prices at Fixed Levels Through Monetary Action." *Federal Reserve Bulletin* 25 (April 1939), 255–9.

"Financial Position and Buying Plans of Consumers, July 1948." *Federal Reserve Bulletin* 34 (November 1948), 1355–9.

"1950 Survey of Consumer Finances." *Federal Reserve Bulletin* 36 (June 1950), 643–54.

"Preliminary Findings of the 1954 Survey of Consumer Finances." *Federal Reserve Bulletin* 40 (March 1954), 246–9.

Bordo, Michael D. "The Bretton Woods International Monetary System: A Historical Overview." In Michael D. Bordo and Barry Eichengreen, eds., *A Retrospective on the Bretton Woods System: Lessons for International Monetary Reform.* Chicago: University of Chicago Press, 1993, 3–98.

The Gold Standard and Related Regimes: Collected Essays. Studies in Macroeconomic History. Cambridge: Cambridge University Press, 1999.

Bordo, Michael D., and Anna J. Schwartz. "Monetary Policy Regimes and Economic Performance: The Historical Record." In John B. Taylor and Michael Woodford, eds., *The Handbook of Macroeconomics*, vol. 1. New York: Elsevier, 1999, 149–234.

Bordo, Michael D., Ehsan Choudhri, and Anna J. Schwartz. "Could Stable Money Have Averted the Great Depression?" *Economic Inquiry* 33 (1995), 484–505.

"Was Expansionary Monetary Policy Feasible During the Great Contraction? An Examination of the Gold Standard Constraint." *Explorations in Economic History* 39 (2002), 1–28.

Bordo, Michael D., Christopher Erceg, and Charles Evans. "Money, Sticky Wages, and the Great Depression." *American Economic Review* 90 (December 2000), 1447–63.

Bremner, Robert P. *Chairman of the Fed: William McChesney Martin, Jr., and the Creation of the American Financial System.* New Haven, CT: Yale University Press, 2004.

Brittan, Samuel. *The Price of Freedom.* New York: St. Martin's Press, 1970.

Broaddus, J. Alfred. "Macroeconomic Principles and Monetary Policy." Federal Reserve Bank of Richmond *Economic Quarterly* 90 (Winter 2004), 1–9.

Broaddus, J. Alfred, Jr., and Marvin Goodfriend. "Foreign Exchange Operations and the Federal Reserve." Federal Reserve Bank of Richmond *Annual Report*, 1995.

"Sustaining Price Stability." Federal Reserve Bank of Richmond *Economic Quarterly* 90 (Summer 2004), 3–20.

Bronfenbrenner, Martin, and F. Holtzman. "Survey of Inflation Theory." *American Economic Review* 53 (September 1963), 593–661.

Brunner, Karl, and Allan H. Meltzer. *The Federal Reserve's Attachment to the Free Reserve Concept.* Washington, DC: House Committee on Banking and Currency, Subcommittee on Domestic Finance, Government Printing Office, May 1964.

Bureau of the Census, U.S. Department of Commerce. *Historical Statistics of the United States, Colonial Times to 1970*, Part 1. Washington, DC: Government Printing Office. 1975.

Burger, Albert E. *The Money Supply Process.* Belmont, CA: Wadsworth, 1971.

Burns, Arthur F., "Money Supply in the Conduct of Monetary Policy." *Federal Reserve Bulletin* 59 (November 1973), 791–98.

"Statement" before the Committee on Banking and Currency, House of Representatives. July 30, 1974. *Federal Reserve Bulletin* 60 (August 1974), 554–60.

The Anguish of Central Banking. Belgrade, Yugoslavia: Per Jacobsson Foundation, 1979.

Burns, Arthur F., and Wesley C. Mitchell. *Measuring Business Cycles.* New York: NBER, 1946.

Burns, Arthur F., and Paul A. Samuelson. *Full Employment, Guideposts and Economic Stability.* Washington, DC: American Enterprise Institute, 1967.

Burstein, Ariel, Martin Eichenbaum, and Sergio Rebelo. "Why Is Inflation so Low After Large Devaluations?" Mimeo. Northwestern University, 2003.

BusinessWeek. "The Fed's New Rule Book." May 3, 1999, 46–8.

Calomiris, Charles W. "The IMF's Imprudent Role as Lender of Last Resort." *The Cato Journal* 17 (Winter 1998), 275–94.

Carlson, John A. "A Study of Price Forecasts." *Annals of Economic and Social Measurement* 6 (Winter 1977), 27–56.

Chandler, Lester. *Benjamin Strong, Central Banker.* Washington, DC: Brookings Institution, 1958.

Chang, Roberto. "Is Low Unemployment Inflationary?" Federal Reserve Bank of Atlanta *Economic Review* (1st quarter 1997), 1–13.

Chari, V. V., Lawrence J. Christiano, and Martin Eichenbaum. "Expectation Traps and Discretion." *Journal of Economic Theory* 81 (1998), 462–92.

Cho, In-Koo, Thomas J. Sargent, and Noah Williams. "Escaping Nash Inflation." *Review of Economic Studies* 69 (2002), 1–40.

Christiano, Lawrence J., and Christopher Gust. "The Expectations Trap Hypothesis." Federal Reserve Bank of Chicago *Economic Perspectives* 25 (2nd quarter 2000), 21–39.

Citicorp. *Economic Week.* Various issues.

Clarida, Richard, Jordi Gali, and Mark Gertler. "Monetary Policy Rules and Macroeconomic Stability: Evidence and Some Theory." *Quarterly Journal of Economics* 115 (February 2000), 147–80.

Congressional Quarterly. *Almanac.* "1966 Bank Interest Rates." *Congress and the Nation.* II 1965–1968. Washington, DC: Congressional Quarterly, 259–60.

Weekly. Washington, DC: Congressional Quarterly, various issues.

Cook, Timothy, "Determinants of the Federal Funds Rate: 1979–1982." Federal Reserve Bank of Richmond *Economic Review* 75 (January/February 1989), 3–19.

Cook, Timothy, and Thomas Q. Hahn. "The Information Content of Discount Rate Announcements and Their Effect on Market Interest Rates." *Journal of Money Credit and Banking* 20 (1988), 167–80.

Croushore, Dean, and Tom Stark. "A Real-Time Data Set for Macroeconomists." Federal Reserve Bank of Philadelphia Working Paper No. 99-XX, May 1999.

Darin, Robert, and Robert L. Hetzel. "A Shift-Adjusted M2 Indicator for Monetary Policy." Federal Reserve Bank of Richmond *Economic Review* 80 (Summer 1994), 25–47.

"An Empirical Measure of the Real Rate of Interest." Federal Reserve Bank of Richmond *Economic Review* 81 (Winter 1995), 17–47.

Davis, Richard G. "Monetary Aggregates and the Use of 'Intermediate Targets' in Monetary Policy." Washington, DC: Board of Governors of the Federal Reserve System, *New Monetary Control Procedures* I (February 1981), 1–44.

Dell'Ariccia, Gioanni, Isabel Schnabel, and Jeromin Zettlemeyer. "How Do Official Bailouts Affect the Risk of Investing in Emerging Markets?" *Journal of Money, Credit, and Banking* 38 (October 2006), 1689–714.

DeLong, J. Bradford. "America's Peacetime Inflation: The 1970s." In Christina Romer and David Romer, eds., *Reducing Inflation: Motivation and Strategy.* Chicago: University of Chicago Press, 1997, 247–76.

Despres, Emile, Milton Friedman, Albert G. Hart, Paul A. Samuelson, and Donald H. Wallace. "The Problem of Economic Instability." *American Economic Review* 40 (September 1950), 505–38.

Dotsey, Michael. "Monetary Policy, Secrecy, and Federal Funds Rate Behavior." *Journal of Monetary Economics* 20 (December 1987), 463–74.

Eccles, Marriner S. "The Recession of 1937–8". In Sidney Hyman, ed. *Beckoning Frontiers: Public and Personal Recollections*. New York: Alfred A. Knopf, 1951, 287–323.

Eichengreen, Barry. *Golden Fetters: The Gold Standard and the Great Depression, 1919–1939*. Oxford: Oxford University Press, 1995.

Euromoney. "A Superpower Falls Apart." September 1998, 56–8.

Fannie Mae Economics Department. "Money and Capital Markets," January 16, 1987.

Federal Reserve Bank of New York. *Quarterly Review*, various issues.

Open Market Operations and Securities Market Developments, various issues.

Report of Open Market Operations and Money Market Conditions, various issues.

Feldstein, Martin, and Joel Slemrod. "Inflation and the Excess Taxation of Capital Gains on Corporate Stock." *National Tax Journal* 31 (June 1978, part 2), 107–18.

Feldstein, Martin, and Lawrence Summers. "Inflation and the Taxation of Capital Income in the Corporate Sector." *National Tax Journal* 32 (December 1979, issue 4), 445–70.

Fellner, William, Kenneth W. Clarkson, and John H. Moore. *"Correcting Taxes for Inflation."* Washington, DC: American Enterprise Institute for Public Policy Research, 1975.

Financial Times. "Fed Chief Says Recession May Be Worst since 1945." October 15, 1992, 1.

"S Korea Rescue Raises Uncomfortable Questions." January 2, 1998, 3.

"Camdessus Warns of 'Biggest Crisis' for IMF." May 6, 1998, 6.

"CSFB Traders Left Seething After Losing Fortune." August 28, 1998, 3.

"Risks as Bank Offers Greater Transparency." October 3, 2000, 27.

"Time for Clarity, Mr. Greenspan," August 12, 2003, 10.

"The Gospel According to 'Saint Paul'." October 23–24, 2004, W3.

Fisher, Irving. *Stable Money: A History of the Movement* (assisted by Hans R. L. Cohrssen). New York: Adelphi Co., 1934.

Forbord, Thomas Austin. *The Abandonment of Bretton Woods: The Political Economy of U.S. International Monetary Policy*. PhD thesis in Political Economy and Government, Harvard University, January 1980.

Foust, Dean. "Visionary Alan Greenspan: An Unlikely Guru: The Fed chairman sees a high-tech economy as a natural inflation fighter." *BusinessWeek*, August 31, 1998, 70.

Fowler, Henry. Remarks before the US Savings and Loan League, February 18, 1966, in U.S. Department of the Treasury. *Annual Report of the Secretary of the Treasury on the State of the Finances for the Year 1967*, Washington, DC: GPO, 1967a, 209.

Supplementary Statement before the Joint Economic Committee, Feburary 6, 1967, in U.S. Department of the Treasary. *Annual Report of the Secretary of the Treasury on the State of the Finances for the Year 1967*, 1967b, 218.

Friedman, Milton. *A Program for Monetary Stability*. New York: Fordham University Press, 1960.

"Real and Pseudo Gold Standards." *The Journal of Law and Economics* 4 (October 1961), 66–79.

"Inflation: Causes and Consequences." (1963). In Milton Friedman, ed., *Dollars and Deficits*. Englewood Cliffs, NJ: Prentice Hall, 1968, 21–71.

"The Role of Monetary Policy." (1968). In Milton Friedman, ed., *The Optimum Quantity of Money and Other Essays*. Chicago: Aldine, 1969, 95–110.

"A Theoretical Framework for Monetary Analysis." In Robert J. Gordon, ed., *Milton Friedman's Monetary Framework: A Debate with his Critics*. Chicago: University of Chicago Press, 1974, 1–62.

"Using Escalators to Help Fight Inflation." In Milton Friedman, *There's No Such Thing as a Free Lunch*. LaSalle, IL: Open Court, 1975, 148–61.

"Nobel Lecture: Inflation and Unemployment." *Journal of Political Economy* 85 (June 1977), 451–72.

"The Quantity Theory of Money." In John Eatwell, Murray Milgate, and Peter Newman, eds., *The New Palgrave Money*. New York: W. W. Norton, 1989, 1–40.

Money Mischief: Episodes in Monetary History. Orlando, FL: Harcourt, Brace, Jovanovich, 1992.

"John Maynard Keynes." Federal Reserve Bank of Richmond *Economic Quarterly* 83 (Spring 1997), 1–23.

"A Natural Experiment in Monetary Policy Covering Three Episodes of Growth and Decline in the Economy and the Stock Market." *Journal of Economic Perspectives* 19 (Fall 2005), 145–50.

Friedman, Milton, and Rose D. Friedman. *Two Lucky People: Memoirs*. Chicago: University of Chicago Press, 1998.

Friedman, Milton, and Anna J. Schwartz. *A Monetary History of the United States, 1867–1960*. Princeton, NJ: Princeton University Press, 1963a.

"Money and Business Cycles." *Review of Economics and Statistics* 45 (February 1963b), 32–64.

Monetary Statistics of the United States. New York: National Bureau of Economic Research, 1970.

Funabashi, Yoichi. *From the Plaza to the Louvre*. Washington, DC: Institute for International Economics, 1988.

Glass, Carter. "Senator Glass' Testimony, May 10, 1932." *Congressional Record – Senate*, 1932, 1984–5.

Global Insight. *U.S. Economic Outlook*, "Summary of the U.S. Economy," various issues.

Goldenweiser, E. A. *American Monetary Policy*. New York: McGraw-Hill, 1951.

Goodfriend, Marvin. "Discount Window Borrowing, Monetary Policy, and the Post-October 6, 1979, Federal Reserve Operating Procedure." *Journal of Monetary Economics* 12 (September 1983), 343–56.

"Interest Rates and the Conduct of Monetary Policy." *Carnegie-Rochester Conference on Public Policy* 34 (Spring 1991), 7–30.

"Interest Rate Policy and the Inflation Scare Problem." Federal Reserve Bank of Richmond *Economic Quarterly* 79 (Winter 1993), 1–24.

"Why We Need An 'Accord' for Federal Reserve Credit Policy." *Journal of Money, Credit, and Banking* 26 (August 1994), 572–84.

"Monetary Policy Comes of Age: A 20th Century Odyssey." Federal Reserve Bank of Richmond *Economic Quarterly* 83 (Winter 1997), 1–22.

"Overcoming the Zero Bound on Interest Rate Policy." *Journal of Money, Credit and Banking* 32 (November 2000, part 2), 1007–35.

"Monetary Policy in the New Neoclassical Synthesis: A Primer." Federal Reserve Bank of Richmond *Economic Quarterly* 90 (Summer 2004a), 3–20.

"The Monetary Policy Debate since October 1979: Lessons for Theory and Practice." *Reflections on Monetary Policy 25 Years After October 1979*. Federal Reserve Bank of St. Louis *Review* 87 (March/April 2005), 243–62.

"Inflation Targeting in the United States?" In Ben S. Bernanke and Michael Woodford, eds., *The Inflation-Targeting Debate*. Chicago: University of Chicago Press, 2005, 311–37.

Goodfriend, Marvin, and Robert G. King. "Financial Deregulation, Monetary Policy and Central Banking." Federal Reserve Bank of Richmond *Economic Review* (May/June 1988), 3–22.

"The New Neoclassical Synthesis." In Ben S. Bernanke and Julio Rotemberg, eds, NBER *Macroeconomics Annual.* Cambridge, MA: MIT Press Journals, 1997.

"The Incredible Volcker Disinflation." *Journal of Monetary Economics* 52 (July 2005), 981–1015.

Goodwin, Craufurd D., and R. Stanley Herren. "The Truman Administration: Problems and Policies Unfold." In Craufurd D. Goodwin, ed., *Exhortation & Controls.* Washington, DC: Brookings Institution, 1975, 9–93.

Gordon, Robert J. "The Time-Varying NAIRU and Its Implications for Economic Policy." *Journal of Economic Perspectives* 11 (Winter 1997), 11–32.

Gramlich, Edward. "An Insider Looks at the Greenspan Fed." *Central Banking* 61 (November 2005), 21–6.

Granger, C. W. J., and P. Newbold. "Spurious Regressions in Econometrics." *Journal of Econometrics* 2 (July 1974), 111–20.

Greenspan, Alan. "Gold and Economic Freedom." In Ayn Rand, ed., *Capitalism: The Unknown Ideal.* New York: Signet, 1967, 96–101.

"Can the U.S. Return to a Gold Standard?" *Wall Street Journal*, September 1, 1981, 30.

Statement before the House Subcommittee on Domestic Monetary Policy of the Committee on Banking, Finance and Urban Affairs, October 25, 1989. *Federal Reserve Bulletin* 75 (December 1989), 795–8.

"Economic Forecasting in the Private and Public Sectors." Remarks before the National Association of Business Economists, Washington DC, September 24, 1990. Board of Governors Library.

Remarks before The Economic Club of New York, New York, April 19, 1993. Board of Governors Library.

Remarks at a Research Conference on Risk Management and Systemic Risk, Washington, DC, November 16, 1995. Board of Governors Library.

"Performance of the U.S. Economy." Committee on the Budget. U.S. Senate, January 21, 1997. *Federal Reserve Bulletin* 83 (March 1997), 195–8.

"Performance of the U.S. Economy." Joint Economic Committee, U.S. Congress. March 20, 1997. Available at: www.federalreserve.gov.

Statement before the House Committee on the Budget, October 8, 1997. *Federal Reserve Bulletin* 83 (December 1997), 963–7.

Remarks at the 34th Annual Conference on Bank Structure and Competition of the Federal Reserve Bank of Chicago, May 7, 1998. Available at: www.federalreserve.gov.

Speech at the Haas Annual Business Faculty Research Dialogue, University of California, Berkeley, September 4, 1998. Available at: www.federalreserve.gov.

Testimony before the U.S. Senate Committee on the Budget, September 23, 1998, in *Federal Reserve Bulletin* 84 (November 1998), 936–8.

"The American Economy in a World Context," 35th Annual Conference on Bank Structure and Competition of the Federal Reserve Bank of Chicago, May 6, 1999. Available at: www.federalreserve.gov.

."Business Data Analysis." Remarks before the New York Association for Business Economics, June 13, 2000. Available at: www.federalreserve.gov.

"Economic Developments." Remarks before the Economic Club of New York, May 24, 2001. Available at: www.federalreserve.gov.

"Risk and Uncertainty in Monetary Policy." *AEA Papers and Proceedings American Economic Review* 94 (May 2004), 33–48.

Nomination Hearing before the Senate Committee on Banking, Housing and Urban Affairs, June 15, 2004. Available at: www.federalreserve.gov.

"Reflections on Central Banking." Remarks at a symposium sponsored by the Federal Reserve Bank of Kansas City, Jackson Hole, Wyoming, August 26, 2005. Available at: www.federalreserve.gov.

"Closing Remarks." Symposium sponsored by the Federal Reserve Bank of Kansas City, Jackson Hole, Wyoming, August 27, 2005. Available at: www.federalreserve.gov.

"Economic Flexibility." Remarks to the National Association for Business Economics Business Economics Annual Meeting, Chicago, September 27, 2005. Available at: www.federalreserve.gov.

"Economic Outlook." Joint Economic Committee, U.S. Congress, November 3, 2005. Available at: www.federalreserve.gov.

Greider, William. *Secrets of the Temple: How the Federal Reserve Runs the Country.* New York: Simon and Schuster, 1987.

Grenville, Stephen (deputy governor of the Reserve Bank of Australia). "The Global Financial System – The Risks of Closure." Speech to Credit Suisse First Boston Australia Conference, Sydney, November 13, 1998.

Haberler, Gottfried, and Thomas D. Willett. *U.S. Balance-of-Payments Policies and International Monetary Reform: A Critical Analysis.* Washington, DC: American Enterprise Institute, September 1968.

Hafer, R. W., and David C. Wheelock. "The Rise and Fall of a Policy Rule: Monetarism at the St. Louis Fed, 1968–1986." Federal Reserve Bank of St. Louis *Review* (January/February 2001), 1–24.

Haldeman, H. R. *The Haldeman Diaries: Inside the Nixon White House.* Santa Monica, CA: Sony, 1994.

Hamilton, James D. "Was the Deflation during the Great Depression Anticipated? Evidence from the Commodity Futures Market." *The American Economic Review* 82 (March 1992), 157–78.

Hargrove, Erwin C., and Samuel A. Morley. *The President and the Council of Economic Advisers.* London: Westview Press, 1984.

Harris, Seymour E. *Economics of the Kennedy Years.* New York: Harper & Row, 1964.

Hetzel, Robert L. "The Federal Reserve System and Control of the Money Supply in the 1970s." *Journal of Money, Credit and Banking* 13 (February 1981), 31–43.

"The October 1979 Regime of Monetary Control and the Behavior of the Money Supply in 1980." *Journal of Money, Credit, and Banking* 14 (May 1982), 234–51.

"The Rules versus Discretion Debate over Monetary Policy in the 1920s." Federal Reserve Bank of Richmond *Economic Review* 71 (November/December 1985), 3–14.

"Monetary Policy in the Early 1980s." Federal Reserve Bank of Richmond *Economic Review* 72 (March/April 1986), 20–32.

"A Mandate for Price Stability." Federal Reserve Bank of Richmond *Economic Review* 76 (March/April 1990a), 45–53.

"Maintaining Price Stability: A Proposal." Federal Reserve Bank of Richmond *Economic Review* 76 (March/April 1990b), 53–5.

"A Better Way to Fight Inflation." *Wall Street Journal*, April 25, 1991, A14.

"Indexed Bonds as an Aid to Monetary Policy." Federal Reserve Bank of Richmond *Economic Review* 78 (January/February 1992), 13–23.

"Sterilized Foreign Exchange Intervention: The Fed Debate in the 1960s," Federal Reserve Bank of Richmond *Economic Quarterly* 82 (Spring 1996), 21–46.

"The Case for a Monetary Rule in a Constitutional Democracy." *Economic Quarterly* 83 (Spring 1997), 45–65.

"Arthur Burns and Inflation." Federal Reserve Bank of Richmond *Economic Quarterly* 84 (Winter 1998), 21–44.

"Japanese Monetary Policy: A Quantity Theory Perspective." Federal Reserve Bank of Richmond *Economic Quarterly* 85 (Winter 1999), 1–25.

"The Taylor Rule: Is It a Useful Guide to Understanding Monetary Policy?" Federal Reserve Bank of Richmond *Economic Quarterly* 86 (Spring 2000), 1–33.

"German Monetary History in the First Half of the Twentieth Century." Federal Reserve Bank of Richmond *Economic Quarterly* 88 (Winter 2002a), 1–35.

"German Monetary History in the Second Half of the Twentieth Century: From the Deutsche Mark to the Euro." Federal Reserve Bank of Richmond *Economic Quarterly* 88 (Spring 2002b), 29–64.

"Japanese Monetary Policy and Deflation." Federal Reserve Bank of Richmond *Economic Quarterly* 89 (Summer 2003), 21–52.

"How Do Central Banks Control Inflation?" Federal Reserve Bank of Richmond *Economic Quarterly* 90 (Summer 2004a), 47–63.

"Price Stability and Japanese Monetary Policy." Bank of Japan *Monetary and Economic Studies* (October 2004b), 1–23.

"What Difference Would an Inflation Target Make?" Federal Reserve Bank of Richmond *Economic Quarterly* 91 (Spring 2005), 45–72.

"Making the Systematic Part of Monetary Policy Transparent." Federal Reserve Bank of Richmond *Economic Quarterly* 92 (Summer 2006), 255–90.

"The Contributions of Milton Friedman to Economics." Federal Reserve Bank of Richmond *Economic Quarterly* 93 (Winter 2007a), 1–30.

"The Case for Inflation Targeting." *Cato Journal* 27 (Spring/Summer 2007b), 273–81.

"Discretion versus Rules: Lessons from the Volcker–Greenspan Era." In Martin T. Bohl, Pierre L. Siklos, and Mark T. Wohar, eds., *Frontiers in Central Banking.* New York: North Holland-Elsevier, 2008a.

"What Is the Monetary Standard?" Federal Reserve Bank of Richmond *Economic Quarterly* 94 (2008b).

Hetzel, Robert L., and Ralph F. Leach. "The Treasury–Fed Accord: A New Narrative Account." Federal Reserve Bank of Richmond *Economic Quarterly* 87 (Winter 2001a), 33–55.

"After the Accord: Reminiscences on the Birth of the Modern Fed." Federal Reserve Bank of Richmond *Economic Quarterly* 87 (Winter 2001b), 57–64.

Hetzel, Robert L., and Yash Mehra. "The Behavior of Money Demand in the 1980s." *Journal of Money, Credit, and Banking* 21 (November 1989), 455–63.

Hoey, Richard B. "Decision Makers Poll." *Barclays de Zoete Wedd,* April 8, 1991, 6.

Hoover Archives. Milton Friedman Papers, Hoover Institution, Palo Alto, CA.

Hoover, Herbert. *The Memoirs of Herbert Hoover: The Great Depression 1929–1941.* New York: Macmillan Company, 1952.

Humphrey, Thomas M. "Monetary Policy Frameworks and Indicators for the Federal Reserve in the 1920s." Federal Reserve Bank of Richmond *Economic Quarterly* 87 (Winter 2001), 65–92.

Hutchison, Michael M. "Aggregate Demand, Uncertainty and Oil Prices: The 1990 Oil Shock in Comparative Perspective." Bank for International Settlements Economic Papers, No. 31, August 1991.

International Monetary Fund (IMF). "Management Welcomes Board Decision to Provide Additional Credits for Russia." *IMF Survey,* August 3, 1998.

International Capital Markets: Developments, Prospects, and Key Policy Issues, Washington, DC, August 1995 and September 1998.

James, Harold. *The German Slump: Politics and Economics 1924–1936.* Oxford: Clarendon Press, 1986.

Jastram, Roy W. *The Golden Constant.* New York: Wiley, 1977.

Johnson, Harry G. "Balance of Payments Controls and Guidelines for Trade and Investment." In George P. Shultz and Robert C. Aliber, eds., *Guidelines, Informal Controls, and the Marketplace.* Chicago: University of Chicago Press, 1966.

Kaminsky, Graciela L., and Karen K. Lewis. "Does Foreign Exchange Intervention Signal Future Monetary Policy?" *Journal of Monetary Economics* 37 (April 1996), 285–312.

Kane, Edward J. "Politicians against the Prime – The Dual Rate Fiasco." *The Bankers Magazine* 157 (Spring 1974, issue 2), 88–95.

Kettl, Donald F. *Leadership at the Fed.* New Haven, CT: Yale University Press, 1986.

King, Robert G., James H. Stock, and Mark W. Watson. "Temporal Instability of the Unemployment-Inflation Relationship." Federal Reserve Bank of Chicago *Economic Perspectives* (May/June 1995), 2–12.

Kohn, Donald L. "Inflation Targeting." *Inflation Targeting: Prospects and Problems.* Federal Reserve Bank of St. Louis *Review* 86 (July/August 2004), 179–83.

    "Comment." In Ben S. Bernanke and Michael Woodford, eds., *The Inflation-Targeting Debate.* Chicago: University of Chicago Press, 2005, 311–37.

Koopmans, Tjalling. "Measurement Without Theory." *The Review of Economic Statistics* 28 (August 1947), 161–72.

Kosters, Marvin H. "*Controls and Inflation: The Economic Stabilization Program in Retrospect.*" Washington, DC: American Enterprise Institute for Public Policy Research, 1975.

Kozicki, Sharon. "How Useful Are Taylor Rules for Monetary Policy?" Federal Reserve Bank of Kansas City *Economic Review* 84 (2nd quarter 1999), 5–25.

Krueger, Anne O. "Whither the World Bank and the IMF." *Journal of Economic Literature* 36 (December 1998), 1983–2020.

Kuttner, Kenneth, and Adam S. Posen. "The Difficulty of Discerning What's Too Tight: Taylor Rules and Japanese Monetary Policy." *North American Journal of Economics and Finance* 15 (March 2004), 53–74.

Kydland, Finn E., and Edward C. Prescott. "Rules Rather than Discretion: The Inconsistency of Optimal Plans." *Journal of Political Economy* 85 (June 1977), 473–91.

Lambert, Richard. "Inside the MPC." Bank of England *Quarterly Bulletin* 45 (Spring 2005), 56–65.

Leduc, Sylvain. "How Inflation Hawks Escape Expectations Traps." Federal Reserve Bank of Philadelphia *Business Review* (1st quarter 2003), 1–20.

Leijonhufvud, Axel. *On Keynesian Economics and the Economics of Keynes.* New York: Oxford University Press, 1968.

Levin, Fred J., and Paul Meek. "Implementing the New Operating Procedures: The View from the Trading Desk." In *New Monetary Control Procedures* I. Washington, DC: Board of Governors of the Federal Reserve System, February 1981, 1–39.

Lindsey, David E. *A Modern History of FOMC Communication: 1975–2002.* Board of Governors of the Federal Reserve System, June 24, 2003 (publicly available 2009).

Lindsey, David E., Athanasios Orphanides, and Robert H. Rasche. "The Reform of October 1979: How It Happened and Why." *Reflections on Monetary Policy 25 Years After October 1979.* Federal Reserve Bank of St. Louis *Review* 87 (March/April 2005), 187–235.

Lucas, Robert E. "Expectations and the Neutrality of Money (1972)"; "Econometric Policy Evaluation: A Critique (1976)"; and "Rules, Discretion, and the Role of the Economic Advisor (1980)." In Robert E. Lucas, Jr., *Studies in Business-Cycle Theory*. Cambridge, MA: MIT Press, 1981, 66–89, 104–30, 248–61.

McCallum, Bennett T. "Could a Monetary Base Rule Have Prevented the Great Depression?" *Journal of Monetary Economics* 26 (1990), 3–26.

"Recent Developments in Monetary Policy Analysis: The Roles of Theory and Evidence." Federal Reserve Bank of Richmond *Economic Quarterly* 88 (Winter 2002), 67–96.

McGinley, Laurie. "The Good News: Interest Rates Are Down – That's Also the Bad News." *Wall Street Journal*, October 30, 1985, 31.

Maisel, Sherman J. *Managing the Dollar*. New York: Norton, 1973.

Martin, William McChesney, Jr. "The Transition to Free Markets." Remarks at The Economic Club of Detroit, Detroit, MI, April 13, 1953. Speeches at Board of Governors library.

Address. Federal Reserve Bank of Boston. Boston, MA, May 6, 1953.

"Monetary Policy and the Federal Reserve System." *Proceedings of the Fifteenth Annual Pacific Northwest Conference on Banking*. Pullman, WA, April 8, 1954.

Address. New York Group of the Investment Bankers Association of America. New York City, October 19, 1955.

"New Horizons in Money and Banking." Round Tables for Business Executives, New School for Social Research, January 12, 1956.

"Winning the Battle against Inflation." Statement before the Committee on Finance. U.S. Senate, August 13, 1957. *Federal Reserve Bulletin* 43 (August 1957), 866–77.

Remarks. 91st Annual Meeting of the Richmond Chamber of Commerce, January 9, 1958.

"The Battle against Recession." Statement before the Committee on Finance. U.S. Senate, April 22, 1958, *Federal Reserve Bulletin* 44 (May 1958), 540–4.

Remarks. The Executives' Club of Chicago, Chicago, December 12, 1958.

"A System of Flexible Exchange Rates: Pro and Con," Letter to Wright Patman, April 17, 1962 in Foreign currency memos, 1962, Federal Reserve Bank of Richmond Archives.

"Statements to Congress: Monetary Policy and the Economy." *Federal Reserve Bulletin* (February 1963), 122–30.

"The Federal Reserve's Role in the Economy." *Federal Reserve Bulletin* 51 (December 1965), 1669–74.

Extemporaneous Remarks before the American Society of Newspaper Editors. Washington, DC, April 19, 1968.

"The U.S. Dollar at Home and Abroad." Remarks before the 77th General Meeting of the American Iron and Steel Institute, New York, May 22, 1969.

Mayer, Martin. *The Fate of the Dollar*. New York: Times Books, 1980.

Mayer, Thomas. *Monetary Policy and the Great Inflation in the United States: The Federal Reserve and the Failure of Macroeconomic Policy, 1965–79*. Northampton, MA: Edward Elgar, 1999.

Mehra, Yash P. "The Stability of the M2 Demand Function: Evidence from an Error-Correction Model." *Journal of Money, Credit and Banking* 25 (August 1993), 455–60.

"A Forward-Looking Monetary Policy Reaction Function." Federal Reserve Bank of Richmond *Economic Quarterly* 85 (Spring 1999), 33–53.

"The Bond Rate and Estimated Monetary Policy Rules." *Journal of Economics and Business* 53 (2001), 345–58.

Mehra, Yash P., and Brian Minton. "A Taylor Rule and the Greenspan Era." Federal Reserve Bank of Richmond *Economic Quarterly* 93 (Summer 2007).

Meltzer, Allan H. "The Regulation of Bank Payments Abroad, Another Failure for the Government Balance of Payments Program." In George P. Shultz and Robert C. Aliber, eds., *Guidelines, Informal Controls, and the Marketplace.* Chicago: University of Chicago Press, 1966.

A History of the Federal Reserve, vol. 1, 1913–1951. Chicago: University of Chicago Press, 2003.

Meyer, Laurence H. Remarks at the National Association for Business Economics 40th Anniversary Annual Meeting. Washington, DC, October 5, 1998. Available at: www.federalreserve.gov.

A Term at the Fed – An Insider's View. New York: HarperCollins, 2004.

Mishkin, Frederic S. "The Household Balance Sheet and the Great Depression." *Journal of Economic History* 38 (December 1978), 918–37.

Mitchell, James. "Should We Be Surprised by the Unreliability of Real-Time Output Gap Estimates? Density Estimates for the Eurozone." National Institute of Economic and Social Research, December 18, 2003.

Modigliani, Franco. "Rediscovery of Money – Discussion." *Papers and Proceedings. American Economic Review* 65 (May 1975), 179–81.

Modigliani, Franco, and Lucas Papademos. "Targets for Monetary Policy in the Coming Year." *Brookings Papers on Economic Activity* 1 (1975), 141–63.

Moreno, Ramon, Gloria Pasadilla, and Eli Remolona. "Asia's Financial Crisis: Lessons and Policy Responses." Federal Reserve Bank of San Francisco, Pacific Basin Working Paper Series, Working Paper No. PB98–02, July 1998.

Morgan Guaranty Survey. "Competition and the Wage-Price Guideposts." October 1964, 3–10.

Morrison, George R. *Liquidity Preferences of Commercial Banks.* Chicago: University of Chicago Press, 1966.

Muehring, Kevin. "It's Summers' Time." *Institutional Investor* (December 1997), 49–61.

"The Fire Next Time." *Institutional Investor* (September 1998), 74–94.

Nelson, Edward. "The Great Inflation of the Seventies: What Really Happened?" *Advances in Macroeconomics* 5 (2005, issue 1), Article 3. Available at: www.bepress.com/bejm/advances/vol5/iss1/art3.

Nelson, Edward, and Kalin Nikolov. "U.K. Inflation in the 1970s and 1980s: The Role of Output Gap Mismeasurement." *Journal of Economics and Business* 55 (2003), 353–70.

New York Times. "Martin Sees Crisis in U.S. Inflation; Urges a Tax Rise." April 20, 1968, A1.

"Bond Prices Continue Sharp Fall." September 3, 1987, D1.

"U.S. Said to Allow Decline of Dollar against the Mark." October 18, 1987, 1.

"Foreigners Called Key to Rates." October 19, 1987, D1.

"Fed Chief Says Economy Is Resisting Remedies." October 15, 1992, D2.

"Mexico's Trading Allies Play Financial Bodyguard." December 12, 1994, D2.

"I.M.F. Head: He Speaks, and Money Talks." April 2, 1996, 1.

"The Economic Stakes in Asia." November 1, 1997, A4.

"Small Banks May Pose Setback to Korea Plan." January 2, 1998, C4.

"One Korean Certainty: No More Business as Usual." January 4, 1998, 4.

"Shocks and Aftershocks: The Bear Is Rampant in the Markets for Riskier Bonds." September 17, 1998, C1.

"Brazil Makes Fast Recovery From Brink of Economic Collapse." September 24, 1998, A10.

"Long-Term Capital Bailout Spotlights a Fed 'Radical'." November 2, 1998, B1.

"Fed Thinks Globally, Acts Locally, to Lukewarm Response." November 18, 1998, C1.

"Fed Cuts Key Rates Again in 3d Attack on Global Slump." November 18, 1998, A1.

"Greenspan Is Upbeat on Economy and Stirs Hope of More Rate Cuts." June 4, 2003, C1.

Nordhaus, William. "A Map for the Road from Dunkirk." *New York Times*, March 21, 1982, F3.

Okun, Arthur M. Interviews I (March 20, 1969) and II (April 15, 1969), Johnson Library. *The Political Economy of Prosperity*. Washington, DC: Brookings Institution, 1970.

"Efficient Disinflation Policies." *American Economic Review* 68 (May 1978), 348–52.

Orphanides, Athanasios. "Monetary Policy Rules and the Great Inflation." *American Economic Review* 92 (May 2002), 115–20.

"The Quest for Prosperity without Inflation." *Journal of Monetary Economics* 50 (April 2003a), 633–63.

"Monetary Policy Evaluation with Noisy Information." *Journal of Monetary Economics* 50 (April 2003b), 605–31.

"Historical Monetary Policy Analysis and the Taylor Rule." *Journal of Monetary Economics* 50 (July 2003c), 983–1022.

Orphanides, Athanasios, and Simon van Norden. "The Unreliability of Output Gap Estimates in Real Time." *Review of Economics and Statistics* 84 (November 2002), 569–83.

Patinkin, Don. "Some Observations of the Inflationary Process." In J. Flanders and A. Razin, eds., *Development in an Inflationary World*. New York: Academic Press, 1981, 31–4.

Pechman, Joseph. "Oral History Interview with Walter Heller, Kermit Gordon, James Tobin, Gardner Ackley, and Paul Samuelson." Fort, Ritchie, MD: August 1, 1964, John F. Kennedy Library.

Perry, George L. *Unemployment, Money Wage Rates, and Inflation*. Cambridge, MA: MIT Press, 1966.

Phillips, A. W. "The Relation Between Unemployment and the Rate of Change of Money Wage Rates in the United Kingdom, 1861–1957." 25 *Economica* (November 1958), 283–300.

Pigou, A. C. "Economic Progress in a Stable Environment" *Economica* 14 (1947), 180–8.

Poole, William. "Monetary Policy During the Recession." *Brookings Papers on Economic Activity* 1 (1975), 123–39.

"Burnsian Monetary Policy: Eight Years of Progress?" *Journal of Finance* 34 (1979), 473–84.

"Understanding the Fed." Federal Reserve Bank of St. Louis *Review* 89 (January/February 2007), 3–13.

Porter, Roger B. *Presidential Decision Making*. Cambridge: Cambridge University Press, 1980.

Posen, Adam. "Deflationary Lessons." *The International Economy* 20 (Winter 2006), 20–7.

Reno, Virginia P., and Daniel N. Price. "Relationship between the Retirement, Disability and Unemployment Insurance Programs: The US Experience." *Social Security Bulletin* 48 (May 1985, issue 5), 24–35.

Richmond Times Dispatch. "U.S., Japan Split on Severity of Turmoil." September 6, 1998, A4.

Riefler, Winfield W. *Money Rates and Money Markets in the United States.* New York: Harper & Brothers, 1930.

Roberts, Priscilla. "'Quis Custodiet Ipsos Custodes?': The Federal Reserve's System's Founding Fathers and Allied Finance in the First World War." *Business History Review* 73 (Winter 1998), 585–620.

"Benjamin Strong, the Federal Reserve, and the Limits to Interwar American Nationalism." Federal Reserve Bank of Richmond *Economic Quarterly* 86 (Spring 2000), 61–98.

Robertson, J. L. "Remarks." Fourth Annual Business and Economic Outlook Conference, Portland, Oregon, December 5, 1966. Board of Governors Library.

Romer, Christina D., and David H. Romer. "A Rehabilitation of Monetary Policy in the 1950's." *American Economic Association Papers and Proceedings* 92 (May 2002), 121–7.

"Choosing the Federal Reserve Chair: Lessons from History." *Journal of Economic Perspectives* 18 (Winter 2004), 129–62.

Rotemberg, Julio J., and Michael Woodford. "An Optimization-Based Econometric Framework for the Evaluation of Monetary Policy." In Ben S. Bernanke and Julio Rotemberg, eds., NBER *Macroeconomics Annual.* Cambridge, MA: MIT Press Journals, 1997, 297–346.

Rudebusch, Glenn D., "How Fast Can the New Economy Grow?" *FRBSF Economic Letter*, February 25, 2000.

Runkle, David E. "Revisionist History: How Data Revisions Distort Economic Policy Research." Federal Reserve Bank of Minneapolis *Quarterly Review* (Fall 1998), 3–12.

Safire, William. *Before the Fall.* New York: Da Capo Press, 1975.

Samuelson, Paul. "Worldwide Stagflation" (1974). In Hiroaki Nagatani and Kate Crowley, eds., *The Collected Scientific Papers of Paul A. Samuelson*, vol. 4, no. 268. Cambridge, MA: MIT Press, 1977, 801–7.

"What Jimmy Should Do." *Newsweek*, January 10, 1977, 58.

"Living with Stagflation" (1979). In Kate Crowley, ed., *The Collected Scientific Papers of Paul A. Samuelson*, vol. 5, no. 379. Cambridge, MA: MIT Press, 1986, 972.

Samuelson, Paul, and Robert Solow. "Analytical Aspects of Anti-Inflation Policy" (1960)." In Joseph Stiglitz, ed., *The Collected Scientific Papers of Paul A. Samuelson.* vol. 2, no. 102. Cambridge, MA: MIT Press, 1966, 1336–53.

Sanders, Hyman, and Joshua Greene. *Indexing the Individual Income Tax for Inflation.* Washington, DC: US GPO, Congressional Budget Office, September 1980.

Sargent, Thomas J. (1971). "A Note on the 'Accelerationist' Controversy." In Robert E. Lucas, Jr., and Thomas J. Sargent, eds., *Rational Expectations and Econometric Practice*, vol 1. Minneapolis: University of Minnesota Press, 1981, 33–38.

"The Ends of Four Big Inflations." In Robert Hall, ed., *Inflation: Causes and Effects.* Chicago: University of Chicago Press, 1982, 41–97.

The Conquest of American Inflation. Princeton, NJ: Princeton University Press, 1999.

Sawamoto, Kuniho, and Nobuyuki Ichikawa. "Implementation of Monetary Policy in Japan." In Tomas J. T. Balino and Carlo Cottarelli, eds., *Frameworks for Monetary Stability.* Washington, DC: International Monetary Fund, 1994, 81–110.

Schreft, Stacey L. "Credit Controls: 1980." Federal Reserve Bank of Richmond *Economic Review* 76 (November/December 1990), 25–55.

Schwartz, Anna. "Understanding 1929–33." In Karl Brunner, ed., *The Great Depression Revisited.* Boston: Nijhoff, 1981, 5–48.

"The Misuse of the Fed's Discount Window." Federal Reserve Bank of Saint Louis *Economic Review* (September/October 1992), 58–69.

"From Obscurity to Notoriety: A Biography of the Exchange Stabilization Fund." *Journal of Money, Credit, and Banking* 29 (May 1997), 135–53.

Seay, George G. "The Federal Reserve System: The Course of the Federal Reserve Banks Before and During the Price Crisis and Readjustment." Address before the North Carolina Bankers' Convention at Pinehurst, April 26–28, 1922, published by the Federal Reserve Bank of Richmond, May 1922. Federal Reserve Bank of Richmond Archives.

"Illustrating the Expanded Condition of Bank Credit." Speech given to the Federal Reserve Bank of Richmond Directors, January 6, 1928. Federal Reserve Bank of Richmond Archives.

Shultz, George P., and Kenneth Dam. *Economic Policy Beyond the Headlines.* New York: W. W. Norton, 1978.

Simpson, Thomas D., and John R. Williams. "Recent Revisions in the Money Stock." *Federal Reserve Bulletin* 67 (July 1981), 539–42.

Sims, Christopher A., and Tao Zha. "Were There Regime Switches in U.S. Monetary Policy." *The American Economic Review* 96 (March 2006), 54–81.

Smith, Adam. *The Wealth of Nations,* Cannan edition. New York: Random House, 1937.

Solomon, Robert. *The International Monetary System, 1945–1981.* New York: Harper & Row, 1982.

Money on the Move: The Revolution in International Finance Since 1980. Princeton, NJ: Princeton University Press, 1999.

Sproul, Allan. "Changing Concepts of Central Banking." In *Money, Trade and Economic Growth: In Honor of John Henry Williams.* New York: Macmillan, 1951, 296–325.

"Monetary Policy and Government Intervention." In Lawrence S. Ritter, ed., *Selected Papers of Allan Sproul.* New York: Federal Reserve Bank of New York, 1980, 37–47.

Staiger, Douglas, James H. Stock, and Mark W. Watson. "Temporal Instability of the Unemployment-Inflation Relationship." Federal Reserve Bank of Chicago *Economic Perspectives* 19 (May/June 1995), 2–12.

Stein, Herbert. *The Fiscal Revolution in America.* Washington, DC: AEI Press, 1990.

Presidential Economics. Washington, DC: AEI Press, 1994.

Stigler, George J. "Administered Prices and Oligopolistic Inflation." *The Journal of Business* 35 (January 1962), 1–13.

Summers, Lawrence S. "How Should Long-Term Monetary Policy Be Determined?" *Journal of Money, Credit and Banking* 23 (August 1991, part 2), 625–31.

Svensson, Lars E. O. "Inflation Forecast Targeting: Implementing and Monitoring Inflation Targets." *European Economic Review* 41 (1997), 1111–46.

Taylor, John B. "Discretion versus Policy Rules in Practice." *Carnegie-Rochester Conference Series on Public Policy* 39 (1993), 195–214.

"A Historical Analysis of Monetary Policy Rules." In John B. Taylor, ed., *Monetary Policy Rules.* Chicago: University of Chicago Press, 1999, 319–47.

Thatcher, Margaret. *The Downing Street Years.* New York: HarperCollins, 1993.

Timberlake, Richard H. "Gold Standards and the Real Bills Doctrine in U.S. Monetary Policy." *Economic Journal Watch* 2 (August 2005), 196–233.

Tobin, James. "Monetary Policy in 1974 and Beyond." *Brookings Papers on Economic Activity* 1 (1974), 219–32.

"There are Three Types of Inflation: We Have Two." *New York Times,* September 6, 1974, 33.

Triffin, Robert. *Gold and the Dollar Crisis*. New Haven, CT: Yale University Press, 1960.

Ueda, Kazuo. "Japanese Monetary Policy from 1970 to 1990: Rules or Discretion?" In Kumiharu Shigehara, ed., *Price Stabilization in the 1990s*. Tokyo: Bank of Japan, 1993.

U.S. Congress. Testimony of Benjamin Strong on April 8, 1926, in *Stabilization*. Hearings before the Committee on Banking and Currency, House Committee on Banking and Currency. 69th Cong. 1st sess., Part 1, 1927.

   Stabilization of Commodity Prices. Hearings before the Subcommittee of the House Committee on Banking and Currency (Goldsborough Committee) on H.R. 10517. *For Increasing and Stabilizing the Price Level and for Other Purposes*. 72nd Cong. 1st sess., Part 2, April 14, 1932.

   Testimony in *Anti-Inflation Program as Recommended in the President's Message of November 17, 1947*. Hearings of the Joint Committee on the Economic Report. 80th Cong. 1st sess., November 25, 1947, 133–69.

   Economic Report of the President, January 1951. Hearings. 82nd Cong. 1st sess., January 22, 24, 25, 29, 31, and February 2, 1951.

   Statement. *January 1958 Economic Report of the President*. Hearings before the Joint Economic Committee. 85th Cong. 2nd sess., February 6, 1958, 383–411.

   Statement of Seymour E. Harris. *January 1959 Economic Report of the President*. Hearings before the Joint Economic Committee. 86th Cong. 1st sess., February 6, 1959, 495–535.

   Statement of William McChesney Martin. *January 1959 Economic Report of the President*. Hearings before the Joint Economic Committee. 86th Cong. 1st sess., February 6, 1959, 495–535.

   The Federal Reserve System after 50 Years. vol. 1. Hearings before the House Subcommittee on Domestic Finance of the Committee on Banking and Currency. 88th Cong., 2nd sess., February 28, 1964.

   Statement of Sherman J. Maisel. *Recent Federal Reserve Action and Economic Policy Coordination*. Hearings before the Joint Economic Committee. 89th Cong. 1st sess., December 13, 1965, 25–34.

   The 1968 Economic Report of the President. Hearings before the Joint Economic Committee. 90th Cong. 2nd sess., February 5, 6, 7, 14, and 15, 1968.

   The 1969 Economic Report of the President. Hearing before the Joint Economic Committee. 91st Cong. 1st sess., February 25, 26, 27, and March 5 and 6, 1969.

   The 1971 Midyear Review of the Economy. Hearings before the Joint Economic Committee. 92nd Cong. 1st. sess., July 7, 8, 20, 21, 22, and 23, 1971.

   Economic Stabilization Legislation. Hearings before the Senate Committee on Banking, Housing and Urban Affairs. 92nd Cong. 1st sess., November 1, 2, 3, 4, and 5, 1971.

   The 1972 Economic Report of the President. Hearings before the Joint Economic Committee. 92nd Cong. 2nd sess., Part 1, February 7, 8, and 9, 1972.

   Economic Stabilization Legislation – 1973. Hearings before the Committee on Banking, Housing, and Urban Affairs, U.S. Senate. 93rd Cong. 1st sess., February 7, 1973, 485–507.

   The 1973 Economic Report of the President. Hearings before the Joint Economic Committee. 93rd Cong. 1st sess., Part 1, February 6, 7, 8, and 12; Part 2, February 13, 14, 20, 22, and 23, 1973.

   Federal Reserve Policy and Inflation and High Interest Rates. Hearings before the House Committee on Banking and Currency. 93rd Cong. 2nd sess., July 16, 17, 18, 30, and August 7 and 8, 1974.

   Review of the Economy and the 1975 Budget. Hearings before the House Committee on the Budget. 93rd Cong. 2nd sess., September 17, 19, and 25, 1974.

Inflation Outlook. Hearing before the Joint Economic Committee. 93rd Cong. 2nd sess., September 26, 1974.

Statement in *Financial and Capacity Needs.* Hearings before the Joint Economic Committee. 93rd Cong. 2nd sess., October 1, 2, 3, and 10, 1974.

Hearing before the Joint Economic Committee. 93rd Cong. 2nd sess., January 6, 1975.

The Economic Situation. Hearing before the Joint Economic Committee. 94th Cong. 1st sess., May 2, 1975.

Statement in *Conduct of Monetary Policy.* Hearings before the House Committee on Banking, Finance, and Urban Affairs. 95th Cong. 1st sess., February 3, 1977, 81–134.

Indexation of Certain Provisions of the Tax Laws. Hearing before the Subcommittee on Taxation and Debt Management Generally of the Committee on Finance. 95th Cong. 2nd sess., April 24, 1978.

The 1979 Joint Economic Report. Report of the Joint Economic Committee on the 1979 Economic Report of the President. 96th Cong. 1st sess., March 22, 1979.

Depository Institutions Deregulation Act of 1979. U.S. Senate, Committee on Banking, Housing, and Urban Affairs, Subcommittee on Financial Institutions, Hearings. 96th Cong. 1st sess., Part II, June 27, 1979.

The Dollar, Inflation and U.S. Monetary Policy. Hearing before the Joint Economic Committee. 96th Cong. 1st sess., October 17, 1979.

1980 Economic Report of the President. Hearings before the Joint Economic Committee. 96th Cong. 2nd sess., February 1, 1980.

The Conduct of Monetary Policy. Hearings before the House Committee on Banking, Finance, and Urban Affairs. 96th Cong. 2nd sess., February 19, 1980.

Federal Reserve's First Monetary Policy Report for 1980. Hearings before the Senate Committee on Banking, Housing, and Urban Affairs. 96th Cong. 2nd sess., February 25 and 26, 1980, 7–17.

Testimony. In *Renomination of Paul A. Volcker.* U.S. Senate, Committee on Banking, Housing, and Urban Affairs. 98th Cong. 1st sess., July 14, 1983.

Federal Reserve's Second Monetary Policy Report for 1983. Hearings before the Senate Committee on Banking, Housing, and Urban Affairs and the Subcommittee on Economic Policy. 98th Cong. 1st sess., July 21 and 28, 1983.

Conduct of Monetary Policy. Hearings before the Subcommittee on Domestic Monetary Policy of the Committee on Banking, Finance, and Urban Affairs. 99th Cong. 1st sess., February 26 and March 5, 1985.

Conduct of Monetary Policy. Hearings before the Subcommittee on Domestic Monetary Policy of the House Committee on Banking, Finance, and Urban Affairs. 99th Cong. 1st sess., July 17, 1985.

Conduct of Monetary Policy. Hearings before the House Committee on Banking, Finance, and Urban Affairs. 99th Cong. 2nd sess., July 29, 1986.

Conduct of Monetary Policy. Hearings before the Subcommittee on Domestic Monetary Policy of the House Committee on Banking, Finance, and Urban Affairs. 100th Cong. 1st sess., February 25 and 26, 1987.

Conduct of Monetary Policy. Hearings before the Subcommittee on Domestic Monetary Policy of the House Committee on Banking, Finance, and Urban Affairs. 100th Cong. 1st sess., July 21, 1987.

Conduct of Monetary Policy. Hearings before the Subcommittee on Domestic Monetary Policy of the House Committee on Banking, Finance, and Urban Affairs. 101th Cong. 1st sess., February 21, 22, and March 1, 1989.

Federal Reserve's First Monetary Policy Report for 1992. Hearing before the Senate Committee on Banking, Housing, and Urban Affairs. 102nd Cong. 2nd sess., February 25, 1992.

Inflation-Indexed Treasury Debt as an Aid to Monetary Policy. Hearings before the House Commerce, Consumer, and Monetary Affairs Subcommittee of the Committee on Government Operations. 102nd Cong. 2nd sess., June 16 and 25, 1992.

Fighting Inflation and Reducing the Deficit: The Role of Inflation-Indexed Treasury Bonds. Thirty-Third Report by the Committee on Government Operations. 102nd Cong. 2nd sess., October 29, 1992.

Federal Reserve's First Monetary Policy Report for 1993. Hearing before the Senate Committee on Banking, Housing, and Urban Affairs. 103rd Cong. 1st sess., February 19, 1993.

Conduct of Monetary Policy. Hearing before the House Subcommittee on Economic Growth and Credit Formation of the Committee on Banking, Finance, and Urban Affairs. 103rd Cong. 1st sess., July 20, 1993.

H.R. 28: The Federal Reserve Accountability Act of 1993. Hearing before the House Committee on Banking, Finance, and Urban Affairs. 103rd Cong. 1st sess., October 19 and 27, 1993.

The 1994 Economic Report of the President: The Economic Outlook. Hearing before the Joint Economic Committee. 103rd Cong. 2nd sess., January 31, 1994.

Conduct of Monetary Policy. Hearing before the Subcommittee on Economic Growth and Credit Formation of the House Committee on Banking, Finance, and Urban Affairs. 103rd Cong. 2nd sess., February 22, 1994.

Interest Rates, Wages, Employment, and Inflation. Hearing before the House Committee on the Budget. 103rd Cong. 2nd sess., June 22, 1994.

Federal Reserve's Semiannual Report on Monetary Policy – 1994. Hearing before the Senate Committee on Banking, Housing, and Urban Affairs. 103rd Cong. 2nd sess., July 20, 1994.

The Economic Outlook for the Nation. Hearing before the Senate Committee on Finance. 104th Cong. 1st sess., January 25, 1995.

Conduct of Monetary Policy. Subcommittee on Domestic and International Monetary Policy, House Committee on Banking and Financial Services. 104th Cong. 2nd sess., February 20, 1995.

Federal Reserve's First Monetary Policy Report for 1995. Hearing before the Senate Committee on Banking, Housing, and Urban Affairs. 104th Cong. 1st sess., February 22, 1995.

Conduct of Monetary Policy. Hearing before the House Subcommittee on Domestic and International Monetary Policy of the Committee on Banking and Financial Services. 104th Cong. 2nd sess., February 20, 1996.

Federal Reserve's Second Monetary Policy Report for 1996. Hearing before the Senate Committee on Banking, Housing, and Urban Affairs. 104th Cong. 2nd sess., July 18, 1996.

Federal Reserve's First Monetary Policy Report for 1997. Hearing before the Senate Committee on Banking, Housing, and Urban Affairs." 105th Cong. 1st sess., February 26, 1997.

Conduct of Monetary Policy, Statement before the House Subcommittee on Domestic and International Monetary Policy, Committee on Banking and Financial Services. July 22, 1997, 131–9.

Federal Reserve's First Monetary Policy Report for 1998. Subcommittee on Domestic and International Monetary Policy, House Committee on Banking and Financial Services. 105th Cong. 2nd sess., February 24, 1998.

Federal Reserve's Second Monetary Policy Report for 1998. Hearing before the Senate Committee on Banking, Housing, and Urban Affairs. 105th Cong. 2nd sess., July 21, 1998.

Conduct of Monetary Policy. Hearing before the House Committee on Banking and Financial Services. 106th Cong. 1st sess., February 24, 1999.

National Summit on High Technology. Hearing before the Joint Economic Committee. 106th Cong. 1st sess., Part 1, June 14, 1999.

The Economic Outlook and Monetary Policy. Hearing before the Joint Economic Committee. 106th Cong. 1st sess., June 17, 1999.

Conduct of Monetary Policy. Hearing before the House Committee on Banking and Financial Services. 106th Cong. 1st sess., July 22, 1999.

Federal Reserve's Second Monetary Policy Report for 1999. Hearing before the Senate Committee on Banking, Housing, and Urban Affairs. 106th Cong. 1st sess., July 28, 1999.

Federal Reserve's First Monetary Policy Report for 2000. Hearing before the Senate Committee on Banking, Housing, and Urban Affairs. 106th Cong. 2nd sess., February 23, 2000.

Federal Reserve's First Monetary Policy Report for 2001. Hearing before the Senate Committee on Banking, Housing, and Urban Affairs. 107th Cong. 1st sess., February 13, 2001.

Conduct of Monetary Policy. Hearing before the House Committee on Financial Services. 107th Cong. 1st sess., February 28, 2001.

Conduct of Monetary Policy. Hearing before the House Committee on Financial Services. 107th Cong. 1st sess., July 18, 2001.

The Economic Outlook: May 2003. Hearing before the Joint Economic Committee. 108th Cong. 2nd sess., May 21, 2003.

Federal Reserve's Second Monetary Policy Report for 2003. Hearing before the Senate Committee on Banking, Housing, and Urban Affairs. 108th Cong. 1st sess., July 16, 2003.

Economic Outlook and Current Fiscal Issues. Hearing before the House Committee on the Budget. 108th Cong. 2nd sess., February 25, 2004.

Monetary Policy and the State of the Economy. Hearing before the House Committee on Financial Services. 109th Cong. 1st sess., July 20, 2005.

U.S. Congress, Congressional Budget Office. *Five-Year Budget Projections: Fiscal Years 1981–1985.* A Report to the Senate and House Committees on the Budget – Part II. Washington, DC: GPO, February 1980.

U.S. Department of Commerce. *Historical Statistics of the United States,* Part 2, "Government Employment and Finance," 1975.

Statistical Abstract of the United States. "National Security and Veterans Affairs," various issues.

U.S. *Economic Report of the President* transmitted to the Congress annually together with the *Annual Report of the Council of Economic Advisers.* Washington, DC: GPO, various issues.

U.S. Social Security Board. *Social Security Bulletin: Annual Statistical Supplement, 1977–9.* Social Security Administration, U.S. Department of Health and Human Services. Washington, DC: GPO, 1979.

U.S. Treasury Department. *Annual Report of the Secretary of the Treasury,* various issues.

Velde, François. "Poor Hand or Poor Play? The Rise and Fall of Inflation in the U.S." Federal Reserve Bank of Chicago *Economic Perspectives* 28 (1st quarter 2004), 34–51.

Volcker, Paul A. *The Rediscovery of the Business Cycle.* New York: Free Press, 1978.

"Statement" before the Subcommittee on Domestic Monetary Policy of the House Committee on Banking, Finance, and Urban Affairs, November 13, 1979. *Federal Reserve Bulletin* 65 (December 1979), 958–65.

Remarks before the National Press Club, Washington, DC, January 2, 1980. Board of Governors Library.

"Statement." In *Recent Monetary Policy Developments.* House Committee on Banking, Finance, and Urban Affairs. Subcommittee on Domestic Monetary Policy. 96th Cong. 2nd sess., November 19, 1980.

"A Rare Opportunity." Remarks before the 43rd Annual Dinner of the Tax Foundation, New York, December 3, 1980. Board of Governors Library.

"Statement" before the House Committee on Banking, Finance, and Urban Affairs, July 21, 1981. *Federal Reserve Bulletin* 67 (August 1981), 613–18.

"Statement" before the House Committee on Ways and Means, February 23, 1982. *Federal Reserve Bulletin* 68 (March 1982), 167–70.

"Statement" before the Joint Economic Committee, June 15, 1982. *Federal Reserve Bulletin* 68 (July 1982), 405–9.

"Statement" before the Joint Economic Committee, November 24, 1982. *Federal Reserve Bulletin* 68 (December 1982), 747–53.

"Statement" before the House Committee on Banking, Finance and Urban Affairs, Febuary 2, 1983. *Federal Reserve Bulletin* 69 (February 1983), 80–9.

"Statement" before the House Committee on Banking, Finance and Urban Affairs, February 2, 1983. *Federal Reserve Bulletin* 69 (February 1983), 80–9.

"Statement" before the Senate Committee on Banking, Finance, and Urban Affairs, February 16, 1983. *Federal Reserve Bulletin* 69 (March 1983), 167–74.

"We Can Survive Prosperity." Remarks at the Joint Meeting of the American Economic Association–American Finance Association, San Francisco, December 28, 1983. Board of Governors Library.

Statement before the House Committee on Banking, Finance, and Urban Affairs, February 7, 1984. *Federal Reserve Bulletin* 70 (February 1984), 96–102.

"Coming Out of the Recession: The American Economy in 1984." Remarks at the Executive Dinner Forum Wharton Entrepreneurial Center, Philadelphia, April 30, 1984. Board of Governors Library.

"Monetary Policy" and "Summary of Discussion." In Martin Feldstein, ed., *American Economic Policy in the 1980s.* Chicago: University of Chicago Press, 1994, 145–51, 157–64.

"An Interview with Paul A. Volcker." Interviewed by Perry Mehrling. *Macroeconomic Dynamics* 5 (June 2001), 434–60.

Testimony in House of Lords. Session 2002–3, 42nd Report. Select Committee on the European Union. "Is the European Central Bank Working?" October 30, 2003.

Interview conducted by PBS for *Commanding Heights*, September 20, 2006. Available at: http://www.pbs.org/wgbh/commandingheights/shared/minitextlo/int_paulvolcker.html.

Volcker, Paul A., and Toyoo Gyohten. *Changing Fortunes: The World's Money and the Threat to American Leadership.* New York: Random House, 1992.

Wall Street Journal. "Treasury Bond Prices Take Biggest Fall in Six Months as Worry about Dollar Grows." March 31, 1987, 55.

"Bond Prices Jump the Tracks of Stability.," April 6, 1987, 40.

"Some Reagan Officials Fear Fed Steps to Support Dollar Could Fuel Recession." April 17, 1987, 3.

"Fed Keeps Rates Stable to Pressure Tokyo, Aide Says." April 22, 1987, 2.

"A Tougher Trade Law Seems Likely as Anger Rises in Much of U.S." April 27, 1987, 1.

"Dollar Looms Bigger in the Fed's Decisions, at Risk of a Recession." May 19, 1987, 1.

"Nominee Greenspan Shares Volcker's Goals But Not Yet His Clout." June 3, 1987, 1.

"Congress's Failure to Fix Budget Law Makes Major Cuts Unlikely This Year." August 10, 1987, 3.

"Bond Prices Jumble as Dollar's Plunge Prompts Additional Fears on Inflation." August 19, 1987, 27.

"Fed Chief Warns of Higher Rates Caused by Fears." October 5, 1987, 2.

"Baker Denies U.S. Changed Currency Rate." October 19, 1987, 3.

"The Plunge in Stocks Has Experts Guessing about Market's Course." October 19, 1987, 1.

"Foreign Ardor Cools Toward US Stocks After Market's Dive." October 26, 1987, 1.

"Long-Term Rates Fall at Last as Worries of Inflation Abate." July 31, 1992, A1.

"Dollar Intervention Signals Concerns about Rising Rates, Falling Currency." May 2, 1994, A2.

"Rubin Says Global Investors Don't Suffer Enough." September 19, 1997, A2.

"French and Swiss Join Effort to Aid Korean Banks." December 31, 1997, A6.

"Growth Estimates Trimmed for Latin American." September 8, 1998, A20.

"How the Salesmanship and Brainpower Failed at Long-Term Capital." November 16, 1998, A19.

"So Long Supply and Demand: There's a New Economy out There – and It Looks Nothing Like the Old One." January 1, 2000, R31.

"Latest Fed Rate Cut Takes on a Contagion of Low Confidence." February 1, 2001, 1.

"How Nasdaq's Mighty Have Fallen." March 5, 2001, C1.

"Bond-Market Rout Could Pose a Hurdle to Economic Recovery." July 24, 2003, A4.

Warburton, Clark. *Depression, Inflation, and Monetary Policy: Selected Papers, 1945–1953.* Baltimore: Johns Hopkins University Press, 1966.

Washington Bond and Money Market Report, various issues.

Washington Post. "Despite Reform Plan, Indonesian Currency Still Falling." January 17, 1998, 1.

Wells, Wyatt C. *Economist in an Uncertain World, Arthur F. Burns and the Federal Reserve, 1970–78.* New York: Columbia University Press, 1994.

Wheelock, David C. *The Strategy and Consistency of Federal Reserve Monetary Policy, 1924–1933.* Cambridge: Cambridge University Press, 1991.

Wolman, Alexander L. "Staggered Price Setting and the Zero Bound on Nominal Interest Rates." Federal Reserve Bank of Richmond *Economic Quarterly* 84 (Fall 1998), 1–24.

Wood, John H. *A History of Central Banking in Great Britain and the United States.* New York: Cambridge University Press, 2005.

"William McChesney Martin, Jr. A Reevaluation." Federal Reserve Bank of Richmond *Region Focus* 10 (Winter 2006), 2–7.

Woodford, Michael. *Interest and Prices: Foundations of a Theory of Monetary Policy.* Princeton, NJ: Princeton University Press, 2003.

Woolley, John T. *Monetary Politics: The Federal Reserve and the Politics of Monetary Policy.* New York: Cambridge University Press, 1984.

World Bank. Global Economic Prospects 1998/99, Beyond Financial Crisis. December 1998.

Yeager, Leland B. *International Monetary Relations: Theory, History and Policy.* New York: Harper & Row, 1976.

"From Gold to the ECU: The International Monetary System in Retrospect." In Kevin Dowd and Richard H. Timberlake, eds., *Money and the Nation State*. New Brunswick, NJ: Transaction Publishers, 1998, 77–104.

Yellen, Janet L. "Policymaking and the FOMC: Transparency and Continuity." *FRBSF Economic Letter*, September 2, 2005.

"Enhancing Fed Credibility" Luncheon Keynote Speech to the Annual Washington Policy Conference, March 13, 2006. Available at: www.frbsf.org/news/speeches.

Index

379

Hawkins, Augustus F., 117
Hayes, Alfred, 51, 84, 113–14
hedge funds. *See* Long Term Capital
    Management (LTCM)
Heller, Walter, 60, 68–9, 71, 85–6
Herren, R. Stanley, 35, 37
Hoey, Richard B., 46
Holmes, Allan, 98
Hoover, Herbert, 34
Humphrey–Hawkins full employment
    bill
    as activist legislation, 117–18
    Greenspan testimony, 218, 219, 253–4
    macroeconomic goals, 130
    and policy communication, 130–1
    political pressure for, 122–3
Humphrey, Hubert H., 117

IMF. *See* International Monetary Fund
    (IMF)
inflation
    financial market expectations, 5
    Greenspan on, 4
    intrinsic persistence of, 7
    Keynesian views on, 319
    monetary growth, 99
    prosperity trade-off, 4, 334
    public expectations of, 5
    special-factors explanations, 93–4
    stop–go monetary policy, 4
inflation, fiscal pressure interplay
    monetary policy expansion, 143
    personal tax/receipts, 143–5
    social program spending, 143
    unemployment/social security
        relationship, 145–7
inflation, nonmonetary forces
    full employment, 60–1
    wage-price guideposts, 61–5
inflation, political economy of
    credit union share drafts, 135
    dual prime rate, 134–5
    government expenditures, 137
    government revenues, 136–7
    inflation as tax, 132, 136–43
    "low" interest rate pressure, 134
    money market certificates, 135
    NOW accounts, 135, 332
    political costs, 143

Reg Q ceilings, 135–6
    savings bonds, 134
    tax revolt, 147–8
    transfer payment growth, 137–43
inflation, post-WWII
    aggregate demand vs. speculation, 49
    vs. deflation expectations, 40–2, 45
    government bonds/rates, 52–5
    interest rates, 35, 37–40, 45
    Korean War period, 45
    monetary deceleration, 42–5, 55,
        322
    monetary policy effects, 40
    political views, 40
    price controls, 42
    recession fears, 35, 37
inflation scares
    bond-rate increases, 185–7
    dollar depreciation, 183–4
    Greenspan appointment, 185
    Louvre Accord, 182–3
inflation, tax revenues
    base money stock, 148
    capital gains, 149
    corporate income tax, 149
    personal tax/receipts, 148–9
    relative contributions, 149
    Treasury debt payments, 148
interest equalization tax, 104
interest rate forecasts. *See* real rate of
    interest forecasts
International Monetary Fund (IMF),
    208–10. *See also* Asian crisis;
    emerging-market debt crisis; Long
    Term Capital Management (LTCM);
    Mexican crisis; Russian crisis

Japan, deflation experience, 246–7,
    250–1
Johnson administration
    1960s political/social imperatives, 67
    balance of payments, 69
    British pound crisis response, 73
    Great Society/Vietnam War financing,
        69
    income redistribution programs, 132
    interest rate increase hostility, 70
    Martin's monetary policy
        experiments, 312–13

9 780521 88132